Andreas Wald, Christoph Fay, Ronald Gleich (eds.)

Introduction to Aviation Management

Aviation Management

edited by

Prof. Dr. Ronald Gleich
Strascheg Institute for Innovation and Entrepreneurship
EBS Business School
EBS Universität für Wirtschaft und Recht

and

Prof. Dr. Andreas Wald
School of Business and Law
University of Agder

Volume 3

LIT

Introduction to Aviation Management

edited by

Andreas Wald, Christoph Fay
and Ronald Gleich

LIT

Bibliographic information published by the Deutsche Nationalbibliothek
The Deutsche Nationalbibliothek lists this publication in the Deutsche Nationalbibliografie; detailed bibliographic data are available in the Internet at http://dnb.d-nb.de.

3rd, revised edition 2015

ISBN 978-3-643-90693-9

A catalogue record for this book is available from the British Library

Klosbachstr. 107
CH-8032 Zürich
Tel. +41 (0) 44-251 75 05 Fax +41 (0) 44-251 75 06
E-Mail: zuerich@lit-verlag.ch http://www.lit-verlag.ch
Distribution:
In the UK: Global Book Marketing, e-mail: mo@centralbooks.com
In North America: International Specialized Book Services, e-mail: orders@isbs.com
In Germany: LIT Verlag Fresnostr. 2, D-48159 Münster
Tel. +49 (0) 2 51-620 32 22, Fax +49 (0) 2 51-922 60 99, E-mail: vertrieb@lit-verlag.de
In Austria: Medienlogistik Pichler-ÖBZ, e-mail: mlo@medien-logistik.at
e-books are available at www.litwebshop.de

From the editors

Dear Reader

With our series Aviation Management we focus on work that addresses current topics in this research field. The purpose of this series is the discussion of new ideas in Aviation Management.

Since the exchange between research and practice is of special concern to us, the main focus of the series will be on work with high practical relevance. Thus, different contributions either result from direct cooperation with business partners or originate from empirical research findings leading to new concepts and ideas in the field of Aviation Management. In addition, the new series will offer a forum for presenting historical developments, state-of-the-art knowledge, future-oriented technologies and processes, as well as empirical findings obtained from different methodological approaches, either of a quantitative or qualitative nature.

Many contributions to this series provide findings from outstanding dissertations and post-doctoral theses dealing with managerial questions or challenges concerning the field of Aviation Management. Furthermore, the series takes up topical areas of interest in edited volumes, comprising contributions from renowned researchers and practitioners.

We kindly invite you to send in manuscripts – either in German or in English. The editors will decide jointly on their publication.

We hope you will enjoy reading this volume. If you have any suggestions or questions, please do not hesitate to contact us directly.

Yours sincerely,

Prof. Dr. Ronald Gleich
EBS Universität für Wirtschaft und Recht
EBS Business School (EBS)
Wiesbaden, Germany
ronald.gleich@ebs.edu

Prof. Dr. Andreas Wald
University of Agder
School of Business and Law
Kristiansand, Norway
andreas.wald@uia.no

Table of Contents

Airline Specific Management Functions

General Management Functions in the Airline Business

The authors

Tim Brauer
Mr. Brauer is Manager Corporate Sourcing at Deutsche Lufthansa AG, Frankfurt, Germany.

Harald Deprosse
Mr. Deprosse has held various management positions at Lufthansa German Airlines, Frankfurt / Main, Germany. Currently he is Managing Director Miles & More GmbH.

Ulf Diefenbach
Mr. Diefenbach is Research Assistant and Doctoral Candidate at the Aviation Management Center at EBS Universität für Wirtschaft und Recht, Wiesbaden, Germany.

Thomas Dionisius
Mr. Dionisius is director revenue management at Lufthansa German Airlines, Frankfurt / Main, Germany. He has worked in various functions within Revenue Management and currently heads the Pricing and Forecasting for short-haul flights, flights to the US and Canada and global price products.

Christoph Fay
Mr. Fay is Head of Public Affairs, Human Resources at Lufthansa German Airlines.

Prof. Dr. Ronald Gleich
Mr. Gleich is Professor and Head of the Strascheg Institute for Innovation & Entrepreneurship at EBS Universität für Wirtschaft und Recht, Wiesbaden, Germany and Managing Partner of the Horváth Academy, Stuttgart, Germany.

Michael Händel
Mr. Händel has worked in various functions at Lufthansa German Airlines, Frankfurt / Main, Germany. Currently he is Director Network Planning Hub Munich.

Jörg Hennemann
Mr. Hennemann is the Vice President Revenue Management and Distribution of Lufthansa, Frankfurt, Germany.

Stefan Holztrattner
Mr. Holztrattner is a freelance aviation management and business administration teacher, Chatou, Ile-de-France, France.

Prof. Dr. Klaus Jäckel
Mr. Jäckel works for Deutsche Lufthansa AG as Project Director Airline Group, Alliances and Cooperations. At the same time he is Professor for Aviation Management at the University of Applied Sciences in Worms, Germany.

Patrick Keidel
Mr. Keidel has worked for Fraport since 2002. He was a member of Fraport's Investor Relations team until he joined the Airport Retail and Real Estate department in 2006. He is currently involved in the commercial management and strategy of the retail sector at Frankfurt Airport.

Dr. Benjamin Koch
Mr. Koch is Director Corporate & Business Services Europe within Lufthansa AG's finance organization. He previously worked with the company's worldwide shared services, corporate strategy, network management and consulting departments in Cologne and Frankfurt / Main, Germany.

Thomas Kropp
Mr. Kropp is Senior Vice President of Deutsche Lufthansa AG and Head of Corporate International Relations and Government Affairs.

Dr. Peter Malanik
Mr. Malanik is a former member of the executive board and Co-CEO of Austrian Airlines AG, Vienna, Austria. He lectures on aviation management at the University of Economics, Vienna and is CEO of an international executive search company.

Paul McKnight
Mr. McKnight is a retired airport management consultant with California-based Jacobs Consultancy Inc. Mr. McKnight also lectured in Air Transportation Economics in the Commercial Aviation Management Program at Western University in London, Canada. He holds a degree in industrial engineering and an MBA.

Dr. Peter A. Meincke
Mr. Meincke is an analyst and researcher at the DLR – German Aerospace Center, Air Transport and Airport Research in Cologne, Germany.

Martin Nubert
Mr. Nubert (Graduate Industrial Engineer) has been working for Lufthansa Cargo Airlines in the departments of technical operations, flight operations and operations control center since 2002. Currently he is head of performance- and quality management for hub operations Frankfurt within Lufthansa German Airlines.

Marc Oedekoven
Mr. Oedekoven is the owner and MD of KIBIX Logistics GmbH in Cologne. He is also the Chairman of the IQS Group in Langenbach (Munich). Previously, he has held various management positions within the Lufthansa Group in Frankfurt, Dubai and Singapore. He holds a degree of Master of Economics and MBA and he is lecturer at the European Business School Oestrich Winkel, at the International University of Bad Honnef as well as at the Europaeische Fachhochschule Bruehl/Cologne.

Dr. Maximilian Rothkopf
Mr. Rothkopf is a partner at a leading top management consultancy. He focuses on strategic and commercial topics in transport and logistics industries.

Dr. Peter Schentler
Mr. Schentler is Senior Project Manager at Horváth & Partners Management Consultants in Vienna.

Benedikt Schnellbächer
Mr. Schnellbächer is Research Assistant and Doctoral Candidate at the Strascheg Institute for Innovation and Entrepreneurship at EBS Universität für Wirtschaft und Recht, Wiesbaden, Germany.

Alexander Tkotz
Mr. Tkotz works as a Managing Consultant in the Competence Center Controlling & Finance at Horváth & Partners Management Consultants. Besides that he is a doctoral candidate with the focus on innovation control at the SIIE at EBS Universität für Wirtschaft und Recht.

Dr. Jan Vespermann
Mr. Vespermann is Head of Business Development at Germanwings GmbH in Cologne, Germany. He previously was a Management Trainee and a member of the Corporate Strategy Department at Deutsche Lufthansa AG.

Prof. Dr. Andreas Wald
Mr. Wald is Professor of Strategy at the School of Business and Law of the University of Agder in Kristiansand, Norway, and Adjunct Professor of Aviation Management at EBS Universität für Wirtschaft und Recht, Wiesbaden, Germany.

Introduction

Andreas Wald, Christoph Fay, Ronald Gleich

"I really don't know one plane from the other.

To me, they are all marginal costs with wings"

Alfred E. Kahn (McCraw, 1984)

The authors

Dr. Andreas Wald is Professor of Strategy at the School of Business and Law of the University of Agder in Kristiansand, Norway and Adjunct Professor at EBS Universität für Wirtschaft und Recht, Wiesbaden, Germany.

Christoph Fay is Head of Public Affairs, Human Resources at Lufthansa German Airlines.

Dr. Ronald Gleich is Professor and Head of the Strascheg Institute for Innovation & Entrepreneurship at EBS Universität für Wirtschaft und Recht, Wiesbaden, Germany and Managing Partner of the Horváth Academy, Stuttgart, Germany.

A. AVIATION MANAGEMENT AS FIELD OF STUDY

Cut-throat competition, tiny profit margins, soaring fuel prices, a high share of fix costs, pressure from environmental groups and regulative authorities, distorted deregulation, consolidation, strong unions and the transformation of established business models are key factors aviation managers have to deal with (Doganis, 2001; Cento, 2009; Clark, 2010). These factors are also the subject of extensive academic research. Dynamism and complexity have made the aviation industry a fascinating field of study.

The volume at hand provides an introductory reader to the field of aviation management. Instead of creating a more traditional textbook, we chose the format of an edited volume. This approach has allowed us to bring together industry experts and academics. Each of them has contributed knowledge from their special fields of interest and practice. To avoid unnecessary repetition, we have left out general chapters on management.

The third edition is substantially revised work. All chapters have been updated, and, if necessary extended for including more recent developments of the dynamic aviation industry. Two new chapters – on global alliances and on aviation project management - have been added that cover important topics in the field. The chapter on aviation law that was part of the first and second edition has been excluded, as important legal aspects are already covered in the different chapters on aviation management.

B. INTRODUCTION TO AVIATION MANAGEMENT

This volume is divided into four sections. The first section introduces the fundamental structures, processes, players and economic background of the aviation industry. In their chapter, The Air Transport System, *Vespermann* and *Holztrattner* elaborate on the economic and social relevance of the industry and describe the major stakeholders and interrelationships. On this basis they provide an overview of the aviation value chain. In the followig chapter, Airline Economics, *McKnight* provides an introduction to the basic economic concepts of air travel. He discusses the fundamental metrics, principles, processes, and cost structures of airlines.

The second section is devoted to major input factors of the airline industry. *Nubert* introduces the reader to the fundamental technical and physical characteristics of modern aircraft. In his chapter, Aircraft - Types, Operations and Performance, he explains the major technical and structural components of aircraft and the organizational requirements of flight operations management.

In the chapter Airport Management - Types, Functions, Facilities and Accessibility, *Meincke* and *Tkotz*, focus on the ground infrastructure. They compare different national classifications of airport types and explain the main functions, operations, and facilities of airports. More specifically, *Keidel's* chapter, Airports - Management and Strategy, deals with the different business segments of airports. The author concentrates on the non-aviation segments, i.e. commercial activities such as retail.

The third section of the volume includes chapters relating to airline-specific management functions. Based on a brief history of civil aviation, *Koch* discusses some particular characteristics of airline strategy. In his chapter Aviation Strategy and Business Models, he further describes the strategic aspect of different airline business models and provides an outlook on their further development and on the general development of the airline industry structure. *Hennemann* and *Malanik* address another highly important aspect of the airline industry in Cooperation and Alliances. The authors demonstrate how cooperation and alliances can be a means of securing further growth and network expansion in a regulated environment. They present the different forms of airline cooperation and discuss possible future developments within the existing alliances. Building on the chapter of *Hennemann* and *Malanik*, the new chapter Global Alliances in the Airline Industry – a Model for the Future? written by *Jäckel* further elaborates on the structures, processes, and management of the leading global airline alliances.

Network Planning and Slot Management are among the most important management functions of an airline. *Deprosse* and *Händel* explain how the airline industry characteristics influence the processes of network planning and elaborate on the fundamental planning procedures for network development and network scheduling. The second part of their chapter introduces slot management and explains its importance in network scheduling. Network scheduling and network development provide the underlying basis for the maximization of an airline's revenues by means of capacity steering and pricing. These two functions, together with the necessary IT-infrastructure, are discussed in Revenue Management, introduced by *Dionisius*. He identifies the influencing factors of revenue management and explains the main elements of pricing and tools for forecasting, capacity steering and overbooking.

Taking a more general perspective in Aviation Policy *Kropp* maps the historical origins of aviation policy and shows how they have shaped current developments and continue to do so in the future. He discusses the major actors and processes and deals with the underlying legislation of aviation together with future issues, such as environment and sustainability, safety and security and consumer protection. *Oedekoven* dedicates himself to a domain which is often neglected in writings on the airline industry: Air Cargo Management. He underlines the economic significance of airfreight and illuminates the high complexity and dynamics of the market environment in this business field. Furthermore, he presents the different players within the air cargo industry and explains the production process.

In the last section of this volume the perspective shifts to general management functions, which, due to the highly competitive environment of the aviation industry, deserve more detailed treatment. *Gleich, Tkotz* and *Schentler* illustrate the importance and the design of management control systems and performance measurement. In their chapter Performance Measurement in the Airline Industry they also develop a framework for airline performance measurement.

The special characteristics of service innovation and its application to the airline industry is the topic of the last chapter, Innovation Management. The authors, *Rothkopf* and *Wald*, accentuate the importance of innovation for airlines, but also allude to the difficulties in developing and implementing service innovations successfully. Furthermore, they show how airlines can strategically approach innovation to generate value and how they can set up organizational structures and processes for supporting innovation. The last chapter, Aviation Project Management, has been newly added to the third edition. *Diefenbach, Schnellbächer*, and *Brauer* consider project management as an increasingly important management function and skill. They introduce the fundamental tools and concepts of project management and relate them to the aviation context.

Bibliography and further reading

Cento, A. (2009): The Airline Industry - Challenges in the 21st Century, Heidelberg.

Clark, P. (2010): Stormy Skies: Airlines in Crisis, Farnham.

Doganis, R. (2001): The Airline Business in the Twenty-first Century, London.

McCraw, T. K. (1984): Prophets of Regulation, Cambridge: The Belknap Press of Harvard University Press.

Section 1:
The Fundamental Principles of the Air Transport Industry

The Air Transport System

Jan Vespermann, Stefan Holztrattner

Table of contents

You should be able to

- describe the economic and social relevance of the airline industry
- give some background information regarding the four major actors in the air transportation industry – airlines, airports, institutions, and the aircraft industry
- explain the relations between the different actors and the individual actors' roles

The authors

Dr. Jan Vespermann is Head of Business Development at Germanwings GmbH in Cologne, Germany. He previously was a Management Trainee and a member of the Corporate Strategy Department at Deutsche Lufthansa AG.

Stefan Holztrattner is working as a freelance aviation management and business administration teacher, Chatou, Ile-de-France, France.

Abstract

Its economic importance, its dynamism and complexity make the aviation industry an interesting field of study. The ongoing liberalization of markets, rapid technological changes and the establishment of new businesses constantly raise new questions about theory and practice. Current and future developments in aviation are shaped by industry actors and structures - in short, the air transport system.

With this contribution we aim to give an overview of the air transport system. While this first chapter elaborates on the economic and social relevance of the air transportation industry, the second chapter focuses on the different industry stakeholders and the relationships between them. The last chapter provides a conclusion.

A. THE AIR TRANSPORT INDUSTRY - ECONOMIC AND SOCIAL RELEVANCE

Strong growth in aviation industry

The aviation industry has grown at the enormous rate of about 5% per annum over the past 50 years. Today, the world's airlines carry about 40 million tons of freight and more than 2 billion people each year (Macintosh & Wallace, 2008). While some air transportation markets in the Middle East and the Asia Pacific region are expected to continue to grow strongly by annual rates of 6.6% and 6.4% respectively, other more saturated markets, particularly in North America and Europe, are expected to develop only at reduced rates of 2.6% and 4.0% a year. The growth in international aviationis estimated to remain a global phenomenon, with an average projected growth rate of 5.0% annually until 2033 (Boeing, 2014). By size, Europe is the world's largest aviation market (29.3% of world traffic) followed by Asia Pacific (26.1%) and North America (22.2%).

	Revenue Passenger Kilometer (bn)			Total airplane fleet		
	2013	2033e	CAGR (%)	2013	2033e	CAGR (%)
Asia Pacific	1,506	5,175	6.4	5,470	15,220	5.2
North America	1,281	2,140	2.6	6,650	9,120	1.6
Europe	1,691	3,681	4.0	4,350	7,710	2.9
Middle East	324	1,159	6.6	1,180	3,360	5.4
Latin America	433	1,320	5.7	1,380	3,530	4.8
CIS	276	662	4.5	1,180	1,820	2.2
Africa	261	827	5.9	700	1,420	3.6
World	5,772	14,965	5.0	20,910	42,180	3.6

Table 1: Forecasts for traffic numbers and airline fleet [1] (Boeing, 2014)

1 Worldwide traffic in RPK (revenue passenger kilometer) within and between regions. Traffic between regions is allocated according to departing flights. Growth discrepancies between RPK and airplane fleet are ascribed to changes in aircraft size and projected seat load factors.

Direct, indirect, induced, catalyzed and perpetuity impacts of aviation

The economic relevance of aviation has direct, indirect, induced, catalyzed and perpetuity impacts (Whitelegg & Cambridge, 2004). All institutions directly involved in air traffic operations – such as manufacturers, airlines, airports and service providers – have a direct impact on economic activities. Overall, direct effects are estimated to represent almost 5.5 million direct jobs and contribute about USD 400 billion to global gross domestic product (GDP).[2] Services closely related to air transportation, such as catering, aviation fuel suppliers or travel agencies, have an indirect economic effect, generating another estimated 6.3 million jobs worldwide, and contributing about USD 465 billion to the global GDP. The buying power of direct or indirect air transport employees is defined as the induced impact. This effect is estimated to support another 2.9 million jobs around the globe, accounting for about USD 220 billion of the global GDP. An additional industry impact is generated through catalytic or spinoff benefits, referring to economic activities of other industries whose development and growth depends on air transport operations (e.g. the tourist industry). Furthermore, air transportation triggers world trade and enables global expansion of companies - the perpetuity effect.

Social benefits

Next to its economic relevance, air transport leads to social benefits (Brueckener & Girvin, 2008). Employment opportunities contribute to social welfare on local and regional levels, improving living standards and lifestyles (Janic, 2007). As a means of mass transportation the industry supports the connection between different countries and cultures. In doing so, cultural understanding is supported and multicultural cooperation increased. Air transport often provides access to inaccessible places, delivering necessary goods and services. While both the economic and social effects of air transportation contribute significantly to global prosperity and social welfare, these benefits come at the cost of negative ecological impacts (Janic, 2007). The next section will introduce the key players in the aviation industry.

B. STAKEHOLDERS IN THE AIRLINE INDUSTRY

Demand side of air transportation

While this article focuses on the institutions that together form the supply side of the aviation industry, a brief look at the demand side may be worthwhile as well. The demand side of the aviation industry can be distinguished between people flying for business purposes (who demand frequent flights to a wide range of destinations, seek quality service and are willing to pay a premium for these benefits), and leisure travelers (who seek the lowest prices and are less concerned with service offered, flight frequency or number of destinations served) (Costa, Harned & Lundquist, 2002). More specifically leisure travelers can be categorized as vacation travelers, special event travelers and people visiting relatives and friends. Generally, there is an increasing heterogeneity of passengers, as business passengers also use offers intended for leisure travelers (Huse & Evangelho, 2007).

---

2 Subsequent numbers from Air Transport Action Group (ATAG, 2008).

The aviation supply side and its individual actors are introduced in the following sections.

Airlines, airports, aircraft industry and institutions as major stakeholders

In the aviation industry, four main groups of actors – airlines, airports, the aircraft industry and institutions – can be identified (Figure 1):

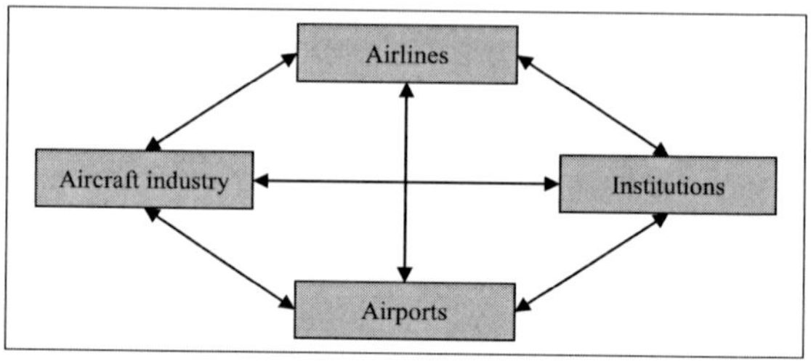

Figure 1: Stakeholders in the aviation industry (Own illustration)

Aviation value chain

While these four groups represent the major stakeholders that shape the aviation industry, the value chain can be refined and extended as in Figure 2 with airlines and airports at the center of the chain.

We can identify capacity and technical service providers for the airlines and operational service providers. Aircraft and engine manufacturers as well as leasing companies and MRO (maintenance, repair and overhaul) providers belong to the capacity providers. All sectors below the airlines in the value chain, i.e. airports, ground handlers and caterers etc. are operational service providers for the airlines. The following illustration displays the aviation industry value chain and gives an overview of the aviation industry's main sectors from a specific airline point of view.

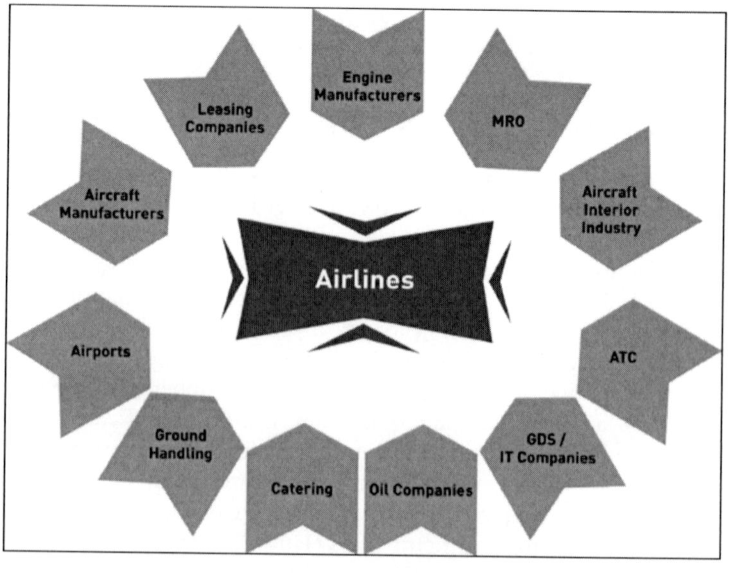

Figure 2: The aviation industry value chain (Own illustration)

B. 1 Airlines

Airlines differ in terms of regional focus, function, business model, and ownership

Airlines represent the most visible group of actors in the aviation industry. Essentially, every airline offers the same core service – the transport from A to B. However, fundamental differences among airlines exist in terms of regional focus, main function (passenger or cargo), the underlying business model as well as the ownership structure. Compared to the pre-liberalization era, where three kinds of operating models were predominant – network carriers, charter carriers and regional airlines - today's competitive environment has changed dramatically.

Passenger airlines provide services prior to, during, and after a flight. Meffert & Bruhn (1995) distinguish between basic, expected features and additional features that do not necessarily have to be provided by the airline. As a consequence, the airlines category is by no means homogeneous. Similar to other industries, there are strong tendencies away from a 'vanishing middle market' in the airline industry, as described by Knudsen, Randel & Rugholm (2005).

Airline business models

The most important economic actors are the international passenger airlines or 'network carriers'. Their business model is generally based on a hub and spoke network. The airlines use one or several airports that primarily focus on transfer traffic. With a carefully synchronized balance between inbound and outbound flights throughout the day, passengers can connect flights (or freight companies can exchange cargo) all day long.

Catchment area hub system

Figure 3 and Figure 4 show the two predominant hub models. The catchment area hub uses one catchment area as the central turning point of a hub. It is mainly used for long distance connecting traffic. European airports like Paris Charles de Gaulle CDG (for Air France) or Frankfurt Airport FRA (for Lufthansa) can be considered to be catchment area hubs.

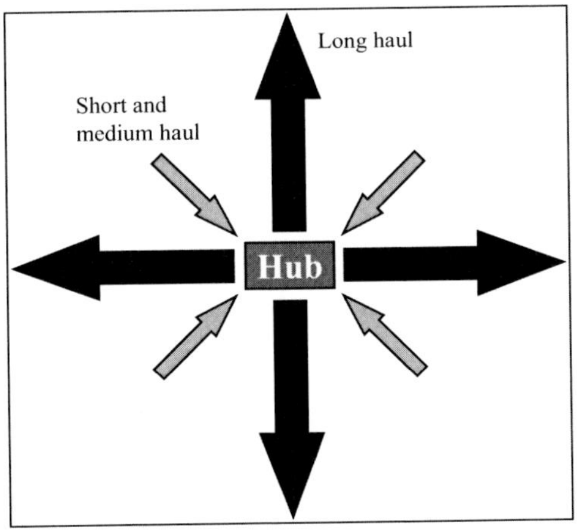

Figure 3: Catchment area hub system (Own illustration)

Hour-glass hub system

The hour-glass hub is generally located towards the middle of important traffic flows and is often used for continental and intercontinental connecting traffic. Dallas Fort Worth Airport DFW (for American Airlines), Atlanta Airport ATL (for Delta Airlines), Chicago O'Hare International ORD (for United) or Dubai International Airport DXB (for Emirates) works as hourglass platforms for their respective airlines.

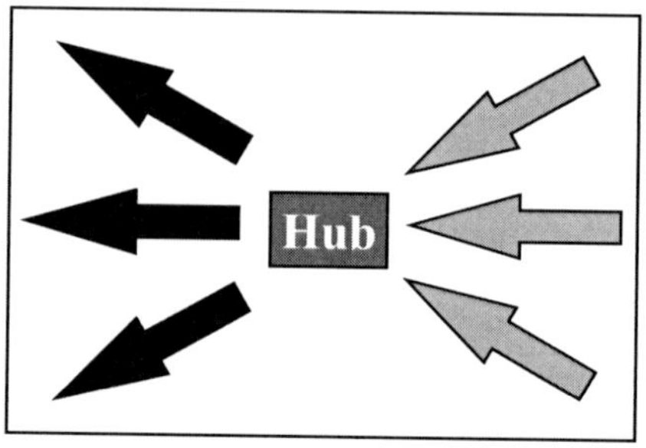

Figure 4: Hour-glass hub system (Own illustration)

Network carrier

Delta Airlines, American Airlines or United are the major network carriers operating out of the US-American market. Air France-KLM, Lufthansa and IAG (incl. British Airways and Iberia) are the dominant networks airlines in the European market. In the Middle East, Asia and Australia, Emirates, Singapore Airlines and Qantas for example, exercise the network model. While the US Carriers have a long tradition of being privately owned, European carriers were originally mostly state-owned and have been privatized only recently (British Airways 1987, Lufthansa 1997, Air France 1999). Some, like Air France, are still partly state-owned nowadays.

Network niche carrier

A modification of the traditional network carriers are the 'network niche carriers', which have had to streamline and adapt the established network model due to their small size and the increasing competition that no longer supported a large and global network (e.g. SAS, Austrian Airlines, Swiss, Alitalia). Generally these carriers are members of one of the three major airlines alliances (Star Alliance, Sky Team, and Oneworld).

Charter airlines and low-cost carrier

Other relevant business models on the passenger side are charter airlines (e.g. Condor, Tuifly) as well as the rapidly growing group of low-cost carriers (e.g. Southwest, Ryanair, Air Asia). They have become the biggest airlines in terms of passengers in their relevant market segment, e.g. Southwest Airlines today is the biggest domestic airline in the USA with more than 108 million passengers in 2013.

In contrast to the traditional network carriers, this group of airlines focuses on high volume short- to medium haul routes based on very lean operations and a minimum service ('no frills') approach.

The low-cost activity circle as shown below in Figure 5 summarizes typical elements of the low-cost airlines' different approaches in comparison to the traditional ('legacy') airlines. The sector itself is far from being homogenous, so in reality each low-cost airline will have integrated many of these elements in its business model, but not all of them. The European low-cost carrier Ryanair, for example, predominantly uses smaller (and cheaper) secondary airports while its competitor easyJet flies to major European airports and thus competes more directly with the established airlines.

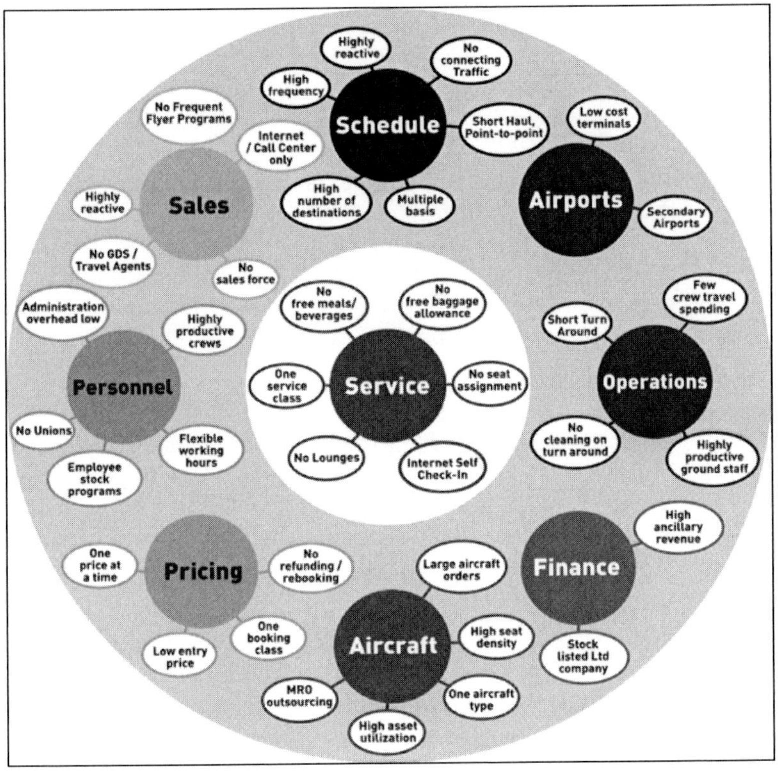

Figure 5: The low-cost activity circle (Own illustration)

Smaller regional carriers (e.g. in Europe, BA City Flyer, flyBe, Air Nostrum) pursue a different business model by focusing on linking remote areas with thin flows, or on feeding into the hubs of the network carriers. They face increasing competition from the aforementioned low-cost airlines.

In 2007 and 2008, first attempts to transfer the success of traditional low-cost carrier (LCC) to the long haul market were made (e.g. Air Asia X). Depending on the type of carrier, the product consists of one (e.g. LCC) to up to four service classes (Economy, Premium Economy, Business Class and First Class) for a long haul carrier. While the core product, the transport, is the same for all classes, the service and comfort levels vary among the different classes. Today, in passenger air transportation, the most common business model is the full-service network model, however, in 2007, LCCs were already accounting for almost 30% of the seats within Europe and the US and for a smaller share in Asia (International Air Transport Association [IATA], 2007).

Convergence of business models

In the short and medium haul sector an increasing convergence of business models can be observed, especially as the airlines' corporate customers have become increasingly price sensitive and the traditional carriers have been forced to defend their market share by offering cheaper and more 'flexible' economy fares. Low-cost airlines on the other hand are increasingly reaching out to lucrative business travelers (e.g. easyJet).

On the cargo business side, we find airlines that focus exclusively on airfreight (e.g. Korean Cargo, Lufthansa Cargo, and Cargolux).

Airline revenue structure

For a traditional airline, the fare for the transport is the main source of revenue. LCCs, by contrast, rely on ancillary revenues on top of the fare, e.g. catering or the charge for credit card usage. LCCs pursue unbundled pricing strategies, where every additional service has to be purchased by the passenger. The majority of traditional airlines still offer all-inclusive prices (O'Connell & Williams, 2005).

Airline cost structure

An airline's cost structure is characterized by high fixed costs (e.g. personnel, ownership costs, administration and distribution or engineering) and low variable costs (e.g. passenger dependent costs: catering or airport fees; and flight dependent costs: fuel or navigation charges). Fixed costs are primarily driven by lease and debt payments for aircraft assets, whereas fuel is the most important driver of variable costs. The high fixed cost nature of the business also highlights the importance of liquidity (Rothkopf, 2009).

Fierce competition and high cyclicality of air transport industry

The aviation industry is one of the most competitive industries around. To describe the competitive environment of the aviation industry, Doganis (2005) used the word 'paradox'. The air transportation industry is characterized by long-term growth, although the industry's profitability is very low. Other features of the industry are its cyclical development, with years of high profits regularly followed by years of substantial losses. Due to the high fixed cost structure and the cyclicality, the airline business relies on a boom time business model (Gillen & Lall, 2004). Contrastingly, the airline industry is an extremely capital intensive industry with very specific investments in long-term assets that create high exit barriers. The industry is also extremely vulnerable to external shocks.

Low profit margins on average

The large dependence on commodity prices (e.g. fuel) and increasing liberalization are key factors influencing further industry development. Competition and schedule and network inflexibility often lead to price wars and oversupply. Due to falling ticket prices the growth of the industry is coupled with a decline in revenues. This leads to cost control, cost reduction and constant innovation at airlines being prioritized. While the cyclical development and vulnerability to external shocks impacts on all players in the aviation industry, profit margins of airlines regularly fall short of those for airports, caterers, aircraft manufacturers and ground service providers (Doganis, 2005). Historical returns in the airline business have been low, and are comparable to those in commodity industries (Gillen & Lall, 2004). Overall, few airlines earn their cost of capital. However, in terms of profitability, there are high variances among airlines. A number of airlines have profits and above-average growth rates, largely independent from economic cycles and the chosen business model. Airlines such as Southwest and Singapore Airlines, for instance, show that this is possible both in the low-cost and premium segment (Heracleous, Wirtz & Pangarkar, 2006).

Airlines often claim that their low profitability arises from a 'hostile' environment where airlines are sandwiched between monopolistic or oligopolistic providers that make much higher profit margins on 'the back of the airlines' as shown in the aviation value chain

This complaint is partly true with regard to aircraft manufacturers (duopoly for large wide body aircraft), leasing companies (dominance of two companies), airports (natural monopolies), fuel companies (oligopoly), global distribution systems (worldwide three main providers) and air traffic control providers (monopolies).

Airline leasing market dominated by the 'Big Two'

The aircraft leasing market seems to have a polypolistic structure at first sight with about 70 active companies (Aviation Strategy, 2008) operating up to the 2008 financial crisis. Looking more closely, however, we see that in a market comprising of about 6,800 leased aircraft worldwide, the 15 biggest companies have 75% of the market out of which the two biggest companies, GECAS (General Electric Commercial Aviation Services) and ILFC (International Lease Finance Corporation), together own or manage about 55% of the top 15 companies' aircraft (Aviation Strategy, 2008). This position remained unrivalled for a long time due to the fact that the two companies were the biggest single customers of both Boeing and Airbus and occupied a large number of production slots making it difficult for other competitors to enter this lucrative business. The 2008 financial crisis and, as a consequence, the credit crunch has led to severe difficulties for the parent companies of the leasing market leaders, General Electric (GECAS) and AIG (ILFC), and the emergence of new and stronger competitors from the Gulf region (DAE Dubai Aerospace Company, Al Waha Capital) and from China (BOC Aviation), which might challenge the dominant position of the two market leaders (Halstead, 2008).

B. 2 Aircraft industry

Market duopoly

While airlines act in a polypolistic market, the aircraft manufacturing industry is characterized by an oligopolistic market environment. Apart from regional sub-markets and smaller planes, the market for large aircraft is mainly dominated by Airbus and Boeing and hence can be seen as a duopoly (Newhouse, 2007). After the acquisition of McDonnell Douglas by Boeing in 1997 and the integration of subsidiaries at Airbus in 2001, these two manufacturers have become the only major suppliers of larger wide body aircraft today. Profit margins for aircraft manufacturers are higher than those of airlines and airports; however, compared to the total manufacturing industry, they are below average (Doganis, 2005).

High capital requirements and long production cycles

The characteristic features of the industry are extremely high capital requirements, high entry and exit barriers, dynamic economies of scale, a high R&D intensity, and relatively long periods between initial investment and returning cash flows on aircraft sales (Wells & Wensveen, 2004). As a consequence, prices for aircrafts must be calculated on the basis of sales forecasts a long time before the aircraft is sold. Also, due to the dynamic economies of scale, production costs vary greatly depending on the output. Thus, an exact prediction of production levels is critical. Overall, the high investments, the long planning horizon and the dependence on the cyclical demand for aircraft significantly increases the manufacturers' business risks (Clarke, 2001). The launch costs of the Boeing 787, for example, are estimated to be well over US$ 13 billion. To reduce the business risk, Boeing had decided to source over 70% of the value added through an international network of suppliers (Pritchard & Macpherson, 2004). Today, however, this fact is regarded as one of the main causes for a delay in the delivery schedule. For the production of the wide body A380 at Airbus, production structures and associated problems were similar. The individual components of the aircraft are produced at the various European locations, then shipped and assembled in Toulouse/France, requiring an extremely high level of coordination.

Subsidies

Since both in the US and the EU the two major aircraft manufacturers have a very high industrial importance, they are granted substantial subsidies, often violating the rules of the World Trade Organization (WTO). In the case of the aforementioned Boeing 787, for example, this led to a complaint from the EU at the WTO (Pritchard & Macpherson, 2004). Airbus has been supported by subsidies as well, from its early beginnings to its current aircraft developments. Tensions between the EU and the US were not reduced through bilateral agreements made in 1992; agreements intended to limit direct and indirect subsidies for the development of new aircraft (Irvin & Pavcnik, 2004).

B. 3 Airports

High specificity of investment

Airports complement airlines as providers of ground infrastructure, such as runways and terminals. However, unlike airlines, airports are not able to quickly respond to fundamental changes in the market environment. Reasons for this are found both in the extraordinarily high specificity of the infrastructure investment and the ownership structure of airports. A vast number of national and international airports are still under public ownership; significant privatization trends have only been observable in the recent past (Graham, 2003). These privatizations are often different forms of concession models for operating an airport (Graham, 2003).

Airport business models

Like airlines, airports are not a homogeneous group, but differ – among others things – in terms of their size, function and regional reach. Airports such as Chicago O'Hare, London Heathrow or Singapore Changi are international hubs ('mega-hubs'), which concentrate inter-regional and international transport, and serve as a starting and finishing point for intercontinental long haul services. Intra-regional services (e.g. intra-European or intra-American air transportation) are the focus of secondary airports, which generally also offer connections to some international long haul mega-hubs. Feeder flights to international or regional hubs are also the focus of regional airports, which are usually served only by smaller aircraft. Overall, there is a high degree of concentration of passenger flows at airports, with the 100 biggest airports worldwide accounting for more than 60% of all passengers (Airports Council International [ACI], 2008). By number however, small airfields are the largest group among all airports. Small airfields serve general aviation, such as private business aviation and leisure/sports flying.

Importance of non-aviation revenues

Depending on the size, function and location of an airport, the importance of different business areas varies. Particularly at major international airports, traditional revenue sources such as landing fees and ground handling services only represent a small part of all income sources. For a large number of airports, non-aviation income sources such as parking and real estate represent more than half of total revenues (Graham, 2003; Jarach, 2005). Profit margins at airports are both significantly higher and more constant compared to those of airlines (Doganis, 2005). However, the intense international competition between airlines also has its impact on airport earnings. The rising market power particularly of low-cost carriers at regional airports puts pressure on revenues. In Europe, for example, a large number of smaller regional airports have already generated losses and thus operate at the taxpayers' expense.

Conflict with airlines

Airports often pursue interests divergent to those of airlines. For example, airports want to maximize the stay of the passengers in order to maximize the revenues of airport shopping while airlines have an incentive to keep the airport stay as short as possible (Rothkopf, 2009).

B. 4 Institutions

Separation between public vs. private and national vs. supranational institutions

In addition to airlines, airports and aircraft manufacturers, a number of institutions are major actors within the air transport system. One common classification distinguishes between public and private institutions and national and supranational institutions. Within this classification one can further differentiate with regard to the primary functions of the institution. National public institutions such as the Federal Aviation Administration (FAA) primarily act as norm-setting and monitoring organizations. The main task of national weather service providers and air traffic control is to offer services for the efficient and safe operation of air traffic. Similarly, one can distinguish between institutions at the national and the supranational level. Supranational public institutions such as the European Civil Aviation Conference (ECAC), and the European Aviation Safety Agency (EASA), focus on norm-setting and regulation in air transportation. Air traffic providers, like Eurocontrol, by contrast, are primarily service providers. Private institutions are not allowed to set binding norms and rules. Their main functions are member advocacy and the creation of a platform for its members. An example is the Association of European Airlines (AEA), offering a forum for exchange of information between its members, and representing and lobbying its members' interests towards stakeholders within the entire aviation industry. We briefly introduce the major institutions in aviation.

IATA

An important international institution in aviation is the International Air Transport Association (IATA). It serves as an umbrella organization for its member airlines. Its main function is the settlement of tickets on the basis of the interline agreements (IATA Clearing House) and the standardization of new processes introduced into the industry. Furthermore, some contracts with service providers (e.g. ticket producers, travel agencies) are directly negotiated and closed by IATA. However, the IATA is not allowed to interfere with the commercial activities of a member. Since its huge member base makes it difficult and time-consuming to reach solutions, expert groups from IATA generally prepare decisions. Decisions are then put down in resolutions that become binding for each member. The so called 'recommended practices', in contrast, only provide advice to the airlines. Overall, the IATA has lost its significance in recent years, partly due to its lost role as a tariff coordinator. The increasing deregulation of the airline industry, the emergence of new competitors from the low-cost segment, and the rising importance of large airline alliances have also contributed to this development.

ICAO

The International Civil Aviation Organization (ICAO) acts as a specialized agency within the United Nations (UN). The ICAO is structured into regional offices that serve different air traffic regions. It is a body that sets standards and recommends practices for the industry, particularly with regard to air navigation and inspection procedures.

ACI

Airports are globally represented by the Airport Council International (ACI). The institution is structured into six geographical territories operating under the ACI brand. The ACI has about 600 members operating at 1,650 airports, including all important airports worldwide. The institution's main purpose is to foster the cooperation between its members and external bodies, such as governments, airlines and aircraft manufacturers. The ACI also acts as a lobbying group to the public, for example by creating awareness of the economic and social benefits airports bring to regions, communities and individuals. The ACI tries to set international standards by exchanging best practices via conferences, trainings, and seminars. To stimulate business development, the institution provides its members with industry knowledge in airport management and operations.

C. CONCLUSION

The air transportation industry was introduced as a highly complex industry, characterized by high growth numbers, intense competition and low profit margins. Air transportation has important economic and social relevance, expected to increase even more in the future. The aviation industry is shaped by four main actors: airlines, airports, institutions and the aircraft industry.

The airline market can best be described as heterogeneous with its players having many different business models, functions and regional focuses. While the airline industry is growing strongly, it is suffering from low profit margins and fierce competition. Airports on the other hand have been able to realize more stable revenue streams. They are, however, also experiencing increased competition and pressure from airlines. Airports are characterized by a high specificity of their investments and an increasing amount of revenues stemming from non-aviation income sources. The aircraft industry is – apart from some smaller manufacturers for regional aircrafts – a duopolistic market, requiring high capital investments and long production cycles. The aircraft manufacturing industry in both the US and Europe is publicly subsidized. The airline industry is shaped by a variety of different institutions and organizations. One can distinguish between public vs. private institutions and national vs. supranational institutions. While public institutions, such as the ICAO, serve as norm-setting and monitoring, private organizations such as the ACI serve as a platform for member exchange and advocacy.

Review Questions

- Explain the economic relevance of the air transportation industry. What do direct, indirect, induced, catalyzed and perpetuity effects stand for?
- Who are the four major stakeholders in the aviation industry? Give an example for each of these stakeholders.
- What are the different airline business models? What differentiates these business models?
- Why are airports – unlike airlines – generally unable to react quickly to changes in their market environment?
- What differentiates mega-hubs, secondary airports and regional airports?
- What is meant by non-aviation revenues?
- Is the market for aircraft manufacturers oligopolistic or duopolistic? Who are the major players in this market?
- Explain the difference between national and supranational institutions in the aviation industry. Give an example for each of them.

Bibliography and further reading

Air Transport Action Group [ATAG] (2008): The economic and social benefits of air transport 2008, Geneva.

Airports Council International [ACI] (2008): International traffic report 2007, Geneva.

Aviation Strategy (2008): Leasing market past its peak – but still robust, London.

Boeing (2014): Current Market Outlook 2014-2033. Market Analysis, Seattle.

Brueckner, J. K. / Girvin, R. (2008): Airport noise regulation, airline service quality, and social welfare, in: Transportation Research Part B (Methodological), Vol. 42, No. 1, p. 19-37.

Clarke, P. (2001): Buying the Big Jets – Fleet planning for airlines, Aldershot.

Costa, P. R. / Harned, D. S. / Lundquist, J. T. (2002): Rethinking the aviation industry, in: The McKinsey Quarterly (Special Edition: Risk and Resilience), p. 88-100.

Doganis, R. (2005): Flying Off Course – The Economics Of International Airlines, 2nd edition, New York.

Gillen, D. / Lall, A. (2004): Competitive advantage of low-cost carriers: some implications for airports, in: Journal of Air Transport Management - Proceedings of the Hamburg Aviation Conference 2003, Vol. 10, No. 1, p. 41-50.

Graham, A. (2003): Managing Airports – An international perspective, 2nd edition, Liancre Hill.

Halstead, J. (2008): Global financial crisis: Aviation repercussions, in: Aviation strategy, No. 132, p. 1-3.

Heracleous, L. / Wirtz, J. / Pangarkar, N. (2006): Flying High In a Competitive Industry. Cost-effective service excellence at Singapore Airlines, Singapore.

Huse, C. / Evangelho, F. (2007): Investigating business traveler heterogeneity: Low-cost vs. full-service airline users?, in: Transportation Research Part E: Logistics and Transportation Review - Selected papers of the 2005 ATRS Conference, Vol. 43, No. 3, p. 259-68.

International Air Transport Association [IATA] (2007): Annual Report 2007, Montreal / Geneva.

Irvin, D. A. / Pavcnik, N. (2004): Airbus versus Boeing revisited: international competition in the aircraft market, in: Journal of International Economics, Vol. 64, p. 223-245.

Janic, M. (2007): The Sustainability of Air Transportation: A Quantitative Analysis and Assessment, Aldershot.

Jarach, D. (2005): Airport marketing. Strategies to Cope with the New Millennium Environment, Aldershot.

Knudsen, T. / Randel, A. / Rugholm, J. (2005): The vanishing middle market, in: McKinsey Quarterly, No. 4, p. 6-9.

Macintosh, A. / Wallace, L. (2008): International aviation emissions to 2025: Can emissions be stabilized without restricting demand? in: Energy Policy, Vol. 37, p. 264-273.

Meffert, H. / Bruhn, M. (1995): Dienstleistungsmarketing – Grundlagen, Konzepte, Methoden, Wiesbaden.

Newhouse, J. (2007): Boeing versus Airbus – The Inside Story of the Greatest International Competition in Business, New York.

O'Connell, J. F. / Williams, G. (2005): Passengers' perceptions of low-cost airlines and full service carriers: A case study involving Ryanair, Aer Lingus, Air Asia and Malaysia Airlines, in: Journal of Air Transport Management, Vol. 11. No. 4, p. 259-272.

Pritchard, D. / MacPherson, A. (2004): Industrial Subsidies and the Politics of World Trade – The Case of the Boeing 7e7, in: The Industrial Geographer, Vol. 1, No. 2, p. 57-73.

Rothkopf, M. (2009): Innovation in commoditized service industries – an empirical case study analysis in the passenger airline industry, Münster.

Wells, A. T. / Wensveen, J. G. (2004): Air Transportation – A Management Perspective, 5th edition, Belmont.

Whitelegg, J. / Cambridge, H. (2004): Aviation and Sustainability, Stockholm.

Airline Economics

Paul McKnight

Table of contents

You should be able to

- explain the difference between air travel demand and air passenger traffic
- describe the difference between a flight route and a city-pair market
- explain why airlines measure traffic and capacity using complicated kilometer-based metrics rather than just the number of passengers carried and seats flown
- show how airline marginal costs affect competitive fare levels and excess capacity in the industry
- describe in detail the concepts of airline unit revenue and unit cost
- differentiate between economies of scale, scope, and density
- explain the effect of leverage on airline profitability
- show how air cargo economics differs from that which affects passenger transport

The author

Paul McKnight is a retired airport management consultant with California-based LeighFisher Inc. He specialized in the analysis of airline service and forecasting of airline traffic flows. Mr. McKnight also lectured in Air Transportation Economics in the Commercial Aviation Management Program at Western University in London, Canada. He holds a degree in industrial engineering and an MBA.

Abstract

This chapter discusses first the demand for air travel and the service and fare factors that affect the number of air passengers. This is followed by a description of airline revenues and costs, as well as the measurement of airline profitability, and a brief discussion of the economics of air cargo and all-cargo airlines. The chapter helps the reader to acquire a basic framework for understanding the more detailed, airline industry-specific material presented in subsequent chapters and, perhaps, the economics of other industries, as well.

A. INTRODUCTION

Basic economic concepts are necessary for airline managers

Although numerous basic concepts are presented in general economics and accounting courses, it is not uncommon for many students to come away from their academic studies without a clear idea of the relevance of those concepts to the real world. Do demand and supply curves really represent something that actually happens? Does anyone make use of price/volume relationships in practice? Does it matter whether costs are fixed or variable? This chapter will help the reader to appreciate how many of the economic and accounting concepts are used by managers in the airline industry.

A metric's absolute value often is less useful than its timelines and comparisons

It is worth noting here that the absolute values of individual economic metrics (measures) often have less significance than the changes in those metrics over time and against other metrics. For example, quantifying a country's Gross Domestic Product provides little useful value in itself, but determining how it has changed in recent years or comparing it to the GDP of other countries can provide useful information.

B. AIR TRAVEL DEMAND VERSUS AIR PASSENGER TRAFFIC

Demand and traffic are not the same

In applying basic economic concepts to the field of airline transportation, a critical distinction in terminology between demand and traffic can be made here.

Definition of air travel demand and air passenger traffic

Many writers on economic subjects use the terms demand and sales/revenue interchangeably. This can lead to lack of clarity when applied to airline economics. A more concise differentiation is that air travel demand represents the need or desire to travel by air between two points – that is, the potential number of air journeys – whereas air passenger traffic represents the actual number of passengers that travel by air.

Air travel demand is fluid and immeasurable. It is a fluid concept because, as an airline trip becomes more convenient and the airfare is reduced toward zero, the potential number of passenger journeys increases exponentially. Demand varies depending on a number of parameters. It cannot be measured because, unlike air passenger traffic, it is not observable. In spite of these limitations, the concept of air travel demand is a useful and relevant one.

Factors affecting air travel demand

It is also important to differentiate the factors that affect demand from those that affect airline passenger traffic. The primary factors affecting air travel demand between any two communities (A and B, say) are the following:

- **Community of interest between A and B**: if A is a northern city with cold winters, for example, while B has a tropical climate, there is a potential for seasonal vacation air travel. If A is a center of industry or government and B is an outlying regional city, there may be business air travel between the two communities.
- **Distance between A and B**: the longer the distance, or the greater the difficulty of travelling via surface modes (due to oceans or mountains, for example), the more likely that travelers will choose the air mode.
- **Populations of A and B, including their respective catchment areas**: attempts to quantify this relationship, using the simplistic gravity model, have hypothesized that air travel demand is directly proportional to the product of the populations at A and B. While such a relationship has never been validated, it at least captures one aspect of demand, i.e. that there is much more air travel potential between two larger cities than between two smaller ones.
- **Personal income levels at A and B**: air travel for non-business reasons tends to be discretionary and funded by disposable income. Higher income levels tend to be associated with more disposable income and, hence, more non-business trips by air.
- **Employment parameters at A and B**: white-collar industries (e.g. financial, trade, education) tend to generate more business air travel than blue-collar ones (e.g. construction, agriculture). All things remaining equal, however, rising levels of employment tend to increase air travel demand, while increasing levels of unemployment tend to depress air travel demand.
- **Economic health of A and B and their respective regions / countries**: a robust and growing economy fosters growth in demand for air travel – directly, for business-related air travel and, less directly, for non-business air travel.
- **Political environment at A and B**: certain countries restrict their citizens' travel, particularly to other countries, and also that of incoming foreigners. Instability, violence, and war tend to depress national economies and increase fear for residents and visitors alike. Both situations dampen air travel demand.

Although it is very difficult to measure the impact of each of these factors on air travel demand, an understanding of the factors is essential for airline management. After all, it is from the demand pool that airlines attract passengers for their flights.

Demand is independent of airline service and fares

Air travel demand is independent of the level of airline service and fares offered. These factors do not affect air travel demand per se – rather, they determine the proportion of potential demand that is translated into air passenger traffic.

Potential demand vs. air passenger traffic

In contrast to air travel demand, air passenger traffic is both finite and measurable. Passengers represent a subset of air travel demand; they can be counted, and their numbers will always be less than total potential demand.

Figure 1 shows that the volume of air passenger traffic is higher in more developed economies. Note, however, that the chart relates trips per capita to a factor that affects demand, not traffic. The originators of the chart can be forgiven, perhaps, given that the chart was developed for marketing purposes, for making the leap of logic required: namely, that gains in per capita gross national product increase the size of the demand pool from which air passenger traffic is drawn.

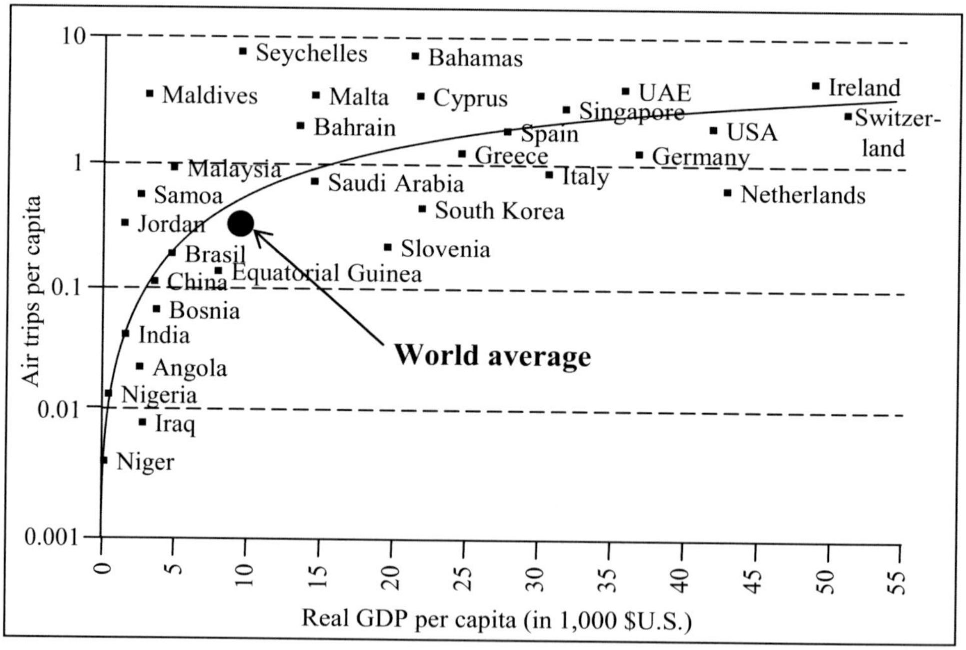

Figure 1: Relationship of air travel to international economies (Sources: IATA, PaxIS, Global Insight, Airbus)

Air passenger traffic lags the economic cycles

The same process results in air passenger traffic within a given country, or an integrated set of countries such as the European Union, varying with cyclical changes in GDP. As shown in Figure 2, however, air passenger traffic typically lags the GDP cycle. Traffic tends to decline several months after the economy begins to show weakness, in part due to the substantial sale of advance airline tickets, and also because of the time it takes for the economic downturn to reveal itself and affect consumer behavior and business travel budgets.

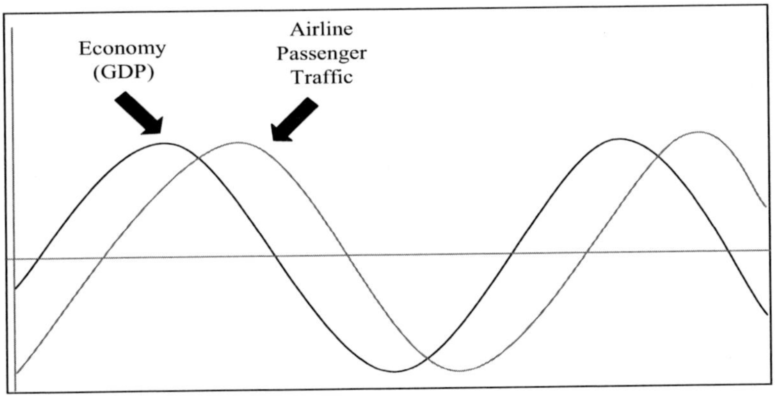

Figure 2: Traffic tends to lag economic fluctuations (Own illustration)

Measurement of air passenger traffic

The measurement of air passenger traffic can be surprisingly complex, as shown by the multiplicity of traffic measures in Box A. A passenger is not a person - a passenger is something that a person does. For example, a person on a multiple-stage itinerary can be counted in various ways: 1 round-trip, 2 one-way trips, 4 flight boardings (enplanements), and 5 flight legs traveled (assuming one of the flights makes an enroute stop). Each measure poses combinability issues when a picture of total traffic is needed. If the enplanement metric is used, for example, then a passenger who flies on a nonstop flight from A to B will be counted once, while a passenger traveling from A to B who makes an enroute connection will be counted twice. And a passenger boarding a 300-km flight will be counted as equivalent to a passenger taking a 3,000-km flight.

Revenue passenger kilometer a measure of airline traffic

To address the latter problem, the industry developed a measure that weights each passenger by the number of kilometers traveled. It was further refined to measure only the number of revenue (i.e. paying) passengers, in order to omit the non-revenue (i.e. non-paying) passengers, such as deadheading crew and promotional pass-holders. The resulting metric is known as revenue passenger kilometers or RPK for short, and is used worldwide as the standard measure of traffic carried.[1]

---

1 In the United States and other countries that have not officially adopted the International System of Units (the metric system), the airline industry uses miles rather than kilometers. Hence, revenue passenger miles (RPM). Other kilometer-related metrics introduced in subsequent pages also tend to be denominated in miles in those countries.

Box A:
Passenger Traffic Metrics

Air travelers	Number of individual persons who made air trips
Passenger trips	Number of completed air passenger journeys, including some that are one-way only
One-way trips	Number of one-way passenger trip equivalents, where a round-trip is counted as 2 one-way trips
Flight legs flown	Number of passengers on board all departing flights
Enplanements	Number of passengers boarded on each flight, including both originating and connecting passengers
Origin-Destination	Number of passengers carried that originated at one city of a city pair and terminated at the other city, and vice versa, regardless of flight routing (nonstop, one-stop, multi-stop, or connection)
Revenue Passenger-Kilometers (RPK)	Number of kilometers flown by all revenue passengers carried (typically referred to as traffic)

Three key factors determine the degree to which air travel demand is converted into actual passengers: air service, airfares, and airport access. The relationship between demand and traffic, and the factors affecting both, are illustrated in Figure 3.

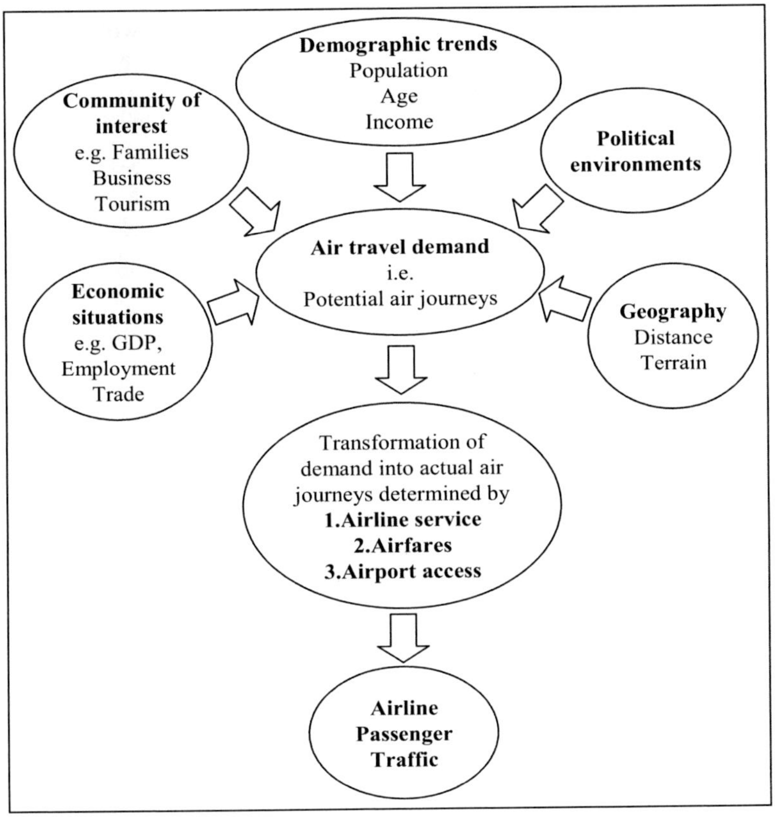

Figure 3: Schematic of factors affecting demand and traffic (Own illustration)

Each of the three traffic factors is discussed further below. Note that airline management controls the first two (service and fares) and sometimes the third (airport access) in areas that are served by more than one airport.

C. AIRLINE SERVICE

In former days airline services were heavily restricted

Until the forces of regulation began to be lifted from the airline industry in the latter quarter of the 20th century, airline service was prescribed by government regulation. Airlines could operate only on routes for which they were specifically designated by their national aviation authorities. The evolution of air charter services was a response to this strict regulation. Economic deregulation of the airline industry took hold in successive countries, beginning in the United States, and resulted in a proliferation of new airlines, expanded service by incumbent airlines, and a steep ramping-up of airline competition.

Scheduled vs. charter services

Commercial air passenger service has two types: scheduled and charter. In scheduled service, an airline publishes a flight schedule and is obliged to operate according to that schedule; the airline bears the risk that it will earn insufficient revenue to cover its costs. In charter air passenger service, an airline operates under a contract with another entity; the airline is paid in advance, and the risk is borne by the chartering entity (typically a tour operator, organization, or individual). The discussion in this chapter relates primarily to scheduled service.

Routes and network

A route is a flight leg, a nonstop link between two airports. An airline's routes together constitute its network, sometimes referred to as its route system. Airline route networks tend to be categorized as either point-to-point or hub-and-spoke, as follows:

- **Point-to-point network**: This type of network is comprised of routes linking several airports in no regular pattern. Its viability primarily relies on the local passenger traffic on each route. Connecting passengers comprise a relatively small proportion of total point-to-point network passenger traffic. Many smaller airlines and low-cost carriers (LCCs) operate networks that are primarily point-to-point in character.
- **Hub-and-spoke network**: This type of network is comprised primarily of routes (spokes) to and from one or more major airport selected by the airline to serve as its hubs. The flight schedules are timed in banks, or complexes, throughout the day to maximize the number of connecting possibilities for the passengers. Connecting passengers make up a sizable proportion of hub-and-spoke network traffic. By funneling passengers through the hub, the airline achieves certain efficiencies; however, an airline typically pays a significant penalty from lower utilization of aircraft and airport-based assets. Most large, scheduled airlines, and some LCCs, operate a form of hub-and-spoke network.

Level of air service

The level of air service (as contrasted with the quality of service) is one of the three key factors that determine how much air travel demand is converted into passenger traffic on a given route. Level of service relates to such features as the number of flights (sometimes referred to as flight frequency), flight timings (both departure and arrival times), flight routings (nonstop, one-stop, or multi-stop), the type of aircraft operated (number of seats, level of comfort, classes of onboard service), and the particular airports served at A and B (in cases where there are alternative airports serving those communities).

Available seat-kilometers: a measure of airline capacity

Like air traffic, the level of air service is measured in several ways, as shown by the air service metrics listed in Box B. A distance-weighted measure of seats operated, namely available seat kilometers (ASK), is used to quantify the amount of service provided and represents the standard measure of capacity provided. The service-related ASK metric is analogous to the traffic-related RPK metric described earlier.

Passenger Load Factor

Air traffic metrics and air service metrics converge in another metric, Passenger Load Factor. On a single flight, the passenger load factor is simply the percentage of seats that are occupied by revenue passengers. For an entire route system, however, both the number of passengers carried and seats flown are weighted by the kilometers that each is flown, yielding the following formula:

Passenger load factor
= *Traffic carried divided by capacity provided*
= *RPK / ASK*

The Passenger Load Factor metric is more complex than it first appears. One reason is that it does not discriminate between different types of passengers. On a given flight, for example, there may be four types of passengers, namely, a) local (O&D) passengers traveling strictly between A and B; b) beyond passengers originating at A who connect with other flights at B; c) behind passengers originating elsewhere who connect with the flight at A and are destined for B; and d) bridge passengers originating elsewhere who connect with the flight at A and connect again with other flights at B.

Load Factor represents a measure of productivity

From a managerial perspective, however, Passenger Load Factor is often used as a scorecard. It represents a broad measure of the productive use of the airline's mobile assets (aircraft and seats). It is also sometimes used as a proxy for system profitability although, as will become clear later in this chapter, load factor can be an inaccurate profit predictor.

Box B:
Airline Service Metrics

Flight frequency	Number of daily flights in each direction on a given route
Seats operated	Total seats available on nonstop flights on a given route
Available Seat-Kilometers (ASK)	Number of kilometers times the number of seats, on each flight (typically referred to as capacity)

An airline does not operate in a vacuum, of course. It typically faces competition from other airlines, particularly on its routes carrying the largest numbers of passengers. Metrics used to gauge levels of competition are listed in Box C.

Shares as measures in competitive markets

Wherever two or more airlines compete, each measures its proportion or share of flights or seats provided and passengers carried in relation to the other carrier(s). Each of these metrics is frequently, if not always quite correctly, referred to as market share. In any discussion of competitive shares, however, it is important to be clear as to what is being measured - activity on a route or passengers in a city-pair market.

Difficulties in computing shares

It is not as simple, or even relevant, for an airline to compute its share of total passengers carried on a route. As described earlier, more than one type of passenger is often carried on a given flight: origin-destination (O&D) passengers that are local to the route (i.e. traveling only from A to B, and vice versa), and other passengers that are carried on a flight between A and B in the course of a journey that involves another origin or destination, or both. A simple share calculation, then, using all passengers on board all flights operated on a route, yields a result that is not useful. This leads to the need for another important concept: the city-pair market.

Shares of O&D passengers in city-pair markets

A city-pair market is the term used to describe the air travel demand, and subsequent O&D passenger traffic, between two communities - regardless of the flight routings used by passengers. Because an airline is unable to link all communities with nonstop service, and often competes using one-stop, multi-stop, or connecting flights, it needs to measure its share of total O&D passengers traveling in a given city-pair market. Strictly speaking, this is the correct use of the term market share.

Box C:
Competition Metrics

Route capacity share	One airline's percentage of total flights or seats operated on a given route
Hirschman-Herfindahl-Index	A relative measure of airline concentration, with respect to either seats on a route or passengers in a city-pair market. Calculated as the sum of the squares of each airline's percentage share of the total. Value ranges from 10,000 (a monopoly) to 0 (an infinite number of competitors).
Airport market share	One airline's percentage of total flights, seats, or passengers at a given airport
City-pair market share	One airline's percentage of total O&D passengers carried by all airlines in a given city-pair market

Degree of concentration e.g. at an airport

Airlines' shares of total flights or seats operated on all routes emanating from a given airport are often of interest to both the airlines and the management of the airport. The Hirschman-Herfindahl Index (HHI) was developed to quantify the degree of concentration of competitors in a given market. HHI facilitates comparison of the level of airline concentration on routes and at airports. Most airports selected by airlines to serve as their hubs, for example, exhibit a high level of airline concentration.

The S-curve effect

One example of the importance of flight frequency and airline market shares on a route is an observed phenomenon called the S-curve effect. As an airline increases its share of flights on a given route, the increase in its share of local traffic is not linear - it exhibits an S-curve pattern. See illustration in Figure 4. Consequently, there is an incentive for an airline to establish more than a minimal share of the service offered on each route it serves.

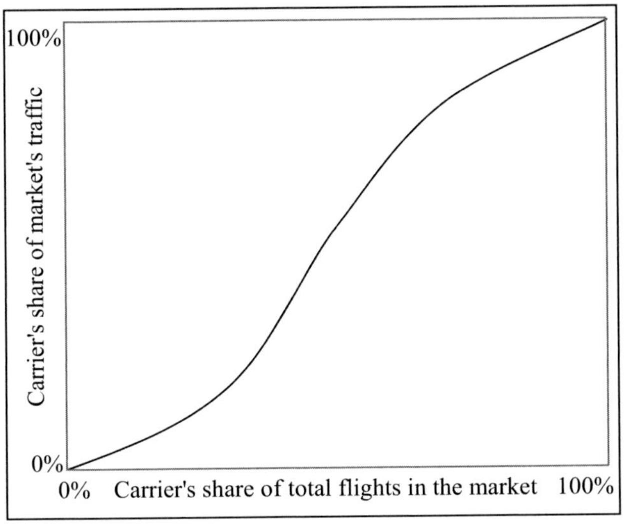

Figure 4: Flight frequency S-curve
(Own illustration)

D. AIRLINE FARES

Fare setting in former days...

As economic regulation of the scheduled airline industry evolved in North America and elsewhere after WWII, there was only one domestic fare available for each city-pair, and all airlines charged the same amount. Changes to the standard fare, to reflect changes in the airline's input costs, were subject to the approval of government regulatory authorities. The standard domestic airline fare was generally set in accordance with a version of the following formula:

...was rather simplistic

Fare = Trip charge + (rate per km. x city-pair nonstop distance)

This formula had several advantages for the industry and its regulators, including:

- It was easy to understand and simple to apply
- It recognized that there were fixed and variable costs in providing the service
- Fare increases could be accomplished by adjusting upward the fixed component (trip charge), the variable parameter (Rate per km.), or both
- It put all airlines on a level playing field with respect to fares charged

The linear nature of the fare formula is illustrated in the upper chart of Figure 5. Charting the fare-per-kilometer result of the formula (as shown in the upper chart of Figure 5) shows that the fare paid by the air traveler declined, on a per-kilometer basis, as trip distance increased. As airline pricing became more sophisticated, and various premium and discount fare types were introduced, they were typically calculated as a percentage of the standard fare.

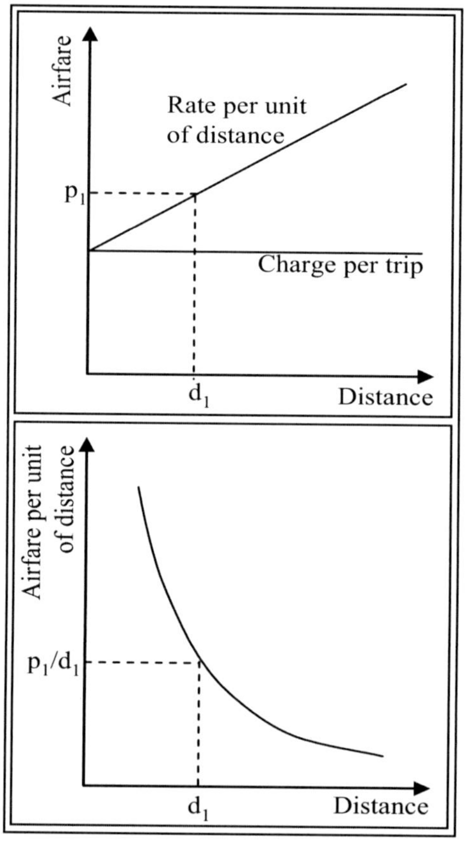

Figure 5: Relationship of distance flown to airfare charged (Own illustration)

Nowadays air fares also reflect e.g. market factors and competition

With the advent of economic deregulation in the airline industry (1978 in the US, later in other countries), airlines were free to set fares reflecting not only costs but also market and competitive factors. The free-market fare-setting experience was new to most airline managers. Among other things, they learned that:

- Making fare information more readily available to air travel consumers makes for a much more competitive marketplace. Establishment of airline websites in order to sidestep the relatively costly travel agency channel of distribution, for example, has made pricing more transparent and facilitated shopping around for travelers for the lowest fare. This has put downward pressure on airline fares and, arguably, cost the airlines more in lost revenue than they have saved on travel agency commissions.
- Although fares must be set at competitive levels, fare levels do not necessarily need to match those charged by competitors. Air travel consumers make value trade-offs between alternative airline service offerings. Some travelers are willing to pay more for nonstop service, for example, versus multi-stop or connecting flights connecting the same city-pair. Other travelers are willing

to modify their travel plans or forego certain service frills in order to obtain a lower fare.

- Offering a number of different fares in each city-pair market, with varying fare levels and qualifying conditions, can attract additional customers. If managed carefully, these can increase load factors and improve profitability.

New entrants introduced price competition

In the regulated era, airline fares were set generally on a cost-plus basis, i.e. at levels intended by the regulatory authorities to ensure that airlines made a fair profit margin. After route and pricing regulation was lifted, numerous new airlines entered the industry, offering lower fares and threatening the continued existence of the older legacy airlines. Although the competing fare levels were clearly below cost for them, the older airlines learned to compete by offering (and heavily promoting) matching fares while limiting the number of seats available for sale at those lower levels.

Market segmentation leads to numerous fare levels

Most airlines now offer numerous types of fares, targeted at various segments of the air travel market and differentiated by such limitations as round-trip travel, advance purchase, and minimum stay at destination - and the number of seats available for most fare types on each flight is limited. While such fare structures may provide fare discounts to some travelers who would have been willing to pay more, they attract new customers who otherwise would not travel by air. The key to offering a differentiated mix of fare levels is to ensure that the average fare paid on each flight exceeds the airline's per-passenger cost of providing the flight.

Development of frequent flyer programs

Another development by airlines in the regulated era is the frequent flyer program (FFP). It rewards travelers who make repeated trips with an opportunity to earn free trips. FFPs are targeted primarily at those business travelers who do not incur the cost of their trips personally, and who have some control over which airline's flights they utilize. The FFP has proven to be a powerful tool at building customer loyalty and defending against low-fare competitors. Although FFP rewards are generally regarded by air travelers as free, they are really nothing more than a volume discount; fares paid by all travelers are higher than they would be otherwise.

New fees and charges

In recent years, the air travel pricing environment has seen the introduction of new fees and charges, including the following:

- **Fuel surcharges.** Since the days of cheap oil, in the 1990s and early 2000s, the price of jet fuel has tended to rise faster than airline fares. As the cost of jet fuel increased from about 15% to over 30% of the airlines' total operating costs, a separate fuel-related charge was imposed by many airlines. Although regulations in many developed countries require that the airlines include the fuel surcharge in any public fare advertisements, keeping the surcharge separate from the fare shields it from fare discounts negotiated with corporations. Passengers making free FFP reward trips are typically required to pay the fuel surcharge.

- **Airport-related charges.** As governance of airports around the world has increasingly moved away from government subsidy toward self-sufficiency, many airports have imposed fees on passengers using their facilities. After the 2001 terrorist attacks in the US, for example, the level of security screening of passengers was increased significantly at all airports and the cost passed along to air travelers.
- **Government charges.** Even though many national governments have passed the responsibility (and cost) of operating airports to quasi-public and private organizations, they continue to impose taxes of various kinds on air travelers. Some of these taxes do not relate to the costs of the air transportation system at all and are controversial, such as the tax on airline tickets launched in 2006 by France and several other countries directed at helping poorer countries fight lethal AIDS, malaria, and tuberculosis epidemics.
- **Ancillary fees.** Innovative, menu-based pricing approaches taken by several relatively new airlines have been adopted by many of the older, more established airlines. The common thread is the decoupling of many service features that have traditionally been included in airline fares. Passengers who want to check baggage, have preferred seating locations, enjoy a meal or soft drink, or have the comfort of a pillow or blanket, are now sometimes paying separately for each service and amenity.

International airfares had been controlled by IATA

International airfares have evolved differently than domestic airfares. Shortly after World War II, the major airlines providing international service across the world met to consider, among other matters, the control of international airfares. Although they were unable to reach a consensus, they decided that the governments of two countries linked by airline service must approve the airfares charged by the airlines providing the service. Setting of the airfares was left to be regulated by procedures established by their newly-formed trade association, the International Air Transport Association (IATA). The resulting process was cumbersome and costly and, although it had the benefit of producing a coherent and worldwide structure of interrelated passenger fares and cargo rates, it meant that prices were to be set by an association of producers - the international airlines. In other industries, price fixing by an industry cartel tends to be viewed by governments as illegal, but this practice continued into the late 1970s when IATA's pricing machinery began to disintegrate in the face of competitive pressures and a movement, industry-wide, towards economic deregulation.

Liberalization began in the late 1970s

Since 1978, fare-setting in many international air transport markets has been liberalized. While the traditional IATA- system is still used to set airfares between many countries across the world, an unfettered fare-setting environment prevails in an increasing number of country-pairs where so-called open skies bilateral agreements have been adopted. Consequently, most international airlines have to work under two different regulatory regimes when it comes to setting airfares.

Common metrics used in the monitoring of airline fares are laid out in Box D. Average fare and fare yield data are used by airlines in managing the availability of discount-fare seats and in evaluating the relative profitability of serving markets.

Box D:
Airline Fare Metrics

Total fare paid*	Total fare paid by a traveler for his/her air journey, whether a round-trip or one-way itinerary
Average fare paid*	The average amount paid by air travelers in a given market - may be based on round-trips or a one-way equivalency
Fare yield*	Fare paid per kilometer traveled, calculated as: i) the sum of one-way fares paid in a given market divided by total RPMs, or ii) the average fare paid divided by the average passenger trip distance

*Note: may include taxes and some of the new fees and charges noted in the narrative.

The asterisked note in Box D hints at one of the challenges for both airlines, and those outside the airline industry, in monitoring and comparing fare data from various sources - the data often includes differing fare elements. In addition, while reported airline fares often incorporate fuel surcharges and airport-related charges, taxes may or may not be included. It is important, when examining average fare data, to ascertain the extent to which zero-fare reward trips, ancillary fees, and taxes are included in the calculation. Ancillary fees are often collected when passengers check-in for their flights and, consequently, are not included in the reported fare paid. Finally, airlines are required to report detailed fare data to their governments only in the United States, so that, elsewhere, reliable fare data is generally difficult for outsiders to obtain.

E. AIRPORT ACCESS

The third factor affecting the amount of air travel demand that is converted into passenger traffic is not as immediately obvious as the two previous factors, service and airfares. It tends to be less influential but still deserves mention here.

Customers take into account the total trip cost

This factor relates to the passengers' actual (and perceived) cost to travel from their points of departure (home, office, and hotel) to the airport of departure and from the arrival airport to their individual destinations. An increase in tolls or congestion delay on the highways leading to and from the airports can raise the access cost. While it might be argued that such things are unlikely dissuade a given passenger from traveling, a certain percentage of passengers on the margin will elect not to make airline trips. On a larger scale, and all other factors being equal, relocation of an airport to a more remote location can reduce the volume of passenger traffic.

Trip cost (including time) and passenger numbers are inversely correlated

The basis for this relationship between the time / cost of getting to and from the airport and the number of passengers who will make a flight from that airport is the classic demand curve. See Figure 6. Given that all people put some value on their time, albeit some a higher value than others, the curve explains why an increase in time to reach the airport can reduce air travel demand and result in fewer passengers. It is worth noting that an increase in congestion (i.e. delays on the airport roadways or parking lots, inside the terminal, on the runways, or enroute from origin to destination) also pushes the demand curve to the left. Conversely, the relationship depicted in Figure 6 explains why the introduction of faster aircraft in earlier decades stimulated air traffic.

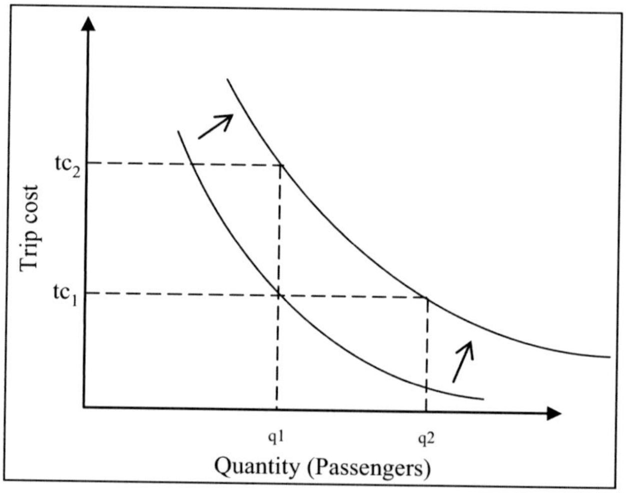

Figure 6: Effect of travel time on price and quantity relationship (Own illustration)

Choice between alternative airports

Many air travelers who live within reasonable driving distance of one or more alternatives to the local airport have a choice of airports. An example would be residents of, or visitors to, Cincinnati, Ohio, who have ready access to alternative airports within an hour's drive (Dayton) and within two hours (Louisville, Indianapolis, and Columbus). Differences in the service and fare offerings to the intended destination at those airports can leave the ease, cost, and time of driving to the airports as a key deciding factor. In the same way, the existence of multiple alternative airports serving the origin or destination cities (e.g. London, Paris, Milan, New York, Chicago, and Washington DC) can affect travel decisions.

F. AIRLINE REVENUE

Like any other business enterprise, an airline strives to maximize revenue in order to produce optimum profits. For a passenger airline, that includes attracting as many passengers, and deriving as much fare yield from each of those passengers, as it can.

To gain profits many factors need to be considered

Most airlines expend a great deal of effort building passenger volume. They focus on aircraft selection, route structure, schedule design, pricing strategy, competitive analysis, and aggressive sales and advertising. Airline profit margins tend to be thin, however, and often the difference between profit and loss comes down to effective management of passenger revenue.

Revenue management

Revenue management essentially involves the dynamic adjustment of seat inventory and fare availability on every flight on every route on every day for which reservations are being accepted (typically a rolling 11-12 months in advance). The objective is to fine-tune the mix of fares paid by passengers on each flight in a way that maximizes total fare revenue in each case. Now that most airlines have unbundled their fare structures, this challenging process now includes consideration of how to maximize ancillary fee revenue.

Other revenue sources such as cargo or ground handling

Other revenue sources are tapped by an airline. Chief among these is air cargo, comprised of mail and freight. Cargo carried in the belly compartments of a passenger aircraft augments the revenue earned from passengers in the main compartment. For a freighter aircraft, however, cargo revenue must be sufficient to offset all of the operating costs. Larger airlines also derive revenue from providing ground handling, personnel training, information technology, and aircraft maintenance services for other airlines. In addition, many major airlines have used their frequent-flyer programs as sources of significant revenues by working with credit card issuers to offer non-flight rewards and target non-business travelers.

Unit revenue

A key revenue metric used by passenger airlines is commonly referred to as unit revenue. It is calculated as operating revenue divided by ASKs, and is sometimes referred to as RASK (revenue per available seat kilometer). Watched carefully by airline management, changes in RASK chart the airline's progress by wringing revenue from each seat-kilometer flown. Airline management compares unit revenue against unit cost, a metric that is introduced later, in tracking overall profitability.

G. AIRLINE COSTS

The topic of airline costs is a large and complex one. This discussion is not intended to be exhaustive, but it will touch upon key cost relationships that will be discussed later in this book.

Fixed costs and variable costs

A useful way to view airline costs is by whether particular costs are fixed or variable. The term 'fixed' does not mean that the costs do not change over time, because virtually all costs do, but rather that they do not change with levels of activity. For example, the cost of the airline headquarters building does not change as the number of flights fluctuates, so that cost is regarded as fixed. On the other hand, changes in flight activity directly affect total landing fees incurred and the amount of jet fuel consumed, so these costs are termed variable.

Airlines typically face a high proportion of fixed costs

Fixed costs make up a high proportion of the total cost of an airline's operation. The implications of this are many. One obvious implication is that the profitability of an airline is dependent on obtaining high utilization of its productive assets (aircraft, people, and facilities). Another implication is that, when business conditions deteriorate rapidly, it is difficult for airlines to respond rapidly by reducing costs. Airlines are highly sensitive to fluctuations in traffic; increases in passenger volumes can drive up profits markedly, but passenger declines can generate losses quickly. This latter phenomenon will be revisited later in the chapter in the discussion about operating leverage.

Mixed costs

Actually, most costs are mixed, with both fixed and variable characteristics. This is illustrated in the following examples:

- Pilots are paid at an hourly rate and can be furloughed during periods of low demand, but their union contracts typically stipulate that operating pilots will be compensated for a minimum number of hours each month, whether or not they fly that number of hours. The contract typically specifies a maximum number of hours that can be flown each month, as well, so as the airline expands, it incurs the costs of initial training for new pilots. In addition, each pilot employed by the airline poses costs, which are largely fixed, such as supervision, recurrent training, and health and pension benefits.
- The cost of aircraft ownership is typically regarded as a fixed cost, given that loan or lease payments must be made each month regardless of the level of aircraft utilization. However, the size of the fleet can be reduced by selling aircraft in the event of a traffic downturn, and more aircraft can be acquired if traffic volumes increase. The reader is cautioned not to fall into the trap of regarding aircraft purchased with borrowed capital as posing fixed costs and leased aircraft representing variable costs; while the two methods of financing differ, the obligations they impose on the airline are similar.
- Rental payments for passenger gate lounges and loading bridges are fixed, in the sense that they are constant regardless of the number of flights or passengers processed at a given gate each day. Over time, however, the airline can negotiate with the airport to increase or reduce the number of gates leased.
- Costs related to taking passenger telephone reservations (still a material cost for many airlines despite increased online bookings)

have a significant variable component, in that the number of hourly-paid reservations staff can be reduced or increased as passenger call volumes change. However, the information systems and technology that support the reservations process represent a sizeable fixed cost - one that cannot be readily reduced if traffic declines.

- General overheads (including headquarters offices, sales and advertising, insurance, staff not involved with daily aircraft or passenger operations, and so on) are almost always regarded as a fixed cost. Clearly, though, virtually all of the component costs could be modified if circumstances warranted.

Cost structure of a flight

An airline's overall fixed/variable cost mix translates to a comparable fixed / variable cost makeup for operating an individual flight (see upper chart of Figure 7). The costs involved in operating any flight, including airport costs, landing fee, and aircraft ownership costs, are common to every flight, regardless of the distance flown. Once the aircraft is in the air, the flight incurs mostly fuel and crew costs. That yields a declining cost per seat-kilometer, as the distance flown increases as shown on lower chart of Figure 7.

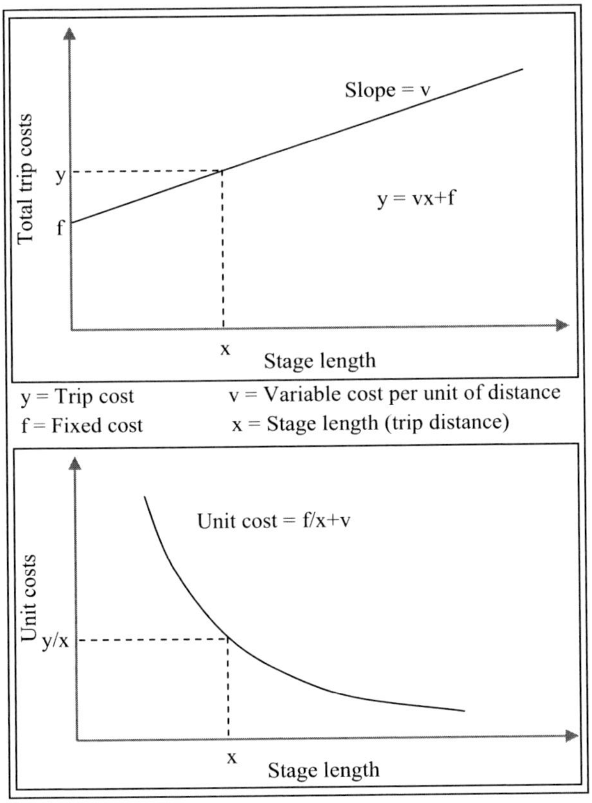

Figure 7: Components of trip costs and derivation of unit costs (Own illustration)

Higher utilization lowers average costs

The same logic reveals a similar declining relationship between the airline's costs per passenger and the load factor. The greater the percentage of seats occupied on any flight, the lower the average cost per passenger will be. As shown in Figure 8, the intersection of the declining cost curve and a horizontal line, representing the average fare paid by all of the passengers on the flight, defines the break-even load factor (BELF). Additional passengers carried in excess of the BELF level produce a profit for that flight, while failure to achieve the BELF level results in a loss.

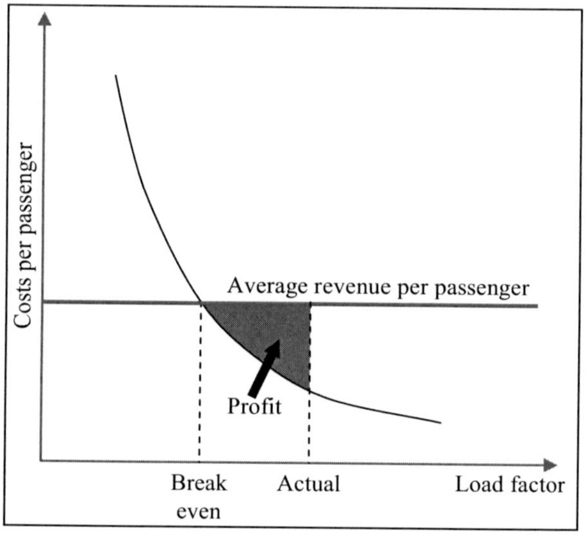

Figure 8: Relationship of load factor and profit (Own illustration)

Unit costs

In addition to many different types of costs and various subtotals thereof (e.g. direct costs, indirect costs, operating costs, non-operating costs), airlines use a measure of unit cost that bears a similarity to the unit revenue metric described earlier. Unit cost is calculated by dividing total operating cost by the number of ASKs operated. This metric is sometimes referred to as CASK (cost per available seat kilometer). Changes in unit cost (CASK) are closely monitored by airline management.

Given the earlier discussion about fixed and variable costs, the reader may wonder why airlines would use a metric in which all costs, both fixed and variable, would be related to the number of ASKs. Why not, for example, develop a metric that represents only variable cost per ASK? The question is a valid one. For practical reasons, however, and given that most costs have both a fixed and variable component, airlines do not make widespread use of such a metric.

Airline marginal costs are low

The preponderance of fixed costs in an airline's cost structure results in rather low marginal costs, where marginal cost equals the cost of producing one more unit of activity (e.g. flight operated, passenger carried). If an airline has a crewed aircraft sitting idle for a period during the day, for example, the marginal cost of operating one more flight tends to be relatively small. This is the key factor underlying a chronic problem for the airline industry: excess capacity. Similarly, if an aircraft has unoccupied seats just prior to departure time, the marginal cost of carrying additional passengers is relatively small. This explains why an airline can offer extremely low (and hence, highly competitive) fares for any seats expected to be empty when the flight departs. It is essential for anyone learning about airline economics to understand the significance of the industry's low marginal costs.

Economies of scale, scope, and density

In addition to simply attempting to minimize each cost for which they are responsible, airline managers often seek to reduce the company's unit costs by achieving one or more of the following three economies: scale, scope, or density.

- **Economies of scale** are achieved when unit costs decline as output increases. At a university, for example, this might equate to adding more faculties or expanding departments to attract and accommodate more students. An airline that expands its network (number of airports served), with the intent of reducing its unit costs, seeks economies of scale. With increasing size, however, airlines often must add overhead and more complex managing processes, resulting in higher-than-proportional increases in costs. Indeed, some industry observers argue that the airline industry does not provide meaningful economies of scale - otherwise, how can larger more-established airlines tendency to have higher unit costs than smaller new-entrant airlines be explained?
- **Economies of scope** are achieved when unit costs decline as the range of products increases. At a university, for example, this might equate to having each faculty broaden its programs or share resources in joint programs. An airline that decides to broaden its service offering (e.g. offer an additional onboard class of service, or begin carrying cargo) or its geographical coverage (e.g. operate multi-stop flights, or provide new nonstop flights between airports already served) seeks economies of scope. Entering into a global alliance also achieves such economies for an airline.
- **Economies of density** are achieved when unit costs decline as output from a given facility increases. At a university, for example, this might equate to enlarging class enrolments. An airline that increases the volume of traffic within its existing network, by offering more flights or operating larger aircraft on existing routes, seeks economies of density. The hub-and-spoke style of network achieves economies of density by funneling passengers from several origin cities onto a single flight to a given destination.

H. AIRLINE BUSINESS MODELS

Three basic business models

There are three primary business models used in the airline industry, although some airlines exhibit characteristics of more than one model. Table 1 summarizes the three business models and the differences in business premise, physical characteristics, and economics.

	Regional "feeder" airline	"Legacy" network airline	Low-cost carrier (LCC)
Business premise	Short-haul service for O&D passengers & connections to/from major hub*	Full mainline service to O&D & conneting passengers + member of global alliance	Low-fare service mostly to O&D passengers & intraline (only) connections
Geographic Scope: European Airlines	Intra European	Europe + worldwide	Mostly Europe and adjecent countries
North American Airlines	Mostly US, some Canada and Mexico	Nort America + worldwide	Mostly US, some Canada, Mexico, Caribbean, Latin America
Aircraft Operated	Regional jets + turboprop aircraft	Jet aircraft both narrow- and widebody	Narrowbody jets + some regional jets
Premium-fare Service	No, but carry premium connecting passengers	Yes, high reliance on premium fare revenue	No
Revenue Yield per RPK	Rel. High	Rel. High	Rel. Low
Unit (per ASK) Revenue	High	Rel. High	Rel. Low
Unit (per ASK) Cost	High	Rel. High	Rel. Low

* Typically operated under a capacity-purchase agreement with a major carrier

Table 1: Comparison of scheduled airline business models (Own illustration)

Regional airlines

Regional airlines typically operate short haul routes using smaller aircraft mainly serving point-to-point O&D passengers. Regional airlines that have close commercial relationships with a large network airline feed passenger traffic to and from one or more of the major airline's airport hubs. Under such an arrangement, flight schedules are usually prescribed by the major airline to ensure optimum passenger connecting times. Consequently, aircraft utilization is seldom optimal, and this, together with the operation of smaller aircraft, makes for high unit costs. Offsetting this cost penalty are often a) a substantial proportion of higher-yield business passengers and b) a capacity-purchase agreement with the major airline that provides some assurance that revenue will cover costs.

Network airlines

Network airlines, sometimes referred to as legacy airlines, are usually well-established, full-service carriers that aim to provide all things to all passengers. These airlines operate larger jet aircraft on mostly medium and long haul routes and tend to rely heavily on revenue from long haul and premium-fare passengers. Network airlines typically have relatively high unit revenue matched by relatively high unit costs. Most network airlines gain economies of scope by joining one of the three global alliances (Star Alliance, Oneworld, or SkyTeam) which expands the range of their networks and enables them to offer more competitive long haul fares.

Low-cost carriers

Low-cost carriers (often referred to as LCCs) are distinguished by a relatively low-fare offer and a lower level of unit costs than for either of the other two business models. Low unit costs are achieved primarily by strict internal cost discipline and high productivity (i.e. utilization of assets). These airlines accommodate passenger connections between their own flights, but only occasionally enter into interlining or alliance relationships with other airlines.

I. AIRLINE PROFITABILITY

Airlines can estimate profitability on unit level

As is true for every business, airline profits equal total revenue minus total cost. For airlines, however, another gauge of profitability is the unit margin: the difference between unit revenue (RASK) and unit cost (CASK). The unit margin is a ready approximation of the average amount of profit the airline has achieved for each unit of capacity (ASK) flown.

Determining profitability of a single leg is difficult

A challenging task for most airlines is to determine the profitability of a given route. On occasion, for example, management may review all routes operated with a view to cutting service on the worst performing ones. This is a difficult exercise for two main reasons. First, good accounting practice requires that fare revenue be allocated to the flight legs where it was earned. For passengers who paid a single fare but traveled on more than one flight leg, it must be decided how to apportion that fare revenue to each of the flight legs traveled. Some airline networks are more complex than others, so meeting this challenge varies in complexity for each airline. Not surprisingly, the approach used by each airline to assign revenue by route also varies.

Contribution to fixed costs and profit

Secondly, good accounting practice requires that costs also be allocated to the flight legs where they are incurred. However, some of the costs associated with a given route are fixed costs, have a value to several routes, or for other reasons are not readily apportioned. A commonly used solution to this dilemma is to identify the variable costs incurred on the route and to subtract them from the revenue earned on the route, as described earlier. The result is termed Contribution to Fixed Costs and Profit. While it does not identify route profit per se, it is calculated much more readily and can serve as a proxy - particularly when the objective is to rank all of the routes and identify the least lucrative ones.

Airline profits tend to be volatile

Airline profits are generally characterized as volatile, meaning that they tend to be highly variable from one period to another. One way that airline industry volatility reveals itself is that, when the overall economy (i.e. GDP) shows weakness, airline profits tend to plummet to a greater degree, and vice versa when the economy is strong. This is known as 'procyclicality', although it is more important to understand the concept than to remember the term! Income elasticity of the US airline industry has been estimated at 2.0, meaning that airline industry profit tends to change at roughly twice the percentage change in GDP. Earlier in the chapter, it was noted that changes in passenger traffic tend to lag changes in the economy; it should come as no surprise, then, that changes in airline profits also tend to lag changes in the economy.

Leverage affects airline profitability

Airlines have two ways to manage their profitability that are not as obvious as simply generating more revenue and reducing costs. Both of the ways involve leverage, which acts to magnify the degree of profitability or loss, as the case may be. Leverage increases both upside profit potential and downside risk. It is not an absolute - its significance lies in its relative degree. For example, is an airline more or less leveraged than its competitors? How much more (or less) leveraged is the airline now than it was a year ago? There are two types of leverage: operating leverage and financial leverage.

Operating leverage

Operating leverage is a measure of how much an airline's operating profit changes in response to a change in revenue. Essentially, operating leverage relates to the relative levels of fixed and variable costs. Given their generally high level of fixed costs, operating leverage for most airlines tends to be high relative to companies in many other industries. High operating leverage requires that the airline accurately predict future traffic levels, because it is on the basis of that forecast that the airline commits to fixed obligations (e.g. aircraft, facilities, staff) in order to handle that traffic. If actual traffic exceeds the airline's traffic forecast, the airline will show high profits; on the other hand, if the airline under-performs its traffic forecast, the airline may experience heavy losses.

Financial leverage

While operating leverage is related to the cost structure in the firm, financial leverage is related to how the firm is financed (i.e. debt capital vs. equity capital). Financial leverage is a measure of how much an airline's per-share net profit changes in response to a change in operating profit. An easier way to address financial leverage is to consider the relative proportions of debt and equity (the debt/equity ratio); the higher the proportion of debt, the more the company is leveraged financially. Airlines raise their financial leverage when they believe that the investment climate will be favorable and that the value of their company will grow. Use of financial leverage enables an airline to increase the return on capital invested by the shareholders, since the cost of debt capital tends to be fixed, but it raises the company's level of risk.

In general, management tends to increase an airline's overall degree of leverage in response to positive future prospects and, conversely, to reduce it in the face of negative prospects. Changing the degree of operating leverage involves shifting the mix of fixed and variable costs, while changing the degree of financial leverage involves shifting the debt/equity ratio. There are a number of levers available to management to accomplish both actions; the key is to take those actions at the appropriate time.

Adjust leverage as conditions change

J. AIR CARGO

Air cargo traffic is measured in a similar way to air passenger traffic, that is, by revenue tonne kilometers (RTKs). Of all air cargo traffic carried worldwide, nearly 80% is carried from one continent to another. Only 2% of all international cargo tonnage is carried by air, but that air portion represents 30% of the total value of international cargo transported. Since 1970, worldwide air cargo traffic has grown at 2.5 times the rate of global GDP growth - an average of 8% per year for RTKs compared to 3% for RPKs.

Revenue tonne kilometer: a measure of air cargo traffic

As was the case with passenger travel, demand for air cargo service is related to factors such as the relative strength of the economy at the origin and destination, specific industry concentrations, relative currency values, and distance. But realization of that demand as cargo traffic is highly dependent upon uplift capacity and routes served, as well as the level of air cargo rates vs. those offered by competing surface modes.

Air cargo demand analogous to air travel demand

Air cargo is transported by three types of aircraft operators:

Types of air cargo operators

- **Combination airlines**, so-called because they carry both passengers and cargo on the same aircraft. The cargo product is offered to produce additional revenue on already-scheduled passenger flights. Examples are Lufthansa and Korean Air.
- **All-cargo operators**, which carry only cargo on freighter aircraft. Cargo is often carried under contract but, in any case, only from airport to airport. The shipper must arrange for the cargo to be transported via truck to the originating airport and delivered by surface modes to the consignee at the destination. Examples are Cargolux, Nippon Cargo, and Polar Air Cargo.
- **Integrators**, which offer shippers complete dock-to-dock service, including ground transport of the shipment at each end of the journey. These operators rely for their success on time-definite delivery of the shipment and, in turn, charge a premium for the service. Examples are FedEx and UPS.

Even within the industry, the economics of air cargo are not as widely understood as for passengers, but they can be highly relevant to passenger airlines. Although LCCs tend to carry little, if any, cargo, many of the larger network airlines derive a material proportion of their total revenue from cargo - only about 5% on average for US network airlines, but as much as 15% for some large European network airlines and up to 30% for certain Asian network airlines.

Air cargo has a low visibility in the industry

There are several reasons why air cargo tends to have relatively low visibility in the industry. Most airline managers have little experience with cargo and do not appreciate its value or potential for their company. Many airline managers regard the cargo component as less interesting and simply a by-product of passenger operations (i.e. using belly compartment space that would otherwise go unused). Finally, the availability of reliable cargo data is poor to non-existent, while detailed passenger data tends to be much more widely available.

Summarized below are some key economic factors related to air cargo.

Air cargo is a premium service

Air cargo commands a price premium over transport by surface modes. It is important to note that it is the delivery premise - not the transport mode - that causes shippers to be willing to pay the premium air cargo price. Shippers often cite the time value of money as a pressing reason for preferring air cargo services over surface modes of transport, as the faster shipment time often increases sales and offsets inventory carrying costs. Because air cargo operators offer secure and reliable, time-definite delivery of goods, it is the mode of choice for shippers of such things as:

- Live cargo (e.g. racehorses, livestock)
- Perishable goods (e.g. seafood, flowers) that are subject to spoilage when shipped via surface modes
- Time-sensitive goods (e.g. fashion goods, legal documents) that may be subject to costly delays when shipped via surface modes
- High-value goods (e.g. art, gems, precious metals) that are vulnerable to damage and theft when shipped via surface modes

Tradeoff between cargo carriage and fuel carried (flight range)

On longer haul passenger flights, airlines sometimes face a tradeoff between the amounts of cargo, passengers, and fuel that will be carried. In order to carry sufficient fuel and reserves to reach the destination, and given that every aircraft has a maximum takeoff weight, an airline must manage its payload (passengers and cargo) accordingly. The relationship is shown in the payload/range chart in Figure 9. Carrying all of the cargo for which commitments have been made on a particular nonstop flight, for example, may require dumping some passengers. Alternatively, if all of the cargo and passengers are to be carried, the flight may have to make a refueling stop en route to its destination.

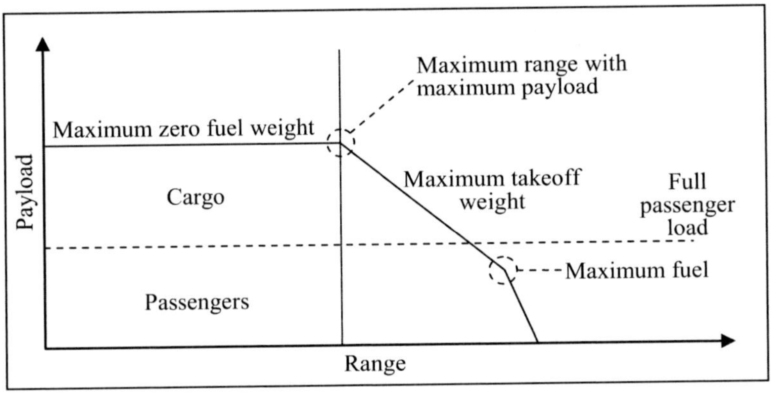

Figure 9: Aircraft payload vs. nonstop range (Own illustration)

Cargo density affects rate charged

A related factor is air cargo density (i.e. the weight per unit of volume). For example, a flight carrying a large shipment of flowers may bulk out (fill all usable cargo space onboard the aircraft) before it reaches its maximum allowable payload weight. On the other hand, a flight carrying a shipment of gold bars may depart at maximum gross weight and yet have considerable unused cargo space remaining. For these reasons, an airline must take density into account in determining its commodity-based cargo rates.

Challenges due to peaks and unidirectional nature of air cargo

Air cargo presents some unique peaking challenges. Whereas passengers typically make round trips, cargo is unidirectional. Trading patterns affect the directional flows. For example, twice as much air cargo is shipped from Asia to North America as is shipped in the opposite direction and this tends to create a cargo capacity shortfall on eastbound trans-Pacific flights. Cargo demand is sometimes highly seasonal (e.g. flowers for Mother's Day, electronics for the Christmas shopping period), and this tends to exacerbate the directional peaking. Air cargo operators typically adjust their charges to take these peaks into account, in an attempt to bring supply and demand into balance.

Cargo shippers are indifferent to shipment routing

Routing of a cargo shipment is flexible. As long as the delivery premise is met, the shipment routing is not relevant to the shipper. This often leaves cargo operators with a range of options, including indirect, multi-leg flight itineraries and use of surface modes for a portion (or all) of the shipment journey.

Air cargo pricing is often negotiated

Pricing of a cargo shipment is negotiable. Partly as a result of routing flexibility, partly because pricing of cargo services has tended to be less regulated and monitored than is the case with passenger services, and partly because there can be several intermediaries involved in handling a cargo shipment, the pricing of air cargo services is often negotiated between the parties rather than based on a set rate structure.

Profitability of air cargo

Determination of air cargo profitability is complex and controversial. There are numerous ways used by passenger airlines to measure the profit generated from their air cargo activity and, in turn, several ways to assess the profit achieved by a given mixed passenger/cargo flight. Most of the differences derive from whether air cargo revenue is offset by a portion of the cost of operating the flight on which it is transported, or by whether air cargo revenue is regarded simply as ancillary net revenue (less cargo-related costs) that offsets the airline's overall fixed costs. The profit measure is much simpler for all-cargo airlines, of course.

\- - - - - - - - -

This concludes the introduction to airline economics. In the chapters that follow, many of these economic concepts will be used in a variety of contexts. The reader may find it useful to return to this chapter, as needed, to review the fundamental relationships.

Review Questions

- What is the difference between the concepts of air travel demand and air passenger traffic, and what are the factors affecting each concept?
- What are the various metrics used to measure a) passenger traffic, b) airline service capacity, c) airline competition, and d) airline fares?
- What is the difference between a flight route and a city-pair market?
- Why do airlines measure traffic and capacity using complicated kilometer-based metrics, rather than just the number of passengers carried and seats flown?
- How is the concept of marginal costs related to each of a) competitive fare levels and b) excess capacity?
- How are the concepts of unit revenue and unit cost relevant to airline economics?
- Explain the differences between economies of scale, scope, and density, as they apply to the airline industry.
- What are the defining characteristics of a) regional airlines, b) network airlines, and c) low-cost carriers?
- How do air cargo economics differ from those affecting passenger transport?

Section 2: Infrastructure and Major Input Factors

Aircraft – Types, Operations, and Performance

Martin Nubert

Table of contents

You should be able to

- explain what basic physical principles enable an aircraft to fly
- explain an aircraft's major technical and structural components
- explain how a modern turbofan engine works
- draw an outline of the structural requirements for a commercial flight operations management organization
- sum up the major tasks and processes a operations management organization is responsible for and name the major internal and external details regarding the regulatory environment for the flight operations organization
- allocate main cost drivers induced by the operation of aircraft

The author

Martin Nubert (Graduate Industrial Engineer) has been working for Lufthansa Cargo Airlines in the departments of technical operations, flight operations and operations control center since 2002. After appointments within the departments of ground product management and airport infrastructure development he is actually head of performance- and quality management for hub operations Frankfurt within Lufthansa German Airlines.

Abstract

When thinking about Aviation Management one might in preference refer to the attractive disciplines such as network planning, yield management, sales and marketing. As an airline's core competence, flight operations are usually viewed as being limited to the black box, and not as an interesting field in itself. Nonetheless, the multiple tasks within flight operations management require a sound and dependable knowledge of the economic and technical characteristics of aircraft to manage this highly cost intensive resource as well as the crew to assure a safe, reliable and economic production of flights.

The following chapter first gives an overview of the basic physical and technical aspects of aircraft operations followed by a description of organizational requirements for the branch of flight operations management within a commercial airline. Whenever reasonable, the whole picture consisting of effects on the organizational implementation, operational needs and the resulting economic challenges is presented. Although the content is just a snapshot of this comprehensive management task, it will nevertheless provide the reader with all basic information needed to understand the elementary structures and principles inside the former black box.

A. BASIC AERODYNAMIC ASPECTS AND FUNDAMENTAL PRINCIPLES OF AIRCRAFT TECHNOLOGY

A. 1 Bernoulli's principle

According to the continuity equation[1] the amount of a fluid passing a tube is equal to the quantity sent into it. If the diameter of this tube remains stable, the velocity of the flow (v_{flow}) remains stable as well. This changes when the diameter is decreased continuously towards the tube's end, which results in a continual increase in the velocity of the flow. A change to the cross-sectional area and its resulting change of the velocity are negatively inverted, i.e. if the cross-sectional area is halved, the velocity is doubled.

Flow velocity determines the ratio of the pressure components

This is valid if the total pressure p_{total} within this system remains stable. Nevertheless p_{total} consists of two different components: the dynamic (p_{dyn}) and the static pressure component (p_{stat}). If p_{stat} is measured at locations with a small diameter the pressure is revealed to be lower than at locations with a wider diameter, which means that at sections with a higher velocity of flow, p_{stat} is also reduced. Simultaneously p_{dyn} is higher at these points with a higher velocity of flow,

[1] The continuity equation is a mathematical statement that at any steady state within a process the rate at which mass enters a system is equal to the rate at which mass leaves the system.

finally leading to the conclusion that the sum of p_{stat} and p_{dyn} remains the same but p_{stat} and p_{dyn} change negatively reciprocal towards each other. This can be demonstrated by analyzing pressure components in a Venturi tube as shown in Figure 1.

This interrelation was first discovered by Daniel Bernoulli (1700 – 1782). It is one of the basic principles in fluid and aero dynamics and helps to explain processes on an airplane's wing which enables it to fly.

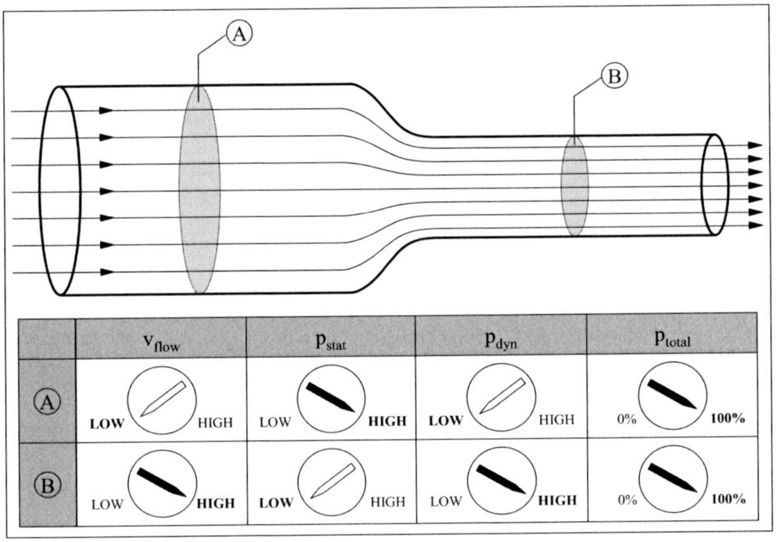

Figure 1: Venturi-Tube
(Own illustration based on Mies, 1996)

A. 2 Lift

The difference between the pressure components leads to the resulting lift force

Due to the curvature of a classical airplane wing, particles of the air have a different velocity when moving from the wing's leading edge to the trailing edge depending on their position above or below the airfoil. Particles on the upper side will have a higher velocity than the ones on the lower side, as they have to pass a longer distance due to the increased curvature. This is based on the principle of continuity which requires particles leaving the stagnation point of the leading edge at the same time to reach the trailing edge simultaneously. Following Bernoulli's principle the different velocities induce a difference in pressure components on the upper and lower side of the wing. This difference in pressure finally leads to the resulting lift force as illustrated in Figure 2.

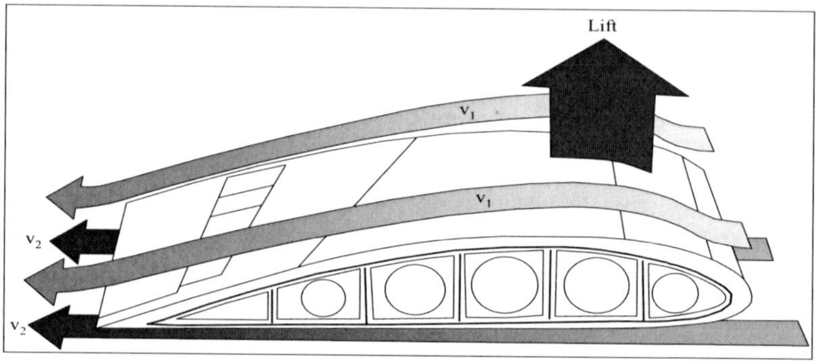

Figure 2: Basic airfoil aerodynamics (Own illustration based on DKL, 2004)

The amount of lift depends on different factors. First of all the wing profile, its curvature and the induced difference in velocity of the flow influence the resulting forces – if the difference increases (for example by increasing the airspeed) lift increases as well. Air density or the total wing area of an aircraft, are additional factors determining the lift component.

The amount of lift can be varied by changing the aircraft's angle of attack

To increase the lift force during take-off or flight, one option is to adjust the angle of attack. This is the angle between the direction of the airflow and the chord of the wing profile (line from leading to trailing edge). If the angle of attack is increased the airflow has to follow an increased curvature on the upper side so the lift is increased due to a higher difference in static pressure. Gain of lift is increased with linear dependence on the increasing angle of attack. But this is not unlimited: if the angle of attack exceeds a critical value the energy of the airflow is insufficient to overcome the curvature – the flow becomes turbulent and detached from the airfoil so there is no lift anymore. This critical condition is called 'stall'.

A. 3 Drag

Creating lift on an airfoil always induces another force: drag. There are four main types of drag on an aircraft:

- Form drag
- Friction drag
- Interferential drag
- Induced drag

Induced drag is a major determinant for the capacity at larger airports

Induced drag is of particular importance. The difference in pressure between the upper and lower side of the wing induces an additional airflow at the wing tip – this flow tries to compensate the pressure gradient. The higher value of static pressure at the lower side of the wing induces a circular flow around the wing tip. This flow has a direction of rotation towards the fuselage. In combination with the forward movement of the aircraft this results in vortices which the aircraft leaves behind. This primarily results in additional drag the aircraft has to overcome. Furthermore, these wake turbulences endanger succeeding aircraft and are a serious problem at airports where these vortices require safety distances between aircraft: a fact that additionally determines an airport's capacity.

The four types of drag add up to the total drag of an aircraft which is dependent on the size of the aircraft, the speed of the surrounding airflow, the angle of attack and the air density. The major rule is: more lift = more drag!

A. 4 Movements and flight controls of the aircraft

An aircraft's movements are specified according to the axis they refer to. These axes are perpendicular to each others; their intersection is located at the center of gravity (CG).

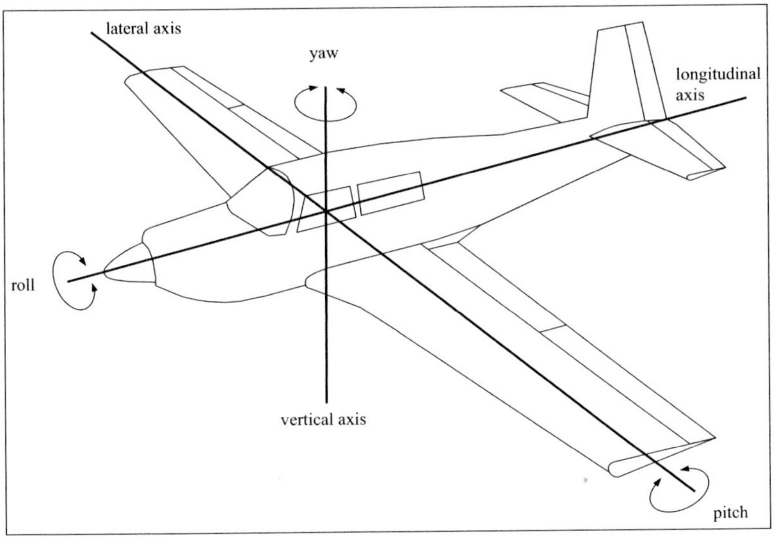

Figure 3: Axes and movements of an aircraft (Own illustration based on Mies, 1996)

Flight controls

The primary flight controls induce a direct movement on the aircraft's attitude and/or position:

- Ailerons
- Elevator
- Rudder

Using the ailerons creates a rolling movement around the longitudinal axis of the aircraft - the airplane banks to the left or the right which initiates a turn. This is due to the increasing and decreasing lift at the wings. Left and right ailerons move simultaneously in opposite directions. Depending on the aircraft type, ailerons are situated at the outer or inner area of the wings (outboard ailerons, inboard ailerons).

The rudder is mounted at the trailing edge of the fin at the aft section of the airplane (empennage). By treading the right rudder pedal in the cockpit the rudder moves to the right and vice versa. If the rudder moves to the right the airplane's nose also yaws to the right. The rudder movement is for example used during the touchdown and take-off phases of the flight to adjust the airplane to the runway's center line.

At the trailing edge of the stabilizer (aft section of the airplane, empennage) the elevator is situated. If the elevator moves downwards, lift is increased and the tail moves upwards, i.e. the aircraft pitches around its lateral axis. Pitching the nose down lowers the angle of attack and decreases the amount of lift. This effect is inverted if the elevator moves upwards pitching the nose up. Additional to influencing lift production by pitching the nose up or down, the airspeed can be increased or decreased.

Secondary flight controls induce a change of lift, drag and/or trim:

- Flaps and slats
- Stabilizer
- Spoilers and speed brakes

Flaps and slats are elements of the wing mounted at the leading (slats) and the trailing (flaps) edges. During cruise flight they usually are retracted - their application mainly takes place during take-off and landing. If slats and flaps are deployed they increase curvature and total area of the wing. This in effect increases lift and drag and enables the airplane to take-off and land with lower airspeed. Due to the higher amount of drag, the engine thrust has to be increased. Depending on the type and size of airplane, different slats and flaps are utilized.

The stabilizer is situated on the aircraft's tail. Stabilizer and elevator are mounted to each other such as rudder and fin are. It is possible to move the stabilizer up or down by turning the stabilizer trim wheel in the cockpit. This is helpful as the movement of the center of gravity (CG) during flight (induced by burning the fuel) can be trimmed by moving the elevator up or down, which results in a force at the aircrafts tail.

Spoilers or speed brakes are mounted on the upper surface of the wings. When they are retracted they are completely level to the wing's surface. During descent or after touchdown they will be deployed to eliminate remaining lift and to produce drag for braking action.

A. 5 Engines and APU

Today's modern civil aircraft are powered by turbofan engines which were evolved from the early turbojet engines. A jet engine mainly consists of six major components: fan, compressor, combustion chamber, shafts, turbine, and exhaust nozzle. Figure 4 shows how these components work together.

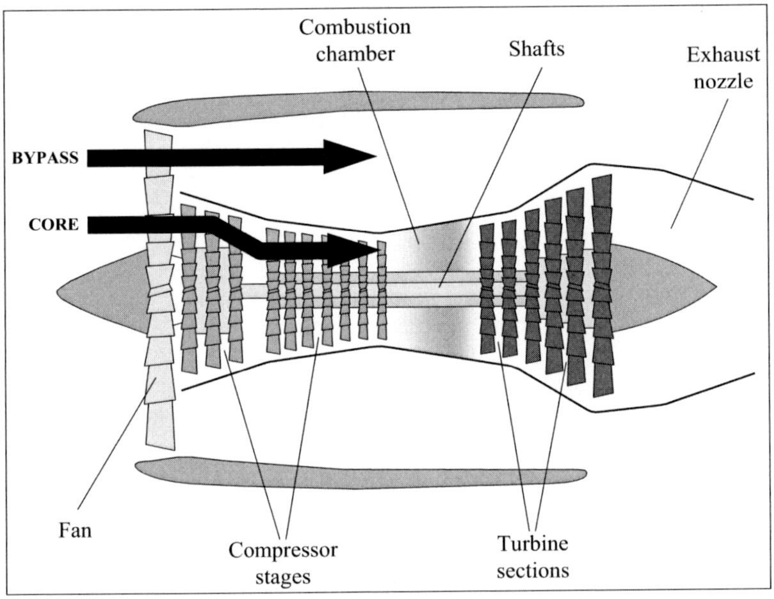

Figure 4: Major components of a high-bypass turbofan engine (Own illustration based on Aainsqatsi, 2009)

Suck, squeeze, bang, blow – the working principle of a turbofan engine

First of all air is sucked into the engine and passes through the fan. Modern bypass engines then divide the airflow behind the fan into a hot and a cold section. While the cold section is routed around the core engine (bypass), the hot section first streams into the compressor section. By transcending through several compressor stages (low to high pressure sections) the air becomes increasingly dense. Within the combustion chamber fuel is added to the compressed air and the mixture is finally ignited. Once ignited the volume of the air increases rapidly and streams into the turbine (now from a high to low pressure section) and energy is delivered to one or several shafts which transfer the energy to the compressor and the fan at the front of the engine. The hot air flow becomes more decompressed and streams into the exhaust nozzle which (in combination with the cold airflow section) induces the thrust. Today's engines have a bypass ratio of 6:1 up to 9:1, which means that six parts of the air pass the cold section while one part passes the hot section. This explains why the exhaust from the cold section is primarily responsible for the resulting thrust force.

The APU delivers electric, pneumatic and hydraulic energy to the aircrafts' systems

The working principle of an auxiliary power unit (APU) situated in the aft section of the fuselage below the empennage is similar to that of a jet engine apart from the fact that an APU mostly uses a radial rather than an axial compressor. An APU primarily supplies the aircraft with electrical, pneumatic and hydraulic energy when the engines are shut off and the aircraft is on the ground. Particularly during the engine starting phase the APU delivers the pressurized air needed. It is possible to operate an aircraft with an inoperative APU but the autarchy of the aircraft is reduced. Electricity and pressurized air is then needed from the ground to compensate for the missing system, and therefore ground power units (GPU) or air start unit (ASU) have to be provided. Latest generations of aircraft, such as the Boeing 787, require APU concepts that primarily deliver electricity to the aircraft's systems. These modern jets have a reduced number of pneumatic and hydraulic systems; electrical components will substitute these heavy-weight elements to reduce weight and costs.

A. 6 Landing gear

The landing gear of an aircraft consists of nose landing gear, the main landing gear and optionally a center landing gear. Main and center landing gears are equipped with effective high-tech brakes made out of carbon fibers, for example. The nose landing gear normally has no brakes. Landing gear needs to be completely overhauled after a certain period of time (hard time) which requires an aircraft downtime of several days. As an option, one aircraft type can be equipped with different configurations of the landing gear. The A320 family for example can be equipped with two or four wheels on one bogey of the main landing gear – this enables operations at destinations with a limited load bearing capacity on the pavement.

B. AIRCRAFT TYPES AND PERFORMANCE

B. 1 Classification of aircraft

There are various classifications of aircraft beginning with the parameter 'lighter than air' or 'heavier than air'. Following a set of classification criteria developed by ICAO, commercial airplanes can finally be found in the category 'heavier than air power driven landplanes'.

This category can further be subdivided to distinguish between commercial aircraft:

- **Manufacturer**: Boeing, Airbus, Bombardier
- **Diameter of fuselage**: widebody, narrowbody
- **Range capability**: long haul, medium haul, short haul
- **Engine type**: turbofan, turboprop
- **Number of jet engines**: twin, tri, quad

B. 2 Commercial aircraft manufacturers

Besides the two big players Airbus and Boeing some other companies offer a variety of commercial aircraft types on the global market. Table 1below presents the most important players in the business and their product ranges:

Company	Main Location	Aircraft
Boeing Commercial Aeroplanes	Seattle / WA, USA	737, 747, 757, 767, 777, 787, MD-80, MD-11, etc.
Airbus S.A.S. (Société par Actions Simplifiée)	Blagnac, France Hamburg, Deutschland	A318-A321, A330, A340, A380, A350, etc.
Embraer S.A.	São José dos Campos, Brazil	ERJ 135, 140, 145 Embraer 170, 175, 190 etc.
Bombardier Aerospace	Quebec, Canada	CRJ 200, 700, 900, 1000 Challenger, Dash 8, etc.
Sukhoi Civil Aircraft	Moscow, Russia	Superjet 100

Table 1: Selection of commercial aircraft manufacturers (Own illustration)

Each aircraft type built by these companies is characterized by an individual profile of performance, capacity etc. according to the classification criteria mentioned above.

B. 3 Aircraft family concepts

In the aviation industry aircraft manufacturers and airlines have a symbiotic relationship. Aircraft companies have recognized that airlines require flexibility and easy interchangeability of aircraft. That is why the concept of aircraft families is an essential feature of a manufacturer's product line.

Aircraft family concepts mainly enable airlines to schedule their crews flexible and efficiently

For example, the airplanes of the A320 / A330 / A340 model series feature a fleet commonality: all aircraft types have the same cockpit layout and technical systems are integrated analogically. Additionally, flight operational procedures are virtually the same for all aircraft types and the fly-by-wire control creates a similar operational feeling even when flying different aircraft types. This aircraft family concept has advantages for the airline operator, especially in terms of crew productivity. If certain procedures and crew training concepts are installed and maintained by the airline, crews can be swapped from one aircraft type to another easily. For the pilots these concepts result in less fatigue, an increased potential for more varied experience and more take-offs, landings and flight hours due to a higher flexibility and productivity. For the airline this results in reduced costs and increased productivity. Less new training is required and optimization of crew scheduling is easier - one pool of pilots and one maintenance organization means that complex operations and scheduling tasks can be performed more efficiently and at lower costs.

B. 4 Aircraft performance

One of the key parameters that describe an airplane's performance can be shown in a payload range diagram. It primarily describes the potential range performance of a specific aircraft type as a function of the payload carried onboard. The three segments of the diagram can be described as follows:

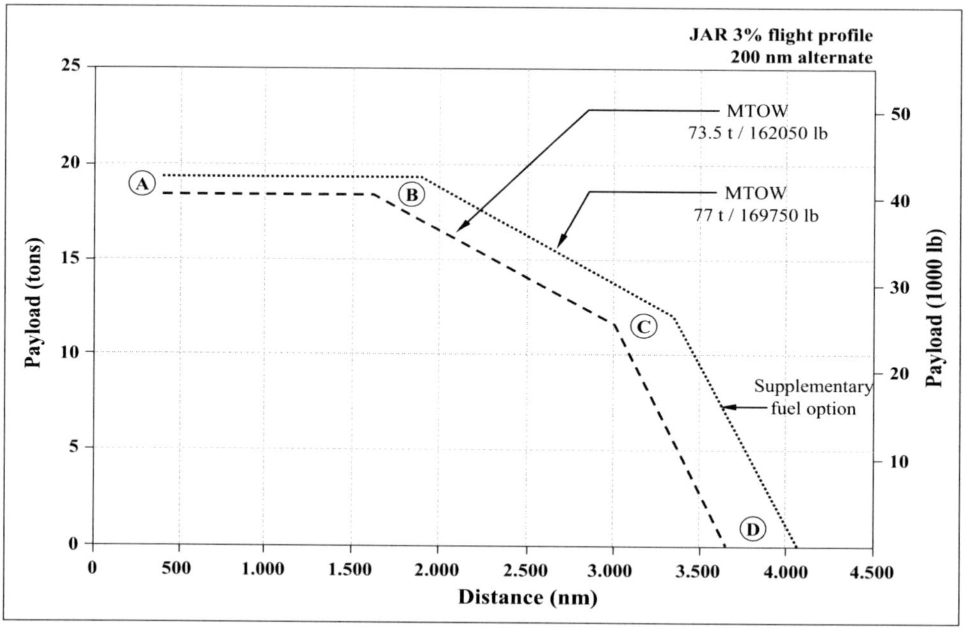

Figure 5: Payload range diagram
(Own illustration based on Airbus, 2008)

The payload range diagram gives an overview of an aircrafts performance

Segment AB reflects the range span with the maximum payload onboard. At point B the maximum range with maximum payload is reached. If the payload is reduced in order to enable a higher amount of fuel in the tanks, range increases along the segment BC. Point C shows the range when the airplane's tanks are full. Therefore segment CD displays an increase in range capability based only on a reduction of payload. At point D there is no payload onboard. It shows the maximum range for this specific aircraft.

The payload range diagram is a basic tool for the fleet strategy of an airline, as it gives a rough impression of this airplane type's strategic suitability for the intended network operations.

As a second parameter the take-off performance of an airplane determines whether it can be operated at specific airports. As length and slope of a runway determine operations for specific airplane types, take-off performance is a second important performance parameter. A take-off performance diagram integrates the interdependency of take-off weight and required field length (runway length). Usually such a diagram offered by the manufacturer contains multiple curves as an airplane can be equipped with different engine types that have different thrust ratings, which influences this performance parameter significantly. It has to be considered that take-off performance is influenced by air temperature and air density conditions at the departure airport as well. Therefore operations at so called 'hot and high' airports (such as Quito/Ecuador for example) require intensive certification processes for new airplane types to assure safe take-off procedures, even in case of engine failure during the take-off phase.

C. COCKPIT

C. 1 Cockpit basics

There are certain aeronautical instruments that can be found in nearly every airplane starting from a Cessna 172 up to an Airbus A380-800. These instruments display the conditions of the most important parameters to the pilot during flight and are arranged in a typical 'basic-T' structure.

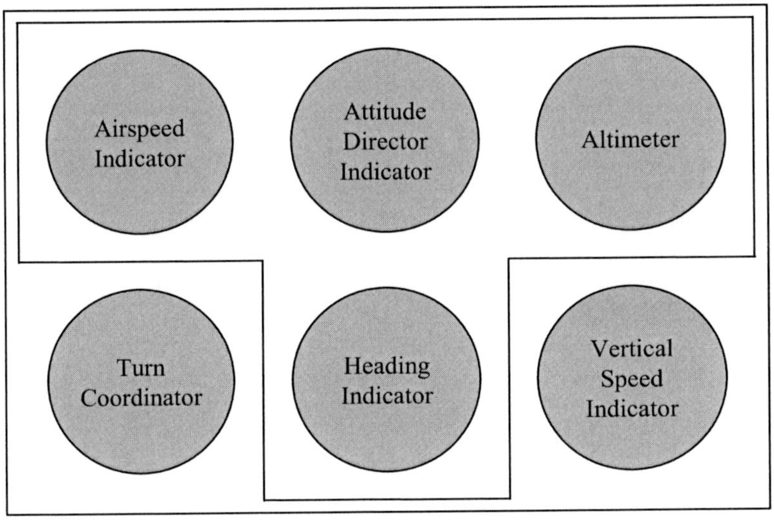

Figure 6: 'Basic-T' arrangement of standard cockpit instruments (Own illustration)

Instruments of the Basic-T can be found in nearly every airplane

The air speed indicator (ASI) displays the speed of the aircraft compared to the surrounding airflow. Sophisticated ASIs are able to display different airspeeds, e.g. the true airspeed (TAS) which considers the density and air temperature for a correct calculation, etc.

Attitude director indicator (ADI), better known as the artificial horizon: Its basic element is a bowl with a blue shaded upper and a brown shaded lower half, the middle of this bowl (where the shades meet) represents the horizon. In front of this movable bowl a small airplane is fixed. The ADI displays this situation based on the airplanes attitude. If the airplane's nose is pitched down, the brown half of the bowl rises up, if the airplane is banked to the left, the artificial horizon on the ADI moves respectively. The fixed small airplane in front of the bowl displays the actual situation of the airplane with reference to the horizon. The ADI is an essential tool, especially in adverse weather conditions, when pilots have no external visual reference.

The altimeter measures the distance of an airplane to a referential surface below. The altimeter delivers different parameters based on that reference level. Height is the distance between the airplane and the terrain height at the reference aerodrome. As an altimeter mainly measures differences in air pressure for the height value, its referential value has to be set to the air pressure at the departure airport. Therefore the altimeter will show a height of zero ft/m at the reference aerodrome. Altitude is the distance between the airplane and mean sea level. Therefore the altimeter's reference value has to be set to a calculated mean sea level air pressure. At the departure airport the altimeter then shows the altitude of the location above sea level. Finally, flight level is primarily used at high cruising altitudes. To display this value, the altimeter has to be set to the international standard atmosphere (ISA) pressure level of 1,013 hPa as a reference value. A standard procedure in civil aviation is to depart from an airport with an altitude value and then switch over to the flight level value when the transition altitude is reached. At this point all aircraft use the same reference height.

Heading indicator: the horizontal course rose displays the heading track of the airplane, i.e. the direction of the airplane's nose with reference to magnetic north. As the position of magnetic north and true geographical north are different, more complex variants of the horizontal course indicator are capable of taking the local value of this difference (deviation) into consideration and displaying the 'true heading' rather than the 'magnetic heading'. It needs to be taken into consideration that a potential cross wind component influences the airplane's track. Therefore the heading value is not equal to the track the airplane finally covers.

Vertical speed indicator (VSI) displays the rate of climb or descend in feet per minute. It measures the change in air pressure while the airplane varies its height, altitude or flight level.

The turn coordinator is primarily used in smaller airplanes. It displays the bank value of the wings and in addition a small ball below the sketched airplane shows whether the centrifugal force is coordinated while turning the plane. This is mainly to control the adverse yaw movement and to correctly control the aircraft's turn. If the pilot does not move the rudder correctly, the small ball moves either to the right or the left as centrifugal forces are not coordinated during this turn.

C. 2 Cockpit layout and system components

The glass cockpits of modern jets with their seeming complexity consisting of panels, displays and switches are impressive. Despite the complexity a basic cockpit structure exists containing different groups of system controls and aeronautical components. These groups are mounted in a certain layout according to international standards. These standards were set up in order to align cockpit layouts of different aircraft families and to create a consistent 'look and feel'.

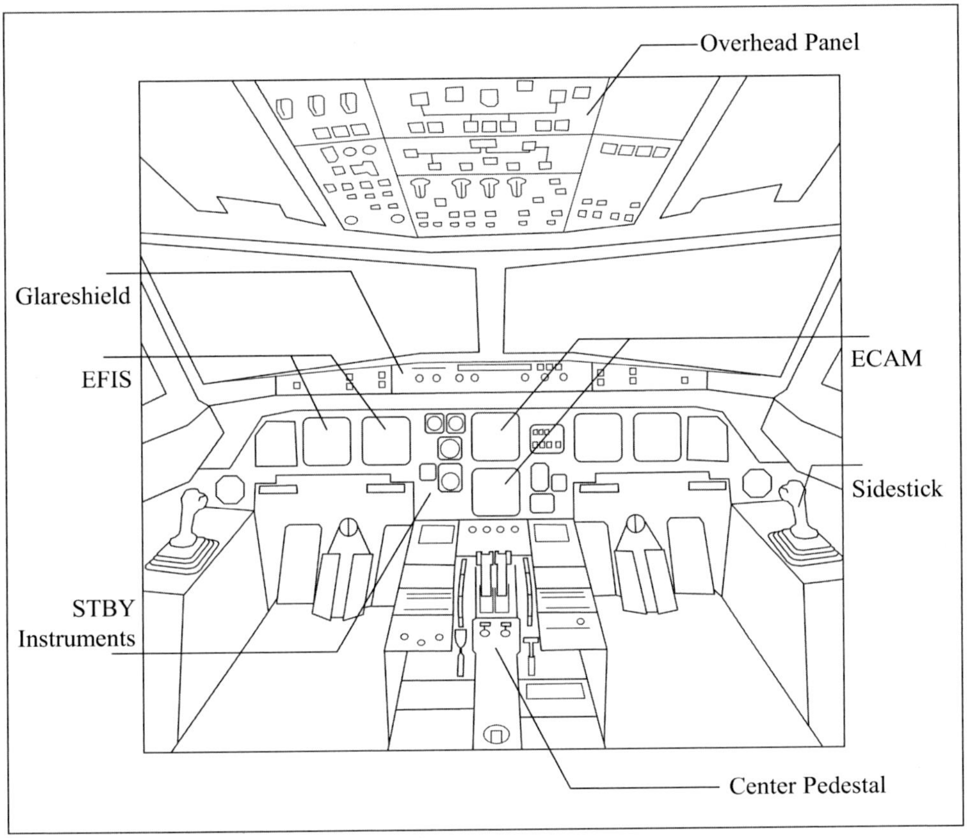

Figure 7: Cockpit layout (A320 family)
(Own illustration)

The electronic flight instrument system (EFIS) is an instrument display system in which the display technology used is electronic rather than electromechanical. An EFIS mainly consists of a primary flight display (PFD) and navigation, sometimes called multi-function display (ND/MFD).

The primary flight display (PFD) primarily displays information regarding the airplane's attitude and its movements. Therefore it integrates most functions of the basic-T, such as attitude director indicator, airspeed indicator, vertical speed indicator and horizontal situation indicator.

Computerized cockpits integrate functions of all basic instruments

Besides these essential components, the PFD integrates information regarding auto-pilot modes, settings of auto thrust or condition of the flight director. The flight director therefore indicates the position of the airplane relative to a preselected flight path by displaying the deviation from this track using a moving horizontal and vertical line in front of the artificial horizon. If the airplane is moving exactly on the preselected track, the two lines build a cross section directly in the center of the artificial horizon.

The navigation display (ND) displays navigational and weather information from multiple systems. Sophisticated NDs allow the aircrew to overlay different information on a map or chart. The main information displayed on the ND is the aircraft's current route plan, weather information from the onboard radar or ground-based sensors, restricted airspace and aircraft traffic. The ND primarily shows information regarding actual navigational information such as ground speed, true airspeed, wind direction and velocity, track and distance to go, estimated time of arrival to the next waypoint, etc. The function of the traffic collision avoidance system (TCAS) can be integrated into the navigation display. The ND shows other airplanes in the vicinity and their main parameters (speed, descent or climb, track) and follows the development of potentially hazardous situations. In case of an 'intruder' (another aircraft crossing the flight track and the danger of a crash occurring), the TCAS changes the color or shape of the data to alert the aircrew to this hazardous situation and recommends a conflict-solving maneuver.

ECAM (electronic centralized aircraft monitoring) from Airbus or EICAS (engine indication and crew alerting system) from Boeing displays information about the aircraft's systems, including its fuel, electrical and engine systems. The displays are often designed to mimic traditional round gauges while also supplying digital readouts of the parameters. Pilots are able to toggle between different pages of the ECAM and EICAS displays to access the information needed. In case of a malfunction or system irregularity ECAM and EICAS automatically display the relevant information on the active display electronics unit (DEU), ECAM and recommend remedial action.

Standby instruments backup essential functions of the EFIS and ECAM/EICAS. Traditional gauges in the middle of the front panel provide information regarding speed, altitude, attitude, and radio navigational info. The center panel additionally accommodates the gear lever and indicator, brake setting and indicator and a clock.

Major elements on the center pedestal are the multicontrol and display unit (MCDU), which is the main interface to the flight management system (FMS); NAV/COM (devices for the tuning of navigational and inter-communicational radios); spoiler/speed brake lever (to control the extension or retraction of the spoilers); display setting knobs (switches and turn knobs to toggle between different display modes of the EFIS, ECAM and/or EICAS); thrust levers (controls the thrust delivered by the engines - during landing reverse thrust can be engaged by these levers as well); and flap setting (lever to control the degree of slat and flap extension).

The overhead panel has control pads for the management of the airplane's basic systems, such as air conditioning, the hydraulic system, the fuel system, electricity and lights. In most cockpits the emergency levers for an engine or APU fire shutdown are also on the overhead panel. By pulling these levers the fuel flow is shut off and one or two fire extinguishers can be activated in the affected engine.

D. FLIGHT OPERATIONS MANAGEMENT

D. 1 Postholder organization

The European Aviation Safety Agency (EASA) has issued a variety of regulations controlling the system of air traffic operations and its related processes within the EASA associated states.

The major guidelines are divided into the following main chapters:

- Airworthiness
- Operation
- Licensing
- Maintenance

The regulations list requirements an airline has to fulfill for the commercial and civil operation of airplanes. Apart from its aim to assure safe, economic and high quality flight operations of the airline's aircraft, they define requirements for the organizational setup of a flight operations unit called the postholder organization.

Postholder organization provides a manager for each flight operations duties

The structure of a postholder organization consists of an Accountable Manager who is the responsible leader of the organization, four associated postholders (flight operations, technical operations, crew training, and ground operations) and a Quality Manager.

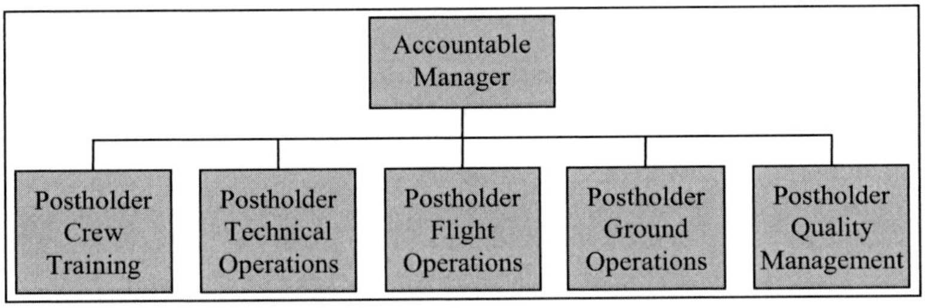

Figure 8: Postholder organization (Own illustration)

The european regulations are mostly assimilated into national law of a state, usually then the original content is transferred into a national law. In the US, the Federal Aviation Administration (FAA) is the corresponding institution and most of the philosophies and concepts of EASA and FAA are comparable or even compatible.

D. 2 Air Operators Certificate (AOC)

To perform commercial air transportation an airline requires approval issued by the national aviation authorities. This permission is the air operators certificate (AOC). The AOC defines all relevant details of the planned airline operation. It contains information about the type of operation, the aircraft's equipment (A/C) or the planned areas of operation. This latter definition is the Operations Specification. A copy of the AOC has to be carried onboard each airplane.

An AOC audit approves the capabilities of the flight operations organization

National authorities carry out an all-encompassing technical and economic inspection of the airline (AOC audit). Important criteria are financial capacity of the airline and the verification of a competent and structured postholder organization. If an AOC has been issued for the first time, it is valid for a limited period. During that period it can be revoked at any time by the national authorities.

D. 3 Operations manual

The Operations Manual is an EU-OPS stipulated document which has to be indited in English and which has to be approved by the legal authorities. It consists of four parts:

- **OM Part A** – General/Basic (basic principles, directives and procedures)
- **OM Part B** – Aeroplane Operating Matters (aircraft type specific procedures)
- **OM Part C** – Route and Aerodrome Instruction and Information (aeronautical charts)
- **OM Part D** – Training (principles, programs, documentation)

The entire Operations Manual has to clearly set regulations for the following aspects of flight operations management:

- Names and responsibilities of all functional elements within flight operations
- Communicational processes within flight operations
- Description of business and operational management processes
- Concepts regarding flight safety and risk prevention
- Description of the quality system
- Description of operational processes on the ground
- Procedures in case of an emergency incident

D. 4 Accountable manager and postholder flight operations

The accountable manager occupies the highest position within the flight operations organization. He is personally responsible to the national authorities for assuring orderly financing, operations and proper maintenance of the fleet. He also has to assure that definite and sustainable processes are established and documented in operations manuals.

The flight operations postholder reports directly to the accountable manager and is superior to all fleets within the organization. He/she defines all processes relevant for flight operations. He/she manages and monitors all activities of his/her own department or those carried out by external providers. All procedural instructions issued by the flight operations postholder are obligatory. He/she may be supported by a fleet captain (managing director for an associated fleet) and/or a technical fleet captain (coordinates the evaluation and implementation of technical system updates or modifications of the existing aircraft, planning and physically performing maintenance and test flights).

E. TECHNICAL OPERATIONS

E. 1 Tasks and setup

The main responsibility of the technical operations department is to assure proper maintenance of the fleet. Basic targets of maintenance are:

- Assurance of a maximum level of operational safety
- Achievement of a maximum technical reliability
- Implementation of an economically optimized maintenance concept.

A main goal for technical operations is the optimization of efficient aircraft utilization by minimizing failure costs due to technical delays or cancellations of flights. Management of maintenance costs is a big challenge for technical operations as the budgetary volume of maintenance for a major airline easily amounts to EUR 1 billion per year.

Technical operation is primarily responsible for aircraft engineering, control of the check schedule and quality assurance

The technical operations postholder is personally accountable to the legal authorities regarding proper maintenance of the fleet. He is the head of department.

A sub team of system engineering takes care of evaluation and implementation of technical instructions, e.g. those provided by the manufacturer such as airworthiness directives (AD notes) or service bulletins (SB). Furthermore the team acts at the interface to the contracted maintenance organization and is the main point of contact for the manufacturer. System engineering is primarily responsible for the development and administration of the individual maintenance schedule.

Maintenance control has to adhere to check intervals as prescribed in the maintenance schedule. The controllers do the preplanning for checks and communicate potential maintenance slots. Maintenance control has a strong interaction with operations control and network planning, as they have to reserve longer aircraft downtimes for base maintenance events. Additional maintenance control is the interface to a production planning department of the maintenance provider.

The establishment of a maintenance contracting team depends on the amount of maintenance outsourcing an airline has. This team primarily coordinates maintenance service procurement. As an option it can be structured into a line and base maintenance division. Regarding economic aspects, maintenance contracting is in charge of market research and optimization of costs in terms of contracted services.

The setup of a quality control team is mandatory.. Main tasks are the inspection of external provider's and internal employee's qualifications; this is why so called quality audits are performed continuously.

The most important document continuing aviation maintenance exposition (CAME) contains detailed process descriptions regarding all maintenance aspects of the airline and is issued by the quality control team.

In accordance with an airline's 'make or buy' philosophy different setup versions of technical operations might exist. Some of the mentioned functions might be sourced out and provided by an external partner. Some of the functions must remain within the airline's responsibility by law (e.g. maintenance control). An assessment also needs to take place to evaluate whether the existence of an additional interface to an external provider is beneficial.

E. 2 Maintenance, repair and overhaul

The term 'maintenance' covers all technical activities. Nevertheless, subdivisions of different measures, such as 'maintenance', 'repair' and 'overhaul' (MRO) are also common.

Maintenance describes prophylactic measures taken to maintain the perfect technical condition of the aircraft. These measures can be divided into: active measures (i.e. lubrication of contact surfaces, refill of fluids, etc.) and condition monitoring of system parts (i.e. visual checks).

Repair is the active elimination of a defect which negatively influences the aircraft's operation. Several levels of importance can be defined, as not every defect immediately leads to a safety relevant issue. This level of importance and the timeline left for rectification is defined by the minimum equipment list (MEL) which is available for every single type of aircraft.

Overhaul sums up comprehensive measures such as checks, inspections, change of parts and, if applicable, rectifications which are mainly bundled into long-term downtimes which are longer than routine maintenance events.

E. 3 Line and base maintenance

The systematic structure of line and base maintenance events is summarized in the maintenance schedule

Line maintenance is done during active operations and can be done at a line station. The aircraft does not have to be taken out of operations on a mid- to long-term basis. The biggest line maintenance event is the 'A-check' which usually takes 12 to 36 hours (depending on A/C-type). Other line maintenance events are transit or ramp checks.

Base maintenance (or heavy maintenance) describes maintenance events that require the aircraft to be taken out of active operations for a longer period of time. Base maintenance events are characterized by a large amount of man-hours needed to carry out all check items. A typical base maintenance event is the 'C-check' which requires a ground time of several days to weeks.

The combination of check intervals for line and heavy maintenance events of an aircraft type is defined in the maintenance schedule. The optimization of the maintenance schedule is an important tool for an airline operator to optimize costs and utilization of the fleet. If the interval of C-checks can be synchronized with the A-check interval, for example, it is possible to merge these events into one ground time instead of having the aircraft on the ground twice.

In addition to the planned maintenance events (scheduled ground time, SGT), non-routine maintenance unfortunately is the daily business of an airline. If a defect occurs which does not affect the aircraft's airworthiness it can stay on line. The MEL then defines whether the airplane can be dispatched and when the defect has to be eliminated or whether the airplane has to remain on the ground. In such a case the aircraft is AOG (aircraft on ground). Airlines might also define the terms of MGT (more ground time) if SGT is insufficient and has to be enlarged to finalize all work or UGT (unscheduled ground time) which might arise out of an AOG situation, e.g. to finally rectify a defect after the aircraft's return to the home base.

E. 4 Maintenance cost drivers and optimization potentials

Monitoring and management of maintenance costs is essential for economical success. Several key drivers have to be watched continuously as they influence maintenance cost structure significantly.

Common maintenance cost drivers can be identified easily

Aircraft utilization (flight hours or 'FH', cycles) directly influences the asset depreciation of the airframe and the wear on the components. Short haul aircraft usually have more cycles per period than long haul aircraft, which induces increased wear on landing gear and engines due to the higher amount of take-offs and landings. Long haul aircraft gain more FH per period than short haul aircraft, which, in effect, causes a higher stress on the structure of fuselage and frame. Therefore maintenance cost structures for long and short haul aircraft can be driven by different maintenance tasks for these individual causes of asset depreciation (i.e. engine overhauls or checks of the airframe structure). Operating reliability of the engines and the total amount of engines within the fleet (including spare engines) determine maintenance costs significantly. A main indicator regarding engine overhauls is the 'time between removals' (TBR), engines should remain in service for a certain amount of cycles (the cycle is the main cause of wear on the engine as it contains take-off and landing phases).

Aircraft types operated. Different aircraft types require different tooling, spare parts, staff training, etc. The more different types of aircraft there are to be maintained the more complex the coordination and production of maintenance services is. Therefore the structure of the fleet might be an important cost driver or saver.

The maintenance schedule of an aircraft type determines the amount of checks necessary and the man-hours needed for each check. The more flexibility the maintenance program allows, the less costs in terms of direct maintenance costs and failure costs due to an unproductive aircraft there are.

Optimization potentials

Due to the large proportion of maintenance costs, optimization potentials have to be identified carefully by the airline management. Basically there are typical starting points which might hold any cost saving potential.

A central question regarding organization of maintenance is the decision to 'make or buy'. As already mentioned outsourcing of different tasks from the technical operations department might offer economic rewards. Smaller airlines in particular purchase complete services, such as system engineering or line maintenance as it is inefficient to provide such a setup for a small amount of aircraft.

Harmonization of the fleet and engine type operated might support the realization of economies of scale. A harmonized fleet means less different tooling, variety of spare parts and skills needed. In addition to these maintenance oriented aspects, a harmonized fleet provides uncomplicated flexibility in terms of swapping A/C in case of operational irregularities. Low-cost carriers usually follow this philosophy.

An escalation of check intervals to expand the timeframe between two check events aims on having fewer checks throughout an A/C lifetime. Additionally this might help to better synchronize intervals of line- and base-maintenance events. Such a measurement has to be approved by the local authorities.

Optimization by design and retrofit

Aircraft manufacturers in some cases develop retrofits to improve technical reliability of a certain aircraft type which then might reduce maintenance effort. A pro-active approach involves modern A/C being provided with build-in test equipment (BITE), which then reduces the demand for additional tooling and time budget during a maintenance event.

F. FLIGHT DISPATCH AND OPERATIONS CONTROL

Flight dispatch and operations control can be seen as the succeeding step of network planning. Both teams take over the coordination of flights on a short-term basis. While dispatch is mainly responsible for the operational flight planning, operations control is the surveillant and managing interface to the flights and the entire route network in its active phase.

F. 1 Tasks of flight dispatch

Flight dispatch primarily provides the operational flight plan (OFP) to cockpit crews

The main tasks of flight dispatch are:

- Preparation of all operational flight plans and other cockpit relevant flight documents
- Centralized ATC slot management in coordination with air traffic control (ATC)
- Inflight assistance to the crews

Major objectives for dispatch are safety, regularity, punctuality and economic efficiency. Dispatch offices of major airlines easily create 1000 flight plans and referring documentation (briefing packages) per day to support flight preparation and operation.

The main steps during the planning process are:

- Analysis and definition of permitted load
- Evaluation of weather forecasts
- Evaluation of technical A/C status and MEL status
- Evaluation of information by Air Traffic Control (ATC)
- Evaluation of available overflight permits
- Definition of the flight routing according to minimum cost aspects
- Calculation of fuel and definition of the minimum take-off fuel
- Application of the flight at air traffic control
- Coordination of ATC slots in coordination with Eurocontrol
- Provision of briefing packages for the crews and consulting (briefing) if requested
- Inflight assistance in case of irregularities

F. 2 Operational flight plan

To summarize all relevant information in one single document and to provide crews and operations control with this information, the operational flight plan (OFP) is issued by dispatch to each individual flight. It generally contains the following information (which is partially defined by the legal authorities such as EASA in Europe):

- A/C tail sign and A/C type
- Date of flight and flight number
- Names of the crew members, task of the crew members
- Departure airport and STD (scheduled time of departure)
- Destination airport (planned and actual) and scheduled time of arrival
- Mode of operation (ETOPS, ferry flight, etc.)
- Routing and waypoints, distances, times and course above ground
- Planned cruising speed and times between control/waypoints
- Estimated and actual times over control/waypoints
- Minimum safety altitude and flight levels, planned altitudes and flight levels
- Fuel monitoring

- Amount of fuel at point of engine start
- Planned alternate airports and (if applicable) alternate departure airports
- Navigational calculations in case of diversions during flight
- Weather information

Today's dispatch offices mainly use IT-based tools to provide the requested OFP. The tools are able to calculate optimized routings by accessing real-time data such as weather, NOTAMs (notification to airmen) and aircraft performance data fully automatically.

F. 3 Economic impact of flight planning

Different optimization premises can be used for flight planning. According to the main principle chosen, it is possible to calculate different flight tracks for a trip from point A to point B:

Flight planning might follow different premises

- Minimum time track (MTT): the routing calculated will lead the aircraft from departure to destination in the shortest possible period of time.
- Minimum fuel track (MFT): the routing calculated will ensure that the aircraft will consume the least possible amount of fuel on that trip.
- Minimum distance track (MDT): the routing is equal to the shortest possible distance.
- Minimum cost track (MCT): the calculated routing will cost the operator the least possible amount of money; all potential cost drivers such as fuel and fees are considered.

F. 4 Tasks and authorities of operations control

The main tasks of Operations Control are:

Operations control manages the daily production of aircraft rotations and coordinates measures in terms of irregularities

- Monitoring and management of flight operations (24h/365 days)
- Trouble shooting and corrective coordination in case of irregularities
- Centralized coordination and information regarding all flight operational issues
- Activation of the crisis management group in case of severe incidents.

Major objectives for the management of flight operations are safety, regularity, punctuality and economic efficiency. Parameters that influence operations negatively, such as adverse weather, technical problems with A/C, strike or short-term airport runway closures, overflight permissions and ATC-slots/night curfews have to be managed by intelligent disposition of the available resources to ensure a high quality flight operation.

F. 5 Ground time, block time, delay and cancellation

Managing aircraft rotations requires the knowledge of several basic terms

Ground time describes the period from chocking the aircraft after arrival at the parking position (on-blocks) until the chocks are removed (off-blocks). The ground time is the period in which the aircraft is unproductive. Therefore airlines tend to minimize ground time as much as possible. A minimum ground time then describes the least amount of time needed to implement the aircraft's turnaround at a station. This minimum ground time primarily depends on the aircraft type plus the infrastructure and staff available at the station.

A block time is the period from removing the chocks at the parking position until chocking the aircraft again at the next destination. It consists of three components:

- Taxi out (off-blocks to airborne)
- Flight time (airborne to touchdown)
- Taxi in (touchdown to on-blocks)

Each one of these components is dependent on different external factors. Taxi times, for example, might differ according to the amount of traffic at an airport, whereas taxi out usually takes longer than the taxi in process, induced by the queues at the runway position. Flight time for one certain leg is dependent on the aircraft's performance, traffic density en route and during approach. Weather, especially jet stream velocities in high altitudes, additionally influences block times severely. Therefore it is possible that a block time for a trip from A to B might be different for different aircraft types or during different seasons. For the schedule this is an additional challenge to guaranteeing punctual performance or even to publishing valid schedule details.

The aircraft schedule describes the planned block and ground times for each aircraft

The synthesis of planned block and ground times is the schedule. If a flight starts at station A the planned moment for off-blocks is defined as a discrete value: STD (scheduled time of departure). Add the planned block time to STD and the result is STA (scheduled time of arrival). The ground time at station B is added to this STA which results in the STD for the trip originating from B. The schedule for one leg (the trip from A to B) can be displayed as follows:

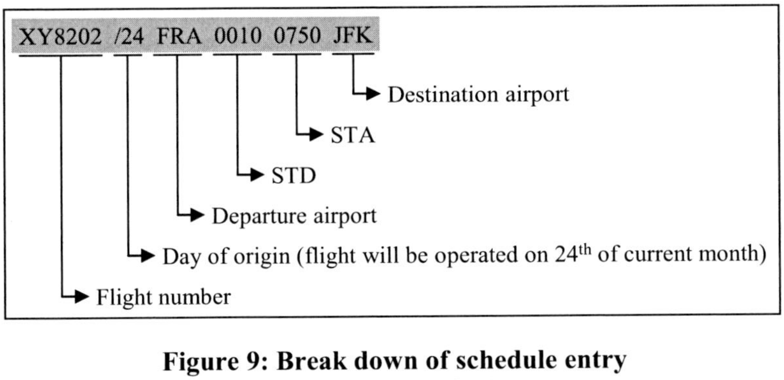

Figure 9: Break down of schedule entry (Own illustration)

The actual values for off- and on-blocks are described by the terms ATA (actual time of arrival) and ATD (actual time of departure). Furthermore, a delay situation might result in issuing an ETD (estimated time of departure) or an ETA (estimated time of arrival); if a flight departs at 0050 UTC (ATD), the plan was 0030 UTC (STD) this results in a departure delay of 20 minutes. If the planned block time is added to the ATD, the estimated time of arrival (ETA) at the next station can be issued.

Monitoring the aircraft or even the fleet schedule by operations control is supported by IT-systems that display all relevant data on a graphic user interface. It displays past, current and future aircraft movements with all details such as STD, ATD, STA, etc. at a glance, so managing delay situations by swapping aircraft or planning of reroutings is easy to deal with. A severe measure of operations control then is the cancellation of a flight, although this might happen due to operational reasons (AOG, weather, etc.).

F. 6 Operational performance

Flight operations are the core production of an airline. Therefore it is essential to monitor their performance. The main performance indicators are punctuality and regularity. Both indicators are influenced by several internal and external factors:

Punctuality is a major indicator to analyzing an airline's operational performance

- Network and schedule: complexity of rotations, planned ground times for a potential buffering of delays
- A/C productivity: cycles and flight hours per day and A/C
- A/C home base absence: A/C availability at the home base for swapping or maintenance
- ATC/weather: external factors ('force majeure') that cannot be influenced and affect all operators
- Aircraft reliability and maintenance schedules: maintenance cycles, AOG ratio, technical condition of the fleet
- Crew: availability of crews, flexibility and guideline of crew disposition

Punctuality is referenced to the planned departure and arrival by comparing the planned values with the actual values. Airlines usually calculate arrival and departure punctuality based on a certain threshold, i.e. a flight is counted as unpunctual if the delay amount is larger than the applied threshold. Common threshold values are 3 minutes and 15 minutes. In order to better analyze delay structures within the operations delay codes might apply. Operations control then has to add a delay code according to the cause from a standardized delay coding list. Usually a number with a range from 0 to 100 has to be chosen, although certain groups define derivative delay causes, e.g. 30-39 = delays due to ground handling or 40-49 = delays due to technical reasons.

The parameter regularity can be used to measure the amount of flights operated in comparison with the amount of flights planned. That is why it is negatively influenced by the cancellation of flights. For the calculation it is necessary to use a 'frozen status' of the schedule which serves as the basic plan for the calculation. For example, this can be the point of time when operations control takes over the responsibility for the flight from the network planners. However, this time value might vary between different airlines. If a flight is cancelled by operations control within this defined timeframe, the value for regularity decreases as it is deducted from the intended production plan.

G. CREW SCHEDULING AND CREW CONTROL

G. 1 Regulatory environment for crew planning

Crew planning manages one of the most cost-intensive resources of the airline

The target of the crew planning process is to assign cockpit and cabin crews to each of the rotations defined by the network planning department. As up to more than twenty individuals have to be assigned for just for one leg (i.e. cockpit plus cabin crew for long haul operations with a 747-400 or A380-800) it is evidently clear that this process is a complex venture to be managed by the airline. The crew planning process itself is confronted with various external influences and regulations that partially decrease the leeway for the crew planners significantly:

Network: the airline's network and its routings is the fundamental basis for crew planning. In only a few cases it is the other way round and network planning does follow optimization premises of crew planning.

Legal requirements: the legal authorities have defined rules and regulations regarding crew duty time limitations to prevent long working hours, which may negatively affect safety. Regulations within the company: at an airline, payment and retention periods of pilots, for example, might be regulated by a certain contract which is usually defined by the company's management in coordination with the acknowledged union. In addition to the legal regulations, these contracts might further decrease the maximum amount of crew duty times and also affect agreements regarding salary, amount of holiday, or even special agreements regarding the crew accommodation at certain destinations such as an additional layover day etc.

G. 2 Crew duty time limitations

The operation of a commercial jetliner requires a sufficient amount of cockpit and cabin crew members. Nowadays the cockpit crew has a captain or commander and one first officer. If the flight time exceeds the maximum amount of the permitted crew duty time, the principle of an augmented crew is applied: an additional first officer or senior first officer joins the cockpit crew to enable one of the team to rest during the flight. The cabin crew is primarily onboard to assure the safety of the passengers in case of an irregular situation. For this reason, the minimum amount of cabin crew members is defined by the maximum amount of passengers onboard. The cabin crew is mainly there to take care of customer service onboard and the number of cabin crew is defined by the service level offered.

As working onboard an airliner is not a nine-to-five job, legal authorities have defined strict regulations an airline has to follow regarding crew planning. The aim of these regulations is to ensure a sufficient amount of crew rest periods enabling the crew members to recover from the stress of flights at night or through several time zones. These regulations might for example refer to the following aspects:

Regulations for the maximum allowable crew duty time are manifold

- Regulation of the maximum crew duty time per day
- Limits on crew overtime (additional duty hours)
- Limits on overtime within a certain period of several consecutive days
- 'No-go' criteria overtime after a certain amount of consecutive legs
- Special regulations if the duty time starts at night
- Regulations regarding the minimum rest period at the home base or en route

G. 3 The crew planning process

The crew planning process starts with the scheduling of aircraft rotations. Firstly, the crew pairing takes place: on every leg the amount of crew members is assigned according to the flights requirements, mainly determined by flight time and aircraft type. The result is the total crew demand for the planning period.

Crew planning proceeds from long- to short-term oriented process steps

Secondly, the result of the crew pairing is matched with the database of the available individual crew members; specific names are planned for the flights. Finally, the crew roster for the following month is created. For this planning step a lot of dependencies have to be considered, such as requested off-days, required training flights, etc.

Having issued the individual crew duty plans, which contain a complete overview, including on-duty legs, briefing schedule, layover periods, off-days and specials, such as appointments for the medical examinations, the crew roster is adjusted on a daily basis in case any crew members are off due to sickness etc. This is done by crew control.

G. 4 Crew productivity

Indicators of crew productivity are valuable both for planning and in real life

Flight crews are a costly resource an airline has to employ efficiently. To measure the productivity of crews the indicator block hours per duty day (BH/DT) is applied. It describes an average value which determines how many block hours a crew member was actively on duty during the reviewed period. The target of this indicator is to monitor how efficient the crew assignment is by taking into consideration that the crew is on duty during a layover period at a line station, but unproductive in terms of generating revenue inflight. Therefore, BH/DT only refers to the productive period onboard an aircraft. Additionally it can be divided between the maximum planable and achievable crew productivity.

The maximum planable crew productivity depends on:

- Legal regulations
- Regulations of the company's contract with the labor union
- The structure of the network
- The structure and amount of the available personnel
- The crew complement

The maximum achievable crew productivity additionally depends on:

- Actual fluctuation
- Modifications of the plan during the actual month
- Actual sickness rate of the crews

Most optimization potentials in terms of crew productivity are dependent on the factors that determine the maximum planable crew productivity. However the implementation of such optimization measures is limited:

- An adaption of the network structure is very restricted, market and customer orientation are the major premises for optimization measures
- An adaption of company contracts depends on the attitude of the labor union / employee's council

H. CREW TRAINING

H. 1 Tasks and setup

The crew training postholder or 'Head of Training according to JAR-FCL 1&4' is responsible for the management of the whole department or (if applicable) of a Type Rating Training Organization (TRTO). He/she reports directly to the accountable manager and is responsible to the governmental authorities in terms of crew training issues.

Additional supporters in his/her team can be a chief flight instructor (responsible for the development, implementation and monitoring of training standards in terms of practical education and training of the crews), a chief ground instructor (responsible for the development, implementation and monitoring of training standards in terms of theoretical education and training of the crews), a manager training operations (planning, management, guidance and monitoring of the actual training processes), and a flight simulator expert and the group of check pilots.

H. 2 Main cost drivers of crew training

Cost drivers for crew training depend on the airline's philosophy to engage ab initio candidates or ready entries

As cockpit crews are another cost intensive cluster within the financial structure of an airline, crew training is optimized by the management whenever possible. Besides the fact that crew training decreases crew productivity, some other cost drivers contribute to the amount of costs induced by crew training:

- Recruitment, selection and training of ab initio candidates
- Recruitment, selection and training of ready-entry candidates
- Re-training (type ratings): induced by fluctuation or by acute demand of capacity
- Loss of productivity due to training
- Rental and operational fees of flight simulators
- Costs induced by training flights (A/C capacity, fuel, fees, etc.)

I. FLIGHT SAFETY, SECURITY AND QUALITY

I. 1 Definitions

Safety, security and quality are usually bundled together, although they focus on different aspects

Safety refers to the reliability of flight operations. Procedures and guidelines have to be developed and established to avoid critical incidents and/or to introduce recovery processes in case of a safety weakness within the whole system of flight operations.

Security concerns the defense of intentional threats from a third which endanger the company's safety. Theft and raids are major subjects in terms of security.

Quality sets requirements for the excellence of services provided by the company. Conflicts with safety requirements might result from certain measures introduced to increase quality which may negatively affect safety processes.

I. 2 Tools and concepts for flight safety management

Resulting from the legal requirements, the basic principle behind risk prevention and the flight safety program is to collect relevant data from several sources and systems to identify trends which might endanger a safe flight operation process. Such data sources might be:

- Ground reports regarding critical incidents on the ground
- Technical logbook entries regarding critical technical defects of the aircraft
- Flight reports by the crew regarding critical incidents inflight

A further essential element of this prevention program is the Flight Operations Data Analysis (FODA). The FODA system is based on a manifold collection of data during operations of the aircraft. This data is saved on a data cartridge which is interconnected with all relevant systems onboard the aircraft. Data saved on the card is analyzed continuously. Recorded parameters are, for example: radio altitude, ground speed, heading, flap setting or headwind component. Besides these parameters, FODA detects abnormal situations such as alert modes of systems, loss of altitude or stall. The recorded data can be analyzed by the operator and finally it is possible to display the flight virtually on a computer screen to re-fly the analyzed situation.

IOSA enables airlines to exchange quality audit

In 2001, the IOSA (IATA Operational Safety Audit) project was initiated. A quality audit involves airline representatives visiting another airline's headquarters to check defined topics of the flight operations and management structure such as documentation and processes. Especially before initiating code share agreements such an audit is a necessary tool for establishing the other airlines standards of safety and quality. By establishing the IOSA program the whole audit environment has become more efficient, as its main purpose is to enable airlines to share the results of their quality audits. An IOSA quality audit has eight areas which cover the whole flight operations management organization. For example, the management system, procedures and regulations, operations control and dispatch. If the auditors raise any findings, the affected airline has to present a recovery plan at short notice. It has to be divided between the first IOSA audit to gain the IOSA approval (IOSA initial) and the IOSA Renewal, which can be carried out 150 days prior to the expiry date of the IOSA registration, valid for two years.

The main benefits of the IOSA program are:

- Reduction of costs and audit resource requirements
- Elimination of audit redundancy through mutual acceptance of audit reports
- Improved operations
- Increased and simplified code-share opportunities
- Continuous updating of standards to reflect regulatory revisions and the evolution of best practices within the industry

Review Questions

- How do pressure components within a laminar airflow change when the flow velocity varies from slow to fast, and how does this effect contribute to the production of lift on an airfoil?
- What are the main elements of a turbofan engine and what is the basic working principle of this engine type?
- Which cockpit instruments are parts of a Basic-T? What is the name of the modern system which integrates these instruments digitally?
- Why is an AOC such an important document for an airline? What does AOC mean? How does an airline get an AOC?
- Flight operations is an important factor in the management of an airline's cost structure. What are essential cost drivers to be dealt with in each department of the flight operations organization?
- Flight planning might follow different premises. What premises do you know and what is the focus of each individual premise?
- What is an indicator of crew productivity and which factors determine the values of maximum planable and maximum achievable crew productivity?
- What are the major benefits of the IOSA principle launched by the IATA in 2001?

Bibliography and further reading

Aainsqatsi, K. (2009): Turbofan engine, http://en.wikipedia.org/wiki/turbofan_engine, retrieved: 10/21/2009.

Airbus (2008): All about the A320 family, Toulouse.

Belobaba, P. / Odoni, A. / Barnhart, C. (2009): The Global Airline Industry, Chichester.

Doganis, R. (2002): Flying Off Course, 3rd Edition, London.

DKL - Dorling Kindersley Limited (2004): Action Pack Flight, London.

Kinnison, H. A. (2004): Aviation Maintenance Management, New York.

Mies, J. (1996): Flugtechnik, Stuttgart.

Hoffer-Gittell, J. (2003): The Southwest Airlines Way, New York.

Sutter, J. / Spenser, J. (2006): 747, New York.

Airports – Types, Functions, Facilities, and Accessibility

Peter A. Meincke, Alexander Tkotz

Table of contents

You should be able to

- name some airport classifications and describe their special categorization as well as differences between the categories
- explain the difference between airside and landside operations and name some of these operations
- show how airport operators generate revenues and which tasks and functions are connected to this
- describe the most important facilities of an airport and give a detailed overview of the different runway and terminal layouts
- describe why access modes are important to airports and why it is important for an access mode planner to know the individual traffic mode split of an airport
- give an overview of possible access modes, their importance and the factors that influence customers in their individual access mode choice

The authors

Dr. Peter A. Meincke is an analyst and researcher at the DLR – German Aerospace Center, Air Transport and Airport Research in Cologne, Germany.

Alexander Tkotz works as a Managing Consultant in the Competence Center Controlling & Finance at Horváth & Partners Management Consultants. Besides that he is a doctoral candidate with the focus on innovation control at the SIIE at EBS Universität für Wirtschaft und Recht.

Abstract

This chapter introduces the types, functions, facilities and access modes of airports from a commercial point of view. Technical components are explained in detail with regard to their economic (e.g. capacity) and operative implications only.

We first give an overview of the different classification criteria and types of airports that are used in different countries and contexts. The subsequent chapters cover main functions and facilities of an airport including landside and airside operations as well as runway and terminal layouts. The last chapter explains the importance of intermodal connections and shows how the choice of travelers for or against an access mode is influenced by the characteristics of the access mode itself. The reader learns how to asses the economic implications of decisions in the highly complex system(s) of an airport.

A. TYPES AND CATEGORIES OF AIRPORTS

Possibilities to differentiate airports

There are plenty of different airport types: rural airstrips, private airstrips, military airports, small community airports, regional community airports, regional airports, major city airports and hub airports. These airport types can be classified in several ways and nearly every nation and air traffic organization has its own classification scheme.[1] Some classifications are rather general in nature and identify airport functions without specifying design standards. Others contain detailed lists of facilities an airport needs in order to achieve a certain classification. The specific classification systems identify airport function, primary economic role and, to a lesser extent, funding category eligibility, and importance for scientific and political transportation issues.

National airport systems

Some of these differentiation criteria can be found in regulations concerning national airport systems. These national airport systems are designed for a particular geography, economic structure and the political goals of each country, and financed to produce maximum benefit from the investment. Some systems are illustrated in the following to show how categories vary to suit different airports and their parameters.

---

[1] Short summary of various airport classifications in literature: EU Commission (airport classes A-D: based on PAX numbers); German Federal Statistical Office (international versus regional airports); German aviation law (airports versus airfields); ACI (airport groups 1-4, based on PAX numbers); Boston Consulting Group (primary hubs, international O&Ds, secondary hubs and O&Ds, regional airports); Oliver Wyman (primary hub, secondary hub, major O&D, low-cost airport, leisure airport); Transport Canada (national air system airports, FAA classification on U.S. airports).

A. 1 British National Airport System (as of 1978)

British National Airport System distinguishes four airport categories

- **Gateway International Airports**: Airports supplying range and frequency of international services, including intercontinental services and full range of domestic services.
- **Regional Airports**: Airports catering to the main air traffic demand of individual regions. They are concerned with the provision of a network of short-haul international services (mainly to Scandinavia and other parts of Europe), a range of charter and domestic services, including links with gateway airports.
- **Local Airports**: Airports providing third-level services (scheduled passenger services operated by aircraft with fewer than 25 seats), catering privately for local needs, concentrating on general aviation with some feeder services and some charter flights.
- **General Aviation Airports**: Airports concerned primarily with the provision of general aviation facilities.

A. 2 United States airport categories

The FAA differentiates on basis of commercial passengers

The United States Federal Aviation Administration (FAA) has established a system for categorizing public use airports that is primarily based on the level of commercial passenger traffic through each facility (see Table 1). It is used to determine whether an airport is eligible for funding through the federal government's Airport Improvement Program (AIP).[2] The FAA categories describe the airport roles and the type of facilities at each airport. To qualify for the AIP an airport needs to fulfill the following criteria:

Airport Improvement Program

- Less than 2,500 scheduled passengers each year
- At least 10 aircraft based there
- Most aircraft are small and operated by private persons or entities

Altogether less than 20% of US airports qualify for the program, though most that do not qualify are private-use-only airfields.

<table>
<tr><th>Common name</th><th>Percentage of annual passenger boardings</th><th colspan="2">Airport classifications</th></tr>
<tr><td>Large hub</td><td>1% or more</td><td rowspan="5">Commercial Service: Public owned airports that have at least 2,500 passenger boardings each calender year and receive scheduled passenger service</td><td rowspan="4">Primary: Have more than 10,000 passenger boardings each year</td></tr>
<tr><td>Medium hub</td><td>At least 0.25%, but less than 1%</td></tr>
<tr><td>Small hub</td><td>At least 0.05%, but less than 0.25%</td></tr>
<tr><td>Nonhub primary</td><td>More than 10,000, but less than 0.05%</td></tr>
<tr><td>Nonprimary commercial service</td><td>At least 2,500 and no more than than 10,000</td><td>Nonprimary</td></tr>
<tr><td>Reliever</td><td>Not applicable</td><td colspan="2">Nonprimary (Except commercial service)</td></tr>
</table>

Table 1: Definition of airport categories by FAA (Federal Aviation Administration [FAA], 2014)

---

2 The AIP is part of the National Plan of Integrated Airport Systems (NPIAS). NPIAS identifies more than 3,400 existing and proposed airports that are significant to national air transportation and thus eligible to receive Federal grants.

Reliever and general aviation airports

Some of the categories in Table 1 need to be defined in more detail: Reliever airports are airports designated by the FAA to relieve congestion at commercial service airports and to provide improved general aviation access to the overall community.[3] These airports may be publicly or privately owned. The remaining airports, while not specifically defined, are commonly described as general aviation airports. This airport type is the largest single group of airports in the U.S. system. The category also includes privately owned, public use airports that enplane 2,500 or more passengers annually and receive scheduled airline service.

Cargo airports

The FAA airport categories also define cargo airports. These are airports that, in addition to other air transportation services, are served by aircraft providing air transportation for cargo, with a total annual landing weight of at least 100 million pounds.

A. 3 EU Commission airport classification

Classification of EU commission

The European Union distinguishes between four airport categories on the basis of the 'Guidelines for financing of airports'. The four airport categories are detailed in Table 2.

Category	Airport classification	PAX per year	Example for German situation
A	Large community airports	10m and more	Berlin-Tegel, Düsseldorf, Frankfurt, München
B	National airports	5m to less than 10m	Berlin-Schönefeld, Köln-Bonn, Stuttgart
C	Large regional airports	1m to less than 5m	Bremen, Hannover, Dresden, Leipzig-Halle, Nürnberg
D	Small regional airports	Less than 1m	Lübeck, Paderborn/Lippstadt, Saarbrücken

Table 2: EU Commission airport classification (Conrady, Fichert & Sterzenbach, 2013)

A. 4 Categories in scientific literature

Scientific literature mainly uses four categories

Scientific literature often differentiates between primary, secondary, tertiariy, and quartiary airports (Hirschhausen, Beckers & Tegner, 2004; Conrady, Fichert & Sterzenbach, 2013):

- **Primary airports**: airports with hub function and a huge amount of transit passengers (e.g. Heathrow, Frankfurt)
- **Secondary airports**: airports that have an large catchment area and are therefore connected to the hub airports of large network carriers (e.g. Milan, Glasgow, Hamburg)
- **Tertiary airports**: all other airports with international services and scheduled feeder services to large hub airports (e.g. Hannover, Nuremberg, Bremen)
- **Quartiary airport**: regional and former military airports often used by low-cost carriers (e.g. Frankfurt-Hahn, Zweibrücken)

[3] Greater Atlanta e.g. has more than 10 reliever airports.

A. 5 Airport classification in Germany

German classification is set up by air traffic law

German air traffic law differentiates between airports, airfields and gliding airfields (see Table 3). Airports and airfields are further subdivided into public and special airports/airfields. It is within each province's jurisdiction to permit the building and operation of an airport, airfield or gliding field.

Public and special airports

The differentiation between 'public' and 'special' is based on two principles. First, public airports/airfields are (as the name indicates) accessible to everybody; whereas the special airports/airfields are only accessible to closed user groups, such as corporations or military. Second, public airports/airfields require – due to their high traffic volumes – special safety measures which are met by the establishment of airport construction restriction zones.[4]

Airfield	Criteria	Examples
Public airport	With construction restriction zone accessible for public air traffic	All international German airports (Hamburg, Frankfurt, Cologne-Bonn, Munich, etc.)
Special airport	With construction restriction zone only accessible to certain users	Private company airport of Fairchild-Dornier at Oberpfaffenhofen
Public airfield	Without construction restriction zone accessible for public air traffic	Bonn-Hangelar, Egelsbach, Helgoland-Düne; some are connected to line operation: Friedrichshafen, Hof, etc.
Special airfield	Without construction restriction zone only accessible to certain users	Private company airport of EADS Airbus at Hamburg-Finkenwerder
Gliding airfield		Bad Wörishofen, Bergheim, Wasserkuppe

Table 3: German airport classification system (Maurer, 2006)

Besides the classification according to German air traffic law there are some other classifications in use in Germany.

Alternative classification by DFS

The German authority for air traffic control (DFS) counts 16 international airports because the federal government has a political interest in these airports. As a consequence, air traffic control is active at these airports (Conrady, Fichert & Sterzenbach, 2013).

Alternative classification by ADV

Building on different criteria, the German Airports Association (ADV) counts 21 international airports. The ADV criteria for an international airport are:

ADV criteria

- Valid license as public airport or public airfield
- National scheduled services
- Scheduled and charter services with foreign destinations
- Air traffic control
- Yearly PAX numbers that are at least as large as the average passenger numbers generated by two airports that were already part of the association in the year 1991

[4] A construction restriction zone is an area around an airport in which construction of premises is not permitted unless approved by air traffic authority.

Regional airport

The term 'regional airport' is also used, though it is not defined by law. ADV and the German air traffic authority use the term for regional airports or airfields with scheduled traffic that is not already part of the international airports. The difference to the international airports is that regional airports have the right to conduct air traffic control (ATC) themselves, whereas ATC at international airports has to be conducted by the German authority for air traffic control.

A. 6 Important facts about the basic airport types

Common classification

To sum up, we give a short overview of the basic airport types and their characteristics used hereafter. This classification is one of the most common when discussing airport-related topics.

Hub airport

Hub airports:

- Large passenger numbers
- Great share of transit passengers
- Huge catchment area (supported by intermodal long range traffic such as rail)
- Airport infrastructure for long-distance flights (e.g. length of runway min. 3,300 meters, facilities to service large aircraft)
- Optimized premises for fast transfer and minimum connecting time as well as short cargo turnaround times
- Sufficient capacities (check-in, terminal, gates, etc.) to handle large passenger quantities
- No or only few restrictions for take-off and landings
- High potential for growth

Secondary airport

Secondary Airports (international airports):

- Bigger airports in terms of passenger numbers
- Small number of transfer passengers
- Considerable number of international services
- Many point-to-point services
- Feeder function for large hubs
- Huge regional catchment area

Regional airport

Regional Airports:

- Small airports in terms of passenger numbers
- No transfer passengers
- Regionally limited catchment area
- Mainly direct flights and feeder services

B. FUNCTIONS OF AIRPORTS

B. 1 Core function and business model

Today, airports are very complex and interconnected service providers, dependent on cooperation with different companies, authorities and other institutions.

Aviation is core work

The (traditional) core function of an airport is the operation of premises for servicing and handling aircraft, passengers, cargo and mail. This includes supply and operation of ground handling facilities, apron, runways, maintenance areas, gates, people movers, baggage handling, car parks, waiting areas, warehousing, storage space, areas for security and social purposes, and many more. The activity of ground handling is certainly part of the traditional airport core function, although some airport operators see ground handling itself as an independent business unit since they were forced to give up their monopolies due to deregulation.

Non-Aviation as supplement

Furthermore, what an airport offers also includes non-aviation services. These are mainly the supply of space for shopping, convention centers, hotels, restaurants and business centers. The non-aviation revenues of an airport are often a major profit driver, and thus an essential part of an airport's business model (Finnsson, 1993).

Non-Aviation becomes more important

The transition from a pure infrastructure provider to an integrated service provider that many airports have gone through was followed by a massive expansion of business activities. Whilst in the past, airports offered only a few shopping facilities mainly focused on the travel-related needs of passengers, a service-oriented international airport today offers a wide range of products and services (e.g. shopping malls and leisure centers) that go far beyond the traditional core function (Hermsen, 1993).

Other business areas

However, the non-aviation business forms only one segment of the extended business model of modern airport operators. A further area of activities comprises service products which include inter-modal connections to rail[5] and road, as well as passenger information systems that enable passengers to retrieve all relevant information for their journey from one source. These services are usually part of the non-aviation segment since they normally only generate small revenues. An important segment of the extended business model is the selling of an airport operator's know-how to foreign markets. The importance of this business segment is growing rapidly. For instance, Frankfurt's airport operator, Fraport AG, runs several airports in other countries and actively offers consulting servives to other airport operators.

B. 2 Airside and landside operations

Mandatory tasks prescribed by law

The mandatory tasks of an airport and its operator in Germany are determined by the operator's license. Fraport's license, for example, predetermines that the airport operator must keep the airport in a reliable condition at all times and is required to take measures (in line with its capabilities) to secure air traffic performance. In addition, the German

[5] The British airport operator BAA, for example, built an express railway for £ 620m. The Heathrow-Express connects Heathrow Airport with Paddington station in the city of London and is fully owned by BAA.

air traffic licensing regulations prescribe general duties for airports in article 45.

Airside services

According to the law a central part of an airport's duties are ground handling services. Under this category different services are mentioned that can be divided into either landside (or check-in) services or airside (or apron) services. The airside services include all services in connection with aircraft dispatch, passenger servicing and cargo handling, e.g. loading and unloading an aircraft, supplying it with fresh water, electricity and kerosene, disposal of waste and excrement, cleaning, baggage handling, transportation of passengers, luggage and cargo between aircraft and terminal, and the providing of aerobridges and airstairs. Furthermore, airside services include building and operation of runways, taxiways and aprons. Figure 1 illustrates some airside services needed to turn around a Boeing 777.

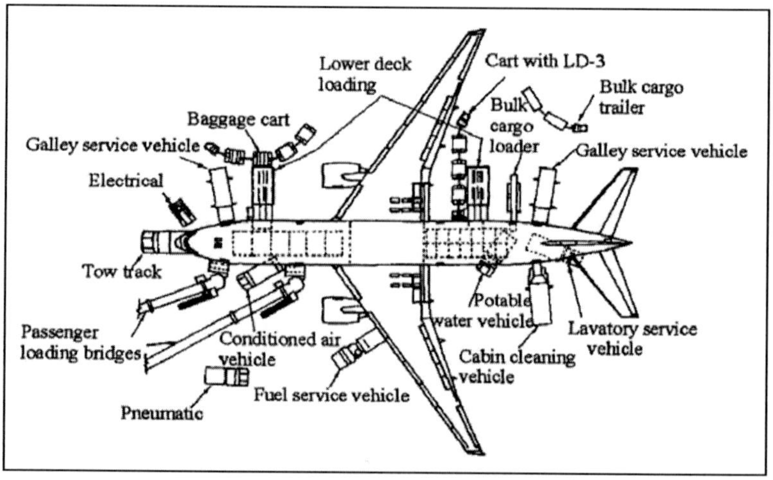

Figure 1: Ground handling services for a Boeing 777 (Boeing, 2008)

Providers of airside or apron services

Airside services can further be distinguished according to the operator providing a certain service. There are four basic constellations:

- Airlines can provide the services needed on their own
- An airline can provide services for other airlines (mostly the home carrier for its alliance partners)
- The airport can provide the services
- Specialized service agents or companies can provide the services

Specialized service companies

Specialized service companies usually offer a full range of ground handling services. To offer a service every provider requires a license, which is usually issued by the airport operator responsible for safety and security.

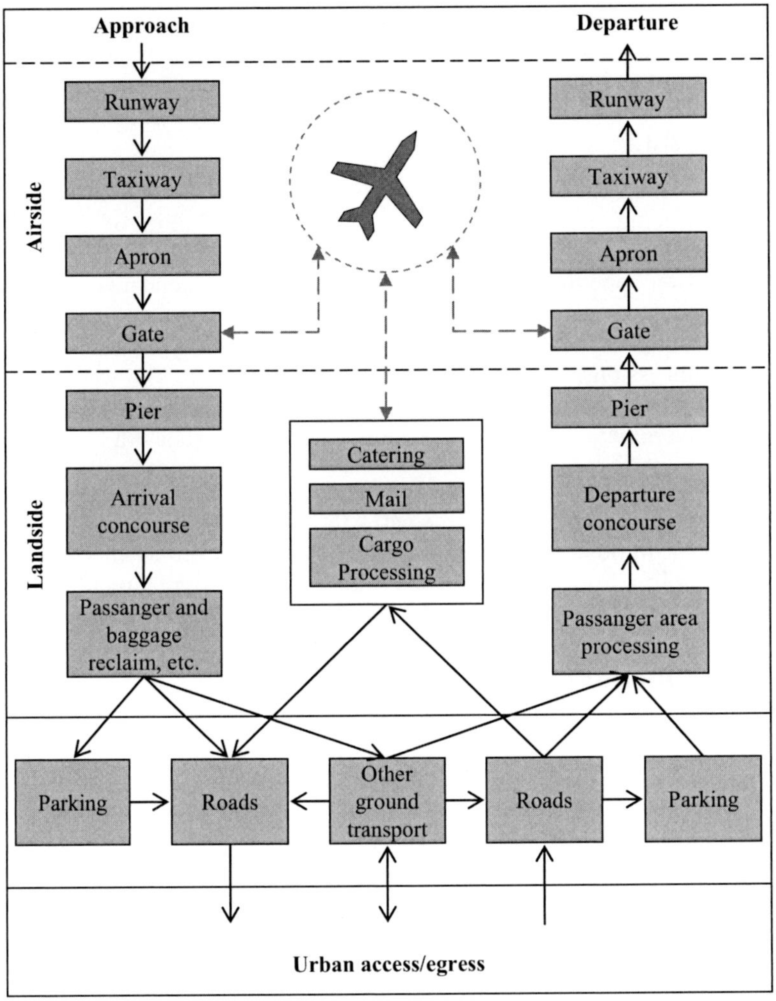

Figure 2: The airport system (Ashford, Stanton & Moore, 2012)

The services are divided into airside and landside and also different buildings and operations at an airport. Therefore it is common to differentiate operation between airside and landside functions (Figure 2).

Landside services

The landside services include renting rooms and spaces as well as giving concessions to run a business at the airport. Another service is the building and operation of premises for any purpose in connection with the airport such as hotels, car parks and convention centers.

B. 3 Different functions subject to airport size

Many small airports that provide little more than a simple passenger terminal for low-volume passenger operations provide barely more than a facility. The operation of the airport is not significantly more complex than that of a railway station or an inter-urban bus station.

The medium- or large-scale airport is, however, much more complex and requires an organization that can cope with such complexity. Airports of a significant size must have an organization that can either supply or administer the following facilities (Ashford, Stanton & Moore, 2012):

- Handling of huge passengers volumes
- Servicing, maintenance and engineering of aircraft of different size
- Airline operations including aircrew, cabin attendants, ground crew, terminal and office staff
- Businesses necessary for the economic stability of the airport (concessions, leasing companies, etc.)
- Aviation support facilities (air traffic control, meteorology, etc.)
- Governmental functions – customs, immigration, health

Large hubs are complex entities that encounter all the problems facing any large organization. In some cases the airport itself may be a large employer, in other cases the authority may act as a broker of services, resulting in a low level of directly authorized employment and a high level of outsourcing (Ashford, Stanton & Moore, 2012).

B. 4 Functions of the terminal

A terminal has three major functions

The terminal itself is a facility that fulfils three distinct functions (Ashford, Mumayiz & Wright, 2011):

- **Change of mode**: provides a physical link between the air vehicle and the surface vehicles designed to accommodate the operating characteristics of the vehicles on the airside and landside respectively
- **Processing**: provides the necessary facilities for ticketing, documentation, and control of passenger and freight
- **Change of movement type**: converts continuous arrivals of freight by truck and departing passengers by car, bus and train into aircraft sized batches that generally depart according to preplanned schedule (Reverse this process for arriving aircraft)

C. AIRPORT FACILITIES

Major airport components

The infrastructure needed to deliver the ground handling services can be divided into three major components: Air traffic facilities, handling facilities and ground traffic facilities (see Table 4). Further facilities are e.g. hotels, forwarding, firefighters, airport administration, customs and other authorities.

In this section we describe some particularly important facilities in more detail. These are runways, taxiways, aprons, and terminals.

Air traffic facilities	Handling facilities	Ground traffic facilities
Runways	***Terminals***	Access- and descent roads
Taxiways	Cargo facilities	Parking
Ramps and aprons		Public transport
Areas for security		Cargo gates

Table 4: Airport components (Hüschelrath, 1998)

C. 1 Runways

Among the most important airport facilities are the runways. In the following we describe runway basics, runway markings, and different runway configurations.

C. 1. 1 Runway basics

Basic principles on building runways

- Runways are typically constructed from gravel, snow, ice, grass, asphalt or concrete, whereas most commercial runways are made of asphalt or concrete
- Runways are normally optimally positioned for prevailing winds, noise, land use, and other determining factors
- The primary runway is oriented towards the prevailing winds
- Crosswind runways are oriented towards the most common crosswind direction(s) to secure a steady level of high service under changing weather conditions
- The length and width of a runway is mainly determined by the type of aircraft it should accommodate. This area of construction is strongly influenced by international regulations, laws, and standards
- Runways should comply with safety regulations such as the ICAO or FAA design standards

Compass layout

Runways are laid out according to magnetic north. In navigation and surveying, all measurement of direction is carried out using the azimuth of a compass. The compass directions are 0/360° for north, 90° for east, 180° for south and 270° for west. A typical compass is illustrated in Figure 3.

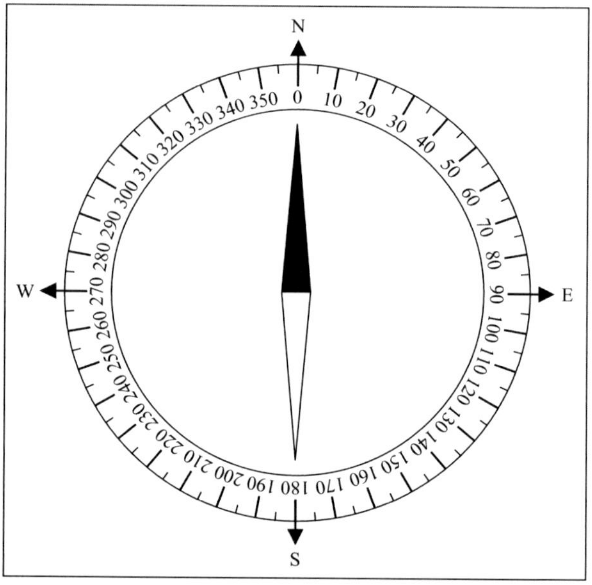

Figure 3: Typical layout of a compass (Own illustration)

C. 1. 2 Runway markings

Runway marking in relation to compass azimuth

A runway's compass azimuth is indicated by a large number painted at each end of the runway. A runway's designation marking indicates the direction in degrees in which the runway lies. The last zero of each number is left out, meaning that 14 is actually close to (if not exactly) 140 degrees or southeast facing. A runway with a marking of 4 has a heading of 40 degrees, that is, a northeast direction. Figure 4 gives an example of a runway. One end of the runway is facing due east: The compass azimuth for due east is 90 degrees (9).The other end of the runway naturally faces due west or 270 degrees (27). Therefore the runway is identified as runway 9/27. In this context it does not matter which direction is the primary operating orientation, the lower number is always identified first. However, during operations the runway is identified only by the number indicating the current operating direction.

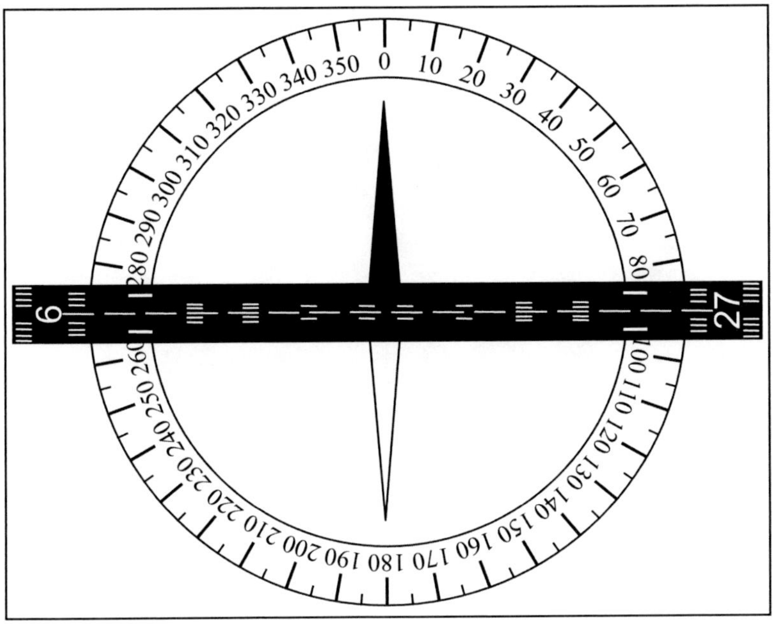

Figure 4: Example runway 9/27
(Own illustration)

Marking of parallel runways with the same orientation

All runways follow this directional layout. If two parallel runways with the same orientation are operated the runway markings are supplemented with L for the left runway and R for the right runway.[6] With three parallel runways the center runway is either marked with a C or one of the outer runways gets a different marking to the next nearest 10 degrees. The same principles apply if four or more runways are operated parallel. Atlanta, for example, has five parallel runways that are all oriented 9/27: Beginning with the most northerly runway the first two runways have the marking 8/26 (supplemented with corresponding L and R) the next two runways have the marking 9/27 (supplemented with corresponding L and R) and the most southerly runway has the marking 10/28.

Figure 5 is an illustration of the complex runway system with different runway orientations and markings at Chicago O'Hare International Airport. Note that the runway 10/28 used to be the parallel runway of 9R/27L. Because a third parallel runway with orientation 9/27 was built in the northern part of the area the markings of the two existent runways had to be changed.

---

[6] The L and R markings are assigned from the viewing direction of an approaching aircraft. Therefore a runway in parallel setup will have an L on the one end and an R on the other end; the second runway will have the L and R distributed vice versa.

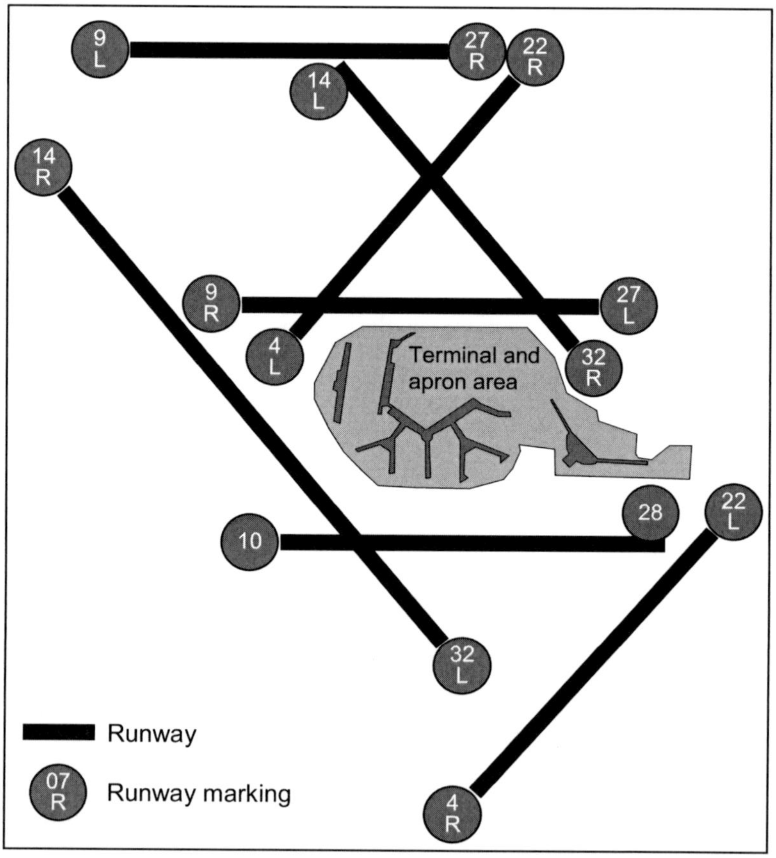

Figure 5: Example of runway system at Chicago O'Hare International Airport (Own illustration)

Visual runway markings

Besides the runway designation marking there are several other equally important visual markings. Each runway has a center-line with regular gaps giving guidance during take-off and landing. Even in front of the designation marking there is the threshold zone painted on the edge of both runway ends. The threshold consists of four to sixteen stripes depending on the runway width. Following the runway marking there is the touchdown zone starting 500 feet away from the runways edge. It consists of six stripes. Fixed distance markers or runway aiming points (two wide stripes) follow at 1,000 feet. They are intended to help the pilot aiming during approach. At 1,500 and 2,000 feet there are additional markers consisting of four stripes. After that each additional 500 feet are marked (up to 3,000 feet from runway edge or till the runways midpoint, whatever is reached first). Figure 6 shows a plan of the above described visual markings.

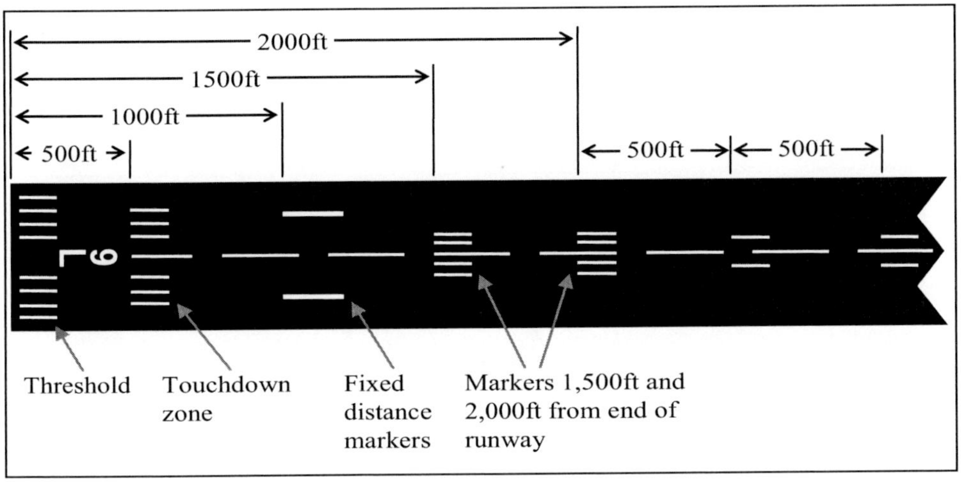

Figure 6: Visual runway markings (Own illustration)

Further visual and non-visual runway markings

In addition to the visual runway markings painted on the pavement there are also runway lights and approach lightning systems that also fall into the category of visual runway markings. Precision and non-precision instrument markings are also included in the runway. For further details refer to e.g. Young & Wells (2011) or de Neufville et. al. (2013).

C. 1. 3 Basic runway configurations

Runway configuration determines capacity

For air traffic and airport capacity the runway configuration is critical. Position, quantity, length, width and distance between two runways are decisive for the quantity of flights an airport can handle per hour. The capacity of a runway can change dramatically if it is either operated solely under instrument flight rules (IFR) or operated solely under visual flight rules (VFR). The basic configurations will be explained on the following pages. The classification presented follows the FAA classification.

Excursion:
Instrument flight rules (IFR) and visual flight rules (VFR)

On flights using instruments the flight attitude is controlled via instruments in the airplane only. A reference to outer indicators like the natural horizon is not necessarily needed. This makes flight through clouds or fog possible. The instrument flight makes flying independent form weather conditions and thus enables adherence to flight schedules. Weather conditions that make a flight under visual flight rules (VFR) impossible are called Instrument Meteorological Conditions.

In Germany every commercial flight with more than 14 tons of maximum take off weight or more than 19 passengers must be conducted following IFR.

C.1.3.1 Single runway

Single runway

Figure 7 depicts the simplest basic runway configuration. It is one runway optimally positioned for prevailing winds, noise, land use and other determining factors.

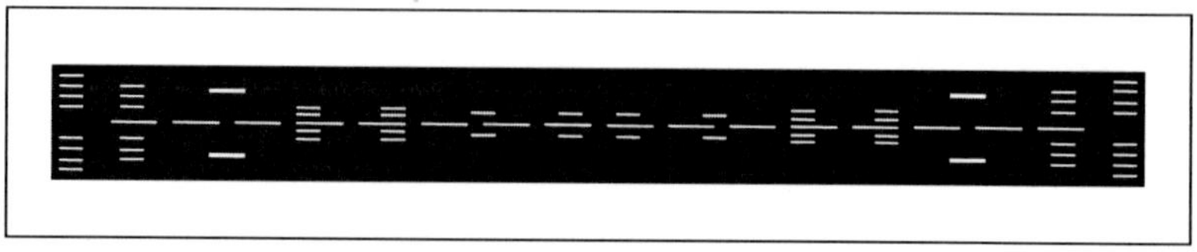

Figure 7: Single runway (Own illustration)

During VFR conditions, this runway should accommodate up to 100 light aircraft operations per hour. While under IFR conditions, it would accommodate 50 to 60 operations per hour depending on the mix of traffic and navigational aids available at that airport (International Civil Aviation Organization [ICAO], 2008).

C.1.3.2 Parallel runways

Parallel runways

Parallel runways are at least two runways with the same geographical orientation. There are four types of parallel runways which are named according to their proximity to each other. The distance between two runways is measured from the neighboring runway's median strip as point of reference. The terms 'close', 'intermediate' and 'far' are used to identify different configurations. The distance between two runways determines the possible usage and thus the capacity a runway system offers:

Types of parallel runways

- **Closed parallel runways** are spaced from between a minimum of 700 feet to less than 2,500 feet apart. They cannot be operated independently, so the capacity is equal to a single runway's capacity and can handle 50 to 60 operations per hour during IFR.
- **Intermediate parallel runways are** spaced from between 2,500 feet to less than 4,300 feet apart. In IFR conditions arrivals on one runway are independent of the departures on the other runway. The combined capacity can range from between 60 to 75 operations per hour.
- **Far parallel runways**: are at least 4,300 feet apart. In IFR conditions the two runways can be operated independently for both arrivals and departures.[7] The combined capacity can range from 100 to 120 operations per hour.
- **Dual-lane runways**: Dual-lane runways consist of two sets of parallel runways with attendant exit taxiways. Although each runway pair can be used for mixed operations, the desirable mode of operation is to dedicate the runways farthest from the terminal

[7] The 4,300 feet are an FAA specification. ICAO for example specifies only 3,000 feet between runway's center-lines. However, some countries even require 5,000 feet or more.

building (outer) for arrival and the runways closest to the terminal building (inner) for departures. The combined capacity depends on which of the three aforementioned parallel runway configurations is chosen for each runway pair.

The four parallel runway configurations are shown in Figure 8.

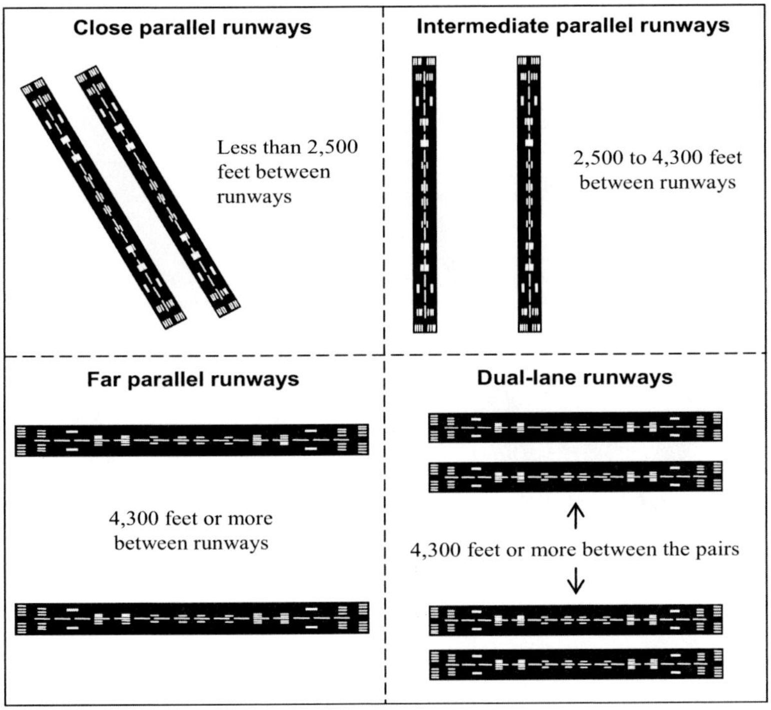

Figure 8: Parallel runways (Own illustration)

Capacity estimation of dual-lane runways

The FAA estimates that a dual-lane runway can handle at least 70% more traffic than a single runway in VFR conditions and 60% more traffic than a single runway in IFR conditions. Capacity was found to be insensitive to center-line spacing between the runways from 1,000 to 2,499 feet. It is therefore recommended that the two runways are spaced not less than 1,000 feet apart to secure operations for large aircraft.

Staggered thresholds

Sometimes it may be desirable to stagger the thresholds of parallel runways. The staggering maybe necessary because of the shape of the acreage available for runway construction or it may be desirable for reducing the taxiing distance for landed aircraft. An advantage of staggered runways is that parallel approaching aircraft are separated by height since the aircraft approaching the closer runway if flying parallel has a lower altitude to the aircraft aiming for the farther runway. Since staggered runways consume more precious land this may be a disadvantage for airports with tight area restrictions.

C.1.3.3 Open-V runways

Open-V runways

Two runways with different orientations that do not intersect form a shape that looks like an open-V, hence the name open-V runways. Depending on the direction of operations open-V runways are also referred to 'diverging' or 'converging'.

This configuration is useful when there is little to no wind as it allows both runways to be used at the same time. When the wind becomes strong in one direction only one runway will be used. When takeoffs and landings are made away from the two closer ends, the number of operations per hour significantly increases (Figure 9).

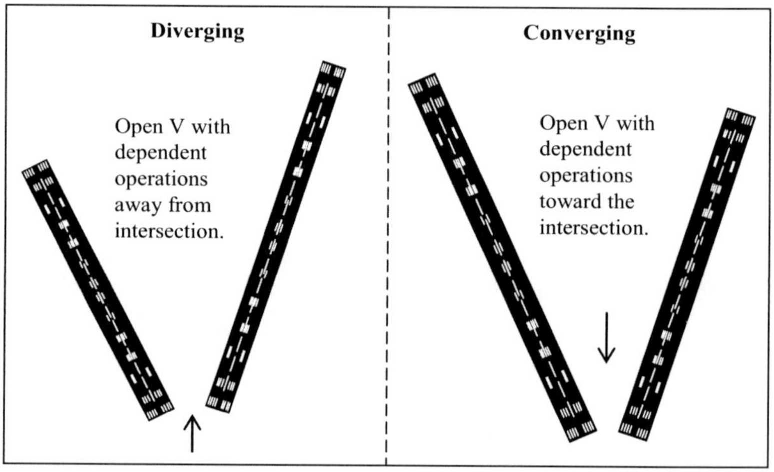

Figure 9: Open-V runways (Own illustration)

C.1.3.4 Intersecting runways

Intersecting runways

Two or more runways that cross each other are classified as intersecting runways. This type of configuration is used when there are relatively strong prevailing winds from more than one direction during the year. When the winds are strong from one direction, operations will be limited to one runway. With relatively light winds, both runways can be used simultaneously. The capacity of two intersecting runways depends mainly on the location of the intersection (midway or near the ends) and on the direction the runway is operated. The greatest capacity for operations is accomplished when the intersection is close to the take-off end and the landing threshold as shown in Figure 10 (Young & Wells, 2011).

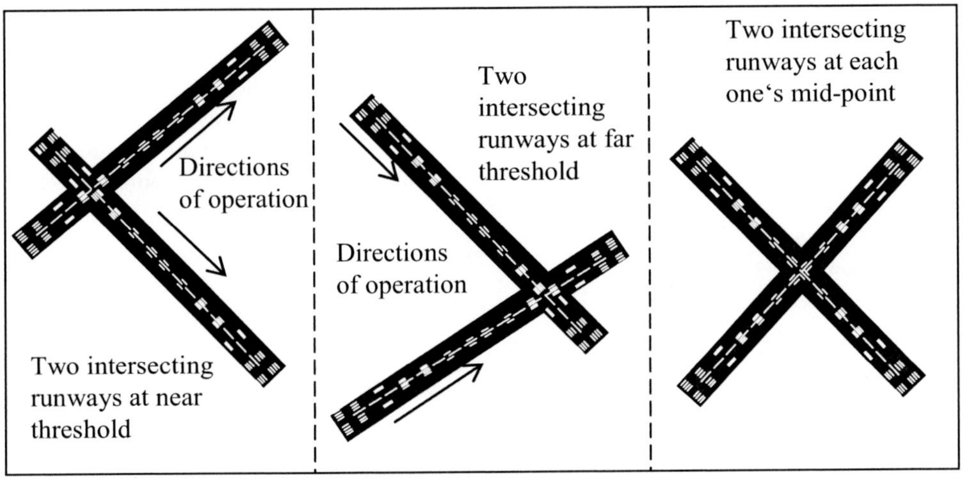

Figure 10: Intersecting runways
(Own illustration)

C. 2 Taxiways

Taxiways connect runways with aprons

A taxiway is a path on an airport connecting runways with ramps, hangars, terminals and other facilities. Because of their total length[8] taxiways are the second major component of the airfield. They usually have hard surfaces such as asphalt or concrete, although smaller airports sometimes use gravel or grass. Busy airports typically construct express exit taxiways in order to allow aircraft to leave the runway at higher speeds. This allows the aircraft to vacate the runway quicker, permitting another aircraft to land in a shorter space of time.

Taxiways have different functions

Basically there are four different taxiway configurations:

- **Entrance Taxiways** lead to one end of the runway and are used by departing aircraft to reach their take-off position.
- **Bypass Taxiways** allow aircraft to bypass other aircraft (for example, during last departure preparations) on their way to the runway.
- **Exit Taxiways**: each runway normally has several exit taxiways distributed along it. A landing aircraft should be able to leave the runway as soon as it has decreased its speed enough, allowing the next aircraft to land or depart. For this purpose express exit taxiways are also used at busy airports. These are normally built at an angle of 30 to 45 degrees to the runway allowing aircraft to leave the runway at higher speed and therefore earlier.
- **Parallel Taxiways** run parallel to a runway.

---

8 At major airports taxiways can easily exceed 20 km in length. Especially at airports with dual-lane runways that have several express exit taxiways and full length parallel taxiways the total length of taxiways can exceed the total runway length by far. For example, the airport in Dallas/Fort Worth has about 25 km of runways and nearly 80 km of taxiways.

Taxiways can be designated to more than one function

Taxiways often cannot be categorized into above-mentioned functions. For example, at many airports there are several entrance taxiways that also serve as bypass taxiways. Another example is a layout with two parallel taxiways adjacent to one runway. Of course, they can also be used as bypass taxiways. In Figure 11 you can see an example for taxiway layout showing runway 8L/26R at Munich International Airport and its dedicated taxiways.

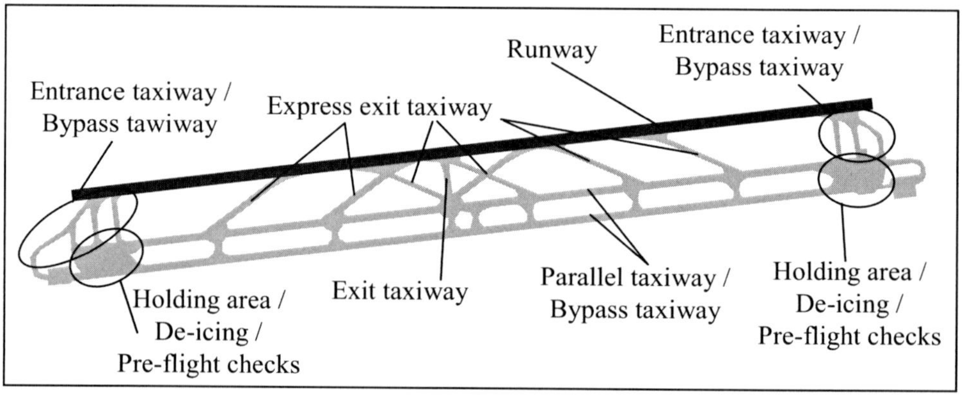

Figure 11: Taxiways at runway 8L/26R at Munich Airport (Own illustration)

Principles for the planning of taxiways

Taxiways are planned with the following principles in mind (Young & Wells, 2011):

- Aircraft that have just landed should not interfere with aircraft taxiing to take off
- Taxi routes should provide the shortest distance between aircraft parking areas and runways
- At busy airports, exit taxiways should be located at various points along runways so that landing aircraft can leave the runways as quickly as possible
- A taxiway designed to permit higher turn-off speeds reduces the time a landing aircraft is on the runway. Such taxiways are called high-speed exit taxiways and are typically aligned at 30 to 45 degree angles connecting the runway with the parallel taxiway
- When possible, taxiways are planned so as not to cross an active runway

C. 3 Airport ramp or apron

Aprons and ramps are used for servicing aircraft

The airport ramp or apron is usually the area where aircraft are parked, unloaded, loaded, refueled, and boarded. Although the use of the apron is covered by strict regulations, it is typically more accessible to users than the runway or taxiway. However, the apron is not open to the general public and a license is required to gain access. The words 'apron' and 'ramp' are used interchangeably in most circumstances. Generally, the pre-flight activities are completed on the ramps; and areas for parking and maintenance are called aprons. Passenger gates are the main feature of a terminal ramp.

Aprons use is regulated

The use of the apron may be controlled by the apron management service (apron control or apron advisory), which would typically provide a coordination service between the users. The apron is designated by the ICAO as not being part of the maneuvering area. All vehicles, aircraft and people using the apron are referred to as apron traffic.

Aprons design requirements

Aprons are usually designed to meet the following requirements (Kazda & Caves, 2007):

- Support the safe guidance of aircraft to the assigned position
- Shortest possible distance between taxiways and stands
- Aircraft should be able to move independently from each other
- Sufficient number of ramps and stands to cope with aircraft handling in peak times
- Quick aircraft turnaround should be possible
- Neighboring stands/ramps should be designed to adequately dispatch adjacent aircraft without interfering each other's operations
- Aprons should provide enough space for maneuvering and parking ground handling equipment
- Possible future extensions of the facilities should be considered

C. 4 Terminals

Terminals link airside and landside

The terminal builds the link or interface between the airside and the landside. It comprises all the facilities and equipment needed to serve passengers and handle their luggage. Furthermore airlines, handling agents and travel agencies typically run offices at the airport to be close to their customers.

Five basic terminal configurations

There are many types of terminal configurations in use at airports around the globe. However, five basic configurations can be identified: simple terminal, linear concept, pier finger concept, satellite concept and transporter concept. Each will be described in the following. For further information about inner layout of terminals including passenger flows and distribution of space for different facilities see, for example, Young & Wells (2011) or Kazda & Caves (2007).

Most terminals are mixtures of basic concepts

In reality 'pure' terminal concepts are seldom to be found, since most airports have grown over the years and have therefore had to expand their capacity continuously. In most cases different concepts are applied and intermingled with each other to meet the needs and requirements both of capacity goals and geographical situation. Alongside passenger terminals, different cargo terminal concepts can also be defined, but they will not be dealt with in this chapter.

C. 4. 1 Simple terminal and open apron

Simple terminal or open apron

The simple terminal or open apron configuration consists of only one building holding all the relevant facilities like ticketing, check-in area, waiting area, and luggage handling. Aircraft are parked on the apron next to the terminal. In most cases passengers have to walk to the aircraft and board via stairs. This configuration is often used at very small airports and some older regional airports (Figure 12).

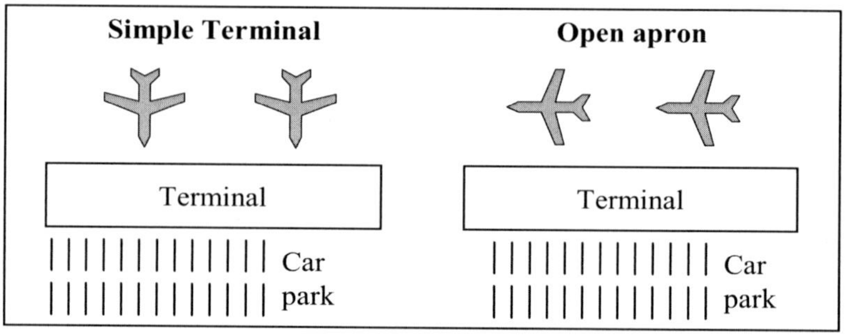

Figure 12: Simple terminal or open apron (Own illustration)

C. 4. 2 Linear Terminal and curvilinear terminal

Linear terminal concept

The linear concept is a further development of the simple terminal concept with more gates and more space in the terminal building. On the landside next to the terminal there is a short-term parking area (sometimes referred to as kiss and ride area) to pick up and drop off passengers quickly. On the airside the aircraft are parked directly at the terminal. Passengers usually board via an aerobridge. This concept has no need for long fingers, piers or satellites (see following concepts). Since there are normally no centralized facilities in linear terminals, all necessary facilities and equipment to handle passengers and their baggage must be ready at various positions in the building.

Advantages and disadvantages

This layout, which is also called 'drive-in-airport', has the advantage of short distances for passengers that arrive by car, since they can park near the entrance next to the assigned check-in area and gate. At larger airports, however, this has the disadvantage of long distances for connecting passengers. Therefore the linear concept is mostly applied to smaller airports with little connecting traffic. From an airport operator's point of view, another disadvantage, especially at large airports, is the necessity to have passenger processing facilities at several positions within the terminal. Finally, due to decentralized passenger flows shops have less customer contact, and are therefore less profitable compared to other terminal concepts

Curvilinear terminal

The curvilinear terminal is a variant of the linear terminal. The only difference is the shape. Figure 13 shows an illustration of both terminals. Negative curvilinear terminals are also possible as can be seen in Figure 15.

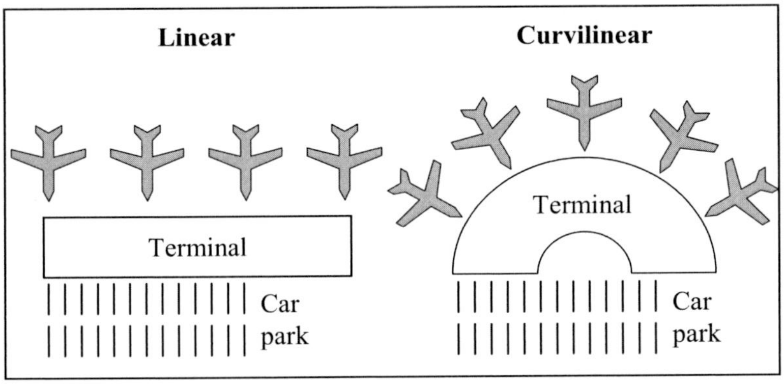

Figure 13: Linear and curvilinear terminal (Own illustration)

An example for a linear terminal is the new terminal 2 at Cologne Bonn Airport as shown in Figure 14. Berlin-Tempelhof airport has an inverted curvilinear terminal combined with an open apron.[9] Figure 15 shows a picture from an open day in 1984. Another example of a curvilinear terminal concept is Dallas/Fort Worth Airport (compare Figure 24)

Figure 14: Terminal 2 at Cologne Bonn Airport (Köln Bonn Airport, 2004)

[9] The airport was closed in 2008. Its premises are nowadays used as urban recreational area.

Figure 15: Inverted curvilinear terminal with open apron at Berlin-Tempelhof airport (Lopez, 1984)

C. 4. 3 Pier finger terminal

Pier finger terminals are used at the majority of airports

Currently, the most commonly used concept worldwide is the pier finger terminal concept which is the consequent next step when increasing capacity at linear terminals (de Neufville et. al., 2013). Like seaports, pier finger terminals have piers (with aerobridges) attached to the main terminal building. This terminal concept offers a significant advantage for airport operators by adding additional gates with the simple extension of a finger. The downside is the huge consumption of precious apron space. However, navigation for passengers (especially transfer passengers) is relatively easy, since all gates are under one roof and no transfer between terminals is needed. The disadvantage lies in the long distances for passengers from the main building where check-in is located to the gate where the aircraft is parked. The more aircrafts can be docked to a pier the longer the walking distances are. Furthermore, aircraft have to taxi into cul-de-sacs to reach their assigned gate. This may result in congestion and delays.

Advantages and disadvantages

Concourses help to centralize certain facilities even at large airports

This terminal configuration was introduced in the 1950s when the simple terminal buildings were extended by adding concourses. A concourse is defined as an open space where paths meet. Passengers are usually processed at the terminal building and then routed down a pier where aircraft are parked in the finger slots or gates for boarding. This setup usually saves space and operating costs, since facilities required for passenger handling and servicing are centralized.

Figure 16 shows possible layouts of the pier finger concept.

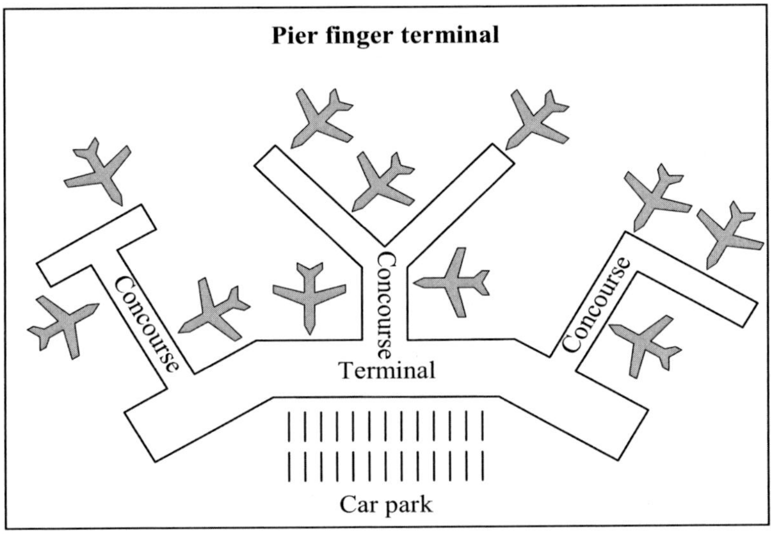

Figure 16: Pier finger terminal (Own illustration)

A good example of the pier finger terminal concept is Schiphol airport in Amsterdam. This airport uses multiple fingers attached to one central terminal building (Figure 17).

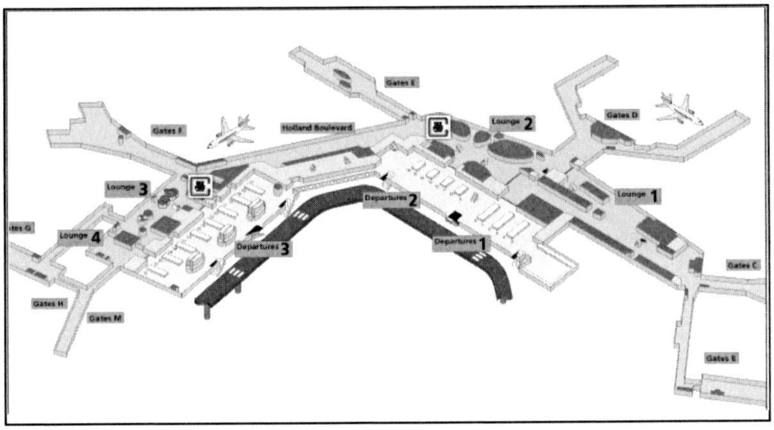

Figure 17: Pier finger terminals at Schiphol Airport, Amsterdam (Schiphol Amsterdam Airport, 2010)

C. 4. 4 Pier satellite terminal and remote satellite terminal

Satellite terminals arrange gates in groups

The satellite terminal concept arranges gates in groups and distributes the different groups, like satellites, around one central building. The difference to pier finger terminals is that gates are concentrated at the end of a concourse without having gates attached to the concourse itself.

Advantages on operations side

All processes around ticketing and check-in are done in the central building. After that, passengers have to proceed to their designated satellite/gate. The connection between the central building and the satellites can either be achieved using normal piers (pier satellite concept) or by an underground connection (remote satellite concept). The advantage of the remote concept is that there is more space for aircraft movement and handling on the apron. Moreover, satellites can be added easily and thus the capacity can be expanded. The disadvantage of the satellite concept is the long distances a passenger must walk to get from one terminal or gate to another. People mover systems are employed in these settings to reduce the walking distances. These systems can be high speed escalators, monorails or electric powered carts. This design concept lends itself to a compact central terminal, but is difficult to expand without disrupting airport operations.

Disadvantages on passenger side

Midfield terminals

Large remote satellite terminals are sometimes also referred to as a midfield terminal concept. Although some designers and even researchers claim midfield terminals to be a separate terminal concept it usually differs from remote satellite terminals only in terms of size. Thus midfield terminals are part of the satellite terminal concept and can be regarded as a scaling-up of capacity needs.

Figure 18 shows a sketch of the two satellite concepts. Figure 19 and Figure 20 show examples for the two concepts at Orlando and Atlanta.

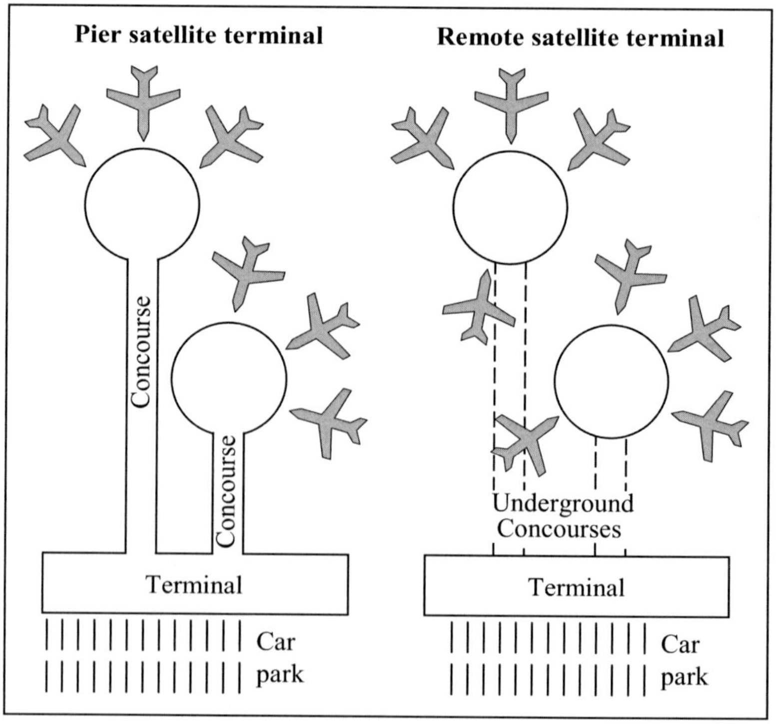

Figure 18: Satellite terminal concepts (Own illustration)

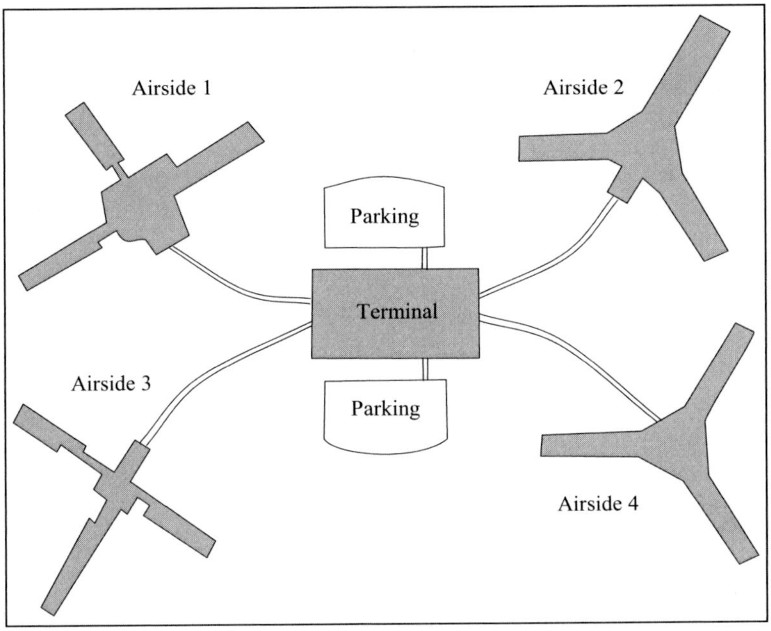

Figure 19: Pier satellite terminal concept at Orlando International Airport (Own illustration)

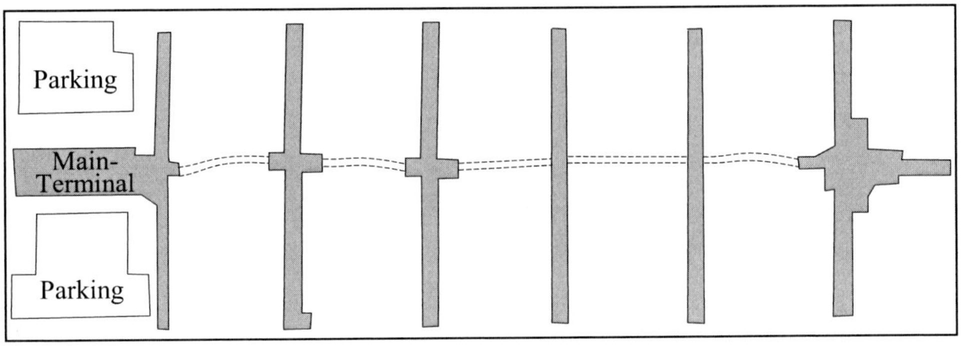

Figure 20: Remote satellite (midfield)-terminals and underground concourses at Hartsfield-Jackson Atlanta International Airport (Own illustration)

C. 4. 5 Transporters and mobile lounges

Transporters move passengers between terminal and aircraft

For this concept passengers are transported from the terminal to the remotely parked airplane and vice versa. Transporters are a broad category of vehicles that move passengers between terminals and aircrafts. Normally these airport buses are designed with low platforms and wide aisles for easy access and require passengers to walk up and down the stairs between the apron and the aircraft cabin (de Neufville et. al., 2013). In Europe, this system of airport busses is used quite frequently at peak times when all gate positions are occupied and additional aircraft have to be dispatched on the apron.

Mobile lounges or transporter terminals

The mobile lounge or transporter terminals (huge elevation platform trucks with a cabin mounted on top) can also be used as holding rooms for waiting passengers at gate positions. With this concept, aircraft can be parked remotely from the terminal buildings, increasing the amount of aircraft enplaning and deplaning passengers at the same time. Airplane taxiing time to and from the runway is decreased as well as the amount of aircraft engine noise around the terminal. Mobile lounges were used in Dulles International Airport in Washington or Mexico City Airport for example but are not in service any more.

Advantages and disadvantages of transporter concept

The most important advantage of mobile lounges is that they protect passengers from weather, jet noise and blast, and also eliminate long walking distances. Furthermore construction costs can be reduced and aircraft can be operated more profitably, since taxiing to and from the terminal is not necessary and turnaround times can be shortened. However, transporters have severe disadvantages that outweigh the advantages. First of all, they are expensive, since the need specially trained staff and constant maintenance including regular refueling. Mobile lounges are expensive to purchase, too. Furthermore, in the case of mobile lounges, a small group of especially skilled workers has the power to shut down the entire airport operations should they go on strike. The more common busses have the disadvantage of providing a lower service level, since passengers usually have to climb stairs and are set of to weather. Figure 21 is an illustration of the transporter concept, and Figure 22 shows a photograph of a mobile lounge that has been used at Dulles Airport.

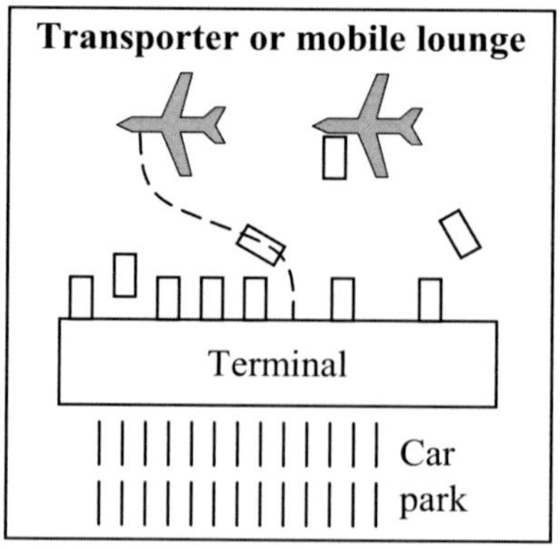

Figure 21: Transporter or mobile lounge concept (Own illustration)

Figure 22: Mobile lounges (Dave, 2008)

Figure 23: Example for future modularized aircraft concepts (Bauhaus Luftfahrt, 2014)

Nevertheless, are mobile lounges not completely outdated as the non-existent usage may suggest. The concept is picked up by research for the future in aviation. The idea is, that aircraft do not provide the passenger cabin any more but are only used as a carrier for standardized modules which can hold either passengers or freight. The passenger modules are designed as fully equipped passenger cabin in which passengers take their assigned seats already at the airport. When boarding is finished the modules are attached to the carrier aircraft. This procedure would lead to much shorter turnaround times since the aircraft does not need to wait until debarking, cleaning and equipping of cabin, and boarding have taken place. Instead it is only a change of already boarded and equipped modules which will be much less time consuming. At the same time debarking can be done at the terminal while the aircraft is already being equipped with the new modules. For passengers this would mean improved comfort since the boarding procedure is not dependent on the presence of the aircraft and thus, the total travel time can be reduced. In effect flight schedules can be more tightly and at the same time more reliable.

C. 4. 6 Factors for selecting a terminal concept

There is no 'one size fits all' in terminal design

Having described the different basic terminal concepts, the next question is which one to choose for a particular airport. There is no general answer to this question, as it depends on many factors. Some of these factors are:

Factors for selecting a terminal concept

- Available area
- Terminal position in respect of runway position
- Possibility to connect to intermodal traffic systems
- Expected passenger volumes
- Mix of aircraft to be handled
- Aspired type of airport
- Flexibility in adapting short-term capacity for peak hours
- Walking distances in the building
- Processing and waiting times
- Minimum connection time for transfer passengers
- Ease of aircraft movements
- Security feasibility
- Ease of navigating passengers through the complex
- Possibility to expand the capacity
- Architecture
- Fixed and variable costs
- Flexibility in distributing available space
- Likelihood of meeting the stakeholders expectations

C.4.6.1 Centralized vs. decentralized terminal systems

Another important decision when designing a terminal or a terminal system is whether it should be centralized or decentralized (although this is an elementary differentiation).

Centralized terminals

In the middle of the last century, many airports were designed as centralized terminal airports. At this time, passenger volumes were small enough for centralized terminals to accommodate all passenger and luggage handling in only one building, while, at the same time, realizing economies of scale on fixed equipment.

Decentralized terminals as reaction to increased traffic volumes

As passenger volumes grew rapidly and many airport terminals reached their capacity limits, terminals had to be expanded or new (then decentralized) ones constructed. The advantage of decentralization is that walking distances are short, and especially transit passengers can profit from short distances and change aircraft more quickly.[10] Decentralized terminals are especially popular with airlines that

[10] ICAO recommends limiting walking distances to a maximum of 300 meters. The distance from the curbside to the check-in counter should not exceed 100 meters.

cumulate a large amount of traffic at a certain airport. These airlines have the possibility to run a whole terminal for their own operations and can therefore adapt all facilities to their special needs and requirements. An example is Terminal 2 at Munich Airport which is operated in cooperation with Lufthansa and used for Star Alliance flights only; also the United, Delta and American terminals at New York's JFK airport. Decentralization normally leads to higher staff requirements, since functions need to be carried out at multiple locations. Beyond that inter-terminal movement needs to be available be it by rail, bus or any other kind of transport system. Moreover a central railway station – connecting the airport to the national rail system – creates inconveniences for most passengers since there are huge distances between the single terminals. Lastly, decentralized terminals are more inflexible than centralized ones. In centralized terminals, for example, check-in counters or gates can be shifted easily from one user to another whereas in decentralized terminals this is usually not possible.

Decentralized concept has more operational challenges

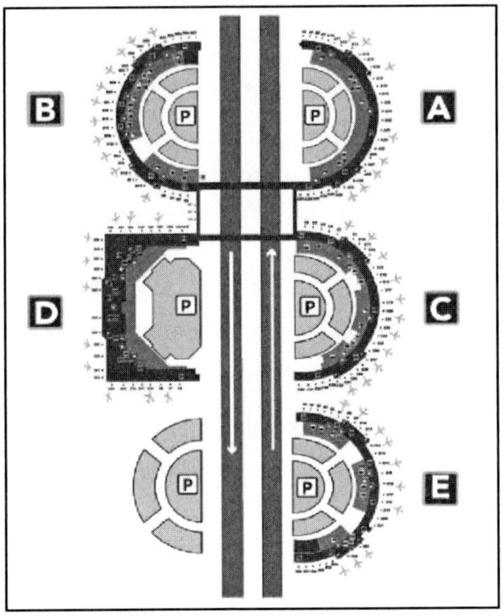

Figure 24: Decentralized terminals at Dallas/Fort Worth (Dallas/Fort Worth International Airport, 2014)

Today, the majority of airports operate on decentralized terminal systems. Examples are Munich Airport, Dallas/Fort Worth (Figure 24) or JFK Airport in New York. Nonetheless, there are still airports operating satisfactorily with a centralized terminal system. Examples are Brussels Airport, Schiphol Airport Amsterdam or Suvarnabhumi Airport in Bangkok (see Figure 25).

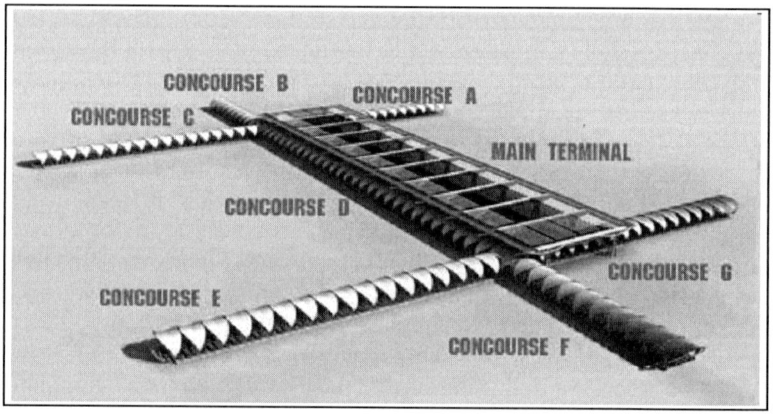

Figure 25: Centralized terminal at Suvarnabhumi Airport Bangkok (Suvarnabhumi Airport, 2010)

C.4.6.2 Centralized vs. decentralized check-in areas

Centralized vs. decentralized check-in areas

While discussing terminal layouts and the question of centralized vs. decentralized terminals we would like to add a few words about the question of centralized vs. decentralized check-in areas.

In most terminals the check-in area is centralized, which means that it is located in a central area of the terminal building where all passengers check-in. After check-in they can go shopping on their way to the departure gate.

In contrast decentralized check-in areas are located directly at the departure gate. This has several advantages and disadvantages.

Advantages

Advantages are:

- Luggage is delivered directly at the aircraft and complex and expensive luggage sorter systems are not necessary
- Road access distances from the curbside to the gate can be very short (e.g. Berlin-Tegel)

Disadvantages

The disadvantages are:

- Passengers have to carry their luggage to the departure gate
- As soon as passengers pass the security control they are stuck in the waiting area at the departure gate. Shopping or other activities are usually not possible
- More personnel is needed since each gate has a check-in, security control and passport control

C. 5 Influences on airport layout

Feasibility study

Before building a new facility or expanding an existing facility, an impact study or feasibility study must be conducted. These studies include a critical assessment of all impact issues from soil to air quality.

Measures against aircraft noise in airport's surroundings

One of the most severe problems is that of aircraft noise at and around an airport. Laying out runways so that air traffic patterns have the least effect on heavily populated areas is a practice now widely employed during runway expansion and when building new airports. Controlling the land use around an airport also helps to reduce the interference of aircraft noise with the public. Noise abatement procedures during take-off and landing make for quieter airport operations. Such procedures consist of faster take-off speeds quickly followed by slowing the engine once airborne over a populated area, then returning the engines to full speed and resuming normal flight operations. This lessens the amount of engine noise over the populated area without adversely affecting the flight. Improvements in engine design have also been a success factor in reducing aircraft noise.

Other emissions of airport operations

Airports can be major contributors to water pollution if suitable treatment facilities are not provided for the various types of airport waste. This waste include domestic sewage, industrial waste, such as oil and fuel spills, and high temperature water degradation that stems from the heat of various power plants in nearly constant use at an airport. These are all factors in runway and airport planning that need to be considered. Many issues are studied before final decisions on airport location and runway layout are determined, among them are cultural and historic, environmental, noise and safety and site pollution issues.

Factors influencing airport layout

When runways (and other facilities) are built, their layout is influenced by many factors:

- Aviation regulations
- Environmental concerns
- Noise level impacts
- Terrain and soil considerations
- Natural and man-made obstructions
- Annual weather patterns
- Size and performance characteristics of the airplanes using the runways

D. ACCESSIBILITY AND INTERMODALITY

Air transportation is dependant on ground transportation

A passenger journey or cargo delivery is always a door-to-door transaction. But air transport can only bring concentrated passenger (and cargo) flows from one airport to another. Thus ground transportation is necessary to collect and bundle all the traffic flows on the way to the airport and to unbundle and distribute the traffic flows once arrived at the final airport.

In this paragraph we will take a look at the different traffic modes passengers use to travel to and from the airport and how their choice is influenced by the different modes.

D. 1 Access systems and their users

Responsibility for airports access system

In the past, the question of airport accessibility was considered to be a question for local transportation authorities only. This attitude was very convenient for airport operators but was, in fact, proved to be wrong. With growing demand for air travel and increasing passenger and flight volumes, airport operators face the challenge of balancing their various potential capacity bottlenecks. Indeed, it is not very wise to have sufficient capacity in terms of runways, gates, terminals, luggage handling facilities and so on, but insufficient capacity in terms of access modes. In such a situation the shortcomings of one capacity crucial facility (the one with the smallest capacity) constricts all other facilities from working efficiently resulting in overcapacities. Therefore airport operators nowadays have a vital interest in bringing their own ideas and knowledge to the development of access modes.

To be able to make a contribution to access mode planning, airport operators must know how each user group uses the different access modes and to what extent.

Access system user groups

The user groups can roughly be divided into passengers originating from or arriving at the airport, the so called 'meeters and greeters', employees, suppliers, and visitors. Transfer passengers of course do not use the access modes unless they have a longer stop over. We will break down the traffic volumes of a fictitious hub airport to give a feeling of the numbers of access mode users.

Example for a fictitious hub airport

Let us imagine a hub airport with approximately 50 million passengers a year of which 50% are transfer passengers. Given the simplified assumption that the demand is equally distributed on each day of a year, the airport and access systems will have to handle roughly 70,000 arriving passengers and 70,000 departing passengers per day (transfer passengers not included). Apart from that there are the meters and greeters. If on average there is only one person meeting and greeting per two passengers this results in another 70,000 access system users per day that use the access mode twice since they have to travel to and from the airport. The third important user group is made up by the employees working at the airport. At large hub airports the number of employees can easily reach 50,000 (including employees of the airport operator, local authorities, departing airlines, different subcontractors, etc.). Assuming that – due to different shift models – each day 60% of these employees are working adding a further 30,000 daily access mode users or 60,000 daily access uses, since every employee travels to and from the airport. Suppliers and visitors make up for a smaller amount of traffic, let us assume another 60,000 daily access mode uses. Altogether, our fictitious airport and its access modes have to accommodate 400,000 access mode uses on an average day. At the first sight this seems to be quite few if the number is divided by the 24 hours in each day. But in reality operating hours may be only 16 or 18 hours a day, and peak times have to be considered. Peak times typically occur in the morning and evening hours when business travelers use the airport. Therefore the access system must also be able to accommodate for these peak times.

D. 2 Traffic split between access modes

Knowing the traffic split is important

Another important aspect an access mode planner needs to know is the traffic split between the different access modes. Since the choice of an access mode is determined by many different factors, which vary at every airport, it is not possible to make a general statement about traffic splits that would fit the majority of airports. Even within one continent or one country it is difficult to make a general statement about this. Among the factors that influence the traffic split at a certain airport are:

Factors influencing the traffic split

- Location of the airport
- Availability and performance of the access modes
- Airport size and facilities
- Range of air services
- Mix of leisure and business travelers
- Passengers preferences
- Cultural backgrounds
- Catchment area

In the following we will give some specific examples of traffic splits. Table 5 starts with an overview of different international airports and their specific traffic splits for the indicated years.

Airport	Hongkong Intern. **HKG**	Tokyo Narita **NRT**	Oslo Gardermoen **OSL**	Stockholm Arlanda **ARL**	London Heathrow **LHR**	Paris Orly **ORY**	Amsterdam Schiphol **AMS**	London Gatwick **LGW**	New York Kennedy **JFK**	Chicago O'Hare **ORD**
Year	2004	2003	2005	2003	2004	2002	2002	2004	2004	1998
Car	7.5%	17.6%	34.0%	35.0%	37.8%	43.0%	45.3%	53.8%	56.2%	79.0%
private			*32.0%*		*35.0%*			*51.4%*		
rental			*2.0%*		*2.8%*			*2.4%*		
Taxi	12.9%		6.0%	21.0%	25.9%	27.0%	9.3%	14.6%	20.7%	
Rail	23.4%	40.8%	40.0%	19.0%	23.5%	13.0%	34.7%	24.6%	12.1%	4.0%
high-speed	*23.4%*		*33.0%*	*19.0%*	*9.3%*					
regional			*7.0%*							
local					*14.2%*					
Bus	47.4%	41.6%	18.0%	19.0%	12.4%	16.0%	8.9%	6.8%	10.9%	17.0%
Other	8.8%		2.0%	6.0%	0.4%	1.0%	1.8%	0.2%	0.1%	

Table 5: Access mode shares for a selection of airports (Kouwenhoven, 2008)

German Air Traveler Survey

In 2003, the German Airports Association (ADV) together with the German Aerospace Center (DLR) conducted the German Air Traveler Survey.[11] In this survey more than 210,000 airline passengers at 22

[11] Follow-up surveys did not show noteworthy differences in traffic split. Thus, we base our remarks on the original study from 2003.

German airports[12] were interviewed about their trip origin, destination, choice of travel mode to the airport, purpose of their journey and continued journey, and person related information. The survey revealed that three quarters of all passengers reached or left the airport by car: 4% with rental car, 19% by taxi, 18% with their own car, and 34% as private car passenger being driven by someone else. The remaining quarter is made up of busses (9%), suburban rail services (11%) and long distance rail services (5%) (Gelhausen & Wilken, 2006). See Figure 26 for an overview of the average traffic split for German airports.

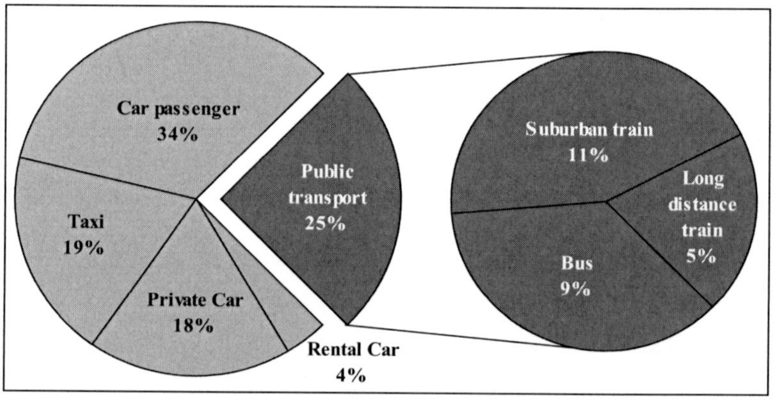

Figure 26: Traffic split between access modes in Germany (Own illustration based on Gelhausen & Wilken, 2006)

Traffic split varies between airports due to different environmental conditions

The traffic split described above represents the German average. At single airports the situation can be significantly different. Some smaller airports, for example, do not have a railway station and are only accessible by car or bus services. Moreover long-distance train services are only available at major German airports. And even the biggest German airport, Frankfurt, is everything but average in terms of traffic split.

The proportion of individuals using public transport to and from Frankfurt is 32%, clearly above the average of 25%. Most of the passengers arriving at Frankfurt airport by means of a public transport come by train. In fact 18% arrive by long-distance train, covering a greater distance than average. Indeed, Frankfurt has the greatest catchment area of any airport in Germany, a consequence of the great number of flight destinations and frequencies offered at that airport[13] (Wilken, Berster & Gelhausen, 2005).

---

12 The three airports in Berlin were counted as one airport.

13 In 2013 Frankfurt recorded nearly half a million movements.

D. 3 Factors affecting model choice

The decision as to which access mode a passenger takes is primarily based on three influencing factors: cost, comfort and convenience (Ashford, Stanton & Moore, 2012).

Car

In most countries a private car is the preferred form of access mode. Therefore airports need to plan for adequate parking areas.[14] Traveling by private car is very convenient since it provides a direct connection between the airport and the place of origin/destination. Luggage can be easily transported even over long distances, and it is possible to park and unload at the curbside next to the check-in area thus shortening walking distances. The disadvantages of using a private car are either the costs for parking at the airport or that someone else is needed to drive the car back after the passenger has been dropped off. Finding parking space may be a problem and the car usually has to be parked in a remote position far away from the terminal. Although shuttle services are normally offered, this may be perceived as inconvenient. Traffic congestion and the possibility of vandalism and theft may be further argument against the use of a private car.

Parking

Taxi

Taxis offer all the advantages of private cars: ease of luggage transport, direct connection between airport and place of origin/destination, reliability and direct access to the curbside next to the check-in area. Finding a parking space and the possibility of theft and vandalism is also not a problem. The two disadvantages that remain are possible road congestions and the high cost.[15] From an airport's perspective taxis have two major aspects. On the one hand curbside occupation stays are short, on the other hand there is no revenue generated by parking fees. A more luxurious form of taxi services are limousine services, offering the same service as taxis with additional comfort at a higher price.

Bus services

A third access mode is bus services. These services can be divided into urban multi-stop bus network services that have an additional stop at the airport en route, and those services connecting e.g. the city center or a remote city directly to the airport. For passengers, bus services have the advantage of direct access to the curbside. The disadvantage is, that passengers need to take another form of transport to connect them with bus service or walk to the next bus stop with their luggage in tow. In exchange, bus services are cheap and highly reliable. If bus lanes are in use, even the problem of congestion is manageable. From an airport's point of view, bus services have special requirements, such as bus terminals and space to load and unload baggage and passengers. At special vacation airports, such as the Canary Islands, most passengers are customers of vacation travel agencies and therefore

Bus terminals

---

[14] For a more comprehensive discussion of parking area planning see e.g. Ashford, Stanton & Moore (2012).

[15] The taxi costs must be evaluated in relation to travel costs for private car use in combination with parking expenses.

take the shuttle bus to and from their hotel. These airports have to design most of their curbside and parking area in order to accommodate for special bus bays. Door-to-door vans that shuttle hotel guests between the airport and hotel are another alternative.

Rail

Rail systems are another important access mode. They can be subdivided into long-distance services, suburban services and dedicated rail services.[16] For passengers, rail services mainly have the same advantages and disadvantages of bus services. One decisive factor that affects passengers' likelihood to choose rail (and airport operators therefore have to keep in mind) is the location of the railway station at the airport. Since rail services inevitably have to terminate at a station they are not as flexible as bus or car. Therefore walking distances at the airport can be long, especially in decentralized terminal systems, and thus baggage handling is correspondingly more difficult. In exchange, rail services are usually better connected to the local and national public transport modes than bus services. For example Heathrow is connected to the public underground system and offers connections to over 250 stations in Greater London. Another interesting aspect of rail services is the possibility of replacing short distance feeder flights with high speed trains (Vespermann & Wald, 2010). This has a positive impact on the environment and on congestion at busy airports where slots are scarce. An example is the German high speed train connection between Cologne and Frankfurt airport. Since the connection was opened up there are no more feeder flights on this route. Lufthansa customers even have the possibility to check-in and drop off their luggage at Cologne's main railway station and do not have to carry their luggage to the airport themselves. However, airport operators and public transport operators have to adapt the trains to the special air passenger needs. Most passengers carry bulky luggage with them and coaches become crowded very quickly if there is no dedicated space to store the luggage. It is therefore essential to adapt the coaches to passenger's specific needs to secure passenger comfort and positive perception of rail services as an access mode.

High speed trains

Other airport access modes

There are also some unconventional means of transport like helicopter, dedicated rail systems or automated metro services. An example of a dedicated rail system is the Shanghai Maglev Transrapid which connects Pudong Airport to Langyong Road station in the city center. From there passengers can use local and national public transport. Another example is the helicopter shuttle service at JFK airport. About 30 daily flights are operated from Manhattan to the airport. Flight time is only 8 minutes. The great disadvantage of unconventional modes of transport is that they are mostly very expensive in terms of infrastructure and operations are costly, too. Additionally, in the case of the helicopter service, noise along with security and safety are serious issues. Another negative aspect is that these modes are not fully integrated into the other surface transport systems.

[16] Dedicated rail services usually connect the airport directly with the city center (normally the main station) without being part of a bigger network.

Review questions

- List the different categories of airports. What is the difference between them?
- How are airports categorized?
- Why does Germany use several different airport classifications?
- Summarize the core functions of an airport. Which tasks are categorized as aviation, and which are non-aviation?
- Why are other business areas besides aviation and non-aviation essential for the future growth of an airport operator?
- Why is it customary to differentiate airport operations between landside and airside? Give some examples for each.
- Who can offer airside services?
- Name the major airport facilities.
- How is a runway related to a compass?
- Give a short overview of visual runway markings and explain how runways with the same compass-orientation are distinguished.
- Which basic runway configurations do you know? What advantages and disadvantages does each layout have?
- What purposes do taxiways serve? Which taxiway configuration is used for which purpose?
- What are apron areas mainly used for?
- Name four basic terminal configurations. Why are these 'pure' concepts so rarely found?
- What were the original functions of an airport terminal?
- From an airport and passenger point of view, why is the terminal layout a crucial factor?
- What advantages do pier finger and pier satellite terminal concepts offer in comparison to simple and linear terminals?
- What is the transporter concept? Where and why is it used? What are the advantages and disadvantages?
- If an airport operator builds a new terminal or terminal system which factors need to be taken into consideration?
- Which environmental circumstances influence the building of an airport / a terminal?
- Why should the access systems be of inherent interest to every airport operator?
- Summarize the most important access modes and explain their particular influence on passenger's transport decisions and access mode share.
- What is a typical access mode share at a typical hub airport?

Bibliography and further reading

Airports Council International [ACI] (2013): International traffic report 2011, Geneva.

Ashford, N. / Stanton, H. P. M. / Moore, C. A. (2012): Airport Operations, 3rd ed., New York.

Asford N. J. / Mumayiz, S. / Wright P. H. (2011): Airport Engineering: Planning, Design and Development of 21st Century Airports, 4th ed., Hoboken.

Air Transport Action Group [ATAG] (2008): The economic and social benefits of air transport, Geneva.

Bauhaus Luftfahrt e.v. (2014): Internal document, Ottobrunn.

Boeing Commercial Airplane Group (2014): Current Market Outlook 2014-2033. Market Analysis, Seattle.

Boeing Commercial Airplane Group (2008): Boeing 777 Airplane Characteristics for Airport Planning, Seattle.

Brueckner, J. K. / Girvin, R. (2008): Airport noise regulation, airline service quality, and social welfare, in: Transportation Research Part B (Methodological), Vol. 42, No. 1, p. 19-37.

Conrady, R / Fichert, F. / Sterzenbach, R. (2013): Luftverkehr, Betriebswirtschaftliches Lehr- und Handbuch, 5th ed., Munich.

Dave (2008): Mobile Lounge, Dallas.

Dallas/Fort Worth International Airport (2014): Terminal Map, Dallas, www.dfwairport.com, retrieved: 06/11/2014.

Doganis, R. (2009): Flying Off Course –Airline Economics and Marketing, 4th ed., New York.

Doganis, R. (1992): The Airport Business, New York.

Federal Aviation Administration [FAA] (2014): Airport Categories, Washington, http://www.faa.gov/airports/planning_capacity/ passenger_allcargo_stats/categories/, retrieved, 06/11/2014.

Finnsson, G. (1993): Move to Privatization of Airports Requires Careful Consideration of Numerous Factors, in: ICAO Journal, Vol. 48, No. 1, p. 18-19.

Forsyth, P. / Gillen, D. W. / Knorr, A. / Mayer, O. G. / Niemeier, H.-M. / Starkie, D. (2004): The Economic Regulation of Airports: Recent Developments in Australia, North America and Europe, Aldershot.

Gelhausen, M. C. / Wilken, D. (2006): Airport and Access Mode Choice – A generalized Nested logit Model Approach, Paper presented at the 10th Air Transport Research Society World Conference 2006 in Nagoya, Japan.

Gillen, D. / Lall, A. (2004): Competitive advantage of low-cost carriers: some implications for airports, in: Journal of Air Transport Management - Proceedings of the Hamburg Aviation Conference, 2003, Vol. 10, No. 1, p. 41-50.

Graham, A (2013): Managing Airports – An international perspective, 4th ed., New York.

Hermsen, W. (1993): Was unterscheidet den Flughafen der Zukunft vom heutigen, in: Schriftenreihe der DVWG e.V., Vol. 154, p. 97-98.

Hirschhausen, C. / Beckers T. / Tegner H. (2004): Privatisation and regulation of German airports, Deutsche Bank Research, Current Issues, Frankfurt am Main.

Hüschelrath, K. (1998): Infrastrukturengpässe im Luftverkehr - Die Vergabe von Start- und Landerechten an Flughäfen, Wiesbaden.

International Air Transport Association [IATA] (2013): Annual Review 2013, Montreal / Geneva.

International Civil Aviation Organization [ICAO] (2008): Aerodrome Design Manual Part 1, Montreal.

Irwin, D. A. / Pavcnik, N. (2004): Airbus versus Boeing revisited: international competition in the aircraft market, in: Journal of International Economics, Vol. 64, No. 2, p. 223-245.

Janic, M. (2007): The Sustainability of Air Transportation: A Quantitative Analysis and Assessment, Aldershot.

Jarach, D. (2005): Airport marketing. Strategies to Cope with the New Millennium Environment, Aldershot.

Kazda, A. / Caves R. E. (2007): Airport Design and Operation, 2nd ed., Oxford.

Knudsen, T. / Randel, A. / Rugholm, J. (2005): The vanishing middle market, in: McKinsey Quarterly Vol. 42, No. 4, p. 6-9.

Köln Bonn Airport (2004): Luftaufnahme Köln Bonn Airport, Köln, http://airport-cgn.de, retrieved: 06/11/2014.

Kouwenhoven, M. (2008): The Role of Accessibility in Passengers' Choice of Airports, in: OECD - International transport forum - Joint transport research center - discussion paper no. 2008-14, The Hague.

Lopez, J (1984): Tempelhof International Airport in 1984, Berlin, http://de.wikipedia.org/wiki/Flughafen_Berlin-Tempelhof, retrieved: 06/11/2014.

Maurer, P. (2006): Luftverkehrsmanagement: Basiswissen, 4th ed., Munich.

Mensen, H. (2013): Handbuch der Luftfahrt, 2nd ed., Berlin.

de Neufville, R / Odoni, A. / Belobaba P. / Reynolds. T. (2013): Airport Systems: Planning, Design and Management, 2nd ed., New York.

Newhouse, J. (2007): Boeing versus Airbus. The Inside Story of the Greatest International Competition in Business, New York.

Nikon (2006): Atlanta Airport, http://commons.wikimedia.org, retrieved: 01/07/2010.

Oechsle, M. (2005): Erweiterung von Geschäftsfeldern im Non-Aviation-Bereich an europäischen Flughäfen unter besonderer Berücksichtigung des Standorts München, München.

Orlando International Airport (2010): Gate locations, Orlando, www.orlandoairports.net, retrieved 01/07/2010.

Schiphol Amsterdam Airport (2010): Plettegrond, Amsterdam, www.schiphol.nl, retrieved: 01/07/2010.

Schulz, A. / Baumann, S. / Wiedenmann, S. (2010): Flughafenmanagement, Wiesbaden.

Suvarnabhumi Airport (2010): Terminal Map, Bangkok, www.bangkokairportonline.com, retrieved: 01/11/2010.

Trumpfheller, M. (2006): Strategisches Flughafenmanagement – Positionierung und Wertschöpfung von Flughafentypen, Wiesbaden

Vespermann, J. / Wald, A. (2010): Long-Term Perspectives of Intermodal Integration at Airports, in: Journal of Airport Management, Vol. 4, Nr, 3.

Wells, A. T. / Wensveen, J. G. (2003): Air Transportation. A Management Perspective, 5th ed., Belmont.

Wilken, D / Berster, P. / Gelhausen M. C. (2005): Airport choice in Germany – New empirical evidence of the German Air Traveler Survey 2003, paper presented at the 9th Air Transport Research Society Conference 2005 in Rio de Janeiro, Brazil.

Young, S. / Wells, A. (2011): Airport Planning and Management, 6th ed., New York.

Airports – Management and Strategy

Patrick M. Keidel

Table of Contents

You should be able to

- summarize the tasks of airport management
- name different business segments and explain their functions within the business model of a modern hub airport
- give a detailed overview of the airport retailing business, and the factors needing to be taken into consideration to ensure successful retailing
- outline possible future developments for modern airports

The author

Patrick M. Keidel has worked for Fraport since 2002. He was a member of Fraport's Investor Relations team until he joined the Airport Retail and Real Estate department in 2006. He is currently involved in the commercial management and strategy of the retail sector at Frankfurt Airport.

Abstract

This chapter provides a brief overview of the essential management functions at a hub airport. The basic business segments are described and their importance for economic success is highlighted. The conflicts between airport core business processes and the business fields relevant for creating an USP (unique selling proposition) in airport competition are discussed, as well as the influences that have resulted in new development trends in the airport industry.

A. STRATEGIC BUSINESS SEGMENTS

Beginning of the airport industry

Where do airports come from? This is the basic question which needs to be answered in order to understand the developments modern airports have had to undergo over the last decades. At the beginning, airports concentrated on the classic airport core businesses: handling passengers and aircraft. Cargo was not an issue in the early days of airports, becoming a big business and earnings contributor a few decades later. In the early days of the industry, the amount on air traffic was too small to implement an airport hub system.

This has changed, and today, air traffic pushes the world economy with attractive growth rates for the future (Figure 1).

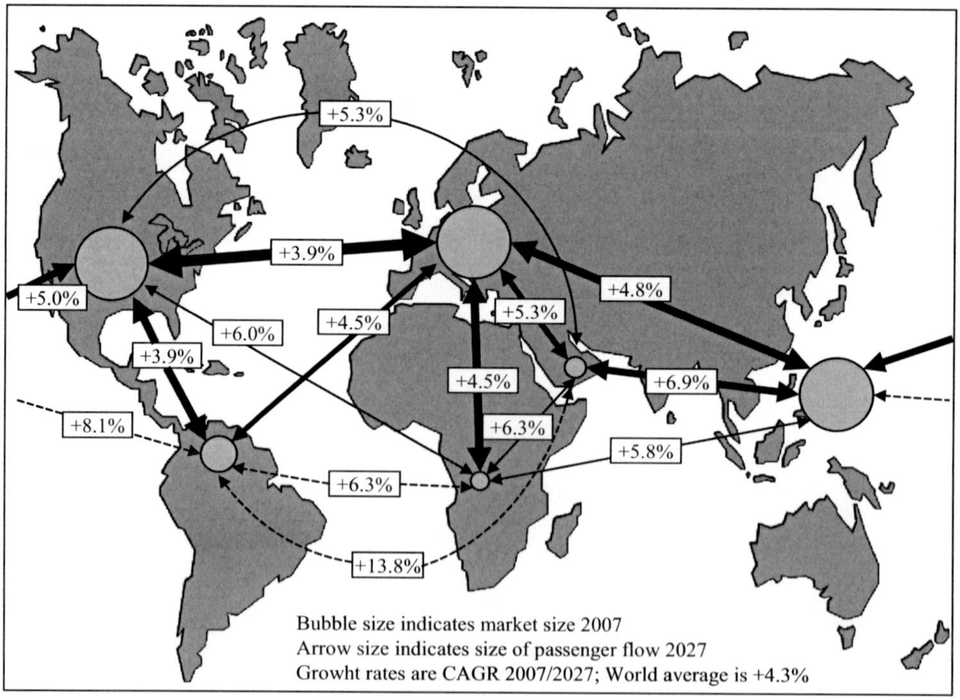

Figure 1: Expected growth rates for global air traffic (Airports Council International [ACI], 2009)

Current strategic business segments of airports

But if the airport business has changed so dramatically what are the strategic business segments of a major hub airport today? At most airports, core business segments are still the aviation and ground handling segments, which are both closely attached to passenger and aircraft handling and terminal operations. Additionally, many international hub airports also run business segments like non-aviation / retail and properties as well as external activities. Table 1 gives an overview of the business segments and associated tasks at Frankfurt Airport.

Aviation	Non-Aviation / retail & properties	Ground handling	External activities
Terminal operations	Retail operations	Baggage operations	Management of holdings and subsidiaries
Security operations	Office space and land development	Cargo operations	
Aviation infrastructure	Non-Aviation infrastructure	Aircraft handling	

Table 1: Business segments and associated tasks (Own illustration)

In the following sections, each business segment is described briefly concentrating on the specifics of each segment.

A. 1 Aviation

Aviation still is the basis of all other airport processes

Aviation is still the core business of every airport. It is the central pillar for all airport processes and is crucial for operating an efficient hub airport. This segment concentrates on the issues of air traffic operations, terminal operations, the airport master planning for passenger and terminal infrastructure and all questions surrounding airport engineering.

Airport charges are regulated

Since airports have an economic status comparable to a monopoly, the aviation market is regulated; meaning airports are not free to calculate the charges for using their infrastructure. Instead, a regulating authority defines the amount airports can charge from third parties, such as airlines, for the usage of airport installations like runways, aprons, etc. There are two approaches the regulating authorities take to calculate airport charges: single till and dual till.

Single till vs. dual till approach

The single till approach considers all costs for the entire airport infrastructure (e.g. apron, runway, terminal, roads, retailing, office rents and so on) to find the regulated price. In contrast to single till, the dual till approach only considers aviation-related costs (landing and take-off charges, passenger charges, security charges, aircraft parking charges) for calculating the charges (Czerny, 2009).

A. 2 Non-aviation / retail and properties

Parts of Non-aviation business segment

The non-aviation business segment is sometimes also called Commercial Activities or Retail and Properties. It consists of the car parks, airport retailing, real estate and others such as energy supply. The non-aviation processes, such as Retail and Properties or Commercial Activities are highly dependable on the perfect functioning of aviation processes. The success of retail and non-aviation processes is reliant on airport infrastructure and passenger handling (Figure 2). We will highlight retailing in more detail on the following pages.

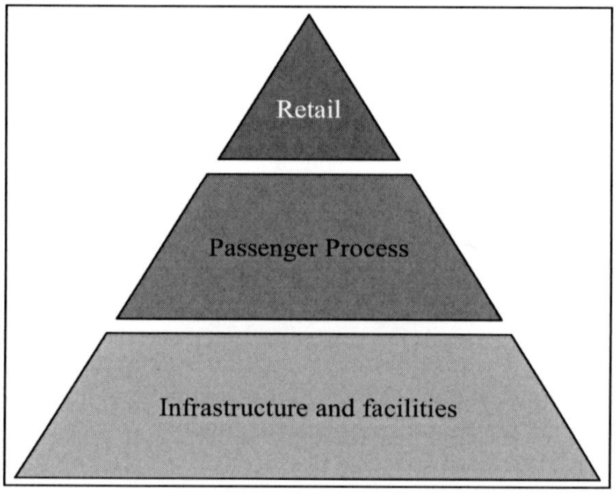

Figure 2: Infrastructure and passengers are the basis for retailing (Own illustration)

A. 3 Ground handling

Ground handling comprises all tasks to turn around an aircraft

Ground handling comprises the management of all demands around the aircraft. This involves the handling of the complex processes between the arrival and departure of every aircraft within a limited timeframe. The activities included in the ground handling core businesses are: ramp services, passenger services and central infrastructure services.

Ramp services:

- Aircraft acceptance
- Supply of handling equipment
- Loading and unloading of aircraft
- Passenger and crew transport
- Baggage, cargo, mail transport
- Ramp supervision
- Moving of aircraft and walk-out assistance
- De-icing/anti-icing services and snow/ice removal
- Safety measures
- Fresh water supply / toilet services
- Cleaning

Passenger services:

- Station representation
- Check-in and boarding
- Ticket service
- Baggage tracing (lost and found)
- Arrival service
- Training
- Crew briefing
- Weight and balance services

Central infrastructure services:

- Total Baggage Management, incl. intermodal handling (AirRail Terminal)
- Baggage facilities and conveyor system
- Baggage customs warehouse
- Baggage security, baggage reconciliation system (BRS)
- Passenger bridges
- 400 Hz ground power
- Fresh water / toilet facilities
- Fuelling and de-icing facilities

Additionally, many airports also offer cargo services as a part of their ground handling.

A. 4 External activities and know-how transfer

Use of know-how to operate other airports

International hub airports have tapped one more source of income over the last years; their know-how is a valuable asset in itself. This means that airports hand out airport operating concessions to other airports or companies with appropriate airport management know-how. These concessions comprise aviation management or total airport management including the commercial business.

B. PARADIGM CHANGE AND DEVELOPMENT TRENDS IN THE AIRPORT BUSINESS

As previously mentioned, airports have come a long way since their first appearance as simple airfields with grass landing strips. Since then, air traffic has evolved from exclusive passenger services only affordable to a few affluent individuals to a mass phenomenon, which is not only limited to passenger services and cargo services. This evolution has also affected the self-conception of airports and their economic situation.

B. 1 Shift of focus

Originally, airports focused on the aviation sector of the business. However, over the last decades, this focus shifted from aviation related services to a broader view as a provider of a comprehensive set of

Non-aviation activities have become more important due to economic reasons

services. This change was caused by simple economic reasons. Since air travel has become a standard for passengers and cargo, airlines have been forced to fight for market shares. One effect of this has been strong competition regarding air travel prices. An extreme result of this competition has been the emergence of low-cost carriers[1] as a new business model. In general, the competition has forced airlines to operate on limited margins and to keep the fares to a minimum. Confronted with this extreme pressure from airlines on the airport infrastructure, airports have been forced to generate income from alternative sources. These sources were found in non-aviation activities like airport retailing, airport advertising and real estate. This development has continued over the last years. Today, non-aviation revenues ensure the viability of modern airports (de Neufville & Odoni, 2003). In the future, airline revenue growth will mainly be achieved in the non-aviation sector (Accenture, 2010).

B. 2 Aviation processes are crucial for non-aviation success

Passengers can only think about shopping if the travel chain works seamlessly

Revenues in the non-aviation sector of airport operations are highly dependent on the quality of aviation processes and a perfect infrastructure setup supporting the needs of airport retailing. This becomes clear when considering the characteristics of airport retailing. Contrary to the normal shopping experience, the mindset of passengers is focused on the travel chain. The following questions guide the passenger through the terminal: Where am I at the moment? Where do I need to go? How long will it take me to pass the boarding pass controls and the security checks? Where is my gate located? How long will it take me to get there? How much time do I have left? Will I catch my plane? Passengers are mainly concerned with the processes and the infrastructure of the airport. Shopping is the last priority for passengers. There is the big difference between airport shopping and everyday shopping: airport shopping is always an impulse driven business. Shops, bars and restaurants have to be orientated towards dragging the attention of the customers away from the airport processes and infrastructures in order to be successful. The better the infrastructure and passenger processes of airports work the better the chances are that airport shopping will attract the attention of potential customers.

B. 3 Importance of dwell time

Once you have the attention of the passengers, you have to give them the right amount of time to satisfy their curiosity and to shop around. Therefore, a balance between aviation and non-aviation operations has to be guaranteed. It is counterproductive if the passenger loses time in the travel chain, for example at security checkpoints, and the processes within the airport retailing also have to be as smooth as possible. If

---

1 For a more comprehensive view on business models please refer to chapter Aviation Strategy and Business Models.

potential customers experience long queues at cashier desks in the shop, they will lose time for additional shopping in other outlets. The amount of time available to potential customers is correlated to the average spending on retail. In fact, the penetration and spending per customer increase the more time a customer has in commercial areas. Hence, dwell time does have a significant impact on turnover (Dolby, 2009). Figure 3 illustrates aviation-related factors which influence the dwell time a passenger has for shopping and other purposes.

The right balance between aviation processes and time for shopping is crucial for turnover

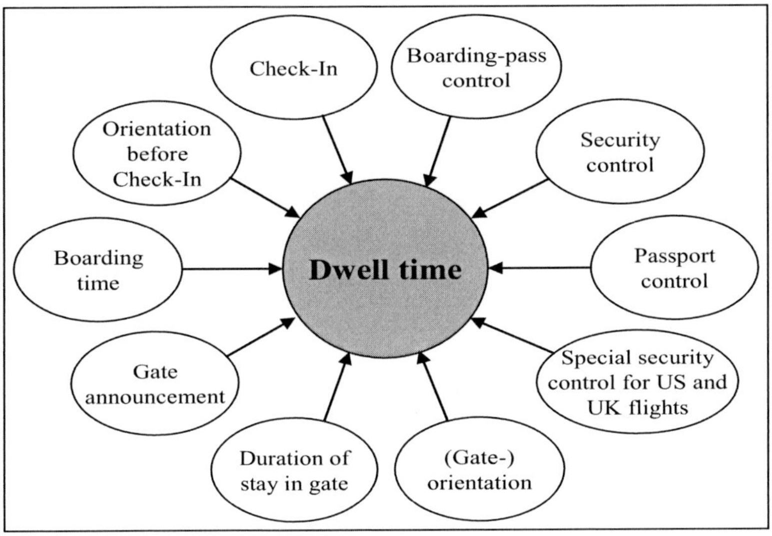

Figure 3; Dwell time (Own illustration)

B. 4 Influence of stress level on retail success

Travelling is stressful. This stress is common for everyone involved in the travel chain, regardless of whether they are a passenger, the flight crew or service personnel. Stress also has a negative impact on the spending behavior of airport retail customers. The higher the stress levels the lower the opportunity for airport retailing. Along the travel process, stress and anticipation levels are correlated and both levels increase during the stay at the airport. At the beginning of the journey, passengers are quite relaxed until they arrive at the airport. Once they have entered the terminal building, the levels of stress and anticipation increase due to the need to orientate, the queues at the check-in counters, loudspeaker messages, crowded hallways and general noise levels. After the check-in process, security checkpoints and gate orientation, in combination with limited time, push stress levels even higher. Rising stress levels, together with a high anticipation, result in a cumulative inability to absorb any information other than the airport and passenger processes. The higher the stress levels the lower the average spending of passengers on airport retailing. Figure 4 gives an overview of passengers' stress levels during the phases of an air journey.

Higher stress level for passengers means lower sales for airport shops

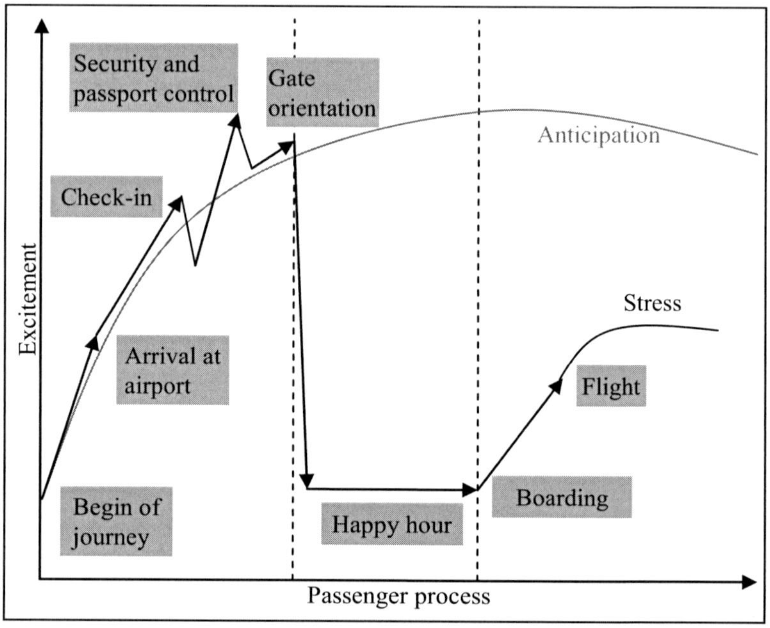

Figure 4: Passengers stress level during a journey (Own illustration)

Ideally a low stress level and high anticipation coincide to achieve maximum revenue

To achieve maximum penetration power for shopping, a high anticipation level in combination with a low stress level is needed. The time the passenger has between entering the area after security checks and gate orientation is ideal for this. In this situation the passenger starts to relax and is therefore open to additional information. The timeframe set by passing the last checkpoints and the beginning of the boarding process represents the airport's retailing happy hour, and in this environment, maximum revenue can be generated (Figure 4).

B. 5 Space allocation in airport retailing: landside vs. airside

Shopping premises placed in the security or airside area are most likely to catch customers' attention

To generate income from airport retailing, the adequate amount of available retail space is only one success factor; the right allocation of retail space is even more important. Since the main influence factors on passenger spending are the dwell time and stress levels, it is important to create the shopping space in terminal areas to accommodate these factors. Passengers' stress levels increase along their journeys to and through an airport but drop to a minimum after passing all checkpoints and arriving at the point of entry on the airside of an airport. The airside comprises the post-security check parts of an airport. In this area the impulse to shop reaches its full potential.

B. 6 Airport retailing operation models

In general, there are four basic operational models for airports to handle their retail business:

Four possible retail operation models

- **Joint Ventures** have the characteristic of direct cooperation between the retail operator and the airport. The strengths of both partners will be utilized in a direct way with a shared risk. Airport operators not only receive a concession but also a share of the earnings of the joint venture. This operation model requires high involvement on both sides.
- **Self operation** (of the retail outlets) represents the model with the highest possible involvement and the maximum risk for the airport operator. It rewards the operator with full and direct performance management opportunities and a direct relation between airport and brand, together with full participation on the economic results.
- **Management contract** is a form of operation setup, in which the airport operator delegates the retail management to a third party. On the one hand there the airport requires no retail know-how and staff involvement is kept to a minimum. On the other hand, there is no direct relation between the airport and the operators and therefore no influence on management of performance. The risk potential for the airport operator is minimal.
- **Concession model** allows airport and retail operators to work directly with each other. Airports generally choose the retail concession partners via a tender process. To find the right partner, a high amount of know-how is needed on airport side. In general, the model comprises a revenue-based rent in combination with a minimum annual guarantee. The concession model is the most common operating model for airport operators.

C. A NEW TREND IN AIRPORT DEVELOPMENT: AIRPORT CITIES

Over the last years, the influence of airports on regional development such as economic infrastructure and urban structures has become increasingly important. Airports are shaping business locations and urban developments as much as highways did in the 20th century or seaports in the 18th century (Kasarda, 2010).

Every airport city starts with basic infrastructure

The approaches towards airport city development start with the airport core buildings and infrastructure such as runways, terminals, and apron. This infrastructure can be seen as the nucleus of a modern airport city. The development process towards an airport city involves basic infrastructure being enhanced in steps by additional facilities, like business centers, cargo terminals and industrial parks, all of which are still linked closely to aviation business.

Next, non-aviation infrastructure will be added. Airport malls, office parks, hotels and conference centers represent the first structures already common to cities. In a further development of these non-aviation facilities, entertainment centers, medical services, warehouses, distributors and landside shopping will be located at the airport. This development reaches its peak with the settlement of manu-

In a further development airports acquire characteristics of normal cities and become cities themselves

facturing companies, sports and recreational services and housing facilities in direct vicinity of the airport. All these services combined represent structures that can be found in a normal inner city environment. With completion of this evolutionary step, the airport itself becomes a city and a destination for travelers. Figure 5 shows the different development stages an international hub airport can take and links these stages to offers and customer groups respectively. In Seoul, Korea, the development of Incheon Airport into a complete Airport City comprises not only all airport-related services, but also recreation and wellness areas, fun parks for kids, medical services with the highest international standards, together with all the aviation-connected services. This kind of development is suitable for international hubs with a large number of passengers and a decent catchment area to feed the services located on landside or outside the terminal buildings.

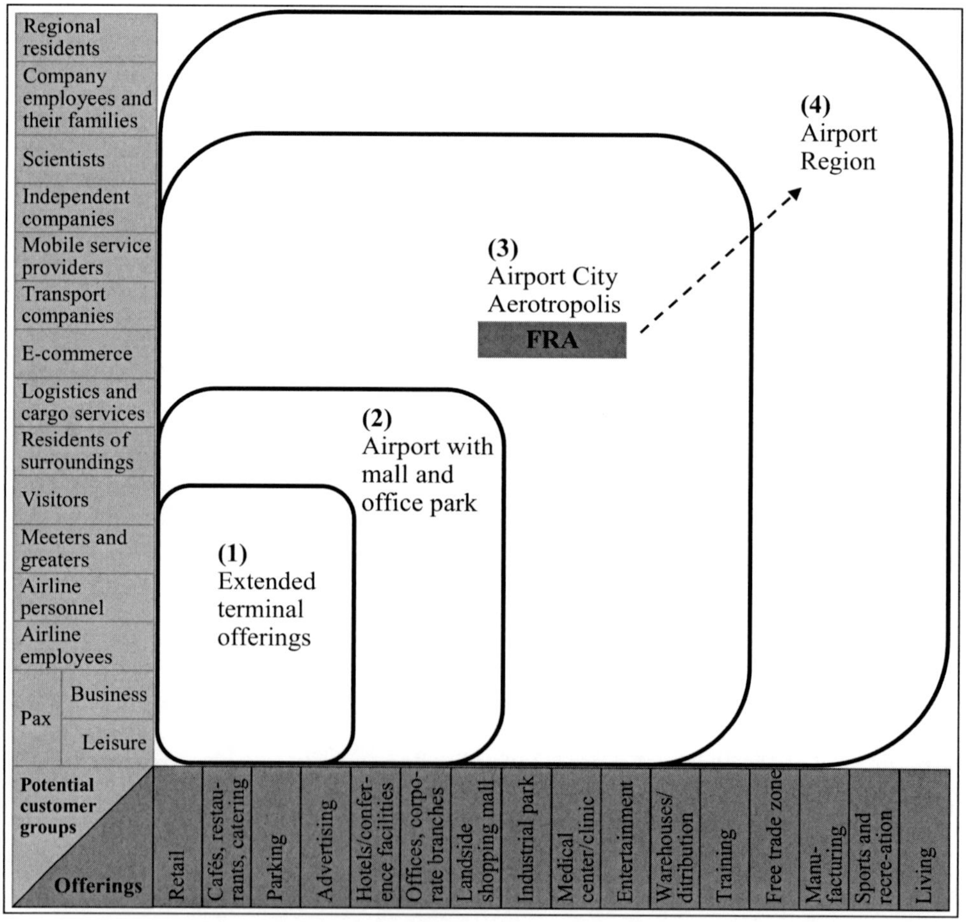

Figure 5: Development towards an airport city and beyond (Own illustration)

Review Questions

- What are the strategic business segments of modern hub airports?
- What caused the paradigm change of modern airports?
- What is meant by dwell time, and why is it so important for retail success?

Bibliography and further reading

Accenture (2010): Airports 2010 Study.

Airports Council International [ACI] (2009): Global Traffic Forecast 2008-2027, Edition 2009, Geneva.

Czerny, A. I. (2006): Price-cap regulation of airports: single-till versus dual-till, in: Journal of Regulatory Economics, Vol. 30, No. 1, p. 85-97.

Dolby, N. (2009): A recession in time, http://www.moodiereport.com /document.php?c_id=1178&doc_id=20595, retrieved: 04/21/2010.

Kasarda, J. D. (2010): no title, www.aerotropolis.com/author.html, retrieved: 04/21/2010.

de Neufville, R. / Odoni A. R. (2003): Airport systems: planning, design and management, New York.

Oechsle, M. (2005): Erweiterung von Geschäftsfeldern im Non-Aviation-Bereich an europäischen Flughäfen unter besonderer Berücksichtigung des Standorts München, München.

Trumpfheller, M. (2006): Strategisches Flughafenmanagement – Positionierung und Wertschöpfung von Flughafentypen, Wiesbaden

Vespermann, J. / Wald, A. (forthcoming 2010): Long-Term Perspectives of Intermodal Integration at Airports, in: Journal of Airport Management, Vol. 4, Nr, 3.

Section 3:
Airline Specific
Management Functions

Aviation Strategy and Business Models

Benjamin Koch

Table of contents

You should be able to

- describe how the aviation and airline market has developed over the past decades based on the existing regulative and legislative framework
- outline how airline partnerships and alliances have developed as a response to the changing market environment
- evaluate how airline business models can be defined and how to differentiate between models
- show which developments have determined the European aviation industry during the first decade of the millennium and what the consequences are
- describe selected current challenges facing airline management which are most likely to have a major impact on future strategic decisions

The author

Dr. Benjamin Koch is Director Corporate & Business Services Europe within Lufthansa AG's finance organization. He previously worked with the company's worldwide shared services, corporate strategy, network management and consulting departments in Cologne and Frankfurt / Main, Germany.

Abstract

This chapter presents an introduction to the broad field of aviation strategy – with a particular focus on airline strategy and airline business models. As covering all fields of relevance and interest in the area of strategy in one chapter is not possible, some brief background about the industry is given – the market and the regulative and legislative developments that have driven the evolution of airlines - providing the basis for a better understanding of today's industry structure. Airline business models closely reflect the different approaches to coping with rules, regulations and limitations and continue driving both competitive behavior and strategy development. Since alliance and partnership approaches are a complement to individual airlines' business model strategies, another focus is the rise and evolution of alliance structures, taking Europe as an example. A brief outlook on the current development and future challenges concludes this chapter.

Since specific areas of airline and aviation management are dealt with in separate chapters of this volume, such as network, airport or air cargo management, this chapter provides a general overview, based on the assumption that the fundamentals of aviation management are already known.

A. FROM THE BEGINNINGS OF CIVIL AVIATION TO DEREGULATION

Many of today's aviation rules go back to the Chicago Convention of 1944

The signing of the Chicago Convention on International Aviation in December 1944 and the following foundation of the International Civil Aviation Organization (ICAO) mark the birth of today's civil aviation (ICAO, 1944), in which the fundamental building blocks for worldwide aviation were laid. Despite their gradual development over the following years and decades, the rules and regulations defined by then still provide the framework for the entire industry. Up until now strict rules regarding competition between airlines and their ownership are the core of the established regulative environment – e.g. traffic rights still depend on majority ownership by national shareholders from the carrier's home country (ICAO, 2009). Such rules set certain limits to both the entrepreneurial developments and the opportunities for international business expansion, and accordingly represent market entry barriers for investors as well as new airlines.

Deregulation started in the late 70s and 80s

Of even greater importance are the developments having started with the US Airline Deregulation Act of 1978, which found their continuation in the liberalization process in the European Union consisting of a three-package program in the years 1987 onwards. Deregulation and liberalization granted access to new market entrants, which had previously strictly been the preserve of well-established legacy carriers. In addition, the development of new business models became possible primarily based on a new interpretation of the mandatory airline product features. Over the following years, setting their hopes on the trans-

Low-cost carriers attack flag carriers

ferability of Southwest Airlines' success in the USA, low-cost carriers also started to conquer the European market. These new carriers have ever since been characterized by avoiding any 'thrill' aspects, in relation to flying as a former luxury that only few could afford, and the consistently low pricing and fares for their passengers. Over the years, low-cost carriers have been successful in building an entirely new aviation market segment, completing the spectrum of service offers, which also comprises the classic flag carriers with their complex hub-and-spoke systems, the regional carriers with their focus on lower populated regions and the tourism-focused charter carriers. The low-cost sector has proven not only to be increasingly strong as a niche market over time, today this youngest airline business model already accounts for about 30% of the continental passenger demand. In Europe, this development has mainly been driven by Irish pioneer Ryanair and British operator easyJet (Lawton, 2002). The following figures show the increasing market presence of low-cost carriers in Europe in terms of flights offered and their network expansion. Regarding the overall market as a whole, the entire growth in provided flights over the past one and a half decades has taken place in the low cost segment, forcing the traditional network carriers in a drawback position.

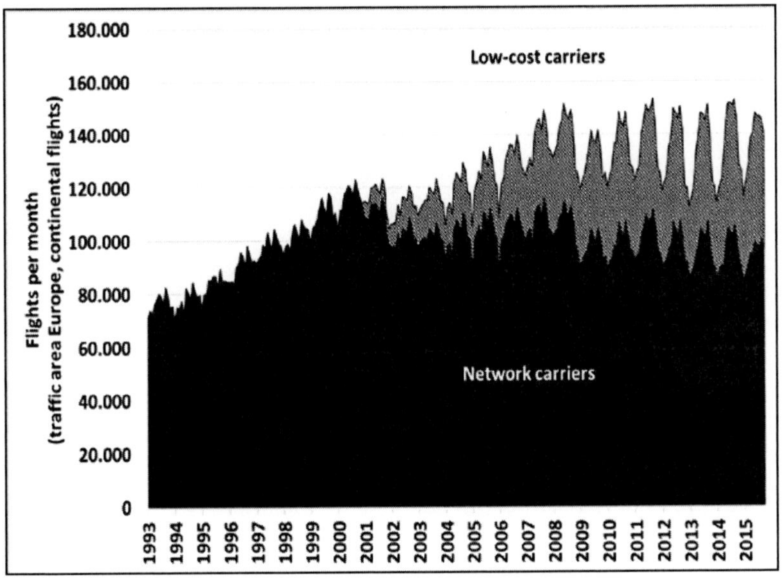

Figure 1: Development of flights offered per month (1993 – 2015) (Own illustration)

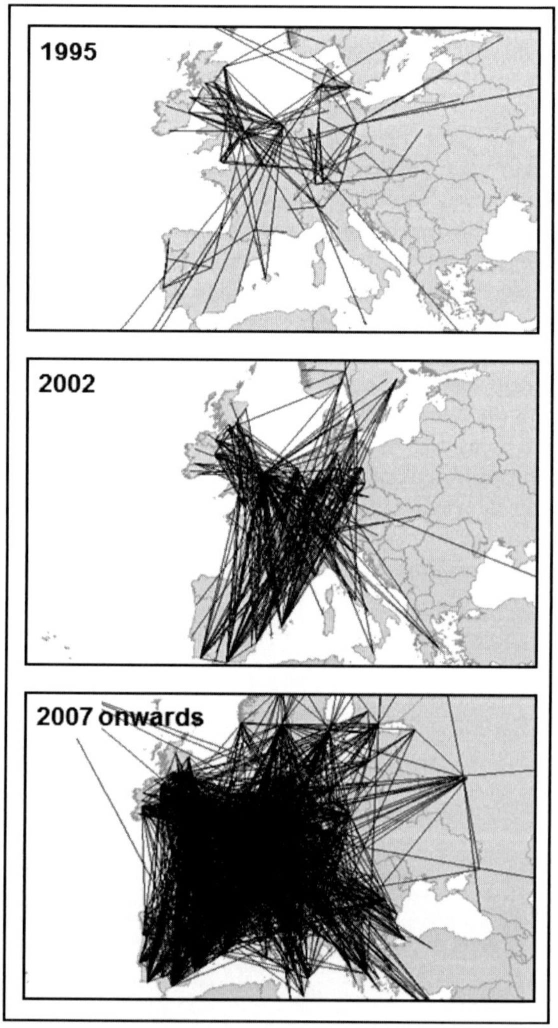

Figure 2: Development of the low-cost carrier network in central Europe (Own illustration)

Low-cost carriers changed the market from the scratch

With the increasing presence of low-cost carriers, fundamentally new market structures came into force (Albers, Heuermann & Koch, 2008). The old, dominant industry mindset focused on high service quality and service standards, combined with the political and infrastructure-related duty of linking the home market with international economic, political and cultural centers (Koch, 2006). The national flag carriers in particular had a duty to guarantee these services, partially relying on the support of regional carriers.

The evolutionary turn of the flight product from luxury to commodity took place with the introduction of the Boeing B747 1970, which, for the first time, made transporting larger numbers of passengers at low operating costs even over long distances possible. The sector to most profit from this development was tourism, gaining access to new markets and customer groups for flight tours.

LCCs opened the market for new customers

While mass tourism and flying at lower costs were basically limited to longer, typically intercontinental routes at the beginning, air travel on continental routes remained a comparably expensive product. The oligopolistic and sometimes even monopolistic market structures established by traditional carriers could thus be maintained – protected by the regulative framework being still in place by that time. This reflected into relatively high fares for customers. It was the market entry of low-cost carriers which substantially changed this situation. They spurred a significant reduction in ticket prices, while also opening up a still increasing number of new markets and niches.[1]

In these early days of liberalization, competition between airlines fell between the extremes of 'network carriers with quality focus' and 'cost focused budget carriers' – a typical duel between quality leaders and cost leaders (Porter, 1996).

Convergence of business models

Interestingly, during the last few years, the European aviation industry has again seen a fundamental evolutionary shift. Convergence of business models and consolidation of airlines have become the main development drivers in the industry. After a few years in which this had been visible in both airline types changing their respective product features, more and more convergence is seen through classic full service carriers transferring large parts of their continental services to specifically developed lower cost subsidiaries while at the same time limiting the full service concept to their hub operations.

To better understand these developments and future challenges in the aviation market, we will first discuss the characteristics of aviation from a strategic point of view, focusing on the passenger airline business. In this context, the various generic business models in place will be introduced, along with a closer look at the convergence phenomenon. Based on these findings we will continue with a more detailed look at response strategies and the outlook for future developments.

B. AVIATION STRATEGY IN DETAIL

Aviation, as discussed in chapter [number], is the general term for a complex system designed to provide transport services for people and

---

1 In the early days of the low-cost airlines it was estimated that up to 75% of all budget passengers had never flown before (market stimulation) and only 25% of passengers were drawn from traditional carriers (cannibalization). The great success of the new business model was also reflected in the sharp rise in passenger numbers over the years: in 2002, low-cost carriers in Germany accounted for about 1 million passengers, while by 2004, about 17.8 million passengers took advantage of the cheaper flight product. Today, Ryanair has grown into the largest carrier for continental services in Europe, transporting over 80 million passengers per year.

goods by the means of air transport. To accomplish the challenge of securing safe and efficient air transport, various actors have to cooperate, act and react in bringing together such different organizations as aircraft manufacturers and aircraft operators (or 'airlines'), air navigation service providers and airport operators, regulators, financial institution, investors and many more.

Consequently, aviation strategy is common to the various individual strategies of each member of the aviation system. To better understand the specifics, it is necessary to base any further investigation into this field on the core purpose of aviation: transport from A to B as illustrated in the following air passenger transport chain.

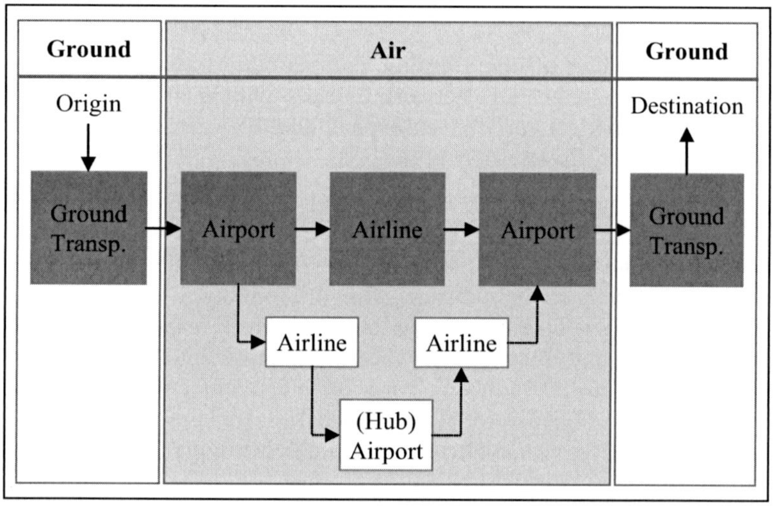

Figure 3: The air passenger transport chain (Own illustration)

Transport chain

The transport chain itself focuses on airlines and airports as the actors within the aviation system who are both the most visible and the closest to the transport of people and goods.[2] In this simplified description, all other organizations are considered to be secondary to transport itself and are not shown here.

Aviation strategy includes airlines and airports

Working within this narrow definition, aviation strategy is a joint strategy between airlines and airports for providing efficient and reliable air transport. It is fundamentally important to understand at this point that airlines and airports cannot continue their respective strategies without each other. No airline can operate without an airport, and no airport would be able to offer any air transport without an operating airline.

---

2 Please note that the air cargo transport chain displays several different characteristics to the air passenger transport chain. Compare e.g. Koch (2006).

While this prerequisite should lead to a generally common approach towards aviation strategy, several fundamental differences between airlines and airports make it necessary to focus on either side's perspective when talking about strategy. The operational and planning horizons of the two companies are too different to be able to create a joint, common strategy.

Airlines and airports have different horizons in terms of planning

Investment periods and amortization periods belong to the most obvious examples for theses differences. Airline network planning practically never accounts for periods of more than 5 years. Operational network planning is even limited to a period of 6 – 12 months. Even for fleet strategy decisions, airlines do not require specific or detailed market considerations, since their assets (the airplanes) can be allocated very flexibly to almost all markets served by the carrier. Airports on the other hand are by definition completely limited to their location. Investments lead to assets made of concrete and steel, which cannot be assigned to other markets or locations if demand shifts. At the same time, the high costs incurred need very long operational periods in order to break even – 20 years or more are typical amortization periods for airports, while airlines can amortize their aircraft in significantly shorter time.[3]

The management and development of airports are discussed in chapter 5 and 6; airport management, in relation to the air cargo business in chapter 13. This chapter will focus on airline strategy in terms of passenger airline strategy. It is immediately obvious that even the narrow field of 'airline strategy' is a catch-all term for a broad set of strategies, which to a large extent are already reflected in the business models applied in the market.

C. BUSINESS MODELS IN THE AIRLINE INDUSTRY

C. 1 Fundamentals of business models

Numerous business models exist

As with most industries, the aviation business is characterized by and thrives for a high degree of diversity. While in the past most airlines acted in a very similar way, built upon the requirements and traditions of flag carriers, with a changing market environment and a growing range of development opportunities, carriers started to diversify. This trend has led to the increasing importance of different products or marketing among the established carriers. Along the lines of Porter's generic competitive strategies, entirely new approaches to running an airline have started to be brought into operation. Besides the ambition to achieve product leadership, the target of being the cost leader has also gained increasing importance.

[3] For more information about specifics and differences between airports and airlines see Koch (2006).

With this development the airline market and aviation has entered a new stage of evolution and competition having changed from competition between equals to competition between business models. Rethinking the way of doing business has taken the evolutionary step from optimizing existing structures towards 'starting all over again'. The beginning of these changes was the invention of new business models – new concepts for the set-up of aviation companies.

So what is a business model? What are its main characteristics? And what are the specifics in the airline business?

Business model basics

In general, a business model defines the way a company and its processes are structured and designed, based on the intention to cater for a specific target market. It contains the available resources, processes and organizational set-up appearing to be most suitable for success. Business models do not only define the way of structuring and running a business, they aim at generating a unique selling proposition to create an advantage over direct competitors. They are intended foremost to differentiate a business from older and – at least in the beginning – more established rivals. Nevertheless, a business model defines the long-term orientation of a company and cannot be replaced by entirely different concepts without wasting earlier achievements. A business model accordingly exceeds the concept of a production or marketing plan, it is the core purpose of a company.

C. 2 Determinants for airline business models

Airline business models comprise six elements

For the airline industry, six criteria should be considered as defining the business model. While three of these criteria – the network concept, scheduling and fleet strategy – describe the basic product of any airline in terms of offering transportation between two places, the other characteristics are primarily customer and thus market oriented. Marketing, product features and the cost and pricing strategy represent classic core functions of efficiently producing and selling a product or service.

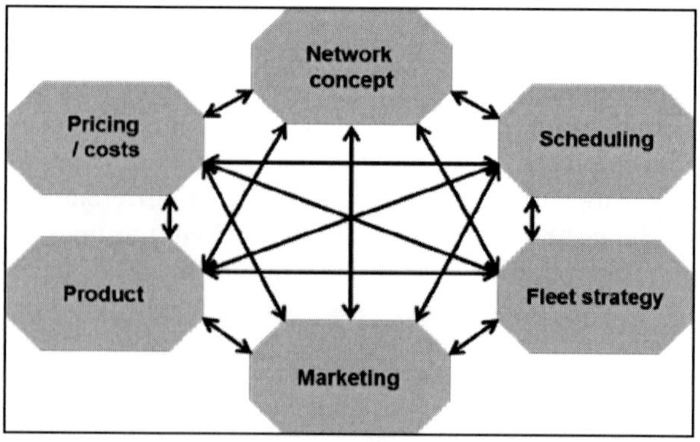

Figure 4: Characteristics of airline business models (Own illustration)

Most of these characteristics are discussed in more detail in other chapters of this book. Thus, here only a brief outline is being provided of what the main concepts are for each characterizing element of airline business models.

C. 2. 1 Network concept

Airports served and network philosophy are the core of a network concept

Two main features characterize the network concept of an airline: the airports served and the network philosophy applied. Airports can basically be distinguished as primary, secondary and tertiary airports (Koch, 2006). Primary airports are mostly hub airports of a significant size located close to a city or business center. Secondary airports are either the smaller airports within an urban region or significantly smaller second airports within an airport system. Finally, tertiary airports are small regional airports, typically found at a certain distance from a large city. They often are converted former military bases and thus far away from densely populated areas.

Range from point-to-point to complex global networks

The network philosophy ranges from pure point-to-point or 'ping-pong' patterns through linear and grid networks to complex global network structures based on a hub-and-spoke or even a multi-hub system. They are primarily driven by the local demand structure an airline targets to serve and are limited by factors such as operating economics, traffic rights, slots and other resources. The network is not only one of the dominant cost drivers of an airline, but it also defines which traffic flows can be attracted and therefore one of the most important drivers of airline revenue. After all, it has to be understood as source of competitive strength or weakness.

C. 2. 2 Scheduling

Optimal service and connectivity

The schedule aims at defining the optimal service pattern to attract as many passengers to the traffic flow or local region as possible – or at least large shares of specific passenger groups. Although constrained by slots, capacities, regulation and legal requirements, offered flight frequency and departure timings leave room for establishing a unique strategy. Core aspects are the time needed to travel from A to B and the adherence of frequent travelers' requirements. In general, scheduling comprises four steps: capacity estimation and planning, frequency planning and fleet and crew assignment.

Furthermore, punctuality is a major success driver. It reflects an airline's reliability and consequently the attractiveness for potential customers and finally the basis for quality oriented prices.

C. 2. 3 Fleet strategy

An airline's fleet strategy is a major driver of its financial planning and furthermore defines the revenue potential the carrier is capable of exploring. Based on internal (i.e. crew availability, financial resources and technical capabilities) and external conditions (i.e. aircraft availability, market for used aircraft, fuel prices and currency values) decisions on the future fleet are taken. This especially includes whether to operate aircraft from one or several manufacturers, to focus on a homogenous fleet or to allow a more heterogeneous fleet, or finally, whether to procure regional, short- or long haul airplanes etc.

Consequently, the fleet sets the framework for the kind of routes operated by an airline, not at last determining available flight ranges and cabin size.

Network requirements and fleet structure need to match

As for all decisions regarding the business model of an airline, there are no set rules regarding the fleet strategy, especially when considering the discussion on a mixed fleet operation. Single type fleets have strong advantages, such as lower training and material costs,[4] and offer the opportunity to easily exchange aircraft at any time. On the other side, this approach leads to a suboptimal capacity allocation for many routes and thus lower load factors and a lack of adaptability to changing demands. Multi-type fleets lead to the obvious disadvantages of higher training and material costs as well as lower discounts with the manufacturers. The main benefits are independence from a specific aircraft supplier and the possibility of assigning an optimized capacity to any single route.

C. 2. 4 Marketing

Distribution channels

A key aspect of each business model, and one of the most important customer interfaces, is the field of marketing. Each business has to choose the right distribution channels, ranging from direct, interactive and personal customer sales (e.g. through their own offices or key account visits) via third party sales to modern sales channels such as internet booking engines or call centers.

Advertisement style

The sales channels chosen have to be supported and mirrored by the advertising style of a company. Advertising has to address the customers and offer them an appropriate way of contacting the company and buying its service, e.g. a ticket. Naturally, the kind of advertising does not only depend on the sales channel promoted, but also on the customer group addressed. Thus, it might differ significantly depending on the target customer group the business model is designed for.

C. 2. 5 Product

Class concept

By defining their products, airlines attempt to appeal to their target customer groups. Product competition between airlines is mainly driven by class concept and the in-flight services offered to the passengers – together with the previously mentioned aspects such as network and fleet. The most obvious distinguishing factor is the number of travel classes offered. While most traditional carriers divide their passengers into first, business and economy class, concepts nowadays range from single class to up to four classes. While the single

---

[4] Material costs mainly include technical costs, e.g. the costs of training and certifying staff for certain aircraft types as well as the costs for holding material stock.

class concept mostly comprises only economy seating (all business class carriers have been economically successful only in rare cases), four class concepts usually integrate an 'economy plus' or 'premium economy' cabin between economy and business class.

The multi-class concept has also increasingly gained importance in the field of ground services, offering a different degree of comfort to passenger groups with different lounges or handling processes.

C. 2. 6 Pricing and costs

Pricing is also used to differentiate from other carriers

The pricing and costs element of an airline's business model is one of the most prominent differentiating factors. Pricing targets the typical or average air fare an airline charges its passengers, leading to general classifications such as low fare airlines versus the classic carriers. Nevertheless, pricing is not only a means of marketing and gaining market shares, it is also used to display quality differences and to capitalize on reputation and brand.

Cost elements

Costs on the other hand are not necessarily linked to pricing – a phenomenon, becoming particularly prevalent between low-fare and low-cost airlines. Cost leadership as an underlying strategy for a business model enables the airline to successfully deliver products and services other companies are not able to provide, opening up additional or new markets to these companies. On the other hand, a higher cost level makes it difficult or even impossible to operate efficiently, posing significant risks to the respective airline. This conflict can easily be observed when classic network carriers match the aggressive pricing of low cost competitors on selected routes: the fares are low, but the costs are not, therefore requiring the respective airline to cross-subsidize between routes.

Nevertheless, costs are to a large extent driven by the other elements of an airline's business model, such as the network concept (hub-and-spoke vs. point-to-point) or the fleet strategy (single vs. multi type fleets, age of fleet). Thus, following a certain business model excludes inhabiting the position as cost leader and poses additional challenges to the respective carrier to generate additional revenues or significantly reduce costs.

Finally, staff costs are also directly impacted by the business model chosen. The more complex the business model is the better qualified the personnel must be to handle the complexity and expected quality. This consequently leads to rising salaries, negatively influencing the airline's cost structure.

Based on these six elements, the most important business models occurring in the passenger and cargo airline markets are outlined in the following. Here, the large variety of concepts and philosophies for approaching the market are being discussed, as well as the continuous evolution of business models in the aviation industry.

D. BUSINESS MODELS IN THE PASSENGER AIRLINE BUSINESS

Five basic business models in the airline industry

In the passenger airline business discussions tend to focus on the differentiation between full service or network carriers and low-cost or low-fare carriers. Nevertheless, at least five generic business models can be distinguished. While charter and regional carriers have played a significant role in the development of the global aviation for many decades – representing the increasing offer of air transport services to both the traveling masses and to smaller regions without large demand volumes – business aviation has only started to gain an increasing importance over the past years.[5]

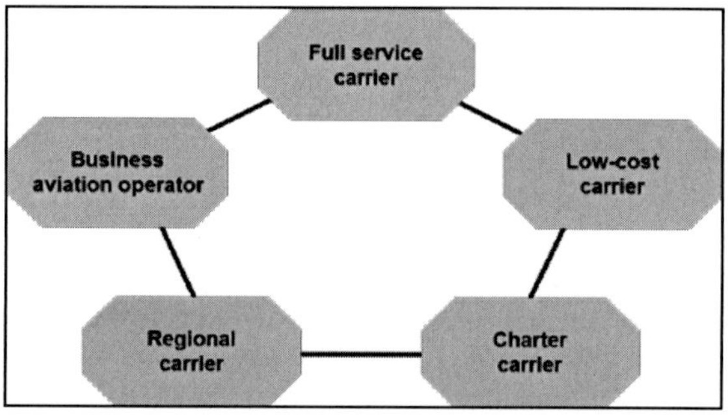

Figure 5: Generic business models in the passenger airline business (Own illustration)

All business models are discussed in greater detail below, based on the key elements of business models introduced above.

D. 1 Network carriers

Most traditional flag carriers operate as network carrier

Network carriers and full service carriers are typically used as synonyms for the same business model and the same group of airlines. These mainly comprise the traditional flag carriers like Lufthansa, Air France, British Airways, or Singapore Airlines – airlines founded or established as part of national infrastructure development. Furthermore, the 'big three' US American carriers are also seen as typical examples of this business model[6]. All of the mentioned carriers as well as the others defined as network carriers focus on the same operational, strategic and economic features: operating a complex network of air services, combining a large number of continental services with

---

5 At least in Europe, business aviation did not gain momentum to a significant degree before the new millennium. In other parts of the world, especially in North America, this segment has a significantly longer history.

6 Over a long period of time, the US American airline market had been dominated by the 'big six' airlines. Nowadays, following a period of intense consolidation and major mergers this has reduced to the three major players United (including former Continental Airlines), Delta (including Northwest) and American Airlines (including US Airways).

a considerable number of intercontinental routes using a hub-and-spoke system. This generally is accompanied by a product strategy based on distinct service class differentiation, offering a full range of services to all passengers. These similarities have led to the synonymous application of the terms mentioned above.

Complex network and large number of continental and intercontinental services

Interestingly, even new entrants apply the network carriers' business model – companies such as Emirates Airlines, Turkish Airlines or Etihad Airways follow the same principles: serving a comprehensive network of destinations (on different continents), while, at the same time, focusing on high service standards. Consequently, the main aspects characterizing the network carrier business model belong to one of these two categories.[7]

Network and fleet are two main elements of network carriers' business model

Network and the fleet employed are two of the main elements defining the network carriers' business model. Network carriers target large catchment areas, while, at the same time, bundling traffic from smaller catchments at their hubs in order to be able to operate profitable intercontinental services. This leads to a focus on primary airports, being those airports belonging to a highly populated urban region or business center, and typically serving several million passengers per year. While these airports guarantee sufficient passenger volumes to fill the number of flights needed to efficiently operate a hub, and thus usually provide the infrastructure needed to cope with the peaks resulting from hub operations (for more detail on hubs see Kraus & Koch, 2005), this strategic focus displays disadvantages when it comes to punctuality. Primary airports, being a preferred destination to all kinds of airlines, tend to suffer from congestion and generate delays and operational bottlenecks. Delays, of course, incur direct costs due to longer block times and lower utilization rates for aircraft or the risk of passengers and crew of missing connecting flights. Indirect costs also result from lower customer satisfaction, being the consequence of having to wait longer than acceptable from the passenger's point-of-view. Exceeding these delay costs, hub-and-spoke systems display significant planning and operational complexity, leading to comparably high production costs.[8]

Congested airports and longer block times are two potential shortcomings

Despite these economically and financially critical aspects, hub operations are about the most valuable asset a network carrier owns. They allow an airline to operate routes which could never be profitably served by local traffic alone. After all, they are the economic basis for a network density clearly exceeding a point-to-point coverage by far.

Hub operations are a valuable asset for bundling traffic

---

7 In all business model descriptions, only selected criteria will be discussed. A summarizing table at the end of each chapter gives a more comprehensive overview of the key elements of each business model.

8 One of the most important cost drivers is the hub operation in peaks or waves. A large number of feeder aircraft needs to arrive on time to allow passengers to change gates and flights allowing a large number of aircraft and flights to leave again. This tends to lead to comparably long ground times for the aircraft, since they always have to wait for their connecting passengers.

Heterogeneous fleet Since the network is designed to link regional, continental and intercontinental routes, the typical network carrier's fleet is rather heterogeneous. Ranging from small regional aircraft to long-range wide-body airplanes, network carriers try to have the right aircraft in place for each single route. This leads to a broad range of available seating capacities and flight ranges, but also implies a multi-manufacturer strategy. Consequently, flight and cabin crews, technical staff, spare parts, handling equipment and personnel and numerous other production factors have to be provided for entirely different aircraft types, adding to the cost base of the carrier.[9]

Apart from the network itself, product features concern the entire passenger service chain and are not limited to class differentiation. The quality of in-flight services and entertainment has become increasingly important in the passengers' choice. Network coverage and total travel times are becoming increasingly similar between the operators, thus these experience factors are growing in importance. This is reflected in many carriers' focus on well-trained, service-oriented staff.

Network concept	Airports	▪ Mostly primary airports, often with capacity constraints ▪ Secondary airports only in order to explore new / high yield markets ▪ Airports typically with large and complex infrastructure
	Network	▪ Hub & spoke network, based on feeder traffic ▪ Turnaround times up to 3 hours
Scheduling	Frequency	▪ Moderate to high ▪ Pattern differs between continental (lower frequencies on weekends) and intercontinental flights (no weekend reductions)
	Punctuality	▪ Average ▪ Highly depending on efficiency and capacity utilization of hub airports
Fleet strategy	Aircraft	▪ Heterogeneous, multi-type fleet ▪ Usually several aircraft manufacturers ▪ Average utilization
	Sectors	▪ Short- to long-range ▪ Continental and intercontinental
Marketing	Distribution	▪ Travel agencies, CRS, direct sales, internet, call centers, …
	Advertisement style	▪ Conservative ▪ Product-feature oriented, increasingly price-oriented
Product	Class concept	▪ Multi-class concept, inc. business / first class (at least intercont) ▪ Comparably low seat density
	In-flight services	▪ Mostly free of charge ▪ In-flight entertainment system, in-flight shopping, seat assignment
Pricing / costs	Fares	▪ Moderate to high ▪ Comlex yield management, including interlining, fare restrictions, …
	Staff	▪ Full bandwith of young and highly experienced ▪ Tarif-based wages, pension fund obligations

Table 1: Key elements of the network carrier business model (Own illustration)

[9] Some carriers attempt to limit these costs by operating a fleet consisting solely of wide-body aircraft. The higher costs of operating 'inappropriate' airplanes on certain routes and offering overcapacities are outweighed by the cost savings resulting from a more limited aircraft fleet. Another equally common approach is employing regional carriers for servicing the smaller planes at an adequate cost basis.

Staff is finally another significant cost driver for network carriers. Linked to their company history and age, these airlines usually have a full bandwidth of employees, ranging from young to the highly experienced. This alone is already to a certain degree a significant cost driver, since seniority is a relevant factor for wage and salary levels.[10] In addition, most of these airlines are also subject to union tariffs. While these do not only tend to be higher than free market salaries, they also imply the risk of strikes – which from time-to-time can severely endanger the company's financial results.

Staff is an important cost driver

D. 2 Low-cost carriers

While it appears to be valid to use the terms 'network carriers' and 'full service carriers' synonymously, a clear distinction between 'low-cost carriers' and 'low-fare carriers' is important. While low-cost carriers follow a business model which is strictly focused at lean, cost-efficient operations, low fare carriers focus on selling tickets at low prices, regardless of their underlying cost structure. To give a brief example: even network carriers such as Lufthansa or KLM Air France offer flight tickets at extremely low rates, sometimes even beating the offers of low-cost carriers for the same routes. This is not the consequence of being able to match the cost structure of a low-cost carrier, but of selling single seats which would otherwise most probably remain unsold. The revenue earned with such tickets might not cover the total costs of production, but it still provides additional revenue to the respective carrier and allows to present the own product to customers which might be convinced by the product quality to return even at higher rates. While this is only an example for dynamic yield management, low-fare airlines tend to have a similar conflict: to be competitive against the low-cost airlines, they need to offer low fares, although their own cost structure does not allow for such a pricing strategy. In the long run, these airlines typically have no alternative to going bankrupt – their business model is not viable.

Low-cost carriers and low-fare carriers are not necessarily the same

Accordingly, we focus here on the real low-cost business model, based on the low-cost model invented by Southwest Airlines and pioneered in Europe by Ryanair (Lawton, 2002). The underlying basis for all features of this business model is the focus on costs and the core product of flying from A to B. All complexity drivers in the network carrier business model are eliminated here: only smaller (secondary, tertiary) airports are served, reducing ground times and the risk of delays; there are no connecting flights offered, the focus is on point-to-point services; aircraft do not fly complex rotations or itineraries, but rather shuttle between their home base and their destinations; aircraft utilization is optimized by limiting the stage length to approximately two hours, thus guaranteeing one or two additional flights per

LCC try to eliminate every complexity in their operations

[10] Another aspect related to this is the matter of pensions. The older the staff the higher the financial obligations which need to be funded either through cash flow or by investing in external pension funds.

day compared to traditional carriers, and also by applying the highest seat density allowed per aircraft. Furthermore, costs are kept to a minimum by operating a single-type fleet, focusing on low-cost distribution channels (internet, call centers) and by making all company processes as simple as possible.

High staff productivity is vital

Staff costs are a different matter. Wages nowadays are very competitive compared to other airlines. Nevertheless, there is no union tariff base to be taken into account, making remuneration systems a lot more flexible; working hours are designed to match the legal limits, thus allowing maximum staff productivity. This is a major difference to the network carriers: they have to take the legal regulations on maximum flight hours per crew member into consideration; union contracts often limit the maximum duty hours even further, thus directly reducing per capita productivity.

Table 2 summarizes some of the most important cost levers for low-cost carriers and their effect compared to network carriers.

Carrier type	Cost item	Cost reduction (%)	Cost per seat
Network carrier			**100**
Low-cost carrier	**Operating advantages:**		
	▪ Higher seating density	-16	84
	▪ Higher aircraft utilisation	-3	81
	▪ Lower crew salaries / expenses	-3	78
	▪ Use of secondary airports	-6	72
	▪ MRO outsourcing / single aircraft type	-2	70
	Product / service features:		
	▪ Minimal station costs, outsourced handling	-10	60
	▪ No free in-flight catering	-6	54
	Marketing differences:		
	▪ No agents' comissions	-8	46
	▪ Reduced sales / reservations costs	-3	43
	Other advantages:		
	▪ Lower administration costs	-2	**41**

Table 2: Cost levers of low-cost carriers (Own illustration based on Doganis, 2003)

Additional revenue sources

Exceeding the strict cost optimization, low-cost carriers are extremely successful in exploring additional revenue sources. These do not only include in-flight shopping offers – which are also popular with network carriers – but also comprise the selling of food and beverages and additional charges, for example for luggage transport, personal service at a check-in desk instead of using the internet check-in and extra charges for credit card payments. Additionally, provisions for marketing hotels, rental cars and other services make up for an increasing share of the low-cost carriers' revenues.

Business models are again converging

Nevertheless, other than in the broad field of network carriers, only a very limited number of airlines strictly follow the pure low-cost model. This is not only reflected in the large number of low-fare carriers, but also in the increasing convergence of business models. Former low-cost carriers have started to adapt features which used to be part of the network carrier business model[11] – and likewise, the full service carriers have started to reduce frills and charge for services or reduce service levels. This trend is discussed in one of the following chapters.

Network concept	Airports	▪ Typically secondary, partially even tertiary ▪ Uncongested airports with usually simple and inexpensive infrastructure
	Network	▪ Point to point focus, mainly ping-pong services ▪ Typically several bases ▪ Short turnaround times (< 30 minutes)
Scheduling	Frequency	▪ High ▪ Only limited differences between weekday and weekend
	Punctuality	▪ Very high
Fleet strategy	Aircraft	▪ Single type fleet (mainly B 737 or A 320) ▪ High utilization (> 11 hours per day)
	Sectors	▪ Short- to medium (typically maximum of 2 hours / 800 km) ▪ Continental routes only
Marketing	Distribution	▪ Focus on direct sales, internet and call centers ▪ CRS, travel agencies etc. very limited
	Advertisement style	▪ Competitive, aggressive ▪ Focus on price and direct comparisn esp. with network carriers
Product	Class concept	▪ Single class (economy only) ▪ High seat density (maximum possible)
	In-flight services	▪ Catering and in-flight sales at high prices ▪ Free seating
Pricing / costs	Fares	▪ Typically low - but very high for short-notice bookings ▪ Simple yield management, no fare restrictions, interlining etc.
	Staff	▪ Competitive wages, usually no tariff-base, stock option programs ▪ High working hours, focus on productivity

Table 3: Key elements of the low-cost carrier business model (Own illustration)

D. 3 Regional carriers

Regional carriers are loosing importance

Regional carriers represent a business model which, at least in the European aviation market, has lost its specific identity and significant parts of its market base. Originally, regional carriers were players in niche markets, linking destinations in smaller regions off the main traffic flows. Bypassing the large hub airports and serving those routes was considered economically unattractive for the large network carriers. Later on, regional carriers had often been integrated into the systems of larger airlines. Most regional carriers have either been acquired by large network carriers or are now working for them as regional partners.[12] Nevertheless, the business model still exists and

Network carriers integrate regional carriers

[11] Even within the current field of successful low-cost carriers such differences can be observed. For example easyJet, the number 2 in Europe after Ryanair, has always focused its operations on primary airports, also targeting business passengers. This has allowed them to constantly generate higher average yields, making up for the higher costs incurred by operating at these non-low-cost airports. See also Lawton (2002).

[12] Acquisitions include e.g. former DLT, now Lufthansa Cityline, by Lufthansa, or just recently VLM by AirFrance/KLM, who are now integrated into the CityJet brand.

shows various specifics and characteristics, making regional carriers a valid player in the market.

Even though the network of most regional players today is determined by their mother company or partner airline, resulting from the regional's function as feeder airline, most networks still show a typical structure. Regional carriers either link secondary airports with each other or connect secondary destinations with a hub airport, thus building the bridge between the local demand and the global offer of a hub carrier.

Smaller aircraft build the backbone of most regional carriers' fleets

Another difference to the network carriers is that regional carriers do not usually focus strongly on the airports' infrastructure. This is mainly due to the fleet operated, which is limited to smaller, regional aircraft, usually with capacities of less than 100 seats. Since both, turboprop and jet aircraft are available in this segment; regional carriers often operate multi-type fleets. Other than the larger jet aircraft these airlines have the advantage of being able to operate from shorter runways and often even have their own staircases. This allows easy and flexible operations at all kinds of airports, without needing to rely on local ground equipment such as passenger bridges. Furthermore, these technical properties make regional aircraft the specialist for several economically attractive airports within a larger airline's network.[13]

On the other hand, the kind of aircraft employed also limits the operational options for regional carriers. Ranges are limited. The lower air speed of turboprop aircraft limits the operational radius even further. Additionally, the small cabin does not allow for a complex class differentiation, reducing the exclusivity of upper classes. Nevertheless, the typical product features of the partner or parent airline are often available.

Staffing

Again, staffing displays some special features for this business model. Due to the large size of many regional carriers wages tend to be tariff-based. Nevertheless, wage levels on average are lower than with network carriers. Several aspects contribute to this. First, flight crew salaries are often defined based on the aircraft size – which is obviously smaller in the regional segment. Second, seniority structures within regional carriers tend to be different from those of networks carriers. Regional carriers are too small to have their own flight training organizations. Consequently, they depend on hiring pilots on the market. Since the larger airlines train their flight crews within their own organizations, and are able to keep them based on seniority systems and privileges, regional carriers tend to be less attractive for these crews. On the other hand, in many cases they are an attractive option for military pilots who lose their licenses at the age of 40 and are looking for options to continue flying. Due to the strict seniority systems in place they are quite frequently unable to join a network carrier and therefore start with a regional airline. This has the advantage for the

---

[13] For example, the airports of Florence / Italy, London City / UK or Antwerp / Belgium can only be served with regional aircraft.

respective carrier of having experienced, well-trained crews at a lower salary level.

Network concept	Airports	▪ Primary (mainly hubs of partner / mother companies) and secondary ▪ No focus on specific infrastructure
	Network	▪ Mainly point to point services, niche markets in smaller regions ▪ Driven by feeder function for network carriers
Scheduling	Frequency	▪ Low to moderate ▪ Weekdays and weekends often witrh different destination portfolio
	Punctuality	▪ Usually high ▪ High impact of share of hub operations
Fleet strategy	Aircraft	▪ Regional aircraft only (< 100 seats) ▪ Turboprop or jet aircraft, consequently often several manufacturers
	Sectors	▪ Short to mid-range ▪ Focus on short-routes-routes
Marketing	Distribution	▪ In niche markets traditional approach: direct sales, travel agencies, … ▪ Majority of sales via network carriers
	Advertisement style	▪ Mainly traditional, conservative ▪ Own advertisement in niche markets only
Product	Class concept	▪ Typically single-class ▪ Medium seat density
	In-flight services	▪ Usually no in flight entertainment system ▪ Other features analogous to network carrier
Pricing / costs	Fares	▪ Moderate to high ▪ High importance of prorating / interlining to long haul routes
	Staff	▪ Experienced, tariff-based ▪ Wages typically below network carrier levels

Table 4: Key elements of the regional carrier business model (Own illustration)

D. 4 Charter carriers

Charter carriers established mass transport

Charter carriers were irreplaceable in making flying a means of mass transport. They transported tourists to the warm water destinations especially around the Mediterranean, often as part of all inclusive tour packages. Although the number of destinations later increased, the charter carriers' mission remained the same.

Fleet is adapted to special needs of transporting tourists

In line with this purpose and mission, the charter carrier business model was created. The fleet follows the requirements of the main destinations served – dependent on the main tour operator and its offers, including only continental or even intercontinental aircraft. Differentiating between classes or passenger groups was also deemed unnecessary, until upper-scale tourism demanded a comfort class cabin at least for long haul flights. In-flight service had to be designed in order to entertain the tourists on board and to give them some 'holiday feeling' – thus meals and beverages used to be free and in-flight entertainment had a certain importance. To keep costs to tight limits and to reduce inconvenience for the traveler, flights operated from the home airport of the traveling tourist groups, flying directly to the final destination without forcing the passengers to change planes in between. Distribution systems and efforts could be kept to a minimum –

flights were typically operated on behalf of a tour operator who sold all flight tickets as well.

Strong seasonality

Accordingly, charter carriers have always faced strong seasonal fluctuations with large demand arising during school breaks and vacation periods and low demand during the rest of the year. This was handled by hiring temporary seasonal staff during the peak months.

Changes in business model

Most of these characteristics are still valid today. Nevertheless, several key elements of the business model have changed significantly. With the rise of low-cost carriers, mainly serving tourism routes, and the growth of network carriers, increasingly operating to tourism destinations as well, the traditional charter business has dramatically eroded. Tour operators do no longer want to take the economic risk of having to sell entire plane-loads and prefer to book contingents on regular, scheduled flights. Furthermore, the higher frequency of scheduled flights compared to one-time charters gives a considerably higher degree of flexibility both to the tour operator as well as to the travelling passenger. Thus, especially in the continental charter market, carriers have lost ever more market share to the new competitors and have been forced to explore new markets. Ethnic traffic, for example, between Turkey, Russia or Eastern and Western Europe, has turned out to be particularly fundamental for these airlines' success.

At the same time, charter carriers have started to change their operational patterns. Instead of relying on the tour operators, they have started to sell single seats on their flights. They also schedule their operations, even though flights very often are not operated daily. Instead of operating pure charter flights their service has become scheduled service and thus a more attractive option not only for tourists, but for other passenger segments as well. Air Berlin is a good example for this strategic turnaround, having started as pure charter carrier and now operating a large network of scheduled services – as well as still being active in the classic charter segment. With this move towards more scheduled operations charter carriers have also moved away from the strict 'no connecting flights' philosophy. Many operators have started to establish hub operations at least for their intercontinental services.[14]

Charter carriers today are thus in many regards different from the original business model. Increasing competition has to a large extent forced the business model out of the (European) market. Successful players have either established scheduled operations – often in the low-cost segment – or are a subsidiary or even a division of large tour operator groups which secure their business.

---

[14] E.g. Condor used to concentrate their intercontinental services in Germany at Munich Airport, feeding their flights with classic continental aircraft from all over Germany. Air Berlin uses its base in Nuremberg for continental hub operations and has even set up a hub at Palma de Mallorca in order to be able to serve a larger number of Iberian destinations.

Network concept	Airports	▪ Primary and secondary airports ▪ Mainly holiday destinations (focus: warm water)
	Network	▪ Point to point ▪ Sometimes bundling of traffic at intercontinenetal base
Scheduling	Frequency	▪ Low ▪ Originally non-scheduled, seasonal variations, highly demand driven
	Punctuality	▪ Below average
Fleet strategy	Aircraft	▪ Multi type fleet ▪ High utilization, often with very low operational reserves
	Sectors	▪ Depending on strategy ▪ Focus on mid- and long haul (including intercontinental)
Marketing	Distribution	▪ Tour operators (flights as part of package) ▪ Travel agents, direct sales for single seats
	Advertisement style	▪ Classic ▪ Destination focus
Product	Class concept	▪ Mainly single class, sometimes long haul fleet with comfort class ▪ High seat density
	In-flight services	▪ Very heterogeneous ▪ Free meals, other service at additional costs
Pricing / costs	Fares	▪ Low, simple structure ▪ Often as part of tour packages only
	Staff	▪ Low basic salaries ▪ Minimum cabin crew, seasonal employment

Table 5: Key elements of the charter carrier business model (Own illustration)

D. 5 Business aviation

Ad-hoc charter flights mainly with small executive jets

'Business aviation' is used as summarizing term for airlines operating ad-hoc charter flights, mainly with small executive jets, for companies or private purposes, mostly independently of any other airline. In this regard, they are a charter business model with an entirely revised focus. They do not target low-cost oriented tourists or any other kind of mass transport, but operate in a niche market offering a clear luxury product. Their core product is not understood to be the transport from A to B, but a combination of exclusivity and time saving. They are exclusive because either single passengers or small groups are being transported; they save time because the direct flight allows the passenger to avoid transferring at one or several hubs, thus reducing total traveling time significantly.

Exclusivity and time as core products

The roots lie in company transportation

The roots of this business model are manifold. First, intra-company transportation used its own aircraft when either significant numbers of internal commuters had to be transported between different locations or production sites[15] or when highly skilled experts had to be trans-

[15] Examples are car manufacturers Ford, which has its own airline connecting the sites in Germany and the United Kingdom; DaimlerChrysler with direct flights between the headquarters in Germany and the United States; or the multinational aviation company EADS with own-company flights between their main sites in the United Kingdom, Germany, France and Spain.

ported to company sites within as short a period of time as possible.[16] Second, business aviation gained momentum in North America, catering for the need for fast transport throughout the country to managers of industries such as financial services or celebrities. Third, the growing interest of individuals in having their own aircraft spurred the development of business aviation, not at least of which through the foundation of part ownership concepts.[17]

Business aviation experienced an upturn

Business aviation has experienced a significant upturn during the past decade, especially due to rising company profits and individual wealth as well as the economy marketing and demanding an ever faster working style. During the past few years, business aviation has even started to be sold as top-end product by network airlines, complementing their feeder network with this kind of luxury, first class plus service.

Differences lie in the business model itself ...

Given its specific customer base, this business segment is defined by different criteria than the other business segments. High fares and the need for product exclusivity allow for typical efficiency measures to be neglected to a large extent. Homogeneity of the fleet is more a question of exchangeability of single aircraft than of productivity, service features are ordered *á la carte,* and since service is a key success factor for the operator, staff quality and thus salaries are seen in a different light to classical airlines.

... and the customers' needs

On the other hand, business aviation operators have to cope with a significantly higher degree of flexibility – there is neither a defined network nor a given schedule – generating significant inefficiencies and low utilization levels. Furthermore, demand is considerably more volatile than with any scheduled service. When an important customer books fewer flights the airline might experience financial difficulties. Considering the recent crises in the financial services and banking sectors, the risk for business aviation operators is obvious.

Thus, business aviation has managed to gain a certain share of the entire air transport market, but will most likely remain a niche product.

---

[16] This is typical especially for the petrochemical and oil exploration industries, where, in cases of emergency or production fall-outs, highly skilled experts need to be brought to various sites globally within hours instead of days.

[17] Part ownership of an aircraft means, that the investor buys a certain share in an aircraft, typically including a pre-defined number of flight hours per year. Additional flight hours, exceeding the budget, can be bought by each investor and are sold to third parties as well.

Network concept	Airports	▪ Any airport requested by customer ▪ Mainly smaller airports with no scheduled flights
	Network	▪ Point to point ▪ Worldwide operations (if not limited to one continent / region)
Scheduling	Frequency	▪ Ad hoc basis ▪ No scheduled flights
	Punctuality	▪ High
Fleet strategy	Aircraft	▪ Typically small to mid-size jets ▪ Large jets with low executive seating with some operators
	Sectors	▪ Short to long-haul ▪ Most operators with focus on continental services
Marketing	Distribution	▪ Direct sales ▪ Fractional ownership
	Advertisement style	▪ Exclusive ▪ Very limited
Product	Class concept	▪ Luxury class ▪ Focus on individualism
	In-flight services	▪ Á la carte ▪ You get what you pay for
Pricing / costs	Fares	▪ Premium ▪ "Value" based
	Staff	▪ Highly trained cabin staff ▪ Experienced flight crews

Table 6: Key elements of the business aviation business model (Own illustration)

E. CONVERGENCE OF BUSINESS MODELS

Today, 'pure' concepts are rarely observed

As previously mentioned, over the past years business models in the airline industry have shown an increasingly strong tendency to converge. Neither 'pure' full service carriers nor 'pure' low-cost carriers are typical in today's aviation market anymore and the same can be observed for charter carriers. Most airlines have developed into hybrids, trying to find and apply the optimal mix of features from various business models. Given their importance for the overall market, the convergence of network and low-cost carriers particularly need to be looked at in more detail.

Costs are a major determinant for success

The low-cost carriers' competitive success against the established full service or network airlines is mainly due to budget airlines concentrating on cost leadership and the full service carriers striving for quality leadership. Achieving and maintaining a considerably lower cost basis than the traditional carriers cannot exclusively be related to a reduction of service offers on board, but is the result of targeting every single element of the production chain and optimizing its cost position. Adding to the individual discussions above, the following table gives a brief overview of airlines' most important cost drivers, which are applied by low-cost carriers to generate competitive advantages especially over network carriers.

Cost driver	Activity	Effects
Fleet structure	▪ focus on typically only one aircraft model	▪ lower training, crew, technical costs ▪ reduced network planning complexity
Aircraft utilization	▪ Higher seat density, more seats per flight / aircraft ▪ only "Ping pong" services between two cities, thus no connection or transfer induced delays ▪ higher aircraft operating hours, due to shorter routes and minimized ground times	▪ lower unit costs ▪ higher revenue potential ▪ reduced complexity
Internationalization	▪ mainly through own bases ▪ fast decentral set-up of operations	▪ no frictions through partner negotiations in international growth
Destinations / airports	▪ secondary / tertiary airports ▪ avoidance of hub airports	▪ lower costs / charges ▪ more efficient, faster processes ▪ less delays
Sales / distribution	▪ mainly internet and call center sales ▪ refund with high charges only	▪ lower distribution costs ▪ low refund rates and costs
Service	▪ no free services, in-flight services etc. for money only ▪ special services such as lounge access at high charges only	▪ lower complexity, lower costs ▪ additional revenues
Personnel	▪ minimum headcount, high degree of flexibility through outsourcing etc. ▪ crew complement limited at safety minimum ▪ cabin crew to clean cabin	▪ lower, flexible personnel costs ▪ reduced costs for external service providers
Processes	▪ process management, continuous optimization / simplification ▪ minimization of ground times, taxi times, etc. ▪ elimination of not mandatory processes (e.g. free seating, no passenger bridges) ▪ no cargo	▪ reduced direct and indirect costs (incl. failure costs) ▪ shorter process running times

Table 7: Cost drivers and drivers of competitive advantage of low-cost carriers (Own illustration based on Lawton, 2002)

Low-cost carriers have started to adopt principles of network carriers…

Considering the entire competitive field of low-cost carriers in Europe, a growing group of actors has turned away from the 'ideal' or pure low-cost model and the consequent optimization of all cost drivers. Today, only Ryanair applies the entire set of cost levers.[18] Even the second-largest European player, easyJet, is already varying several aspects of its original success model. All other low-cost carriers proactively differentiate their product by offering selected services (e.g. seat reservation), switching their operations to larger airports or oper-

[18] Even Ryanair has now started to move away from the strict application of the 'golden rules' by entering primary airports such as Munich or by offering an increasing number of longer flights, thus reducing the number of flight legs possible per day.

ating a heterogeneous fleet, to name a few. Only the focus on larger continental aircraft types, mainly Boeing B737 or the Airbus A320 family, is still a common feature to all relevant companies.[19]

...and network carriers adopt low-cost elements

At the same time, the traditional flag carriers increasingly adapt their products to the low-cost competition. Offering services to smaller airports or introducing lower demand routes, reducing free services, focusing direct sales channels, intensifying aircraft utilization and especially fundamental adaptations of fare and tariff schemes clearly reflect this trend.

As business models converge, network becomes an increasingly important differentiator

Airline business models are increasingly converging. Now, the main differences result from the different network structures (especially the hub-and-spoke structure with its transfer focus) and higher service together with offering a two-class product for business and economy class services. Accordingly, most European airlines currently belong to a hybrid group of carriers facing quality-based competition between them, whilst at the same time trying to implement as many cost reductions as possible.

Recently, the major European network carriers have started to implement the next step towards the convergence of the business models by re-designing their own low-cost platforms. After having tried to get stronger in the market by establishing low-cost subsidiaries and having them operating in direct competition to their own continental services, airlines like Air France and Lufthansa transfer all their non-hub operations to the cost-wise improved low cost subsidiaries. This reduces the service level achievable on board in large parts of the network but keeps the airlines in a competitive position – or brings them back into this state. At the same time, hub services, predominantly being characterized by the classic continental/intercontinental set-up, are improved by investing in improved service and renewed or added service classes. Thus, the difference to the low-cost carriers is continuously being reduced in the continental segment while at the same time differentiation (and competition with new entrants from the Middle East) is intensified in the long-haul market segment.

While airline business models show strong convergence tendencies with regard to pricing and product offer, an analysis of the production structures of the most important European carriers shows that only very few adaptations had been implemented despite the fundamentally changed competition before the above described strategy changes. The basic operational patterns had remained almost unaltered. Low-cost carriers as well as network carriers kept on operating with virtually unchanged average capacities per flight as illustrated in Figure 6.

---

19 One of the very few exceptions from this approach could be seen with Debonair which applied a fleet of smaller BAe 146, offering approximately 80 seats. This fleet strategy, leading to disadvantageous unit costs, is understood as one of the reasons for Debonair's lack of success which finally led to it exiting the market.

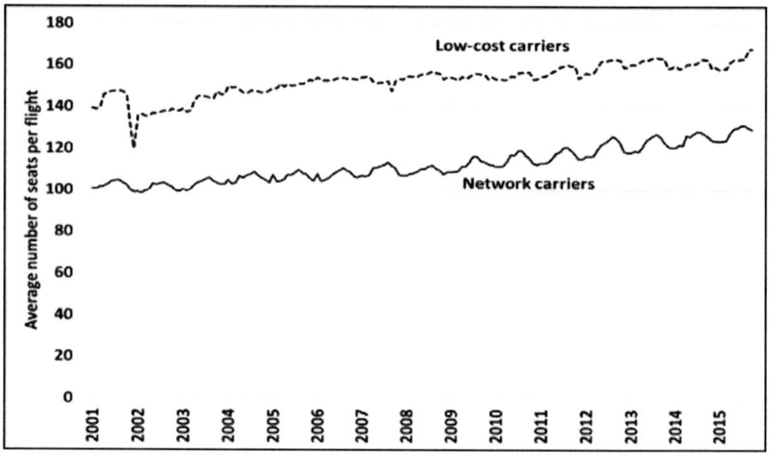

Figure 6: Average seat capacity per European continental flight (Own illustration)

Seat offer per flight

The detailed analysis of the network carrier's operations shows that Swiss had been the first to have managed to significantly increase their average seat offer per flight by replacing smaller regional aircraft with classic continental aircraft like the A320, thus gradually approaching the better cost structures low-cost carriers rely on. All other network carriers needed significantly more years to implement such a development, due to the long lead times and investment costs in fleet renewal programs.

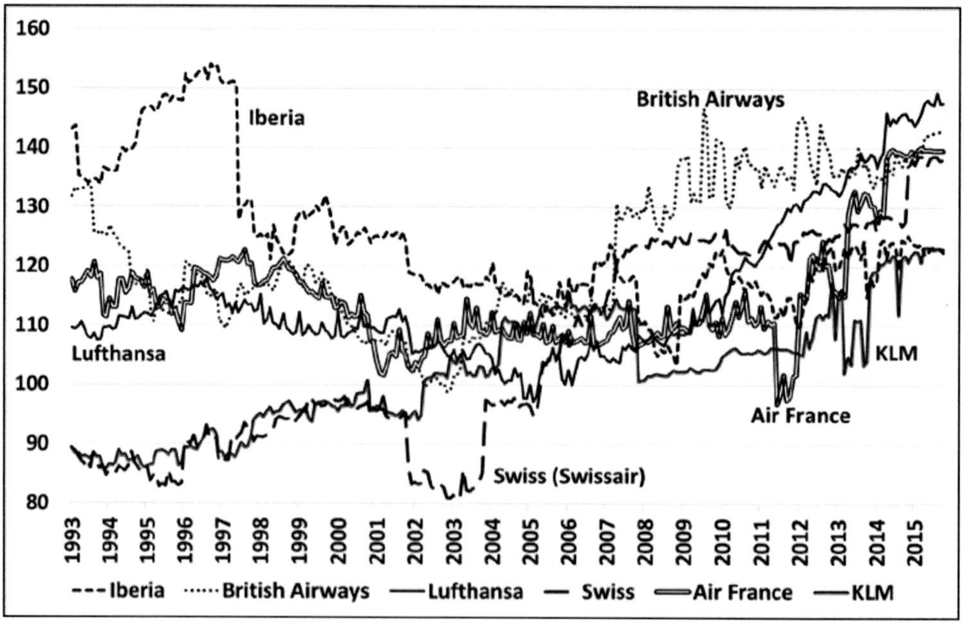

Figure 7: Average seat capacity per European continental flight for leading European network carriers (Own illustration)

Changes in airline industry also affect airports

Despite the consequences of convergence for airline business models, these developments have significant impact on airports as well. While low-cost carriers always require reliable, fast services at a no-frills level, the traditional airlines require a higher service level for their passengers, including services such as lounges or business and first class check-in. For airport operators this means that they have to provide a broad range of different services and facilities for two customer groups – which will also be paid for differently. The following table gives a brief overview of the most important airport services and infrastructure elements depending on the customer airlines' business models.

Cost driver	Traditional airlines' requirements	Low-cost carriers' requierements
Check-in	▪ Own counters, space for check-in kiosks, dedicated check-in for premium passengers (Business / First Class)	▪ Dedicated cute counters, space for check-in kiosks
Service levels	▪ High	▪ Low
Pricing	▪ Adequate prices for received services, but as cheap as possible	▪ No or low charges
Boarding bridges	▪ Yes	▪ No
Terminal layout	▪ Appropriate for serving all passenger requirements and the "air travel experience"	▪ Simple and efficient infrastructure without any frills or money consuming services
Office space	▪ In the terminal for own staff	▪ None, since no own staff present
Lounges	▪ Yes	▪ No
Business centers	▪ Yes	▪ No
Shops and restaurants	▪ Yes, for having the passengers entertained and being taken care of	▪ Yes, as compensation for the airport for lower or not-existing landing and handling charges
Terminal versus apron positions	▪ Terminal prefered	▪ Apron prefered
Turnaround time	▪ Approximately 30 minutes for continental flights	▪ 20-25 minutes
Catering services	▪ Full service	▪ No or limited service
Check-in technology	▪ Through-check-in	▪ Single flight check-in
Baggage handling system	▪ Transfer capability	▪ No special requirements, just single flight service without transit and or through-check-in luggage

Table 8: Differences in airport service requirements (Own illustration)

Taking the different service requirements and the trend of convergence together, airports are facing a challenging situation.

Airports need to segment their airline customers

Customer segmentation and differentiation have gained increasing importance. While some airlines are willing to pay for high quality terminals, facilities and services even in the future, others will increasingly put substantial pressure on airports to lower fares and charges. A growing number of airports have started to distinguish between their airline customers by setting up different facilities for their different needs. This ranges from establishing dedicated low-cost terminals at very low construction costs with only the mandatory operational services to separate premium passenger facilities with excellent services far exceeding the basic offer. While the latter concept can only work in close cooperation with a strong airline willing to pay for such a development, the low-cost approach is independent of specific airline customers. All low-cost carriers are eager to use such facilities and can be expected to positively react to such an infrastructure and product offer.

New airline business models coerce airports into reacting and adapting

On the other hand airport operators need to be ready to react to the newly arisen hybrids. These do expect adequate services, but they are not willing to pay high charges for their utilization. Thus, airport companies need to find ways to provide facilities, offering reliable, efficient, but at the same time inexpensive services. This might be reflected in optimized utilization of commercial potentials as well as inexpensive and flexible construction concepts. Such flexibility allows airport operators to switch the dedication of facilities along changing market demands. For example, passenger terminals can be built with a simple structure allowing the later removal of check-in desks and other equipment and for cargo storage or similar equipment to be built in place of the check-in desks. For higher service level terminals, such concepts could include the provision of commercial areas which could be transformed into operational areas or vice versa.

Thus, the convergence of low-cost carriers and traditional carriers requires major changes in an airport's philosophy of how to respond to market demand changes. On the other hand, it focuses the planning towards opportunities based on flexible and innovative concepts for airport development.

F. RESPONSE STRATEGIES IN THE AVIATION MARKET

F. 1 Alliances and consolidation as response to the changing market environment

Internationalization is a future trend

Besides convergence of business models another trend has turned out to be a fundamental driver for the industry and its structure during the past years: the expansion of core market domains through internationalization (Albers, Heuermann & Koch, 2008). The narrow limits of the regulative framework airline face have led to a situation in which European network carriers have started to seek new opportunities for international expansion – resulting in fundamentally different impacts on the entire market.

The first concepts of taking advantage of the new opportunities resulting from liberalization were rather limited. They allowed an offering of single air services by using new traffic rights within and between other European countries, such as a Lufthansa service on the Torino – Paris route. Since a single route only generates a limited market presence and market power while – at the same time – the established carriers build up strong competition, this approach to internationalize has proven not to be successful. The very few attempts were all discontinued after short time.

Foreign subsidiaries

A different approach to internationalization is the foundation of a subsidiary in a neighboring European country, targeted at gaining market share in the respective country and directing local passengers towards the company's own hub. The most enduring of these attempts has been the development of Deutsche BA, a British Airways subsidiary operating in Germany. Nevertheless, despite substantial investments by its parent company, the airline never became profitable and was finally sold.

Establishing of alliances

Early attempts at establishing alliances

The establishment and development of bi- and multilateral partnerships and alliances was more successful. Again, the first movers on this strategy were not able to survive in the market: the first to establish a comprehensive partnering strategy was Swissair. Realizing that the own home market – Switzerland – would be insufficient for building up and maintaining a profitable global market presence, in 1989, the airline entered into a partnership with Austrian Airlines, Finnair and SAS of Scandinavia, under the brand of European Quality Alliance, thus setting the scene for further alliance developments in the following years (Knorr & Arndt, 2003; Suen, 2002). Swissair soon expanded its partner network to an intercontinental scale by setting up the Global Excellence alliance with Delta and Singapore Airlines. During the 1990s, Swissair even took over the role as first mover in continental consolidation by driving the ALCAZAR project, targeted at deepening the international partnerships through a full merger between the Swiss carrier and its partner airlines Sabena, Austrian Airlines and the Dutch carrier KLM. Multilateral, legal and regulative complexities led to an abortion of this project.

Foundation of Star Alliance oneworld and SkyTeam

All these developments were accompanied by the privatization and near-bankruptcies of numerous European flag carriers. Following their turnaround some of these carriers, especially Lufthansa and SAS, picked-up on the idea of multilateral partnerships. The foundation of Star Alliance in May 1997 by Lufthansa, SAS, United Airlines, Thai Airways and Air Canada finally marked a turning point in the evolution of the competitive structure in international aviation. Since the establishment of these now competing alliances (oneworld from September 1999 and SkyTeam from June 2000), these three multilateral partnerships have become the driving forces in the global airline market, still growing by adding new members to their groupings and thus continuously strengthening their positions.

Cross border consolidation

At the same time, the discussion surrounding cross-border consolidation in the European airline market has never ended; however, legal constraints have prohibited relevant developments and deals. The capital-based reshaping of the market structure did not start before the merger of Air France and KLM in 2004 and the acquisition of Swiss Airlines by Lufthansa in 2005.

The competitive landscape in European aviation has thus fundamentally changed in the first decade of the 21st century. Three business models – network airlines, low-cost carriers and regional carriers – are in increasingly dynamic competition with each other, while competition between network airlines is now dominated by the three global alliances. Furthermore, consolidation has finally gained momentum and started to reshape the industry structure – not least of which spurred by the crises the new century has brought.

F. 2 Europe in the light of airline alliances

Europe is the nucleus of growth for the global airline alliances. It is here where these multilateral partnerships were founded – and here the dynamics of their development can best be observed. The following figure is a comparison of the European alliance landscapes in 2000 and 2014.

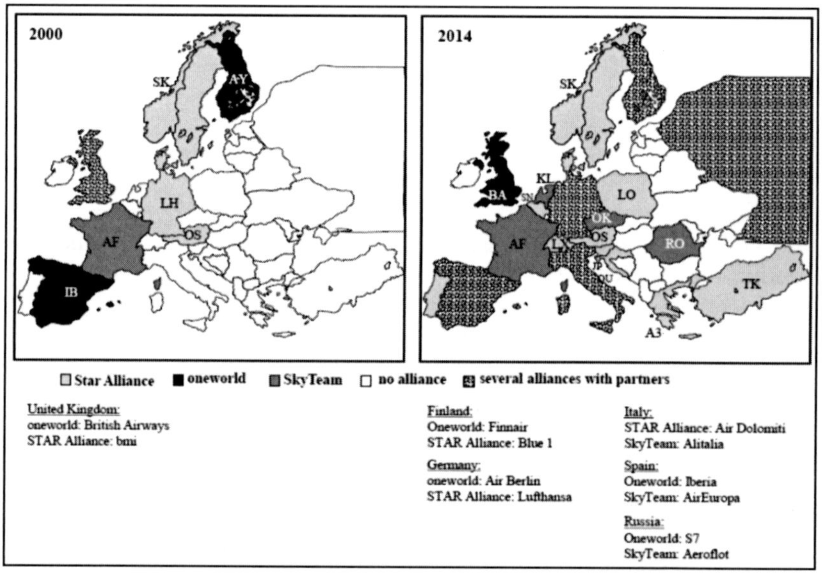

Figure 8: Alliance landscape in Europe in 2000 and 2014 (Own illustration)

Three core observations

Three core observations emerge from the analysis of the European alliance landscape. First, the blank areas marking countries with no alliance partners have been reduced significantly. Only the smaller, economically weaker and in some cases politically unstable Eastern European countries have so far not been integrated into any alliance.[20] The lack of a strong and qualitatively acceptable local airline has particularly slowed down the alliances' expansion into this region –

[20] Ireland and Iceland are the two exceptions from this rule. In the case of Iceland the extremely small home market as well as the geographic location is the reason for there being no alliance integration. Ireland is missing from the alliance landscape, since there is no traditional network carrier anymore. As original low-cost carrier, Ryanair competes strongly against the network carriers' alliances, while Aer Lingus, which used to be member of oneworld, left the alliance in 2007 after becoming a low-cost carrier as well.

despite the limited size of the respective home markets. Second, nowadays in a significant number of countries more than one alliance has been successful in finding a suitable partner of relevant size. While 15 years ago this situation was only present in Great Britain, now more and more markets show that the intense competition between the alliances has even an impact on their domestic and home markets. This development also made it increasingly difficult to secure home markets for an alliance through an exclusive position. While in 2000 this had been possible for almost all major carriers, this is not the case today anymore – not to mention the intense low-cost competition.

Success of alliances was mainly based on prohibition of cross border shareholdings

The success and the rapid expansion of the alliances are mainly based on the prohibition of international, cross-border shareholdings in the strictly regulated European airline market which has been in place for a long time. Furthermore, cooperation, as in an alliance, allows synergy potentials to be exploited while bearing low risks. Particular examples are the coordination of neighborhood traffic between the home countries of participating carriers or selling seats on the partner's flights. A challenge still to be answered is the question of how to optimize the now existing multi-hub structures. In all alliances, the combined hubs still serve basically the same traffic structures, the same target markets than before. This does give the passengers the free choice between member airlines and hubs, but a joint cost reduction and efficiency gains or the efficient combination of member carriers' networks are still rather limited. This allows other competitors like the young airlines from the Gulf region to effectively and efficiently attack the alliance carriers' positions by reducing their transfer requirements to a one-stop journey where the alliance carriers often still require two stops, due to the limited coordination between their subsystems.

Capital investments are becoming increasingly important

As already stated, the development and growth of airline alliances was accompanied by an increasing number of capital investments and tie-ups between European airlines. Besides the opportunity to secure partners for their own alliances, additional synergies could be generated, exceeding those resulting from purely contractual relations and partnerships. This includes the stronger partners' option to protect smaller partners from bankruptcy. Further consolidation developments that would exceed the achieved level of mergers are currently being intensively discussed. The map in the following figure gives a brief overview of these projects and ambitions. In this context another phenomenon is clearly visible that also determines the development and evolution of the airline alliances. The main driving forces of the developments are the three large European carriers, Air France, British Airways and Lufthansa. Due to their size and financial power, they also spur the move to consolidation on the continent. Accordingly, the comparison of the market structures in 2000 and 2014 shows that the market has been rearranged around these three carriers and their airline groups. Nevertheless, in the past five years increasingly other investors such as Etihad Airways of Abu Dhabi / United Arab Emirates and investment companies have started to invest in various carriers across the continent. Those were also the players starting to explore the formerly neglected eastern European carriers.

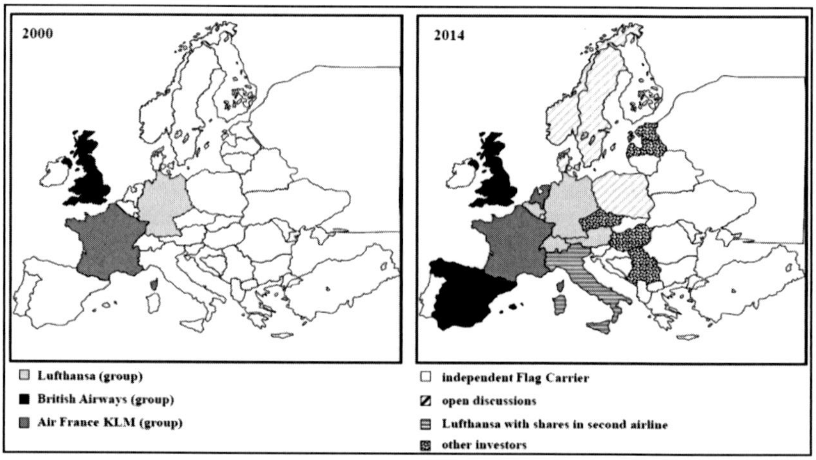

Figure 9: Airline group landscape in Europe in 2000 and 2014 [21] (Own illustration)

F. 3 Crisis as catalyst for industry consolidation

"I've never invested in any airline. I'm an airline manager. I don't invest in airlines. And I always said to the employees of American, 'this is not an appropriate investment. It's a great place to work and it's a great company that does important work. But airlines are not an investment.'"

Robert Crandall, Former CEO, American Airlines[22]

Will the crisis result in consolidation?

In the light of expected consolidation decisions and the dynamically developing alliance landscape, a better understanding of the current industry environment is necessary. Is the recent and current crisis in the aviation industry, spurred by the financial and economic crises, fostering the market consolidation and the restructuring of the competitive aviation environment in Europe?

High fix costs and volatile business are threats

A fundamental driver of consolidation is the fact, that the airline industry, as typical fixed cost intensive industry, is highly dependent on realizing economies of scale. Furthermore, airlines have always faced low profit margins – meaning that highly volatile costs and revenues are a substantial threat to the profitability and survival of particularly smaller companies. Figure 10 shows the cumulated airline results of all ICAO airlines since 1989. Despite growing passenger numbers the

---

[21] Airline groups: AF group: Air France / KLM, Alitalia; BA group: British Airways, Iberia; LH group: Lufthansa, SWISS, Air Dolomiti, Brussels Airlines, Austrian Airlines. Various other investors – financial investors as well as airlines – have taken stakes or full control of the flag or main carriers in the dotted shown countries.

[22] Quoted from Dresner (2009).

industry has not been able to continuously operate profitably. This is not only due to intense competition, but to the aforementioned crises.

Teaming up with a larger partner – especially through merger or acquisition – is often regarded as a safeguard strategy, since it guarantees higher stability and finance ability. At the same time, competitive pressure is reduced and the threat caused by a dominant competitor is at least partially resolved.

Important cost positions

While in the past crisis-related decreases in demand caused turbulence in the European airline market, in 2008 three of the most important airline cost positions gained significant importance. Kerosene, US dollar and financing costs experienced an unprecedented degree of volatility, which posed unknown challenges to all airlines (compare the following figures).

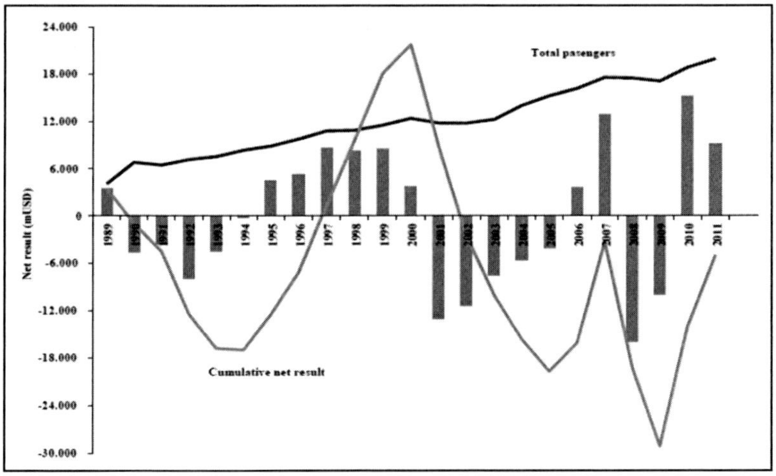

Figure 10: Airline net results and passenger number development 1989 – 2011 (Own illustration based on ICAO data)

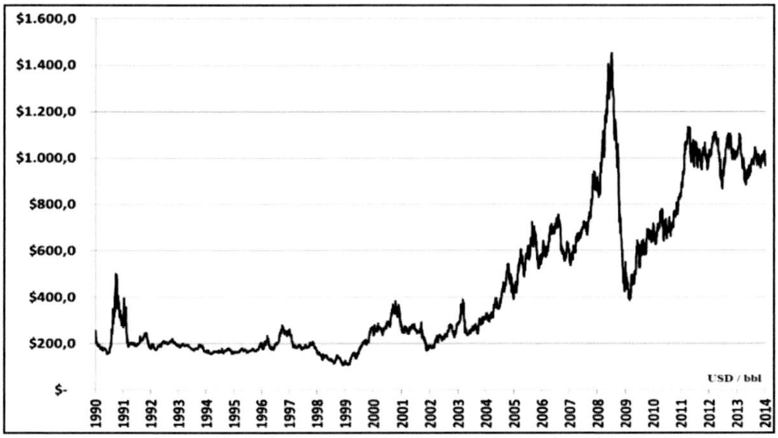

Figure 11: Development of the kerosene price since 1990 in US$ per bbl (Own illustration)

Figure 12: Development of the exchange rate euro / US$ since June 2001 (Own illustration)

80 airlines exited the market in 2008

This shown volatility has not only made planning significantly more difficult for airlines, it has also tested the business models of airlines to their limits. A direct consequence of these developments was the market exit of more than 80 airlines worldwide in 2008 alone – with the majority of the remaining airlines generating losses or at least suffering from severe profit reductions. Even though this peak has not been reached again in the following years, the market exit of airlines remains part of the daily business in the industry.

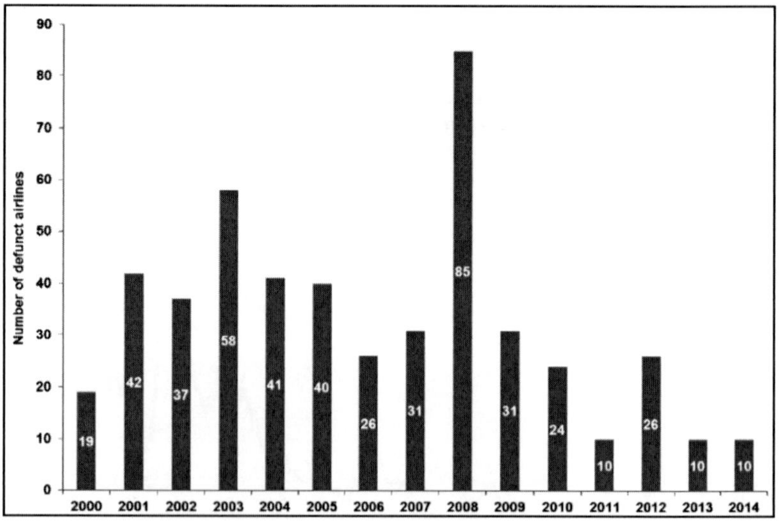

Figure 13: Number of defunct airlines since 2000 (Own illustration)

Capital access may become a future bottleneck

Capital is turning into an increasingly scarce resource and poses ever new challenges to the airlines. Capital access, access to new markets and new revenue sources, are consequently gaining increasing importance to a larger customer portfolios and a lower credit default risk. Valuable markets – markets with high demand for air travel and a high share of high value, high yield demand – are increasingly important for maintaining a competitive position. They will also increasingly become the focus of intensified competition. European airlines have to take the fundamental decision on how to secure market shares and their future development under the given circumstances. Extending influence and strength by joining forces with competitors through alliances or mergers seems to be one of the most promising options in this context.

F. 4 Potential developments to market structure in the European aviation market

Possible developments in the alliance landscape

Today's alliance and shareholding structures in Europe have grown historically. Partners were invited into partnerships or groupings based on economic opportunities or driven by political motivation; acquisitions and mergers have mainly been targeted at additional growth or securing markets. This has led to a very heterogeneous, mixed alliance landscape, with the three main groupings establishing a strong presence throughout Europe. While the target of gaining size with regard to passengers and destinations served has been widely implemented, current considerations focus increasingly on the optimization of the existing alliance constellations. This may include the selective addition of complementary members. Potential criteria for general improvements to the alliance constellation are manifold and can be based, inter alia, on complex considerations with regard to number, heterogeneity or alliance commitment of the partners (Albers, 2005; Gomes-Casseres, 2003). Complementary criteria can be identified which acknowledge the geographical market and network-based nature of the business and its alliances. These are the concepts of friction costs and areas of influence.

Incentive to establish areas of influence

Friction costs are defined as additional costs for airlines resulting from additional and specific efforts to retain extant or gain new customers due to intense competition from airlines of competing alliances in a specific geographic area. Friction costs are high if passengers can easily access alternative flight connections from competing airlines. Access to competitors' flights can be gained through the competitor's strong presence at nearby local airports, where it offers many connections to its own hub, or of course, if the competitor's hub itself can be reached easily by passengers. In areas in which passengers can choose between two airlines due to a similar quality of access, predatory competition takes place. This has a negative impact on possible profit margins for the airlines, but is of course beneficial and desirable for customers due to lower ticket prices. Airlines, however, have an incentive to generate large and closely covered geographic areas (a) in which they establish a dominant position at the airports within this area and (b) from the borders of which competitor dominated airports are hardly accessible – their areas of influence. These can be implemented through mergers and, assuming that allied airlines make use of schedule and capacity coordination as far as allowed by regulatory agencies, also through partnerships.

In the light of these considerations the European alliance landscape can be reviewed again. Taking the situation in 2000 as starting point, a scenario of a friction cost minimal alliance landscape can be derived.

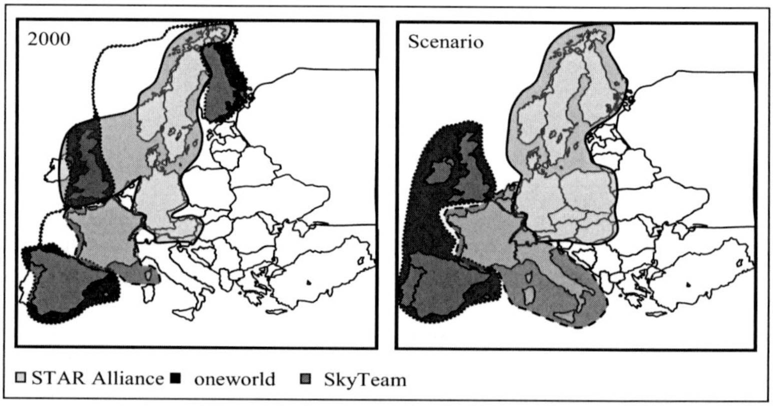

Figure 14: Alliance landscape scenario – areas of influence (Own illustration)

Scenario of future alliance landscape

Based on the three leading airlines the scenario shows three major alliance blocks, which structure the continent in a north-southern direction while avoiding overlaps. Comparing this scenario with today's situation, the weaknesses and shortcomings of the current structure appear obvious. Instead of large interconnected blocks, geographical and strategic 'islands' dominate the competitive picture and lead to a multitude of friction-intense borderlines between the alliances' current areas of influence. Especially in the highly competitive markets of the United Kingdom, Italy, and Spain this weakness is clearly visible.

All this of course does not take into account that the current alliance landscape is being attacked by the non-allied gulf carriers in a completely different way. Taking advantage of their beneficial cost structures and their network pattern connecting all served markets – be it a primary or even tertiary market – directly to the Arab main hub and connect onwards to all other linked destinations they consider entire Europe as catchment area. For them, the original home market is a neglectable size and they need to collect traffic wherever possible in order to establish or keep profitable operations. Nevertheless, while competing with this threat which is as omnipresent as are the low-cost carriers, securing a stable home market is key for the European alliance airlines.

Assumptions on future areas of influence

Based on this status quo, the way the market structure will develop in the upcoming years or which developments should be fostered has to be evaluated. In doing so, we apply the following assumptions:

- International Airline Group, being the mother company of the merged British Airways and Iberia, will continue to be successful in their currently ongoing restructuring efforts and remain a strong and promising market player. The British and Spanish markets will thus be strongly tied up with each other. With the exception of the relatively small market of Portugal, this creates a comprehensive border covering the western edge of Europe.
- The Scandinavian carrier SAS will remain a member of Star Alliance – regardless of any possible change in ownership. The north-south block of Star Alliance throughout Northern and Central Europe can thus be maintained
- Air France / KLM secure the current western to southeastern axis despite the partial take-over of Alitalia by Etihad Airways.

Pressure zone

A consequence of this constellation will be that the future alliance competition and development will take place in a 'pressure zone', covering an area throughout Eastern Europe, ranging from Macedonia and Albania in the south up to Finland and the Baltic in the north. Some of the recent investment development have proven that this is one of the newly interesting areas of the continent, with examples like the investment of Etihad into Air Serbia.

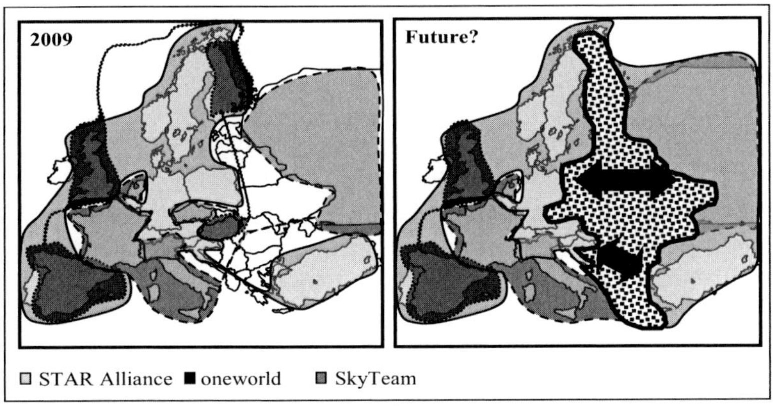

Figure 15: Scenario of future alliance landscape in Europe (Own illustration)

It can hence be expected that over the upcoming years the alliances will attempt to widen their respective areas of influence by expanding geographically. This development will only be slowed by the fact that there are no strong local airlines in the currently underserved countries or that the existing airlines now belong to non-European investors, making it difficult to identify acceptable or available partners in the respective countries or regions.

Star Alliance and SkyTeam are the likely competitors in the pressure zone

Based on the current structure it can be expected that competition in this pressure zone will mainly occur between Star Alliance and SkyTeam. Aside from the British-Spanish axis, oneworld is too weakly represented to play a stronger role in the competition for partners. A direct, geographic link between the alliance's core markets Great Britain and Spain and the partners' home markets of Finland and Hungary does not exist.

Situation in Finland

In Finland, Star Alliance is already represented by Blue 1 and is able to exert significant competitive pressure through the Scandinavian partner SAS, while SkyTeam has a strong presence in Eastern Finland through the Russian partner Aeroflot. Thus, for both alliances expanding their own market presence is an attractive option, which makes it rather probable that competition to attract Finnair away from oneworld into one of the two other groupings will take place. Independent of the Finnish carrier's decision for either alliance, it would become part of a significantly larger and stronger system, offering sound advantages for both the new alliance as well as the airline itself.

Possible investors for LOT and SAS

For Star Alliance, even a contraction of its area of influence is currently conceivable since several of its members are at risk. its Polish member is at risk. Carriers like LOT Polish Airlines and SAS keep on marketing themselves to investors in order to strengthen their own positions. In both cases, the economic and financial conditions make it unclear whether the carriers will be able to survive on its own. At the same time, the intense low-cost competition by carriers such as WIZZair or Norwegian, has shed a dark light on the carriers' perspectives. Even though the German partner Lufthansa is often seen as the preferred investor, Air France / KLM and SkyTeam would be able to significantly strengthen their market presence in Eastern Europe. Nevertheless, both scenarios do not currently seem to be very realistic, given the continuously worsening economic framework.

These examples show that a core characteristic of the previously mentioned pressure zone is the strong presence of SkyTeam both in the western end eastern parts of Central Europe. Star Alliance will have to face the challenge of strengthening and securing its current market position in the upcoming years – be it through further consolidation of grouping members or through adding additional, smaller partners. Otherwise, Star Alliance might soon find itself surrounded by SkyTeam and its members.

From the current viewpoint, future competition in the European airline industry is facing a very diverse situation. After several years in which oneworld appeared to be weaker than the other alliances, all three have established their strongholds and STAR Alliance even appears to be the one with the largest risk of losing valuable partners and markets. At the same time, low cost competitors were successful in forcing all major carriers into complete changes of their business models and will continue to do so. With Norwegian Airlines, who have recently started to even offer long-haul flights, and the Arab carriers competition will also remain to get stronger in the field of intercontinental services. To achieve a new balance in the home markets, changes in the current partnership structures and the ways of operating the alliance systems will have to emerge.

Considering the friction cost criteria, even after the developments and adjustments sketched in the scenario above, an optimal distribution or balance cannot be achieved in the market anymore. A certain degree of friction will remain and keep on determining the competitive structure. The attractive markets of Italy and Spain in particular will also see several alliances with local partners competing for the regions' demand in the future.

F. 5 Consequences for the future of airlines in Europe

In the light of the current consolidation in Europe and the dynamic evolution of the alliance landscape, several implications for the future market and competitive structure can be derived.

Large airlines become even larger

Deregulation and liberalization have opened the path to turn growth through alliances into growth through consolidation. Thus, increasingly larger, multinational airlines emerge, with Air France KLM Group, Lufthansa and British Airways dominating this development. Smaller companies will keep their chances in the new market structure only if they team up with the leading alliances or if they are successful in securing small but profitable market niches for themselves. Midsize airlines will be unable to withstand growing competition and will finally leave the market if they are not engaged by foreign carriers as bridgehead into Europe or as feeder partner for their own hubs. Both those strategies do go along with a far-reaching loss of independence.

Challenges in managing airlines will increase

Consolidation does not integrate airlines, but rather brings together companies with different corporate cultures, different home and target markets and a large variety of legal and political frameworks. The challenge of managing these airlines or airline groups will increasingly be the management of these differences and achieving their harmonization. Only this will allow optimal results and the avoidance of internal cannibalization to be achieved.

Realization of synergies will be the predominant success factor of the new airline groups

Size alone does not deliver competitive strength. Future success factors mainly comprise the ability to reduce the joint cost basis, realize and take advantage of group-wide synergy potentials – e.g. in the fields of administration and procurement – and to maximize revenue synergies. In this context it has yet to be proven how the integration of a group of airlines can be achieved in a way that the consequent rising costs of complexity and redundancy do not erode the synergies gained.

Considering these developments the European airline landscape will fundamentally change over the next years. New concepts for managing the emerging airline groupings have to be developed, and a new capability for leading and sustaining in an unstable environment has to be achieved. The current crisis environment has been catalyst for this development and the industry is likely to remain highly dynamic.

Review Questions

- What are the most important development steps in global aviation in terms of the legislative and regulative framework?
- What are the characterizing elements of an airline business model?
- Which competitive advantages and measures contribute to the success of low-cost carriers compared to network carriers?
- What does the term convergence mean and what is its relevance for today's airline business?
- What major developments are currently driving European aviation the most?
- What impacts can be expected from the current ongoing consolidation in the European airline market?
- What major challenges for airline management result from the shifts in the European airline landscape?

Bibliography and further reading

Albers, S. (2005): The Design of Alliance Governance Systems, Cologne.

Albers, S. / Heuermann, C. / Koch, B. (2008): International Market Entry Strategies of EU and Asia-Pacific Low Fare Airlines. Conference Paper, ATRS World Conference 2008, Athens.

Doganis, R. (2003): Flying off course – The economics of international airlines. 3rd ed., London / New York.

Dresner, M. (2009): Long term challenges for financial stability. Presentation to the 12th Hamburg Aviation Conference, Hamburg.

Gomes-Casseres, B. (2003): Competitive Advantage in Alliance Constellations, in: Strategic Organization, Vol. 1, No. 3, p. 327-335.

International Civil Aviation Organization [ICAO] (2009): Freedoms of the Air, http://www.icao.int/icao/en/trivia/freedoms_air.htm, retrieved: 18/08/2009.

International Civil Aviation Organization [ICAO] (1944): Convention on International Civil Aviation (Chicago Convention). Signed at Chicago on December 7th, 1944, Chicago.

Knorr, A. / Arndt, A. (2003): Swissair's Collapse – An Economic Analysis. Institute for World Economics and International Management, University of Bremen, Bremen.

Koch, B. (2006): Entwicklungsplanung für Flughafengesellschaften. Entscheidungsunterstützung durch die integrierte Marktprognose- und Finanzmodellierung, Cologne.

Kraus, A. / Koch, B. (2005): The Opportunities and Threats of Turning Airports into Hubs, in: Journal of Air Transportation, Vol. 11, No. 2, p. 87 – 112.

Lawton, T. C. (2002): Cleared for Take-Off. Structure and Strategy in the Low Fare Airline Business, Burlington.

Porter, M. (1996): What is Strategy?, in: Harvard Business Review, Vol. 74, No. 6, p. 61 – 78.

Ring, P. S. / van de Ven, A. H. (1994): Development Processes of Cooperative Interorganizational Relationships, in: Academy of Management Review, Vol. 19, No. 1, p. 90-118.

Suen, W. W. (2002): Alliance Strategy and the Fall of Swissair, in: Journal of Air Transport Management, Vol. 8, No. 5, p. 355-363.

Cooperation and Alliances – Opportunity for Growth

Jörg Hennemann, Peter Malanik

Table of contents

You should be able to

- explain why airlines have an inherent need for growth
- explain the basic growth options for airlines
- summarize and give a brief description of the basic forms of airline cooperation
- summarize the enhanced forms of cooperation
- describe the benefit and risk sharing models
- explain an open skies agreement

The authors

Jörg Hennemann is the Vice President Revenue Management and Distribution of Lufthansa, Frankfurt, Germany.

Dr. Peter Malanik is a former member of the executive board and Co-CEO of Austrian Airlines AG, Vienna, Austria. He lectures on aviation management at the University of Economics, Vienna and is CEO of an international executive search company.

Abstract

A recent trend in the airline industry is the emergence of cooperation amongst airlines. The aviation industry exists in an intensely competitive market which is limited by regulatory and infrastructural constraints, drawn by marginal and very cyclical profitability in conjunction with high capital expenditure. But also in fully liberalized aviation markets, airlines are likely to enter cooperation agreements to expand their network, without undertaking sizeable investment. This chapter outlines the forms of cooperation amongst airlines, reflects on the possible tools and highlights another component of airline management tools also discussed in the other chapters in this volume.[1]

A. INTRODUCTION

To a significant degree the growth of an industry depends on its specific circumstances. In the airline industry these circumstances are truly unique.

Airlines need to grow but are often limited

Over the last decades, the global market has shown increasing demand for air travel and cargo, and therefore general growth in the airline business. Airlines inherently, one might even say desperately, seek growth. But restrictions, be they legal or infrastructural, are common.

In the airline industry cooperation are used widely to foster growth

While autonomous growth has its limitations and mergers have been ruled out for legal reasons, cooperation were the only feasible way for global growth for a long time. The industry has so far been very creative in designing cooperation or one could say 'workarounds' with regard to the industry's limitations. Forms of cooperation therefore vary from bilateral, simple agreements to highly sophisticated, multilateral models.

This paper focuses on cooperation as an option for growth in the airline industry. We will briefly touch an airlines' inherent needs for growth, be it due to the global demand or the economic incentive. Furthermore, it is essential to understand the legal and governmental circumstances in which cooperation in aviation industry is set up. Additionally, we will show how growth and cooperation is limited by regulation and competition laws. Central to this chapter is an extensive overview of the various forms of cooperation, from simple interlining to mature multilateral arrangements such as Star Alliance.

What does the future hold? We are confident, this industry may become a 'normal' industry one day with barriers of entry that leave room for newcomers, but also barriers of exit and merger activities as postholders of market efficiency. We also believe that despite this 'normalization' many forms of cooperation dealt with in this paper will prevail as possibilities for growth in the airline industry.

[1] We would like to express our gratitude to Mag. Marco Nussbaumer, whose outstanding work and personal dedication has provided the main reason behind this contribution.

B. COOPERATION OF AIRLINES: AN OPPORTUNITY FOR GROWTH

B. 1 The airlines' inherent need for growth

B. 1. 1 The market view: business is global

"The world is flat" (Friedmann, 2008). For every tangible good there is a tendency to organize the production chain on a global scale, without losing sight of the reasonability and feasibility of the local business perspective. Friedman (2008) indicates that production processes are replaceable and that coordination experts (managers) are needed more than ever. Global coordination processes and the need to coordinate global change management will grow over-proportionally.

Good news for the airline industry. These developments have been and will be major catalysts in air travel demand. Following this path, private travelling is continuously changing and making maximum usage of global and flexible travel options.

Customers demand a global network. To meet this expectation, airlines enter cooperation

While the demand for air travel has become truly global, individual airlines, for various reasons, have only been able to reap limited rewards of it (see below). To defend their position, these airlines need to meet customers' demand for a global network. Given the current limitations on mergers, what could be more obvious than utilizing another airline's network and customer base? Cooperation therefore is a way for airlines to access global traffic streams.[2] A large number of airlines have entered into such cooperation, ranging from marketing agreements and code-shares to alliances and mergers (Kleymann, 2005).

B. 1. 2 The economics

Network costs can be reduced by bundling traffic flows

Network costs are driven by economies of scale, economies of density, economies of scope, and route length. These factors establish the benefits of traffic consolidation. Otherwise, "if there were no cost advantages of consolidating traffic flows, every single passenger would get his own personal flight" (Wojahn, 2001).

Economies of scale (EoS) are defined as:

---

2 According to Oum, Park & Zhang (2000) cooperation allows (1) expansion of seamless service networks (i.e. avoid changing airline); (2) traffic feed between partners; (3) cost efficiency through economies of scale, economies of scope, and traffic density (see chapter B. 1. 2); (4) increased service quality; (5) marketing advantages (pooling of frequent flyer programs).

$$EoS = \frac{Mc}{Ac} \qquad Ac = \frac{Tc}{Q}$$

With:
Mc = marginal costs
Ac = average costs
Tc = total costs
Q = quantity

They tend to occur in industries with high capital costs in which those costs can be distributed across a large number of units of production. Economies of scale are the benefits, in the form of lower unit costs, derived from an increase in capacity utilization, where unit costs come down because fixed costs can be spread over a larger number of units produced. Consequently a doubling of the output requires less than a doubling of the costs. As such we might also think economies of scale as being economies of density on a network level.

Economies of density

Economies of density[3] are defined as the ratio of average cost and marginal cost. Economies of density can also be described as the reciprocal value of Economies of scale. Economies of density arise as a consequence of increasing traffic volume. Hence the seat load factor rises and therefore results in a fixed cost digression. Larger and more efficient aircraft can be deployed on routes with a higher traffic volume, bringing an increase in aircraft utilization with it. Simply meaning economies of density may be interpreted as economies of scale on a single route.

Economies of scope

The concept of economies of scope states that the joint output of two firms is greater than the outputs separately achieved by these firms. In other words, output from a joint production decreases the total cost, while a separate production increases it. The degree of economies of scope (SC) is defined as:

Formula 3: $$SC = \frac{(C(q_1) + C(q_2) + C(q_1 + q_2))}{C(q_1 + q_2)}$$

With
C(q) = cost function for the output q

Thus, a large network is likely to exhibit larger economies of scope and the choice of networks is likely to be important. A firm is likely to enjoy production or cost advantages when it produces two or more products. The advantages result from (Pindyck & Rubinfeld, 2005):

- Joint use of inputs or production facilities
- Joint marketing programs
- Cost savings due to common administration

The following figure shows two product transformation curves:

---

[3] Note: for empirical evidence on the existence of economies of density, see for example Brueckner, Dryer & Spiller (1992) or Caves, Christensen & Tretheway (1984).

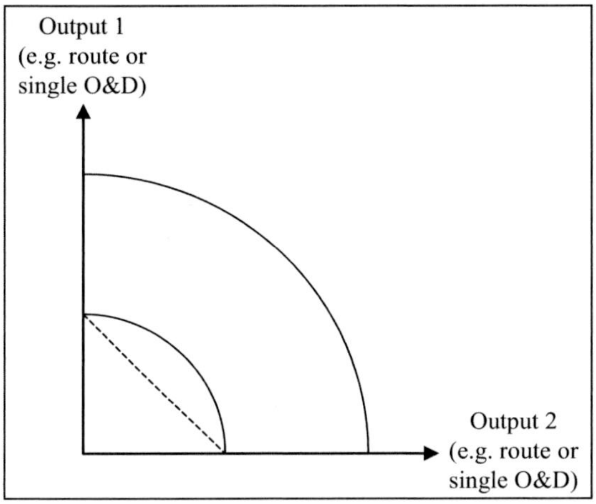

Figure 1: Product transformation curve (Pindyck & Rubinfeld, 2005, p. 240)

Each curve describes the various combinations of two outputs in adherence with the given input. The top curve shows us the output with double the input of the bottom curve. Both curves are concave due to the fact that joint production usually has advantages. They enable a company to produce more output 1 and 2 with the same amount of resources which two companies would need, each producing a separate product. A straight line, on the other hand, would mean that a joint production would entail no gains or losses.

Route length

Lastly, route length directly affects the aircraft unit cost. It decreases as the route length increases, since the fixed costs related to the flights are spread over a larger output and the variable costs do not increase proportionally with distance, rather they show a declining growth rate.

As a consequence of the effects described above, airlines, burdened with high fixed costs, tend to constantly make cheap seats available on the market transforming idle time costs into used capacity costs to reach economies of scale. Of course, there is a point beyond where these positive effects will disappear or even become negative. Airlines may become inflexible and unwieldy if they exceed a certain size. Capital-intensive and high-volume production using 'dedicated' equipment[4] cannot easily be adapted to changes in market demand and product characteristics, which may imply under-utilization or even obsolescence. Large-scale production may offset the original benefits when it comes to economic crisis. Additionally, aircraft delivery reached an all time high when the demand was already decreasing. We identified this as being one of the major drivers causing the repetition of a vicious circle in the industry. Airlines then try to sell the additional capacity at low prices and the above-mentioned cycle repeats itself again.

4 For example an A320 with 150 seats operating constant routes with about 80 passengers on board.

B. 2 Growth and cooperation limitations: international air transport regulations

B. 2. 1 Regulatory issues

The Chicago Convention of 1944 tried to set up a regulatory framework for air transport including the "freedoms of the air"

The basic framework established during the Chicago Convention of 1944, highly regulated the international air transport market. The emergence of Bilateral Air Transport Agreements added further regulation to this market. The principle of air sovereignty is repeated and endorsed from customary law to Article 1 of the Chicago Convention of 1944.[5] Article 6 of the Chicago Convention requires all carriers flying over or into a country, to apply for special permission from that specific country.[6] Article 6 is deemed a monument to the 1944 Chicago Conference's 'failure' to reach a consensus on air transport matters in general and specifically the granting of traffic rights through multilateral exchange (Matte, 1981). This article enshrines the bilateral system of the exchange of traffic rights to a greater extent than its counterpart, Article 1. At the same time the International Air Transport Agreement, also known as First Freedoms Agreement was drawn up. Included in scheduled air transportation are eight 'freedoms of the air'. The first five were established during the Chicago Conference, while the original list was complemented by international air transport law with three new categories (Zylicz, 1992). To summarize, the multilateral International Air Transport Agreement grants greater freedom of movement (International Air Transport Agreement, 1944). In adherence with this agreement, states grant each other five categories of traffic rights:[7]

- **First Freedom**: The right to fly over another country without landing.
- **Second Freedom**: the right to land, due to technical reasons (e.g. refueling) in another country without picking up/setting down passengers.
- **Third Freedom**: the right to carry revenue traffic from your own country (A) to the country (B) of your treaty partner.
- **Fourth Freedom**: The right to carry traffic from country B back to your own country A.
- **Fifth Freedom**: the right of an airline from country A to carry revenue traffic between country B and other countries such as C or D on services starting or ending in its home country A (This

---

5 Article 1: "The contracting States recognize that every State has complete and exclusive sovereignty over the airspace above its territory".

6 Article 6: "No scheduled international air service may be operated over or into the territory of a contracting state except with the special permission or authorization of that state".

7 For further Information regarding the eight freedoms see Groenwege (1998), p. 47-48.

freedom cannot be taken advantage of unless countries C or D also agree).[8]

Only few states signed one of the multilateral agreements concerning air transportation. Thus bilateral agreements gained importance

Only few parties signed the first five freedoms of the Agreement in 1944. Therefore the five commercial rights did not gain universal recognition. Another multilateral agreement, the International Air Service Transit Agreement (1944), was drawn up at the same time. Ultimately, of the five proposed Freedoms, the majority of states attending the Chicago Conference only adopted the first two. From that point on, bilateral systems have been comprised of the same freedoms set out in the bilateral Air Service Agreements. Certain traffic rights were granted to various airlines from every country. Generally, the Third and Fourth Freedom Rights are present in almost all bilateral Air Service Agreements. In an increasing number of agreements the Fifth Freedom is currently undergoing changes. The majority of scheduled air services are presently regulated accordingly.

None of the states have officially recognized the Freedoms mentioned above. The Sixth, Seventh and Eighth Freedoms receive more attention than the original five:[9]

- **Sixth Freedom** states the use by an airline, operating from country A to carry traffic between two other countries using its base A as a transit point.
- **Seventh Freedom** states the right of an airline to operate revenue traffic between points, both lying outside its own home base country.
- **Eighth Freedom** states the right of an airline to pick up and set down passengers or freight between two domestic points in another county on a service originating in its own home country.

Due to the lack of consent at the Chicago Convention, the commercial regulation of international aviation was left to the bilateral interests of individual states. The word 'commercial' should be stressed in as much as, at Chicago, there was no doubt that the air would not be free in the political sense. Since then, states have used bilateral agreements to exchange 'commercial' traffic rights with other states.

B. 2. 2 Bilateral air service agreement (treaty)

Before an airline can operate international services to and from another country, the government must first negotiate a treaty level agreement with the destination country's government. The first major

---

[8] Article 5 offers some leeway in that it allows freedom for non-scheduled flights; it offers no freedom in which scheduled flights can be conducted (Weber & Dinwoodie, 2000).

[9] The Sixth Freedom Right is rarely dealt with explicitly in air services agreements but may be referred to implicitly in memoranda of understanding attached to the agreement. In the application of many bilateral agreements there is also de facto acceptance of such rights. The Seventh and Eighth Freedom rights are granted only in very rare cases.

agreements, Bermuda 1[10] and Bermuda 2[11] were negotiated and agreed upon in 1946 between the United States and the United Kingdom. These treaties, known as bilateral air services, are based on the 'Freedoms of the Air'. Bilateral air service agreements contain the following regulations:

Regulations that are typically found in bilateral agreements

- **Traffic rights**: the routes airlines may fly, including cities that can be served within, between and beyond the bilateral partners.
- **Capacity**: the number of flights that may be operated or number of passengers that may be carried between the bilateral partners.
- **Designation, Ownership and Control**: the number of airlines the bilateral partners may nominate to operate services and the ownership criteria airlines must meet to be designated under the bilateral agreement.[12]
- **Tariffs**: a number of agreements require airlines to submit ticket prices to aeronautical authorities for approval.
- **Freedom of air rights**: these freedoms continue to shape the foundation of rights exchanged in air services. Governments perpetually negotiate new treaties to allow international aviation to grow and expand their carriers' access to new and emerging markets.

Bilateral agreements are always streamlined to the participating countries situations

There is no existing prototype of a Bilateral Air Service Agreement and no two agreements are exactly alike. Each agreement reflects the level of development each country's aviation industry and aviation policy has gone through. Presently, air traffic rights are negotiated by states bilaterally and in some cases multilaterally,[13] with an attempt, by some, to introduce an 'Open Skies' policy. Through the free exchange of air traffic rights between the carriers of consenting states, this policy allows the market to determine prices, routes, and scheduling.

B. 2. 3 Open Skies agreement

An Open Skies agreement allows an airline to enjoy unrestricted traffic rights between any point in the country of origin and any other point within the boundaries of the participating country. It ensures more liberalization in the bilateral agreements than the pre-negotiated

[10] Agreement between the United Kingdom and the United States, 1946.

[11] Agreement Between the Government of the Kingdom of Great Britain and Northern Ireland and the Government of the United States of America Concerning Air Services, 1977.

[12] The substantial ownership and effective control clause states: "A signatory state has the right, to reject the designation of an airline by the other contracting party, if it is not convinced, that the designated airline is substantially owned and effectively controlled by the designating state".

[13] In November 2000, the United States, New Zealand, Singapore, Brunei and Chile concluded the Multilateral Agreement on the Liberalization of International Air Transportation to replace the bilateral agreements between them. The Multilateral Agreement was signed on May 1st, 2001 in Washington, DC. Peru and Samoa have also acceded to the agreement.

routing rights do. The first Open Sky Agreement was signed between the USA and the Netherlands. In recent years the most significant Open Skies Agreement was signed between the USA and the EU. It covers civil aviation between two of the world's biggest markets.

B. 3 Market access, deregulation and liberalization

B. 3. 1 European Union – liberalization of air transport

Situation of airline industry in Europe before liberalization process started

Prior to the liberalization process of European air transport, between 1987 and 1997, the industry was highly regulated and inflexible, having no factual competition between national carriers and fares set through bilateral agreements between states (Brueckner, 2001). A mesh of bilateral air service agreements formed the industry with specified routes, aircraft types, fares and frequencies. In effect, capacity on the majority of routes was artificially restricted, fares were pushed aggressively high, and entry into markets by non-flag carrier airlines was virtually impossible. Various European regions were excluded from agreed route networks due to decisions taken at a national level. They had no possibility of attracting air services and had to rely on connecting services through the emerging network hubs of the flag carriers. The liberalization of European air transport was achieved in three stages:

Liberalization was achieved in three stages

The First Liberalization Package was implemented on 1 January 1988. It allowed scheduled intra-EC air services to cover multiple designations, Fifth Freedom rights, the automatic approval of discount fares, and other such measures towards free market access. It also introduced new competition rules and applied the antitrust rules of the EEC Treaty to EC air transport (EEC Council Regulation, 1987 / 1987a / 1987b). However, this First Package only had "negligible effects on competition in the European Community, resulting in slight reductions in air fares" (Warner, 1993).

The Second Package aimed to expand the liberalization granted in the first one. It came into effect in 1990 and applied a double disapproval rule to full fares.[14] The EC took further steps towards an integrated aviation market (EEC Council Regulation, 1990a / 1990b) by implementing the Third Package, which was the most important of the three. It was implemented on 1 January 1993 and ended on 1 April 1997, "effectively creating a single EC airline market" (Warner, 1993) by lifting pricing restrictions on all fares, abandoning the distinctions between chartered and scheduled carriers, and allowing full access to all routes, including cabotage ones (EEC Council Regulation, 1992). In this way, a single aviation market was created although the EU retained the right to intervene over fares, predatory pricing, and dumping pricing. The EU has been successful in reaching a multilateral open skies environment in air transport.

[14] 'Double disapproval rule' means proposed fares would take effect unless both countries disapproved.

The removal of restrictions on market entry, capacity, frequency and pricing resulted in greater emphasis being placed on the use of normal competition law, to watch out for anti-competitive behavior and abuse of market power. In fact, rules had already been adopted in 1987, which gave the European Commission the power to apply the competition rules of the EU Treaty[15] to air transport services within the EU and to adopt certain group exemptions. The Commission also has exclusive authority to assess competition issues raised by a transaction that falls within the scope of the EU Merger Regulation.

Specific block exemptions, concerning certain categories of agreement in the air transport sector, were adopted and, while some have since been removed, those relating to consultation on passenger tariffs on intra-EU scheduled air services and slot allocation at EU airports, remain in force (Adkins, 1994, p. 10). The effect of these block exemptions has been that operators have not needed to apply to the Commission for an individual exemption each time they are involved in these practices.

State aid to airline industry is limited by a strict EU policy

Early in the liberalization process the Commission adopted a strict policy to apply the EU Treaty's provisions on state aid to the airline industry and, in particular, attached a clear 'one time, last time' condition to any state aid that it approved. In its communication the Commission has left little doubt that a second cash injection, by a government, not in accordance with the 'market economy investor principle' will only be considered in the most exceptional of circumstances and in light of unforeseeable events external to the company (Adkins, 1994, p. 146ff).

B. 3. 2 Deregulation of the North American industry

Since 1938 the Civil Aeronautics Board (CAB) regulated many areas in United States commercial aviation, such as route fares and schedules. The main functions of the CAB was awarding routes to airlines, limiting the entry of air carriers into new markets and regulating fares for passengers (Meyer, Oster & Strong, 1987, p. 9). The Airline Deregulation Act of 1978[16] removed many of these regulations. This changed the face of commercial aviation in the United States. The Act liberalized standards for the establishment of new airlines and gave airlines the freedom to set their own fares and fly whatever domestic routes they chose. The Act also gradually transferred remaining regulatory authority to the US Department of Transportation (DOT) and dissolved the CAB.

---

15 Article 81 prohibits agreements between firms which avoid, restrict or distort competition unless those agreements can be shown to promote technical or economic progress and that consumers enjoy a fair share of the resultant benefits. Article 82 prohibits the abuse of a dominant position.

16 For further details regarding the Airline Deregulation Act of 1978 see Dempsey & Goetz (1998), p. 193ff.

B. 4 Growth options for airlines

Having clarified why airlines seek to grow and what important limitations may keep them from doing this, we now need to categorize how airlines may grow.

There are three growth options for airlines:

- Autonomous growth
- Mergers & acquisitions
- Cooperation

Autonomous growth

The strategy of autonomous growth may imply an organic growth, a start-up or a spin-off of a company. In this context it is necessary to define a differentiated strategy, with the focus on the low-price market segment or the high-quality segment. However, autonomous growth is limited by financial capabilities, management resources, cultural capabilities and infrastructure.

Infrastructural limitations exist both in the air…

Air traffic control systems are the main infrastructural limitations in the air. Whereas there is just one Air Traffic Control System for the whole of the United States, there are 47 (civil and military) Air Traffic Control Systems in Europe. This means that control over the European air space is fragmented into 47 parts. Let us take the route from Brussels to Rome for instance; airplanes have to pass nine control zones. Furthermore, they have to fly around several military zones. The enormous registration effort for each zone and the longer routes result in higher kerosene consumption, thus higher air pollution and higher costs for airlines.

… and on the ground

Airport infrastructure is the limiting factor on the ground. Especially, when hubs have reached the limit of their capacity and sometimes require decades to expand. Moreover, not every location is able to expand. A further factor in infrastructural limitation is personnel shortage, e.g. ground staff or qualified cockpit staff. In addition to these infrastructural limitations, access to slots is problematic. The selective allotment of traffic rights hinders the organic development and growth of airlines.

Merger and acquisition

The strategy of merger and acquisitions aims for the extension of flight routes, optimization of transfer times, consolidation of cost items, increase in market power and purchase of traffic rights (Oum & Zhang, 2001). Firstly, we have a cost rationalization resulting from economies of scale (Brueckner & Spiller, 1991) as a direct benefit of a merger, which concerns sales costs, airport operation costs or maintenance costs. Secondly, redundant routes can be eliminated as a consequence of asset utilization. Thirdly, an airline's competitive position can be improved because of the increasing potential for growth and therefore greater negotiation power.

In fact merger activities do not always have successful perspectives (Button, 1997). Firstly, majority participations from foreign airlines in domestic airlines are often prohibited. Secondly, a merger would extend a market dominating position and therefore there is little chance that they would be permitted in terms of competition policy and competition laws. The roadblock for international mergers and acquisitions is the substantial ownership and effective control clause: "A signatory state has the right, to reject the designation of an airline through the other contracting party, if it is not convinced, that the designated airline is under substantial ownership and effective control of the designating state."[17]

Cooperation

Another growth possibility for airlines – the emphasis of this chapter - is to cooperate with other airlines. In contrast to mergers, cooperation means involved partners remain legally and economically autonomous (Blohm, 1980, p. 1112). After the deregulation of air transport, cooperation became a popular and wide spread strategy for growth. Alliances aim at enlargement of the business spectrum in terms of offered network portfolio and thus market penetration. (Albers, 2000) Qualitative improvement of the core product also achieves a higher degree of brand awareness and a better image. Partner airlines profit mutually from the positive market image of other airlines and thus show an intensified presence in non-domestic markets. Cooperation implicates internal synergy advantages and cost savings because economies of scale and economies of scope can be realized. Additionally, learning effects and competence development accompany cooperation and the share of risk is distributed among all partners.

C. COOPERATION AMONG AIRLINES: THE TOOLBOX

Cooperation is among the most important forms of growth for airlines

The airline industry has traditionally been shaped by a high degree of regulation, not only on the technical, but also on the economic side. On international routes, airlines primarily operate within a very rigid framework set by air services agreements. These are inter-governmental agreements concerning traffic rights between two countries. Air traffic regulation stems from the Paris Convention of 1919, culminating in open sky agreements. The deregulation of the airline industry was an attempt to drive the industry towards the perceived ideal of perfect competition with its supposed benefits of pricing related to costs, optimal output and the disappearance of inefficient producers. However, even after the deregulation of air transport in the US, the European Union and other parts of the world, markets in a global sense are still on the whole far from contestable. Therefore, global cooperation continues to be an important form of growth for airlines. In the following we will discuss the possibilities of cooperation within the airline industry.

---

[17] According to International Air Law and ICAO.

C. 1 Basic forms of cooperation

C. 1. 1 Interlining

Interlining refers to an agreement between individual airlines to handle passengers travelling with itineraries that require multiple airlines.[18] These agreements are basically concluded under the auspices of IATA. They are usually specific to a reservation on the global distribution system (GDS). Interlining agreements differ from code sharing agreements that usually refer to numbering a flight with the airline's prefix even though the flight is operated by another airline.[19] Interlining makes complex routings purchasable at a single point of sale, in a single currency and enlarges the flight options for passengers.

Interlining is used on O&Ds that require distinct airlines

C. 1. 2 Special prorating

Special Prorate Agreements regulate the revenue distribution of fares to one or more carriers involved in the routing.[20] Revenues can be increased by Special Prorate - offering joint fares and establishing competitive tariffs and prices to increase revenues. Furthermore, additional sales can be generated through the special prorate partner.[21]

C. 1. 3 Blocked seat agreements

With a blocked seat agreement (BSA) the marketing partner buys seats on the operating partners' flight and sells them under its own code from a separate inventory (Holloway, 2008, p. 415). With a Hard Block Agreement the marketing carrier bears the whole risk and purchases a fixed number of seats from the operating carrier and sells them under its own code. With a soft block agreement the marketing carrier purchases seats form the operating carrier and sells these under its own code. Unsold seats can be resold under special conditions; therefore the risk is shared between the operating and the marketing carrier.

One airline buys seats on a partner airline's flight and sells them under its own code

---

18 According to Austian Airlines Intranet Definitions.

19 There are three types of Interline Agreements. (1) The Multilateral Interline Traffic Agreement regulates the issuance and acceptance of documents between airlines and is concluded through the concurrence by IATA. (2) The Bilateral Interline Traffic Agreement regulates the issuance and acceptance of documents between the airlines and is concluded directly between two carriers. It enables airlines to include further arrangements such as taxes and other references. (3) The Unilateral Interline Traffic Agreement is comparable with the BITA, but only airline documents will be issued because coupons of the UNITA partners will not be accepted.

20 Amongst other regulations they can specify booking classes and penalty fares for incorrect application.

21 For example Star Round the World including all Star Alliance Airlines.

C. 2 Enhanced forms of cooperation – marketing leverage

Enhanced forms of cooperation are free sale agreements, code share agreements and frequent flyer programs which aim primarily at marketing leverage. Free sale agreements adjust the way in which the partner's seats are sold. There is no convention about a fixed seat contingent; each airline determines its prices on its own and can sell up to the capacity limit. Code-share agreements manage the marketing of two networks. Code sharing enables airlines to publish the same flight under two or more participating airlines' codes. This flight is operated by one of the participating carriers, but is promoted by all participating carriers. Frequent flyer programs cope with the issue of how to bind customers in partnerships and gain their loyalty.

C. 2. 1 Free sale

Each partner can sell seats on flights operated by other partners

Free Sale is an "automated code-share, where the inventory is controlled by the operating carrier."[22] Free sale is a business term describing an advanced sales agreement between the cooperating parties. It embodies a transparent, quick and less complex procedure to entirely sell off the company's own and the partners' capacity. Compared to interlining or BSA, every seat is sold directly and passenger information can be immediately traced back in the reservation systems (Groenwege, 1996). Under the guise of an (individually designed) free sale agreement, both parties are entitled to entirely sell a partner's seat and receive sales commission. Most of the time one partner receives flexible and full access to the entire seat capacity of the other partner, but inventory management remains in the hands of each partner. Generally, though not always, this works in conjunction with an associated code-share agreement.

C. 2. 2 Code sharing

An own flight number is shown on a partner's flight

Code sharing is a business term which first originated in the airline industry. It refers to a practice where one flight operated by an airline is jointly marketed as a flight for one or more airlines.[23] Most major airlines nowadays have code-sharing partners; this has truly become a key feature of the major airline alliances (Holloway, 2008, p. 407).

The term 'code' refers to the identifier used in flight schedules, generally the 2-character IATA airline designator code e.g. LH3543. Flight 3543 operated by LH, might also be sold by airline OS as OS7201 and additionally by LX. Under a code share agreement, participating airlines can provide a common flight number for several reasons: Firstly, a code-share agreement provides clearer routing for the customer,

---

22 According to Lufthansa Definitions Intranet.

23 A code-sharing agreement is a strategic cooperation between two airlines whereby each airline's designated code is shown on its partner's flights. The code-sharing flights are ticketed and provided as if they occurred on one partner airline (Barron, 1997).

allowing a customer to book travel from point A to B through point C under one carrier's code, instead of a customer booking from point A to C under one code, and from point C to B under another code. This is not only a superficial addition - cooperating airlines also strive to synchronize their schedules and coordinate luggage handling, to make transfers between connecting flights less time-consuming. If all the code share agreement participating airlines fly the same route, this method provides an apparent increase in the frequency of service on the route by each airline. Thirdly, there is a perceived additional service to new markets. This provides a method for carriers who do not operate their own aircraft on a given route to gain exposure in the market by displaying their flight numbers.[24] Figure 2 shows a trilateral example of a code-share agreement with significant complexity, flown in the summer schedule 2006:

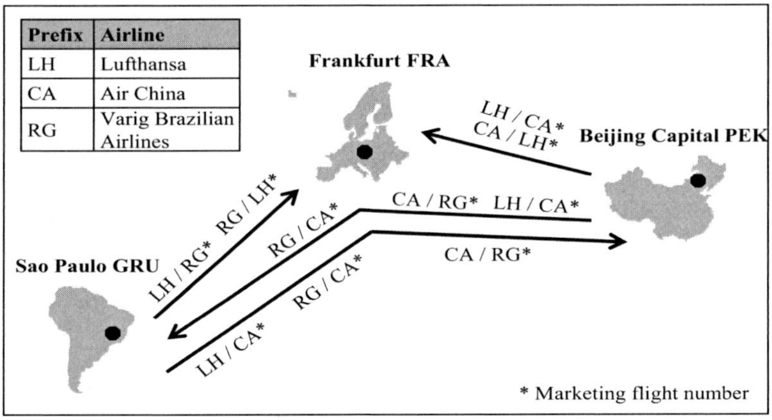

Figure 2: Code share agreement (Own illustration)

C. 2. 3 Frequent flyer programs

A Frequent Flyer Program is an "airline loyalty program that allows the use of credits for future travel."[25] This is a sound marketing leverage for partners to enhance customer retention. It is both an internal instrument and an external service offered by many airlines to reward customer loyalty. Typically, airline customers enrolled in the program accrue points (miles) corresponding to the distance flown on that airline. Accrued points (also known as frequent flyer miles) can be redeemed for free air travel, other goods and services - or for increased

[24] Note: basically there a two major types of codesharing. (1) Complimentary codesharing links the networks of X partner airlines to a complementary network resulting in improved services and coordinated schedules. (2) With parallel codesharing the allied partners serve the same routes to expand the range of frequency and pool their risk (Oum, Park & Zhang, 1996).

[25] According to Lufthansa Definitions Intranet.

benefits, such as upgrades, airport lounge access or priority bookings. In a partnership both partners may agree to accept accrual and redemption of points (miles) reciprocally and thus secure a wider customer base.

C. 3 Benefit and risk sharing models

The advanced developments of cooperation models are benefit- and risk-sharing models. There are a lot of reasons to consider these types of sharing models in airline industry. Firstly, costs and risks can be spread, access to additional revenue resources is improved and economies of scale can be realized. Secondly, an airline's competitive position can be improved through creating a stronger, larger, and virtual unit. Furthermore speed to market and agility can be increased. Last but not least, strategic goals, such as diversification, achieving synergies and the transfer of technology and skills, may come with a benefit- and risk-sharing model (Oum, Park & Zhang, 1996).

C. 3. 1 Franchise agreements

With franchise agreements the franchisee company operates flights for the franchisor. The franchisee bears the economic risk and operates flights with its own workforce and aircraft (Holloway, 2008, p. 417). In the airline industry, direct and immediate control jeopardizes franchising [deals]. This shows that borrowing other industry concepts may not always work out. This approach to sharing risk is therefore no longer used.

C. 3. 2 Revenue sharing and joint venture models

Revenue sharing models manage the sharing of the mutually generated revenues. There are no agreements between the participating airlines regarding the seat contingents. Participating airlines may jointly set prices; resulting revenues are shared in adherence to a conversion table and the utilization risk is borne by all partners conjointly. Revenue sharing formulas are usually an important part of joint ventures.

In a joint venture at least two partners form a new entity that takes over certain tasks

A joint venture is formed by two or more parties undertaking economic activities together. Joint venture models manage the synchronization of vital business elements and have the advantage that partners do not compete against each other[26] - at least on the routes covered by the agreement. It is a legal entity formed between two or more parties undertaking economic activity together. The parties agree to create a new entity by contributing equity and then sharing revenues, expenses and control of the enterprise.

[26] In the case of airline joint ventures, one of the airlines undertakes the revenue management whereas pricing and promotion is undertaken by all involved airlines.

A joint venture has the objective of being effective. This is the incentive and value driver for all partners. Also, the specific arrangement of the joint venture has to be simple and fair. These objectives are, from experience, contradictory - the formula for sharing profits is either simple or fair, seldom both. Choosing the simple formula results in easy, transparent and robust transactional processing although a party might feel disadvantaged by the outcome as important, specific aspects may have been left out. Therefore the parties usually attempt to design a fair model which is always in line with the specifications of all parties. The problem is that this results in complicated and intransparent models which are hard to steer and explain ('black box').

The formula for sharing profits between the partners is often either fair or simple

The joint venture can be exclusively for one specific project but it can also be a continuing business relationship. It is important to mention, that the term 'joint venture' used within the airline industry generally refers to the purpose of the entity and not to a type. Therefore, a joint venture may be cooperation, a limited liability company, a partnership or another legal structure, depending on the number of considerations.

Revenue sharing/joint venture models can be illustrated by the Atlantic Plus (A+) example. Atlantic Plus is an overall business program between United Airlines and Lufthansa and supports a general 'sales without preference' approach. In this model revenues are shared independently from the sales channel applied. All revenues generated on EU/North Atlantic routings are collected monthly in a fund and distributed according to a sharing key. In general this sharing key is based on production contribution (ASK).[27] A+ is a holistic approach including a Balanced Score Card for every business owner.

C. 4 Other forms of cooperation

A Common IT Platform is another form of cooperation. Nowadays, there are several computer reservation systems, for example Amadeus, SABRE or Galileo.[28] The variety of these systems complicates collaboration, which United Airlines and Lufthansa have sought to improve by introducing a common IT platform forward.

Another form of cooperation is to share a common IT platform

---

27 Available Seat Kilometers.

28 The benefits arising from computer reservation systems and commissions to travel agents may be limited by legislation (Adkins, 1994, p. 183).

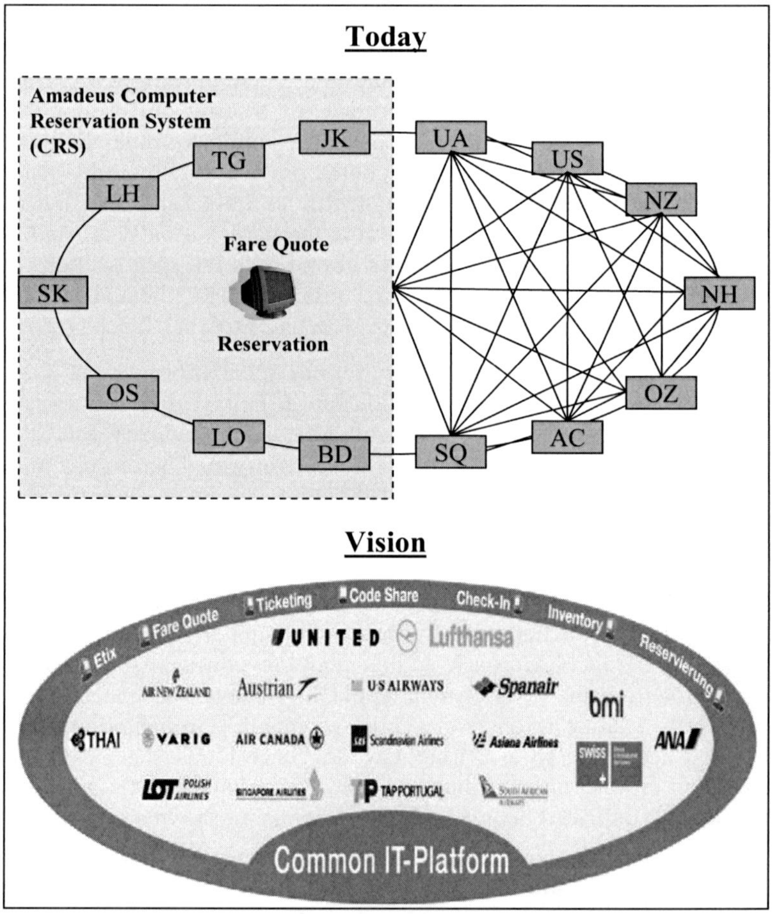

Figure 3: Computerized reservation systems (Own illustration based on Lufthansa Systems)

From the beginning the objective of a Common IT Platform CITP was to conceive, create and introduce a new technology platform for all IT processes related to the vital backbone of every airline.[29] A Common IT Platform would significantly reduce IT and distribution costs. Furthermore, it creates seamless services for customers and improves time to market. A common system comprises the functions of reservation, inventory, ticketing, etix® and fare quote as well as airport customer services. This can result in significant benefits: data duplication will be eliminated and all partners will access the same database. Moreover, no integration will be necessary between partners and thus complexity will be dramatically reduced.

[29] The reservation and customer services at airports.

C. 5 Multilateral cooperation

Competitive forces in the global marketplace increasingly require companies to gain significant market advantages (Ohmae, 1989). Therefore airlines need to collaborate with local and overseas partners (Achrol & Kotler, 1999). The success of a bilateral cooperation lies in the multiplication of positive effects by the number of additional partners.

Multilateral cooperation mostly aim to deliver a seamless travel product to the customers

In the context of aviation, there is no uniform legal definition for the term 'alliance'. In general, an alliance is a commercial agreement in which reciprocal rights are negotiated between two or more airlines from the same or different states. However, the purpose of the agreement can vary from one arrangement to the next (Lelieur, 2003). An alliance links the route networks of two or more airlines, thereby allowing an airline to expand its network overseas without adding new services (Driver, 1999). It intends to offer customers a truly global seamless travel product.

Alliances are the most visible form of multilateral cooperation

We have been observing this form of cooperation since the mid-1990s. In 1997, there were five large airline alliances: Star Alliance, One World, SkyTeam, Qualifyer Group and Wings. Three of them are still active: Star Alliance, Sky Team and One World account for about 70% of the total world airline capacity. Unaligned legacy carriers account for about 20% of the world capacity, with low-cost carriers accounting for the remaining 10%.

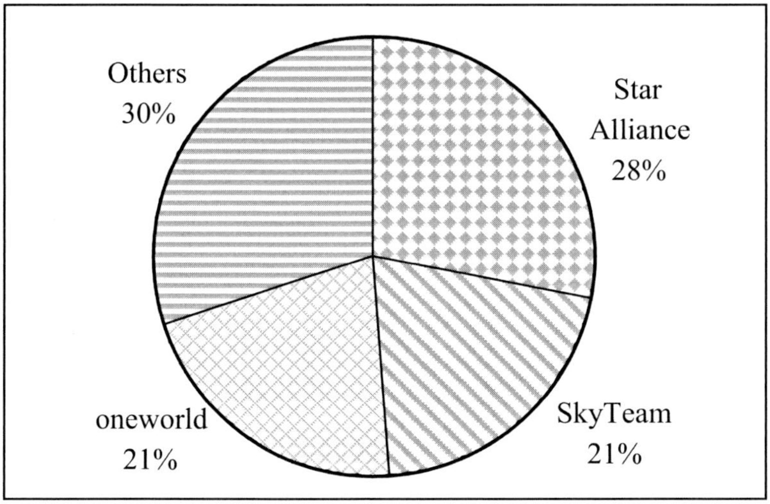

Figure 4: IATA Airlines by alliance group (scheduled RPK 2007) (International Air Transport Association [IATA], 2008)

Star Alliance

Star Alliance is the world's first and largest airline alliance. Since 1997 the core business of this alliance is the cooperation with partners with different regional focuses resulting in a powerful worldwide network. The partners' domestic airports all over the world form a small-meshed net of hubs, which allows seamless travel on a global level. Lufthansa, Air Canada, SAS Scandinavian Airlines, Thai Airways International and United Airlines are founders of this alliance and just five out of 21 full members and further three regional members of this alliance.

SkyTeam

The second largest airline alliance in the world was formed in 2000 by Aeromexico, Air France, Delta Air Lines and Korean Air. Once the integration of Northwest Airlines into Delta Air Lines has been completed, SkyTeam will consist of ten member airlines. In comparison to StarAlliance and OneWorld there are additional cooperation aspects: on the one hand the degree of interaction between the cooperation is as yet relatively underdeveloped. On the other hand, SkyTeam has the advantage of hubs such as Atlanta/Hartsfield or Paris/Charles de Gaulle, each one having a great potential for growth in infrastructural capacity.

OneWorld

OneWorld is the third largest airline alliance in the world and was launched in 1999 by American Airlines, British Airways, Cathay Pacific and Qantas Airways. Now this alliance consists of ten airlines and is the only one with a member in South America and Australia. A mutual cross-ownership between the participating members is its particular characteristic. This participation in terms of minority holdings of leading airlines in smaller airlines leads to closer connectivity between the alliance members.

The following figure shows the alliances' capacity shares within traffic areas:

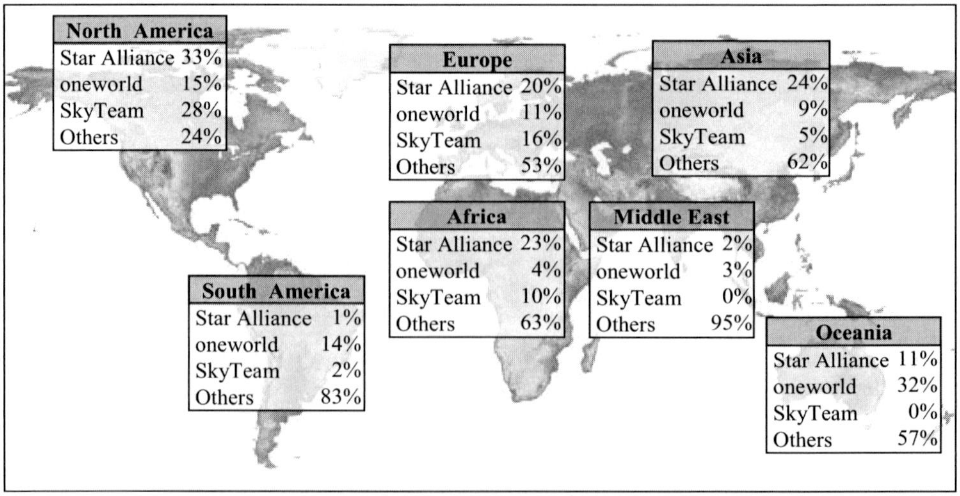

Figure 5: Alliance capacity shares (IATA, 2008)

C. 5. 1 Benefits of alliances

Alliances bring benefits for airlines and customers

Cooperation in the form of alliances has a long-term character and is supposed to strengthen competitive advantages and to protect the competitive position.[30] This leads to standardization and innovation within global alliances and implicates a lot of advantages for airlines as well as for customers.

Airlines benefit e.g. form higher seat load factors, an expanded network, and cost reductions

Airlines benefit from higher seat load factors, which can be achieved by code-sharing and extension of the airline's own flight routes with the partners' flight routes. Furthermore, airlines benefit from joint sales and marketing activities which can strengthen an airline's competitive position. Alliances experience synergy advantages and can quickly react to market developments. Certainly cost reductions can be implemented with optimal purchase of goods and services.[31] Further cost reduction potentials can be accomplished at airport stations due to the joint usage of terminals and lounges, collective staff training, or joint product development.

Customers benefit e.g. form seamless travel, shorter transfer times, and an alliance wide bonus program

There are increased customer benefits through implementation of standardized tools and innovative technologies. The main advantage is the ability to offer seamless travel on a very high level. Passengers profit from a global supply of flight connections. A huge net of coordinated national and international, highly-frequented connecting flights allows shorter transfer routes and times. Additionally, the consumer profits from a coupled customer loyalty and frequent flyer program (Driver, 1999). A participant in any members program can accumulate and redeem miles or points on any other member airline. For example Star Alliance facilitates award travel on any member carrier. Status customers have access to priority travel benefits across the alliance network. More importantly, the possibility to upgrade via the Mileage Upgrade Awards to the next higher cabin class has been introduced between Star partners and amongst different member programs. Customers also benefit from consumer-friendly airport services as preferential treatment at check-in or at the boarding counters. Baggage can be checked through to the final de-boarding point, to allow passengers to enjoy the benefits of access to luxurious lounges. There are price-related benefits for commercial customers as well: corporate plus, SME[32] and convention plus are among these advantages.

---

[30] Alliances are additionally more flexible than mergers; which is required within volatile market conditions (Agusdinata & de Klein, 2002).

[31] Those benefits are partially limited by the big players within an alliance. In fact they do not pass on their purchase power, for example aircraft purchasing, to the smaller alliance members, as they would lose their comparative price / cost advantage.

[32] Small and Medium Enterprises.

C. 5. 2 Risks of the alliance model

The risk of alliance-membership may be sunk costs and problems due to different (corporate) cultures

Alliances also involve some risks for the member-airlines. Depending on the tightness of relationship the participating airlines' entrepreneurial independence can be diminished. Expenses in the form of common sunk costs may occur,[33] and individually built customer relationships may be restricted (Kleymann & Seristö, 2001). Also different company size can lead to interdependencies, and different corporate cultures can be incompatible with each other concerning moral concepts, behavioral patterns or management principles. A global alliance with numerous members needs a very complex decision-making process to keep every member's business choices balanced. However, global alliances face a weightier task than individual airlines do. They have to define a common alliance strategy, achieve consensus with new applicants for membership or build the brand with a common product for the customer, for example.

D. OUTLOOK

The driving forces behind cooperation among airlines have been their need to acquire global access and to provide customers with global coverage.

The prime objective for any airline to become a global player is the expansion of the geographical scope of its network, without undertaking sizeable capital investment. In order to set up efficient global networks, partners and international marketing agreements are needed. These agreements allow airlines to connect their networks and expand their routes beyond their respective territories. Thus the partners can access new markets and therefore provide optimal customer service. The forms of cooperation that are pointed out in this chapter may not all lead to the desired success. Each airline has to decide which type of cooperation and which tool suits it the best.

Changes in political and economic conditions - privatization, deregulation, liberalization, and globalization - have forced the air transport industry into a new era of increased competition. These forces are likely to pressurize airlines into a greater degree of cooperation and towards consolidation.

With its increasing importance in the global economy, air transport should be regulated with a view to maximizing its overall potential. This reality requires a rethinking and readjustment of national ownership, control provisions, bilaterally negotiated traffic rights exchanges, restrictions on cabotage, and other elements in the aviation liberalization process.

---

[33] For example alliance-specific investments like marketing a joint brand, frequent flyer programs etc.

Review Questions

- How do regulatory issues affect growth and cooperation efforts?
- What is the difference between Economies of Scale, Scope and Density?
- Outline the three growth options for airlines. What are the advantages and disadvantages for each of them?
- What is the fundamental aim of mergers and acquisitions? Is there any other possibility to gain market access and traffic?
- Describe the difference between revenue sharing and joint venture models.
- Draw an outline of the risks and benefits of the Alliance model.
- Describe the liberalization of air transport process within the European Union.

Bibliography and further reading

Achrol, R. S. / Kotler, P. (1999): Marketing in the network economy, in: Journal of Marketing, Vol. 63, No. 4, p. 146–163.

Adkins B. (1994): Air Transport and E.C. Competition Law, London.

Agreement between the United Kingdom and the United States, 11 February 1946, 3 U.N.T.S. 253, 60 Stat. 1499, T.I.A.S. No. 1507 [Bermuda I].

Agreement between the Government of the Kingdom of Great Britain and Northern Ireland and the Government of the United States of America Concerning Air Services, 23 July 1977, 28 U.S.T. 5367, T.I.A.S. No. 8641 [Bermuda II].

Agusdinata, B. / de Klein, W. (2002): The dynamics of airline alliances, in: Journal of Air Transport Management, Vol. 8, No. 4, p. 201 – 211.

Albers, S. (2000): Nutzenallokation in strategischen Allianzen von Linienluftfrachtgesellschaften, Working Paper No. 101, 2000, Department of Business Policy and Logistics, University of Cologne, Cologne.

Barron, R. F. (1997): Code-share agreements: a developing trend in US bilateral aviation negotiations, in: Indiana Law Journal, Vol. 72, No. 2, p. 529–543.

Blohm, H. (1980): Kooperation, in Grochla, E. (editor): Handwörterbuch der Organization, p. 1112-1117.

Brueckner, J. K. (2001): The economics of international codesharing: an analysis of airline alliances, in: International Journal of Industrial Organization, Vol. 19, No. 10, p. 1475–1498.

Brueckner, J. K. / Dryer, N. J. / Spiller, P.T. (1992): Fare determination in airline hub-and-spoke networks, in: Rand Journal of Economics, Vol. 23, No. 3, p. 309–333.

Brueckner J. K. / Spiller P. T. (1991): Competition and mergers in airline networks, in: International Journal of Industrial Organization Vol. 9, No. 3. p. 323-342.

Button K. J. (1997): Interactions of global competition, airline strategic alliances and air traffic safety. The Aviation Program. The Institute of Public Policy George Mason University, Fairfax VA.

Caves, D. W. / Christensen, L. R. / Tretheway, M. (1984): Economies of density versus economies of scale: why trunk and local service airline costs differ, in: Rand Journal of Economics, Vol. 15, No. 4, p. 471 – 489.

Convention Portant Réglementation de la Navigation Aérienne (Convention Relating to the Regulation of Aerial Navigation), Paris, October 13, 1919, 11L.N.T.S. 173.

Convention on International Civil Aviation (1944): 15 U.N.T.S. 295, ICAO Doc. 7300/6, ann. 7.

Delfmann, W. / Baum, H. / Auerbach, S. / Albers, S. (2005): Strategic Management in the Aviation Industry, Aldershot.

Dempsey, P. S. / Goetz, A. R. (1998): Airline Deregulation and laissez-faire mythology, Westport.

Doganis, R. (1996): Relaxing Airline Ownership and Investment Rules, in: Air & Space Law, Vol. 21, No. 6, p. 267-270.

Driver, J. C. (1999): Developments in airline marketing practice, in: Journal of Marketing Practice: Applied Marketing Science, Vol. 5, No. 5, p. 134–150.

EEC Council Regulation (1992): Council Regulation of July 23rd, 1992 on Licensing of Air Carriers, OJ Legislation No. 2407.

EEC Council Regulation (1990a): Council Regulation of July 24th, 1990 on Fares for Scheduled Air Services, OJ Legislation No. 2342.

EEC Council Regulation (1990b): Council Regulation of July 24th, 1990 on Access for Air Carriers to Scheduled Intra-Community Air Service Routes and on the Sharing of Passenger Capacity between Air Carriers on Scheduled Air Services between Member States, OJ Legislation No. 2343.

EEC Council Decision (1987): Council Decision of December 14th, 1987 on the Sharing of Passenger Capacity between Air Carriers on Scheduled Air Services between Member States and on Access for Air Carriers to Scheduled Air-Service Routes between Member States, OJ Legislation No. 602.

EEC Council Regulation (1987a): Council Regulation of December 14th, 1987 Laying down the procedure for the Application of the Rules on Competition to Undertakings in the Air Transport Sector OJ Legislation No. 3975.

EEC Council Regulation (1987b): Council Regulation of December 14th, 1987 on the Application of Article 85 (3) of the Treaty to Certain Categories of Agreements and Concerted Practices in the Air Transport Sector OJ Legislation No. 3976.

Friedman, T. L. (2008): The World is Flat – the globalized world in the twenty-first century, London.

Groenewege, A. D. (1996): IATA Compendium of International Civil Aviation, International Air Transport Association, Quebec.

Holloway, S. (2008): Straight and Level: Practical Airline Economics, Aldershot.

International Air Transport Agreement, 7 December 1944, 171 U.N.T.S. 387, US Department of State Publication 2282.

International Air Transport Association [IATA] (2008): World Air Transport Statistics 53rd Edition, Montreal.

International Air Services Transit Agreement, 7 December 1944, 84 U.N.T.S. 389, ICAO Doc. 7500.

Kleymann, B. (2005): The dynamics of multilateral allying: a process perspective on airline alliances, in: Journal of Air Transport Management, Vol. 11, No. 3, p. 135-147.

Kleymann, B. / Seristö, H. (2001): Levels of airline alliance membership: balancing risks and benefits, in: Journal of Air Transport Management, Vol. 7, No. 5, p. 303-310.

Lelieur, I. (2003): Law and Policy of the Substantial Ownership and Effective Control of Airlines, Toronto.

Levine, M. E. / Winston, C. (1985): Intercity transportation route structures under deregulation: some assessments motivated by the airline experience, in: American Economic Review, Papers and Proceedings, Vol. 75, No. 2, p. 57-61.

Matte, N. M. (1981): Treatise on Air-Aeronautical Law, Toronto.

Meyer, J. R. / Oster, C. V. / Strong, J. S. (1987): Deregulation and the future of intercity passenger travel, Cambridge.

Ohmae, K. (1989): Global logic of strategic alliances, in: Harvard Business Review, March – April, Vol. 67 No. 2, p. 143 -154.

Oum T. H. / Park, J. / Zhang, A. (2000): Globalization and Strategic Alliances: the Case of the Airline Industry, London.

Oum, T. H. / Park, J. / Zhang, A. (1996): The effects of airline code sharing agreements on firm conduct and international air fares, in: Journal of Transport Economics and Policy, Vol. 30, No. 2, 187-203.

Oum, T. H. / Zhang, C. (2001): Global airline alliances: international regulatory issues, in: Journal of Air Transport Management, Vol. 7, No. 1, p. 57-62.

Pindyck, R. S. / Rubinfeld, D.L. (2005): Microeconomics, Upper Saddle River NJ.

Single European Act, 28 February 1986, 2 C.M.L.R. 741, 25 I.L.M. 506.

Warner, M. (1993): Liberalize open skies: foreign investment and cabotage restrictions keep non-citizens in second class.

Weber, M. / Dinwoodie, J. (2000): Fifth freedoms and airline alliances. The Role of fifth freedom traffic in an understanding of airline alliances, in: Journal for Air Transport Management, Vol. 6, No. 1, p. 51-60.

Wojahn, O. W. (2001): Airline Networks, Frankfurt.

Zylicz, M. (1992): International Air Transport Law, Dordrecht.

Global Alliances in the Airline Industry – a Model for the Future?

Klaus Jäckel

Table of contents

You should be able to

- explain briefly the history and current status of the three global airline alliances
- understand rules and prerequisites for alliance-membership
- identify main aspects of governance and comment on the specific significance of the decision making in process
- describe the different forms of alliance-typical commercial cooperation and the special role of joint ventures
- explicate the variety of alliance-typical products and services provided for the passenger
- elaborate on various factors – endogenous and exogenous – that potentially destabilize the alliances
- explain why the process of consolidation in the industry is of special significance for the alliances
- build your own opinion and evaluate yourself how the future perspective of global alliances looks like

The author

Dr. Klaus Jäckel works for Deutsche Lufthansa AG as Project Director Airline Group, Alliances and Cooperations. At the same time he is Professor for Aviation Management at the University of Applied Sciences in Worms, Germany.

Abstract

This section builds on the previous chapter of Hennemann & Malanik and further elaborates on the history, governance, challenges and future perspectives of global alliances.

Airline alliances emerged in the late nineties of the last century as a reaction to increased liberalization and strong competition.

Commercial cooperation within the alliances typically comprises interlining and code sharing as well as intensive collaboration in the area of frequent flyer programs and in the area of lounges. This is the basis for an alliance-specific package of services and products for the passenger.

Today the existence and future perspective of global alliances are being challenged by endogenous and exogenous developments.

Moreover the IATA project 'New Distribution Capability' has the potential to massively threaten the future of the global alliances.

For the time being the future prospects of the alliances can be summarized in one word: undetermined.

A. INTRODUCTION

Margins in the international airline industry are notoriously small, competition is extremely intensive, and at the same time dependence of external factors such as economic cyclicality, political or epidemic crisis is high. On top of that massive overcapacities are prevailing in wide parts of the global airline markets.

Against this background and in view of increasing liberalization – especially in the US and in Europe – it was quite natural for the airlines in the nineties of the last century to team up and join forces.

In order to better cope with the competitive challenges the airlines started to create bilateral and multilateral commercial cooperations[1] based on network and sales synergies across the continents.

Nowadays cooperation in global alliances often function as a kind of surrogate for transnational mergers and acquisitions which are no option yet in international airline markets due to restrictive national laws.

The construction of the three alliance-conglomerates (Star Alliance, Oneworld and SkyTeam), is the concrete visible result of a respective global commercial cooperation which started with a handful of found-

---

[1] Before becoming a member of an alliance the airlines normally establish a network of bilateral partnerships which will later be complemented by an alliance-specific, multilateral cooperation on alliance-level. See also chapter C.

ing members. Today the trio builds a comprehensive system of alliance groups with more than 60 member-airlines on a global scale.

However, during the last years there have been some new developments in the airline industry and within the alliances themselves which have substantially influenced the stability and future perspectives for them.

Depending on the further development of these trends even the existence of the alliances needs to be questioned.

The description of relevant issues of these developments in the following will try to clarify what the respective consequences will be for the future prospects of the global alliances.

B. BRIEF HISTORY UND STATUS OF GLOBAL ALLIANCES

B. 1 History

The first group was Star Alliance in May 1997 which was constituted of the founding members United Airlines, Deutsche Lufthansa, Thai Airways, Scandinavian Airlines and Air Canada.

Less than one year later a union of seven airlines surrounding the former Swissair, Austrian Airlines, Sabena and TAP Air Portugal created the so called 'Qualifyer Group', to subtend Star Alliance. However, after Austrian joined Star and the bankruptcy of Swissair the union was dissolved in 2001.

Only two years after the foundation of Star the 'OneWorld" Alliance was created in 1999 with American Airlines, British Airways, Cathay Pacific und Qantas as founding members.

Today three global alliances exist - founded in the late 90ies of the last century as a result of increasing deregulation and competition

Another unsuccessful attempt to build a multilateral airline cooperation was the so called 'Wings Alliance'. Potential members were Northwest Airlines, Continental, KLM and Alitalia. Although there was a network of bilateral cooperations and code sharing, the alliance was never formally established as most members had joined SkyTeam in the meantime.

This last alliance, SkyTeam was founded in the year 2000 by Air France, Korean Air, Delta Airlines and Aeroméxico.[2]

Today, SkyTeam, Star Alliance and OneWorld are the only existing global alliances.

---

2 For a more detailed description of alliance-history and other predecessors such as Alcazar, Atlantic Excellence etc. see for example Iatrou & Oretti (2007).

B. 2 Status

Today (August 2015) the three alliances comprise a total of 62 member airlines – not counting affiliates or other partner airlines.

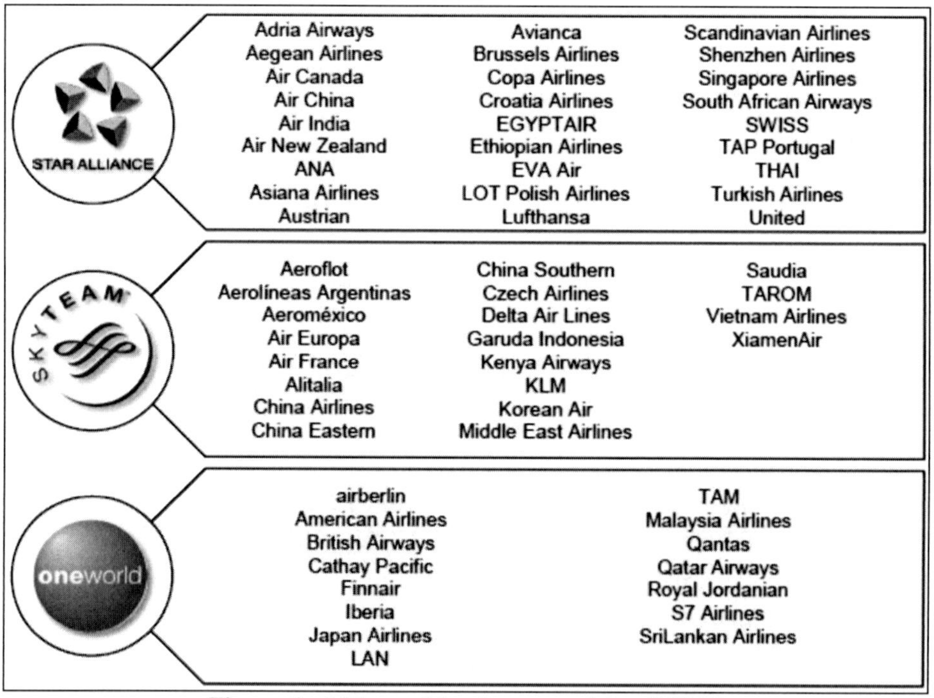

Figure 1: Alliance Members as of April 2015 (Star Alliance, 2015a)

In 2015 the three alliances represent more than 56% of the total air traffic volume in the world as measured by passengers and more than 63% of the Revenue Passenger Kilometers. The higher share reflects a high proportion of intercontinental traffic especially between Europe and the North Atlantic.

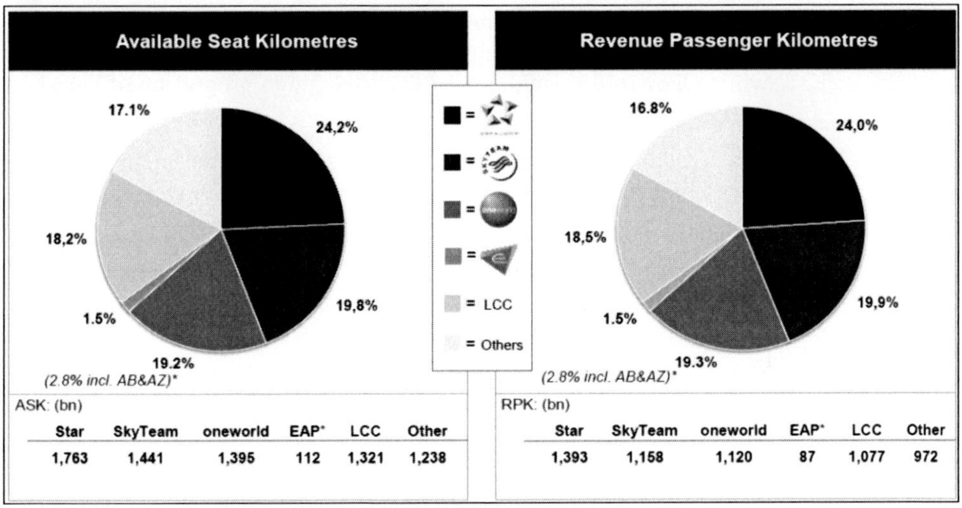

Figure 2: Available Seat Kilometers / Revenue Passenger Kilometers 2015 (Star Alliance, 2015a)

By jointly generating some 500 bn. US$ of operating revenue the global share of the alliances reaches even more than 70%.

The combined number of aircraft amounts to almost 11.000 which transported more than 1.7 bn. passengers in 2014.

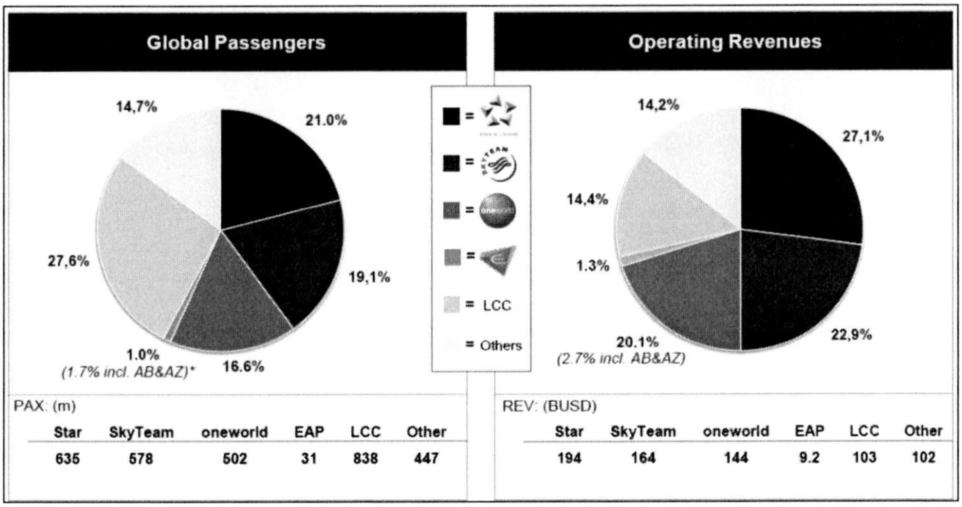

Figure 3: Global Passengers / Operating Revenues 2015 (Star Alliance, 2015a)

As can be seen from the numbers within the alliance-groups Star Alliance and SkyTeam are on a similar level regarding passenger volumes while Oneworld is smaller also due to the high proportion of long-haul traffic.

The number of countries and airports served by the members of the three alliances clearly reveals their truly global coverage:

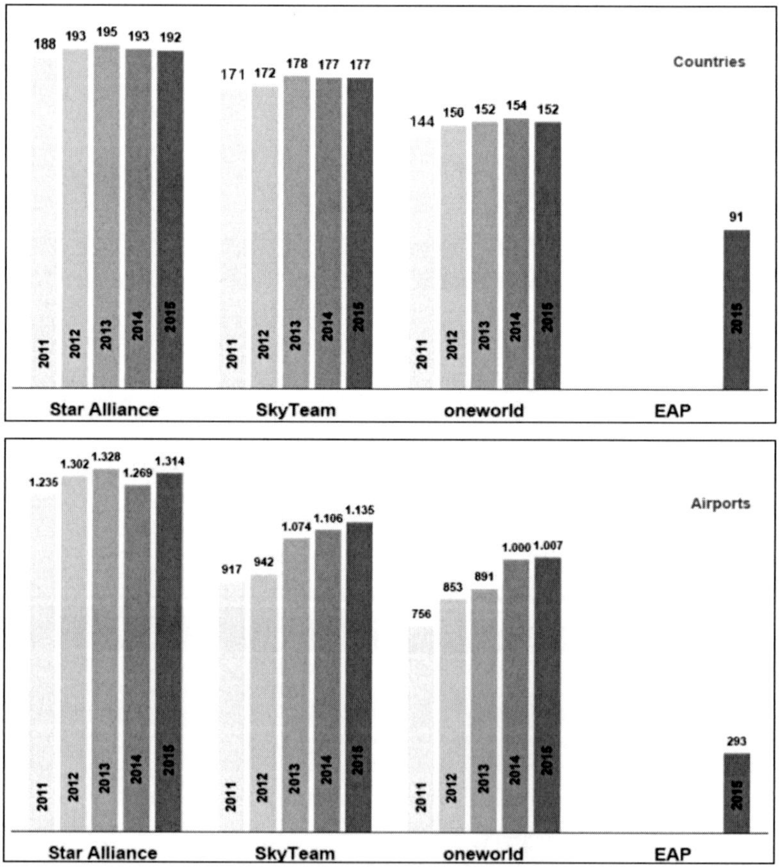

Figure 4: Number of Countries and Airports Served 2015[3] (Star Alliance, 2015a)

[3] Including Etihad Airline Partners Alliance (EAP)

C. ORGANISATIONAL STRUCTURE

C. 1 Membership

Given the enormous significance of the global alliances and the fact that almost all of the world´s biggest leading airlines are members in one of these alliances there is generally a strong interest of airlines to be part of one of these groups.[4]

Apart from safety requirements a wide range of conditions and standards has to be met in order to become a member of a global Alliance

To become a member of one of the alliances joining candidates need to comply with a number of rules and requirements. In that regard the alliances have meanwhile developed a wide range of standards and conditions which have to be fulfilled (at Star Alliance these are called "Core Values") which precisely define a level of quality and safety in the sense of guaranteeing a minimum standard for all members.

In 2012 the webpage of SkyTeam listed more than 100 "membership requirements".[5]

Apart from complying with the general safety-requirements[6] the standards to be met comprise quality aspects in the area of frequent flyer programs, onboard-product, lounges, ground handling processes and the through-check-in of luggage.[7] Incidentally compliance and fulfillment of the mentioned requirements also apply for all incumbent members so that all airlines have to constantly undergo respective procedures in a number of quality audits following detailed schedules. Compliance with the most important standards is normally requested from joining members prior to the beginning of the formal membership. Sometimes however, a certain grace period is granted for less important topics.

The mere joining process for new members – called "New Carrier Integration" at Star Alliance for instance – lasts between 6 and 18 months.[8]

---

4 This is not valid for Low Cost Carriers; for them global alliances normally are of no or minor interest as a membership induces high costs (see chapter C. 1), and moreover increase complexity considerably which leads to even higher costs.

5 "In order to become an official member of SkyTeam, aspiring members first need to meet strict safety, quality, IT and customer service standards. Over 100 membership requirements cover different areas". This is comparable with other alliance such as Star Alliance (SkyTeam, 2015a).

6 Normally a successful conclusion of the so called "IOSA" (IATA Operational Safety Audit) is requested as a „hard" condition for joining.

7 See also chapter E. In case of SkyTeam also the implementation of code sharing on at least one route is a minimum requirement (FAZ.net, 2011).

8 SkyTeam officially speaks of 12 to 18 months (FAZ.net, 2011). Becoming a member of a global alliance in most cases means adoption of a variety of certain operational procedures, IT-applications, revenue-management systems and so on which normally requires extensive implementation processes.

The joining process is ambitious and normally takes between 6 and 18 months

However, in some cases the time between first negotiations and the final joining date amounts to years rather than months. For example TACA in South America had started talks about joining Star Alliance already in 2008 while actual membership did not start before 2012.[9]

It is self-evident that the decision about the acceptance of a new member is also taken prior to the actual joining process. In view of the significance and the impact on incumbent carriers it can be assumed that this decision has to be taken unanimously – which means that in practice each and every member has to give its explicit consent.[10]

Despite the lack of respective public information it can be assumed that a special 'joining-fee' is due for new members when they enter into the alliance.

The cost of this fee has to be added to the costs that are incurred for establishing all the alliance-specific requirements and standards. According to official information of Air Berlin for instance it paid a small double-digit million Euro amount for its membership in Oneworld in the year 2012.[11]

It can be assumed that both, entry into and exit from an alliance is associated with a special fee of some million US$

Likewise a special fee is due upon the exit of a member from a global alliance. The 'exit-fee' is due unless it is waived by a special alliance decision – e.g. in the case when the exit of one member is the consequence of the entrance of a new member. Another case might be that an alliance forces a member to leave and voluntarily abstains from a payment.

Also for this fee it can be assumed that the range is of a one-digit or small two-digit million Euro amount.

On top of these costs each participating airline in the alliance has to pay a regular, annual membership fee which is determined according to internal regulations which are not publicly available.

C. 2 Governance

Governance relates to design and organization of the 'code of conduct' for the business-management of the alliance. In detail it is about definition and determination of rights and responsibilities of the members, conditions for the acceptance of new members, the exit of incumbents and specifically about the general regulation of decision making within the alliance.

---

9 Cf. airliners.de (2012). In the case of Air India the total time between first talks and actual entrance into Star Alliance amounted to more than five years - including a period when the joining process was "suspended".

10 The alliances do not provide public information concerning their internal governance and decision processes. However, voting regulations and majority requirements play an important role when it comes to flexible reaction by and further development of an alliance (see chapter C. 2).

11 Quoted from FAZ (2012, p. 19).

The management of the 'alliance-business' itself lies in the hand of separate legal entities which are founded and sustained by the member airlines of the alliances.

The governance of the alliances regulates decision making, the creation of internal institutions as well as the normal conduct of business

In the case of Star this is the 'Star Alliance GmbH' located in Frankfurt / Main, Germany while for Oneworld it is the 'oneworld Management Company' in New York. Sky Team calls its management team 'Sky Team Central' which is located at the World Trade Center Schiphol, Amsterdam

The employees of these entities form the 'headquarter' of the alliance. They work on all the tasks and topics that have been identified and imposed by the member airlines. According to SkyTeam for example the management-team is responsible for „monitoring the daily operation of the alliance comprising the following areas: marketing, sales, airport-synergies and transfers, cargo, advertising and brand-management, alliance-operation, finance, corporate communications and alliance-administration".[12]

Over the last years the alliances have made enormous efforts to be perceived as a separate and discrete entity which means that they have strived to establish their own brand-identity – Oneworld even operates as a Registered Trademark.

The alliances strive to develop own brand identities

One component of this brand-building strategy for example is to make all participating carriers operate a number of aircraft (as a certain percentage of their fleet) in the official 'livery' of the alliance leaving only small room for the own brand-identification of the specific carrier on the respective aircraft.

The highest institution within the alliances is the assembly of their members´ Chief Executive Officers – as such representing the 'owners' of the respective alliance. This assembly is called „Chief Executive Board" at Star Alliance and "Governing Board" at Oneworld for example. According to Oneworld the executives meet regularly to set strategic direction and review progress. These boards are responsible for all central decisions, regulation of governance and the working-programs of the alliance, finance – and finally the acceptance (or exclusion) of members.[13]

Responsibility for the preparation of alliance-specific topics or decisions and the implementation of agreed strategies, products and projects on alliance level lies in the hands of a different body. In the case of Star Alliance for example this is the "Alliance Management Board" (AMB).

It is composed of the respective alliance-managers of all member airlines who are specifically designated for that task and also have been delegated powers to decide in alliance-relevant issues on behalf of their airline. At the same time AMB-members are responsible for

[12] SkyTeam (2015b).

[13] Oneworld (2015).

Representatives of the member airlines build special alliance-boards to determine the strategic policy of the alliance and take relevant decisions on different levels

the airline-internal implementation of all decisions taken on alliance level.

The ability of each alliance to create flexible structures for quick decision making and joint action will be one of the most important success factors for alliances in the future. Internal and external developments and challenges will not allow long and cumbersome decision making processes any more.

That is why rules and regulations pertaining to decision making and voting rules are a central point in alliance-governance. It is necessary to effectively balance out heterogeneity of a relatively high number of members with different size and often diverse interests.

In detail it is about the definition of decision-areas, in which either the principle of unanimity or a majority system shall prevail. Moreover it has to be decided how 'majority' is defined. In simple models a bare majority is defined as the numerical majority of member airlines, the majority of actual member fees or the majority of specifically defined indicators of size (e.g. Available Seat Kilometers, Revenue Passenger Kilometers, or similar).

The unanimity principle is not adequate to grant efficient decision making

It is self-evident that initially the principle 'one member, one vote' is the preferred method. However, given the number of voting airlines being twenty or even more, the unanimity principle – apart from and sometimes even including deciding about new members – leads to very difficult constellations and complicated, drawn-out decision making processes to find compromises.

It is obvious that rules for efficient decision making are a definite success factor for airline alliances. While in practice there is no formal voting[14] in SkyTeam – Star Alliance has recently implemented a modified more sophisticated voting system to overcome the unanimity principle.

D. COMMERCIAL COOPERATION WITHIN THE ALLIANCES

As in all other forms of commercial collaboration between air carriers the basis of airline specific cooperation within an alliance is interlining. This means that partners establish a comprehensive system of Bilateral Interline Agreements among themselves which grant the mutual acceptance of tickets and additional conditions for the utilization of the partners` networks. These agreements are different from multilateral agreements (for instance the standard of International Air Transport Association, IATA) as they are more flexible and normally

---

[14] Despite the existence of a formal voting regime the members of the alliance refrain from conducting voting-procedures and strive to informally achieve consensus (personal interview of the author with Mauro Oretti, Vice President Sales and Marketing SkyTeam).

provide for more specific individual regulations such as higher number of booking classes, special coverage of code sharing, etc.

Interlining and Special Prorate Agreements are the basic forms of cooperation in all alliances

The system of interlining is complemented by respective Special Prorate Agreements. These agreements define methods how ticket revenue will be split between airline-partners involved in the respective interline passenger itineraries. Typically these agreements contain very favorable conditions regarding the costs for flight legs operated by partners in contrast to those charged to non-members or even competitors. Following the principle of reciprocity the partners thus grant each other direct commercial advantages combined with a relatively high level of seat-availability.[15]

Code sharing is the third and the most visible form of cooperation within the alliances

In general the third level of cooperation among alliance members is a comprehensive system of code sharing. This means that a flight operated by a partner airline, the 'operating flight', will additionally be sold and marketed under the two-letter designator code of a partner airline ('marketing flight'). Again based on reciprocity the partners help each other to better utilize their capacities. By means of through-flight numbers (combination of own operating and marketing flight number) carrier specific pricing is possible with favorable through-fares for the passenger.

The commercial effect of code sharing should not be underestimated: Due to relatively low marginal costs an additional passenger who is sold by a partner generates significant contribution for the profitability of a flight. Air Berlin for instances quantifies the code share revenue generated only by its partner Etihad with a triple-digit million Euro per annum (Düring & Jahberg, 2015).

While at Sky Team – as already mentioned – code sharing is obligatory for all partners within the alliance, this is not the case at Star Alliance[16]; nevertheless almost all airlines have concluded code share contracts among each other which is also valid for OneWorld.

---

[15] Usually the relationship is adverse: availability becomes lower as the prorate-amount decreases.

[16] As an example: Lufthansa and Asiana Airlines are still not sharing codes on each other, also Thai Airways and Singapore Airlines have no code share relationship.

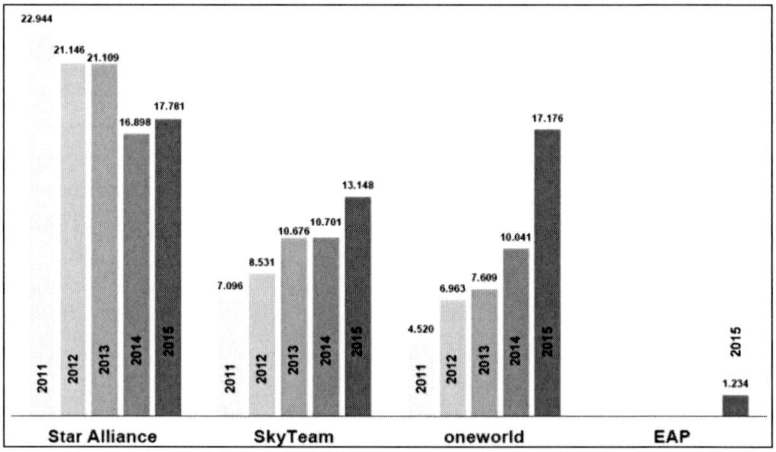

Figure 5: Number of daily intra-alliance code share flights (Star Alliance, 2015a)

In addition to the three mentioned basic areas of cooperation within and between global alliances also other forms of commercial cooperation can occur. The most common ones are so called "Block Seat Agreements" (BSA) or collaboration within the scope of "Sales Incentive Agreements".

Block Seat Agreements are selectively conducted to jointly exploit market chances

In case of a BSA one partner airline acquires a fixed or variable number of seats on a flight (or more flights) operated by the other partner airline. These seats are sold and marketed by the marketing carrier under his own (marketing) flight number, however, contrary to the 'regular' code sharing, under his own risk. By selling the seats in its own risk the marketing carrier in a block seat arrangement helps to reduce the commercial risk of the operating partner. In practice this form of cooperation can enable the operator to maintain a service on a route or take up a new destination into the network which would not have been possible without a BSA.[17]

Sales Incentive Agreements are a complementing form of commercial cooperation

The function of a Sales Incentive Agreement is to create a commercial incentive for one partner to sell the flights of the other partner. These agreements make sense whenever those sales or marketing activities would economically be disadvantageous for one airline so that it would refrain from supporting the partner. Often this instrument is used on routes – typically together with code sharing – where mutual sales activities produce significant imbalances regarding the number of sales generated for the respective partner. Imbalances can be a result of a corresponding capacity-imbalance, a differing

[17] South African Airways and Lufthansa had concluded a Block Seat Agreement on the route Frankfurt-Capetown in order to evaluate if this city-pair can be economically sustained despite the high seasonality in that market. Finally the venture failed and the agreement was not extended.

marketing and sales power or specific schedule and demand constellations.[18]

Thus sales incentive or code share incentive agreements are used to maintain and even increase the level of commercial cooperation which normally would not be beneficial for at least one partner. In practice the incentive is created by granting the marketing-carrier the right to keep a certain percentage of the revenue that he generates for the operating carrier[19]. Instead of a percentage also a fixed amount or a fixed amount per booking class can be agreed as 'incentive'.

The cooperation-level within the alliances is relatively low - members remain competitors

In summary the alliance-typical cooperation is characterized by a relatively high number of partners working together on a relatively low level of integration. The main aspect here is that basically, despite being alliance partners, all members remain competitors – acting on their own behalf, in their own interest and own risk except in the case of the limited area of a block seat cooperation.

This has to be distinguished from a cooperation in the form of a Joint Venture (JV)[20]. In a JV-environment the commercial risk is shared in certain markets or on certain routes and for these joint venture areas the competitive relationship between the participants is no longer existent – the joint venture partners act as one airline.

In order to achieve that status all relevant business processes have to be adapted and harmonized in much more depth which also includes market allocation, capacity- and even price-agreements[21]. This kind of collaboration is substantially more intensive than the 'typical' alliance-cooperation and therefore only possible for a relatively small number of airlines.

---

18 For instance both partners operate a service, one in the morning and one in the evening. If the demand is significantly higher for the evening flight, it will "automatically" attract more bookings also from the non-operating partner airline.

19 The actual rate depends on the given situation and the specific agreement between the partners; normally the range lies between 10 to 30 percent.

20 In the airline industry the term „Joint Venture" is used in a different way than in others. Contrary to the automobile industry for instance where a joint ventures describe the foundation of a joint company as a separate legal entity this is not the case in the airline business. Airline joint ventures are not "visible" as such for the customer and organized inside the business organizations of the JV-partners. In order to differentiate accordingly Oneworld calls those ventures "Joint Business".

21 Apart from being more difficult to install this kind of cooperation requires legal clearance (so called "Anti Trust Immunity") by the cartel- or competition authorities of the affected countries. In the European Union for instance a comprehensive "self-assessment" is necessary; in the US normally approval from the Department of Justice and the Department of Transportation is needed.

Joint ventures have becoming more important during the last years and together with other factors they are a considerable factor to influence the future prospects of the alliances (see chapter F. 1).

E. PRODUCTS AND SERVICES FOR THE PASSENGER

The alliances offer a wide range of additional services and benefits

Based on – and as a direct consequence of – this system of commercial cooperation all alliances offer a variety of benefits, advantages and additional services to their customers, i.e. the passenger.

The following list shows an overview of special services and advantages presented by Oneworld (2015):

- Greater Support
- Global Coverage
- Better Value
- More Miles and Points
- More Rewards and Reognition
- More Lounges
- Smoother Tranfers
- Superior Quality

What is called "Smoother Transfers" pertains to the most important, underlying benefit for a customer which comes from harmonized and jointly optimized route networks on alliance-level.

The goal of this optimization process is to combine networks in a complementary way, minimizing overlap and creating additional travel options by establishing lucrative flight connections with short transit times.

As a result the customer can be offered an ultimate system of 'seamless travel' – accompanied by additional services for a comfortable and pleasant journey. The complementing services pertain to three major areas: services and facilities at the airport, frequent flyer programs and 'joint products'.

Examples for the latter are 'Round the World Tariff' offered by all alliances; Round the World Tickets are fare constructions with a number of flight coupons covering the complete network of all or some participating carriers. Sometimes also so called "Airpasses" are available on a regional level for instance from Star Alliance for China, Africa or North America.[22]

Additionally special packages for corporate travel are offered; e.g. SkyTeam´s so called "Global Corporate Contracts" which "go beyond a standard loyalty program by meeting (the) company´s travel requirements, providing cost savings and a vast network" (SkyTeam, 2015b). Star Alliance offers special services for conventions and for meetings with more than 50 participants (Star Alliance, 2015b).

Special "airpasses" and corporate offers are typical example for joint products

Services at the airports are for instance joint Check In facilities and in some cases the alliances 'co-locate' which means all the airlines bundle their activities in one location and offer their services jointly. The latest example for co-location is London Heathrow where all Star partners operate out of Terminal Two since 2014.

Apart from that lounges play an important role in the service portfolio. Alliance partner mutually give access to their partners´ passengers according to a sophisticated system of recognition. The number of lounges is immense: Star Alliance members offer more than 1.000; Oneworld as well as SkyTeam members more than 600 airport lounges each.

Moreover there are special 'alliance-branded' lounges; for instance SkyTeam will open three new in 2015 bringing it to six own lounges globally.

Joint facilities such as lounges and check-in areas are important examples for alliance products and services at airports

Improving and enlarging the service portfolio is an ongoing business. On the occasion of receiving the Air Transport News Awards the SkyTeam-CEO listed up a number of concrete projects currently being realized which can serve as an example of latest alliance activities in the field of customer services (SkyTeam, 2015d):

- Final implementation of 'SkyPriority'; alliance-standard for Elite Plus-, First- und Business Class-Passengers who can take advantage of special services at more than 1.000 airports.
- Opening of the third SkyTeam Exclusive Lounge in Sydney. Lounges in Dubai, Beijing, and Hong Kong shall follow in the course of the year.
- Realization of the 'SkyTransfer-Initiative', focusing on seamless and efficient transfers for passengers and baggage.
- Implementation of an online tool for participants in frequent flyer programs to book redemption flights of any member airline.
- Introduction of an accelerated process for safety and passport controlling for Top clients at even more airports all over the world

[22] For details see websites of the alliances.

Finally Frequent Flyer Programs (FFP) are an indispensable tool for all alliances to build up customer loyalty and to retain the customer within the own alliance system.

Cooperation in the area of Frequent Flyer Programs is also a characteristic form of cooperation within the alliances to build up customer loyalty

All members of the FFP have the opportunity to collect points or credits with every mile they fly on one of the partners´ flights. Corresponding they can also redeem the credits on all participating airlines within the alliance. By using optimized network of all the alliance members the attractiveness of the FFP increases for the customer as he can take advantage of a significantly higher number of potential destinations and flights to earn or redeem credit points in his individual FFP.

These FFP also include a special system for status-or 'elite'-customers which grants special priority with extra benefits regarding baggage handling, check-in facilities (e.g. red-carpet-treatment) and other advantages.

F. DESTABILIZING FACTORS

Existence and stability of the global alliances have always been challenged by a number of endogenous and exogenous factors. In the last two or three years some new developments can be identified that might increase the impact on the alliances.

F. 1 Endogenous factors

Fluctuation

Airline alliances are not static; from the very beginning a continuous change in membership can be observed. As Star Alliance officials put it: "the Alliance will never be completed. We are dynamic and have to respond to customer needs." (Iatrou & Oretti, 2007, p. 43)

A kind of "natural" fluctuation happens by market exit or merger of member airlines

Some sort of 'natural' fluctuation happens if one of the member airlines is going out of the market and ceases operation. This happened to the Star member Ansett Australia that went out of business already in March 2002. In the meantime there have been more examples like Malev (Oneworld member) and Spanair (Star Alliance member) who both went out of business in 2012.

The same effect is achieved in case of a full merger.[23] There are different examples for that – Shanghai Airlines merged with China Eastern in 2008 - lately the mergers of US Airlines and American Airlines, Continental and United Airlines in the US and LAN Airline Chile and TAM Linhas Aeréas Brazil where only one airline is left.

[23] "Full merger" means that after the merger transaction only one company is left (as opposed to mergers or take-overs with two airlines remaining as for example in the case of Air France / KLM, Lufthansa / Swiss etc.).

On the other hand new members are integrated into the alliances which strive for growth. However, the integration of new members into an alliance – as described above - means a high level of respective activities which take time and efforts.

Fluctuation from the exit of a member is usually considered to be disadvantageous for the alliance because the respective network opportunities and market impact will be lost. In most cases – to make it even worse – in the future respective commercial potentials will be transferred to a competing alliance. For the airlines integration benefits are lost and often sunk costs of alliance membership are incurred. (Jakl & Grimme, 2015)

Once a member has left it is often difficult or even impossible to find an adequate substitute. An example for that is the case when TAM and LAN merged. This led to the exit of TAM from Star Alliance which lost its presence in the most important market in South America. Together with the US Airways-American Airlines merger and subsequent alliance decisions Star Alliance lost some 20% of alliance flights in 2013 (Jakl & Grimme, 2015). Finding a relevant substitute in this case was rather difficult and only in 2015 the integration of Avianca Brazil as a new member started.[24]

Low Hanging Fruit

Given the relatively low level of integration with the commercial cooperation as described in chapter D the alliances have more or less exploited all the respective potential commercial benefits associated with it. Although these benefits are considerable[25] most of the airlines are struggling to maintain profitability – and many small airlines fail.

The given economic potential of cooperation within the framework of global alliances has been exploited to the high degree

The existing framework and structure of the alliances do not allow the members to achieve a deeper level of integration and more benefits: "Alliances provide networks, while the right kind of JV improves the economics of that network." (Thomas, 2014)[26]

The potential to increase revenues for the alliance members seems to be limited: "As the airline industry matures in terms of markets and players, there is increasing evidence that revenue gain is reaching its ceiling and thus current priorities focus on cost-savings through efficiency" (Iatrou & Oretti, 2007, p. 115). The problem is that especially in that field the alliances have not managed to achieve substantial results. One important area of cooperation for example has traditionally been neglected in the alliances: joint procurement. This could pertain to purchase of fuel, inflight amenities, fuel, spare parts, negotiation of airport charges, passenger-seats and even aircraft. Although

---

24 Avianca Brazil as a new member will clearly fall behind the market impact of TAM, LATAM in Brazil respectively.

25 A comprehensive evaluation of the economic benefits is offered by Tugores-García (2012).

26 Thomas, J., quoted from Flight Global (2014).

joint purchasing directly yields substantial commercial advantages the cooperation level and the volumes are poor: In 2000 Star Alliance set itself a target of just 150 mio. US$ in annual savings through joint purchasing, representing just 0.1% of expenses for the whole alliance. (Iatrou & Oretti, 2007, p. 119)

For the time being further economic potential in the area of cost synergies for example by joint procurement seem to be difficult to realize

For SkyTeam their CEO bluntly declares that "we don't´ go as far as joint aircraft procurement, we are too big to create these kinds of traditional synergies, or, for example engine buying" (Wisburn, 2013).[27]

Some carriers in Oneworld however have recognized and acknowledged the significance of joint procurement as IAG (British Airways/Iberia) and Qatar Airways plan to coordinate "aircraft procurement, aircraft engines and potentially maintenance as well" (Walsh, 2015).[28]

Further integration with additional potential for revenues and cost savings would be possible only if capacity planning and network structures could be harmonized and jointly optimized beyond improving connectivity and reducing travel times. Most importantly pricing policies, revenue management facilities and distribution capabilities would need to be aligned.

Joint ventures provide higher economic potential due to deeper integration – however, cartel laws and market conditions pose strong restrictions and limitations for smaller airlines

The problem here is that these business practices are generally considered anti-competitive and therefore normally forbidden under cartel laws. The best way dealing with these issues are joint ventures which, however are very often not a realistic alternative. Given a relatively high number of small or mid-sized carriers, often financially ailing, limited home market volumes and no potential for significant schedule synergies, there is not much room for successful joint ventures. Not to mention the fact that the (realistic) number of joint venture partners is limited to two or three per individual arrangement.

Moreover it has to be acknowledged that the possibility to obtain cartel immunization by so called "Anti Trust Immunity" is of course limited. As a consequence alliance members without joint ventures have a substantial risk of "being reduced to minnows" (Parker, 2013, p. 14).

As we will see, existing joint ventures themselves pose a threat for the stability of alliances.

From cooperation to co-opetition: Increased competition within the alliances

From the 'logic' of global alliances member airlines basically remain competitors and as the Star CEO puts it: "There has always been competition within the alliance (…) there are commercial disputes that come up from time to time" (Schwab, 2013).[29]

---

27 Wisburn, M., quoted from CAPA (2013a).

28 Walsh, W., quoted from Dron (2015).

29 Schwab, M., quoted from CAPA (2013b).

There are however, indications that this wording is becoming 'euphemistic' as economic pressure by heavy competition in and outside the alliances increases.

The best example for this is the relationship between Lufthansa (LH) and Turkish Airlines. Turkish Airlines (TK) operates to 13 destinations in Germany and has continuously expanded its gateway in Istanbul to the second largest international hub of all Star Alliance members (Machatscke, 2015). By making use of this hub TK increasingly attracts passengers from Germany - not only to Turkey but also to markets in North and South East Asia, Middle East and even Africa. Being able to produce at a 30% cost advantage over Lufthansa the commercial impact on the latter is immense as more and more passengers prefer to fly with TK rather than with LH.

As a consequence Lufthansa decided in 2014 to reduce their cooperation with TK to a minimum. The code share agreement was terminated and the conditions of the frequent flyer scheme significantly deteriorated for Turkish. At the same time TK was excluded from Terminal Two in Munich where all the Star partners normally cooperate on the ground.

The negative impact of TK is also perceived by other Star partners in other areas of the world by smaller carriers such as Ethiopian Airways or Egypt Air. They are said to even support the exit of TK out of the alliance. (Machatscke, 2015)

In the case of OneWorld the integration of Qatar Airways as a new member posed a threat for some airlines. Royal Jordanian Airlines may even opt to defect to a rival alliance because its network duplicates Qatar´s in many cases. Some commentators see this as a revelation of the alliance´s key weakness: namely that it is "a disparate collection of airlines that share little strategic overlap". (The Economist, 2012)

Cooperation of alliance members with non-members or members of other alliances cause additional competitive pressure

Moreover competition within the alliances is indirectly effected by members of one alliance cooperating with members of other alliances or (one or more) Gulf carrier(s) – mainly in the form of code sharing.

While for Star Alliance members respective options are restricted (only a maximum of 5% of the available seat kilometers can be offered under code share with members of another alliance[30]) other alliances are more 'generous' and code share agreements with non-aligned partners or even members of other alliances are accepted. According to Rigas Doganis 14% of Star Alliance routes are operated

[30] This is a new rule – until 2014 it was generally prohibited to have such agreements (so called "odd birds") – only for existing contracts a grace period was granted – in all other cases members had to petition special exceptions which were decided on by the other members in complicated negotiations.

with others, while for Oneworld the figure is 38%[31] (Thomas, 2014; see also Figure 6).

Different Levels of Integration

The largest alliance members and increasingly mid-sized carriers cooperate in the form of joint ventures providing them with additional economic benefits and a more powerful position within the alliances

While in 2003 some 10% of all long-haul routes with a length of more than 2,500 nm were under JV-conditions, it was 30% ten years later (Thomas, 2014)[32]. As already mentioned Joint Ventures produce significantly more economic benefits due to a much deeper integration of the participating airlines. As a matter of fact in all three alliances the biggest and strongest carriers are JV partners: Lufthansa and United, American Airlines and British Airways, Air France/KLM and Delta Airlines respectively[33]. All these airlines have a powerful position within their alliance with a respective potential to dominate it as a whole or single alliance partners.

As the example of Oneworld shows, JV-ties are not confined to the core players only. Under the heading: "*Deepening links between airline partners*" Oneworld's web page lists up their latest history:

Joint ventures constitute a "two-tier" system within the alliances. On the one hand this reduces the alliance-attractiveness for JV-partners and on the other hand leaves non-JV-members with the limited potential of the global alliances

"In October 2010, American Airlines, British Airways and Iberia launched a joint business across the North Atlantic, enabling them to offer customers even more benefits. Finnair joined this grouping in July 2013 and American Airlines' merger partner US Airways in April 2014. American Airlines and Japan Airlines launched a similar venture between Asia and North America in April 2011. British Airways and Japan Airlines followed suit, between Europe and Japan, in late 2012, with Finnair joining them in early 2014. American Airlines and Qantas followed suit across the South Pacific in early 2012." (Oneworld, 2015)

Consequently for the JV partners additional benefits of more cooperation will hardly come from increased collaboration with non-JV airlines inside the alliance but from an even deeper integration with existing or new JV partners. The significance of JV for the individual airlines becomes more and more important as expressed for example by the Vice President All Nippon Airways: "the airline's JV with United Airlines is at the core of our strategy and ANA would not be able to serve some US destinations without United's feeder services. Offering connectivity beyond Japan and deploying right-sized aircraft are key to successful operations to secondary cities in the US." (Matsushita, 2015)

Also as a consequence cooperation and engagement in the global alliance will clearly become less important for the biggest and most influential players.

---

[31] Thomas, J., quoted from Flight Global (2014).

[32] Thomas, J., quoted from Flight Global (2014).

[33] Just recently EU institutions indicated their willingness to approve Alitalia´s integration into the venture (Reuters, 2015).

Those airlines with small home markets which are not playing in the 'first alliance league' might increasingly feel uneasy and unsatisfied as they are stuck between the limited potential of alliance-wide cooperation on the one and a lack of access to JV´s on the other hand.

F. 2 Exogenous factors

Impact of Gulf Carriers´ Partner Strategies and Cross-Alliance Ventures

Partnering-activities of the carriers from the Gulf have a strong impact on the stability of the alliances. These strategies massively influence the business practices of the affected members by changing their loyalties vis-à-vis the alliances

The biggest current challenge for the stability of the global alliances as an exogenous factor seems to come from the Gulf carriers´ business strategies: By building up partnership- and even stakeholder-relationships Emirates, Etihad and Qatar Airways exercise direct influence on member airlines of the alliances. By realizing extraordinary growth with successful business models based on 6th Freedom Traffic[34] and supported by their governments[35] the Gulf carriers are attractive cooperation partners for many alliance members – especially for those who have no realistic chances to build joint ventures within the alliance.

The problem for the alliances is that those partner strategies are changing loyalties "and loyalties within the alliance are being undermined by joint ventures which create a two-tier membership structure". (Doganis, 2013)[36]

The first 'blow' happened in 2012 when Qantas, an Oneworld member, agreed to form what they call a "benefits-sharing model" with Emirates ending a 17-year partnership with its alliance partner British Airways. On the trunk routes between Dubai and long-haul flights to London, Asia and Australia/New Zealand 'margin-share', on non-trunk routes a commission-model is applied – so in effect that the model equals a 'true' joint venture which was given anti-trust clearance for 5 years.[37]

---

[34] The 6th "Freedom of the Air" describes the combination of rights from the third and fourth freedom with respect to two different contracting countries - the right of an airline to sell tickets from a contract-state to a third contract-state with the own state being only the place of transit.

[35] At this point it is irrelevant if and in how far these carriers are formally subsidized by their governments; all three Gulf carriers are at least state controlled, enjoy a special "treatment" and are part of the "national strategy".

[36] Doganis, R., quoted from Parker (2013, p.14). In this context "joint ventures" can be different from the models discussed above.

[37] The information is taken from a press release distributed by Emirates/Qantas short after the publication of the deal. In this press release no further details were given, however, statements vis-a-vis the Australian Competition and Consumer Commission gave some insight: "Margin share" in that context means that revenues are pooled and later shared on a net benefits basis which seems to measure how much more each airline

At the same time Qantas changed its hub for European flights from Singapore to Dubai and stopped code sharing with Asian airlines from their hubs to Europe. Not only for the Qantas-CEO this deal marks a 'seismic shift' which will have long lasting impact on the alliance landscape. (Joye, 2014)[38]

While Emirates is strictly following a policy of not joining any global alliance – nor any merger and acquisition programs (Clark, 2015)[39] Qatar Airways is doing exactly the opposite which has been mentioned already. To underline this policy Qatar has even acquired a 9.99% stake in British Airways (IAG) early 2015.

Etihad´s activities are even designed to build up a fourth global alliance with special insights into competing alliances

Etihad is pursuing a much more rigorous strategy by acquiring minority shares of ailing airlines in Europe and Asia. Although Etihad is in all cases only a minor share holder it exercises massive influence on the respective carriers as they receive substantial funding by Etihad.

The system of commercial cooperation between those carriers is very similar to the practice of the global alliances and James Hogan, CEO of Etihad himself called this a fourth global alliance „Etihad Airways Partners“. Consequently Star Alliance has recently integrated Etihad as such in its internal competition monitoring system.

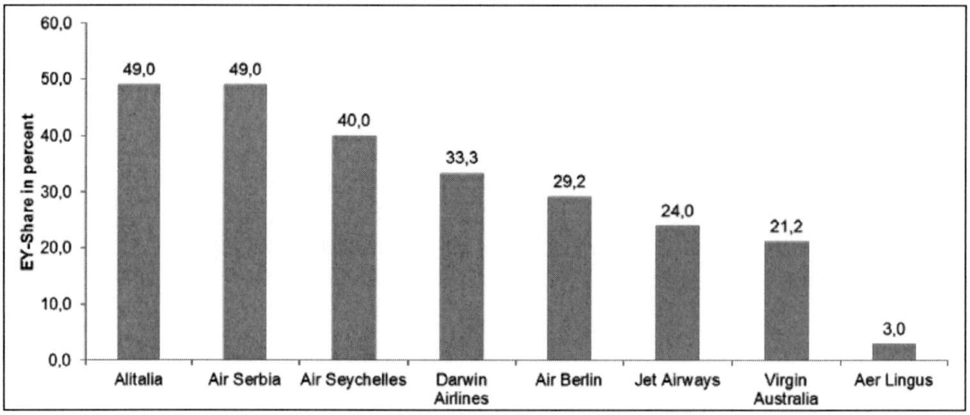

Figure 6: Acquisition-Portfolio Etihad 2015 (Scherff, 2014 / Mouawad, 2015)

By owning small a minority the airlines Etihad has not only tremendous insights in the internal planning and procedures of the respective airlines but also into the relevant topics and decision papers of the alliances; in the case of Alitalia (49%) of SkyTeam and in the case of

earns on that route than it did before the deal. On the non-trunk route the system is similar to a sales incentive agreement (Flightglobal, 2014).

38 Joyce, A., quoted from Flightglobal (2014).

39 Clark, T., quoted from Gulf News Aviation (2015).

Air Berlin 29%) of OneWorld. It will be interesting to see how the affected alliances will react to this constellation in the future.

Some AEA members left the organization due to the connection between Etihad and airlines of the alliances

In April 2015 some airlines demonstrated how strong – and destabilizing – the influence of the Gulf carriers on its subsidies can be for air carrier organizations as a reaction to an initiative of the biggest three US carriers, who had accused the Gulf carriers of receiving unjust subsidies and unfair competition. Important alliance members of SkyTeam and Star Alliance (Air France/KLM – Lufthansa respectively) had supported their American partners in that question also by means of lobbying through the Association of European Airlines (AEA). As a kind of 'joint response' the Gulf Carriers' European affiliates IAG and Air Berlin cancelled their membership in AEA within a couple of days leaving the organization with the necessity to completely restructure its policies and practices for the future[40]. Alitalia is expected to be next to quit AEA.

Cross-alliance strategies seem to become more common and are regarded as a 'normal' behavior; loyalty is not something the alliances can count on: If considerable commercial chances for cooperation are identified airlines will conclude far reaching deals with any potential partner irrespective of the membership in a global alliance.

Loyalty within alliances is diminishing: Cross-alliance strategies – for example in the area of code sharing - seem to become more common and are regarded as a "normal" behavior

Currently – as an example – Air China is talking openly about a venture with Qantas if the Australian Competition and Consumer Commission blocks a deal between China Eastern Airlines and Qantas. The Chairman of the Air China Commercial Committee Huang Bo explained that: "there are lots of very good examples of cross-alliance operations" specifically pointing at the cooperation between the Cathay Pacific and Air China. (Matsushita, 2015)

Garuda Indonesia (SkyTeam) and LOT Polish Airlines (Star Alliance) held a meeting in May 2015 to discuss potential cooperation. The airlines intend to implement a codeshare agreement. (Matsushita, 2015)

Air Berlin and Air France/KLM are also negotiating about intensified commercial cooperation including code share agreement.

Cross-alliance activity becomes visible also in the code share practice which has been demonstrated above – especially in the alliances with no or little restriction in that area respective activity is rising:

---

[40] IAG now announced to become a member in the European Low Fares Airlines Association (ELFAA).

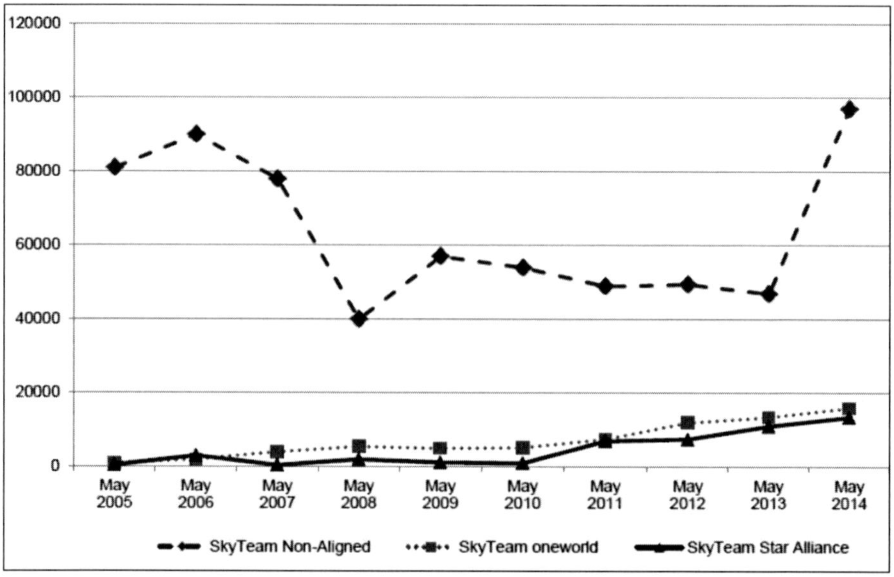

Figure 7: Code share Partnership by Number of Flights outside own Alliance / Example SkyTeam (Own illustration based on Jakl/Grimme, 2015)

In effect alliance-ties will become less and less relevant and membership finally is without obligation. There are no indications that this trend will change in the near future.

Impact of "New Distribution Capability"

New Distribution Capability is an IATA project that redefines communication standards between airlines and distribution partners

This challenge as an external threat to stability is still somewhat 'undetermined'- as for the time being it is in the phase of development and testing. However, it has the potential to massively influence the future prospects and even the existence of the global alliances.

New Distribution Capability (NDC) is an IATA project to define a new communication standard between airlines and distribution partners such as travel agencies, tour operators, global distribution systems and so on. It is designed to integrate more distribution partners and include more products. Another important aspect of NDC is the personalization potential to better understand customer preferences and increase brand loyalty.

So called "Unbundling-strategies"[41] and in times of immense and steadily increasing significance of ancillary revenues in the industry[42]

---

[41] "Unbundling" of services in the airline industry pertains to a business practice where the product "air travel" is separated into single "components" such as mere air transportation, carriage of luggage, inflight catering, seat reservation and other services which are subject to separate pricing as well.

[42] In 2012 53 reporting airlines made more than 27 bn. US$ with ancillaries; while the average profit per passenger was 5,65 US$ the average ancillary

the airlines will focus more and on more comprehensive, sophisticated sales strategies.

So far distribution partners could only book the airlines′ basic product but no additional individual services and products. By means of NDC the airlines create a digital distribution concept which is predicated on their internal availability and schedule system with fare and ancillary portfolio calibrated according to an airline-specific ‘rule-engine‘. Thus a direct agent channel for product merchandizing will be created.

Although NDC has not yet been implemented it has a considerable potential to destabilize the alliances

According to IATA the NDC standard will address the industry′s current distribution limitations (Muller, 2015):

- Product differentiation
- Access to full and rich content
- Greater shopping experience

Although it is too early to finally evaluate the actual impact of NDC some probable consequences can be identified:

In the environment of NDC presumably alliance-specific product features will become less important.

Moreover the NDC standard will contribute that the significance of bilateral interline relationships – most probably - will diminish eventually. The function of interlining (combined commercial utilization of two or more airline-networks) will potentially become obsolete: It could be performed by NDC applications which will directly tab the single airlines` portfolio and combine flights from different airlines together with the respective ‘individualized’ additional service requests.

NDC will reduce or might even make obsolete the function of interlining and also of code sharing in the airline industry and thus take away the basic sources of economic benefits of the alliances

Also the necessity of sharing codes will cease – airline distribution by partner airlines will probably not be needed as in the future NDC directly combines agents and producers.

By losing code share and interlining two basic forms of global airline cooperation disappear which have so far been the basis of the commercial success of airline alliances.

G. CONCLUSIONS AND FUTURE PERSPECTIVES FOR THE ALLIANCES

For the time being the future of global alliances can be summarized in just one word: undetermined.

Alliances are not a target as such, but a migration platform – alliances are not the endgame but transition as a response to the need of merger. (CAPA, 2013a)

---

revenue per passenger (all IATA carriers) was 13,93 US$ in 2012 (Friderici, 2015).

However, the question is: transition into what? If intra-alliance discipline and commitment will become weaker and weaker – as the number of JV's will increase further[43] and if code share and interlining will become obsolete – what is the economic justification of the global alliances for the carriers, inside or outside the joint-venture environment within the alliances?

For the alliances the first consequence is that they urgently need to find a way to response – and re-act to the challenges described above.

It would be naive to assume that the alliances are not aware of all these developments and challenges. However, it is not enough to identify risks and threats but also to come to the correct conclusions and actions. The problem is that joint action is becoming increasingly difficult for the reasons mentioned.

In the context of NDC: the alliances need to define their role in this new 'game'– will they be needed in the communication and distribution process between agents and airlines and what could be their value added? At least Star Alliance is already working on this issue.

As long as global consolidation has not taken place alliance have a future perspective

Generally a future perspective for alliances is probably given as long as they are still 'second best' regarding consolidation in the airline industry. In the best case – as the SkyTeam CEO puts it: "as long as global consolidation is not allowed co-operation on a global platform will be the name of the game." (Wisburn, 2013)[44]

In practice this would give the global alliances a chance to establish a system of deeper integration and closer cooperation especially among the 'non-JV-airlines' to exploit more synergies not only on the revenue side. This is an ambitious task as it would need to be realized mainly without the active support by the large and powerful hub-carriers within the alliances.

Also alliances would need to develop strategies to somehow align with Low Cost Carriers so that members can create a technical minimum standard to combine the different business models in order to make use of additional feeder and de-feeder options. This additional economic potential has so far been neglected and unused.

In a worst case scenario global alliance will become obsolete in a couple of years

However, the current discussions and negotiations between the US and the European Union in the context of TTIP also include questions of liberalizing transnational mergers in the airline industry. As a worst case scenario for the alliances, in a couple of years they will have become obsolete.

---

[43] Both, Lufthansa and Air China as well as Aeroméxico and Delta Airlines are contemplating the next joint ventures already.

[44] Wisburn, M., quoted from CAPA (2013a).

Review Questions

- How would you describe the overall significance of the global alliances in the world-airline industry
- What are the main membership-aspects of joining a global alliance and what are the 'hard conditions' to be met by the candidates?
- Name function and content of governance in global airline alliances. Why is the voting-system so important?
- Describe "Interline" and "Code sharing" as the two basic forms of intra-alliance cooperation.
- What are "Block Seat" and "Incentive" Agreements"?
- Give a brief overview on alliance-typical services and products that are offered to the passengers. What is the ultimate purpose of these products?
- What forms of fluctuation can be detected within alliances and why can this be a problem for them?
- Why is the economic potential of alliance-typical cooperation limited?
- Why have joint ventures a significantly higher economic potential?
- Why is it in most cases not possible to implement them as a general standard within an alliance?
- Why is it a problem that some members in the same alliance have and some do not have a joint venture relationship?
- How do partnering activities of the Gulf carriers affect the global alliance?
- What is the strategy of Etihad in that context and what is the special problem for the affected alliances?
- What does NDC mean and in which areas does it have potentially destabilizing effects on the alliances?
- In which way is the future perspective of alliances related to the further development of consolidation in the international airline industry?
- What is your personal opinion: Will there be global alliances in five years? Give reasons!

Bibliography and further reading

Airliners.de (2012): Star Alliance begrüßt Avianca-TACA und Copa, http://www.airliners.de/star-alliance-begruesst-avianca-taca-und-copa/27423, retrieved: 06/23/2015.

Al Baker, A. (2015): Qatar Air Threatens to Exit OneWorld Alliance, http://skift.com/2015/06/15/qatar-air-threatens-to-exit-oneworld-alliance/, retrieved: 06/23/2015.

CAPA – Center for Aviation (2013a): Airline alliances – what future?, http:// centreforaviation.com/analysis/airline-alliances---what-future-global-multilateral-and-bilateral-partnerships-are-all-evolving-144593, retrieved: 06/15/2015.

CAPA – Center for Aviation (2013b): Lufthansa ends codesharing with Turkish Airlines. A full rift would mean new strategies for each, http://centreforaviation.com/ analysis/lufthansa-ends-codesharing-with-turkish-airlines-a-full-rift-would-mean-new-strategies-for-each-142011, retrieved: 06/22/2015.

Chamberlin, C. (2015): Air China: we're open to Qantas partnership, Australian Business Traveller, http://www.ausbt.com.au/air-china-exec-we-re-open-to-qantas-partnership, retrieved: 06/23/2015.

Dron, A. (2015): IAG hints at future joint aircraft purchase, Air Transport World, 03/11/2015.

Düring, R. / Jahberg, H. (2015): Air Berlin kämpft um seinen Partner Etihad, in: Der Tagesspiegel, 04 /13/2015, p.14.

Flightglobal (2014): Knipp, D. Has Emirates-Qantas been a game-changer?, in: Flightglobal.com.

Frankfurter Allgemeine Zeitung [FAZ] (04/13/2012), p. 19.

Frankfurter Allgemeine Zeitung [FAZ.net] (2011): Skyteam greift Star Alliance an, http://www.faz.net/aktuell/wirtschaft/unternehmen/luftverkehr-skyteam-greift-star-alliance-an-1575657.html, retrieved: 06/31/2015.

Friderici, D. (2015): Destination NDC, IBS-Presentation, ITB-Congress.

Gulf News Aviation (2015): Emirates President Tim Clark in: Emirates to extend Qantas partnership beyond 2018, http://gulfnews.com/business/aviation/emirates-to-extend-qantas-partnership-beyond-2018-1.1494163, retrieved: 04/20/2015.

Iatrou, K. / Oretti, M. (2007): Airline Choices for the Future – From Alliances to Mergers, Hampshire.

Jakl, S. / Grimme, W. (2015): An analysis of airlines' code-sharing practices in strategic alliances between 2005 and 2014, DLR – Institute of Air Transport and Airport Research.

Machatscke, M. (2015): Die Rote Gefahr, in: Manager Magazin, Vol. 45, No. 2, p. 50-53.

Matsushita, T (2015): View From The East. Lufthansa Group Briefing Asia/Pacific, 04/28/2015.

Mouawad, J. (2015): Etihad defends business model, International New York Times, 03.03.2015.

Muller, C. (2015): Toughworks with IATAQ Farelogix – NDC Program, Presentation ITB Congress 2015.

Oneworld (2015): Introduction to oneworld - an alliance of the world's leading airlines working as one, http://de.oneworld.com/news-information/oneworld-fact-sheets/introduction-to-oneworld.com, retrieved: 06/22/2015.

Parker, A. (2013): Gulf carriers destabilise alliances, in: Financial Times Europe, http://www.ft.com/cms/s/0/609582c0-4628-11e3-b495-00144feabdc0.html#axzz3dnIOJXSf, retrieved: 06/16/2015.

Reuters (2015): UPDATE 1-EU to approve Air France-KLM, Delta, Alitalia pact – sources, http://www.reuters.com/article/2015/04/28/eu-airlines-idUSL8N0XP4Z020150428, retrieved: 06/22/2015.

Scherff, D. (2014): Etihad fliegt auf Deutschland, Frankfurter Allgemeine Zeitung 09.03.2014.

SkyTeam (2015a): Airline Member requirements, http://www.skyteam.com/en/about-us/our-members/airline-member-requirements/, retrieved: 06/22/2015.

SkyTeam (2015b): Customer Advantages, (http://www.skyteam.biz/en/customer-advantages/), retrieved: 06/22/2015.

SkyTeam (2015c): Organization – Management, http://www.skyteam.com/de/About-us/Organization/Management/, retrieved: 06/15/2015.

SkyTeam (2015d): SkyTeam Awarded Airline Alliance of the Year by Air Transport News, Amsterdam, http://www.skyteam.com/en/about-us/press/news/news-overview-2015/skyteam-awarded-airline-alliance-of-the-year-by-air-transport-news/, retrieved: 06/23/2015.

Star Alliance (2015a): Facts & Figures, http://www.staralliance.com/assets/doc/en/about/member-airlines/pdf/SCP_Facts%20and%20Figures.pdf, retrieved: 07/28/2015.

Star Alliance (2015b): Tailor-Made Business Travel, http://www.staralliance.com/en/business-solutions/, retrieved: 06/23/2015.

The Economist (2012): Airline alliances – new oneworld order, http://www.economist.com/blogs/gulliver/2012/10/airline-alliances, retrieved: 05/22/2015.

Tugores-García, A. (2012): Analysis of Global Airline Alliances as a Strategy for International Network Development, Master Thesis Massachusetts Institute of Technology.

Wright, R. (2015): Qatar Airways chief steps up battle over protectionism, Financial Times, 06/09/2015, p. 19.

Network Planning and Slot Management

Harald Deprosse, Michael Händel

Table of contents

You should be able to

- show how the specific characteristics of the airline industry shape the process of network planning
- name and evaluate the factors that determine an airline's network
- explain how network development and network scheduling are connected
- differentiate between the underlying phases of network scheduling and outline what happens in these phases
- explain why slot management is important for network scheduling
- explain how slot allocation is managed at coordinated airports and which criteria apply

The authors

Harald Deprosse has held various management positions at Lufthansa German Airlines, Frankfurt/M, Germany. Currently he is Managing Director Miles & More GmbH.

Michael Händel has worked in various functions at Lufthansa German Airlines, Frankfurt / Main, Germany. Currently he is Director Network Planning Hub Munich.

Abstract

This chapter deals with two topics: network planning and (to a lesser extend) slot management.

Part one – network planning – aims to illustrate characteristics, processes, and constraints in airline network planning. It outlines different possible strategic settings for network planning by comparing low-cost carriers with classic network carriers. Furthermore, four economic characteristics, which determine the airline network, are introduced: demand development, yield development, revenue management and cost management. The network planning processes are described starting with a forecast-based network development for the purpose of fleet dimensioning. Network scheduling follows as the next process step, and is introduced in its four phases of basic schedule structurization, optimization, realization, and implementation. The constraints in network planning are described and possible reactions to internal or external influence factors are shown. Finally, current trends of network planning are discussed to reflect changes in the alliance and joint venture-landscape as well as the ongoing consolidation processes.

A slot is a predefined timeframe in which an aircraft may land or take off from an airport. As some of the world's airports operate at their capacity limits, an accepted slot allocation process is necessary. Slot capacity of an airport is determined by its technical (number and location of runways, installed navigation systems, handling capacities) and legal (curfews, flight movement limits etc.) capabilities.

Therefore, the section concerning slot management deals with the characteristics, restrictions and processes in slot management. It describes the restrictions of slot scheduling, which are defined by the International Air Traffic Association (IATA) and, in the following, it outlines a classification scheme for airports. The slot management process is introduced starting with possible priority rules for slot allocation. Slot application, slot coordination and optimization are described as subsequent steps. Finally, current trends in slot management, especially slot trading, are discussed.

A. INTRODUCTION

A. 1 European airline industry before and after liberalization

In restricted markets, competition was extremely limited

Until the early 1990s, almost every state operated its own airline as a national carrier. In the majority of cases these airlines exclusively served their own and often limited home market. Competition with other carriers was extremely limited due to wide spread bilateral air traffic agreements with tight capacity and route restrictions. The size and the network of an airline of this type were hence defined by the size of its home market demand and existing traffic rights.

Continuous liberalization of European air traffic legislation began in the late 1980s and opened up numerous possibilities for national airlines to expand their reach beyond their limited home markets:

Liberalization process was conducted in several packages

- The first liberalization package in 1987 enabled airlines to offer reduced fares, a simplified fare-approval process and eased restrictions on capacity split between countries
- The second liberalization package in 1989 cancelled further restrictions with regard to minimum fares and capacity splits
- The third liberalization package in 1993 abolished all constraints with regards to capacity and routes within the European Union (except cabotage-flights which became unrestricted 1997)
- Bilateral agreements for air-traffic between the European Union and other countries have also tended to become less restricted (e.g. the Open Skies agreement from 2008 between the USA and Europe lifted all capacity and route restrictions on transatlantic flights)

As a result, air traffic within EU and over the North-Atlantic today is completely liberalized whereas traffic between EU and Eastern Europe, Asia and Russia remains more or less restricted.

Airlines have to choose between growth- and niche strategy

In this increasingly deregulated airline market, competition has increased and airlines have had to choose between two basic strategic alignments: remain at their present size and operate in a protected niche-market or grow and explore global markets. However, both strategic alignments have required more accurate methods in designing the airline's network than in the protected times before liberalization.

A. 2 P2P versus network airlines

Establishing of Low-cost Carriers (LCC)

With liberalization, one new strategy arose for European continental airlines: low-cost carriers (LCC). Whereas the 'classic' network carrier operates one or more hubs to bundle passengers in order to reach economies of scale effects, an LCC only operates independent routes with almost no connection system. This is called point-to-point (P2P) as opposed to a hub and spoke concept. Both are shown in Figure 1.

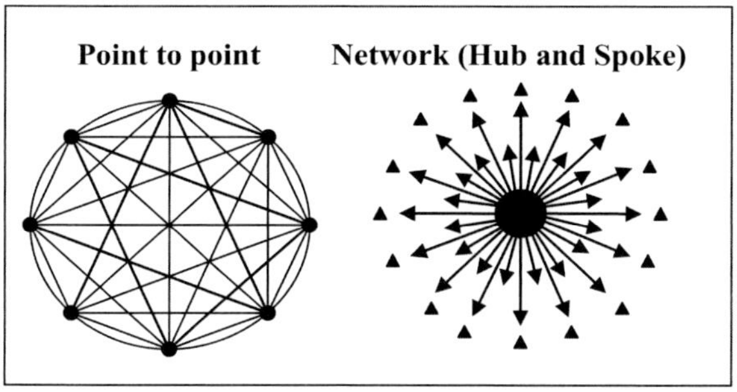

Figure 1: Production concepts of P2P vs. network carrier (Own illustration)

Basic operating principles of LCC

P2P-route portfolio consists of mainly high density short and medium haul routes. The lack of scale effects from neglecting connecting passengers is compensated for by optimizing the remaining cost structure:

- Operation of cost efficient, large continental aircraft suitable only on high demand P2P-routes
- Fleet consisting of one or very few aircraft types
- Operation to uncongested secondary airports in order to reduce aircraft-turnaround times and airport charges/handling cost
- Lean service concepts
- Cost efficient distribution structure
- Stimulation for lack of demand by lowering prices in order to achieve continuously high load factors

The typical LCC operates out of many different bases throughout Europe. Once all suitable P2P-routes are explored from one home base the next base is opened and connected to the system. This model only became possible when airlines were able to operate unrestrictedly between any two cities in the EU. In addition, the possibility of selling tickets via internet from the mid 1990s on was a basic prerequisite for establishing cost efficient distribution structures.

The following comments refer to network planning at a typical large and growing European network carrier.

B. INDUSTRY CHARACTERISTICS

With deregulation eliminating almost all constraining legal factors, today four purely economic characteristics determine an airline's network:

- Major demand concentrated on very few routes
- Decreasing yields
- Necessity of revenue management
- Necessity of cost management

B. 1 Demand

Demand for air traffic is concentrated on very few, large routes (see Figure 2). For intercontinental traffic, many of these routes are transatlantic connections; for continental traffic, they are typically found on domestic routes between the country's largest cities as well as between European metropolitan areas such as London or Paris.

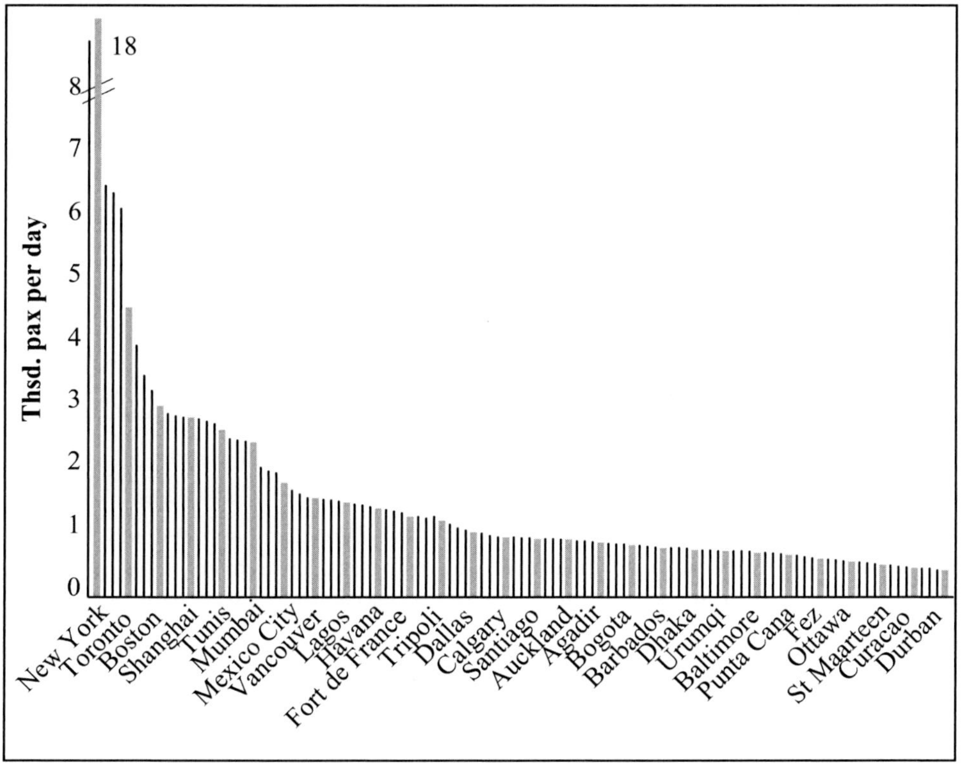

Figure 2: Demand is concentrated on very few routes (Own illustration based on data from CRS)

Demand is bundled via a hub airport

As an airline wishes to offer a broad network in order to provide as many different travel solutions to the customer as possible the relevance of connections grows. Only by connecting different origin and destination cities via one or several hubs can a critical load for routes without sufficient local demand be achieved. Therefore, network management is all about connecting origins and destinations (O&Ds).

B. 2 Yield development

Decreasing yields and increasing RPK

While air traffic demand, measured in revenue passenger kilometers (RPK), has constantly grown in the last 20 years, a continuous decline in the fares paid by the passengers (yield) can be observed since the beginning of deregulation in the early 1990s. Figure 3 summarizes this yield development.

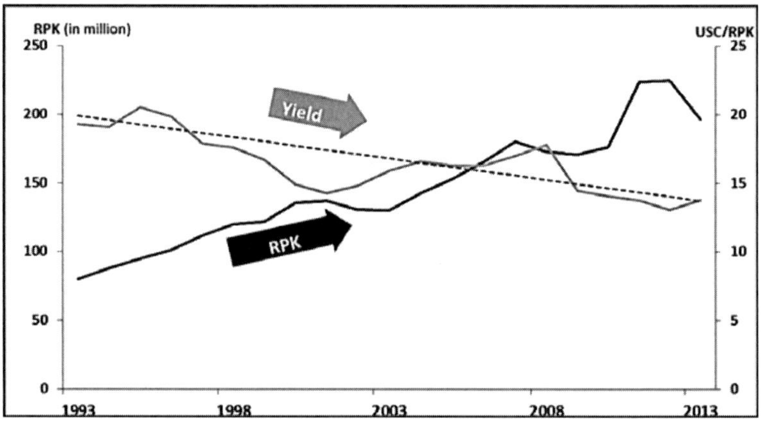

Figure 3: Yield development since 1993 (Own illustration)

An airline therefore has to plan ahead for declining revenues that have to be matched either by a rise in passenger numbers, intelligent ways to soften yield-decline and of course by strict cost management.

B. 3 Revenue management

Revenue management differentiates products and attracts new customers

Declining yields can be countered by efficiently using the demand potential. With accurate revenue management tools and diverse pricing structures, airlines try to skim maximum revenue from the limited available demand. Figure 4 outlines, that a single price (and product) does not maximize revenue, and due to that price segmentation can cause additional revenues and a higher passenger (PAX) volume.

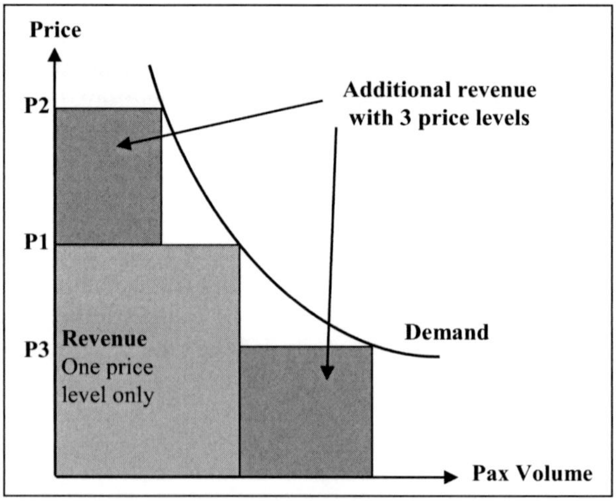

Figure 4: Importance of revenue management (Own illustration)

The tools for effective revenue management and its underlying principles are explained in detail in chapter [number], 'Airline revenue management'.

B. 4 Cost management

The economic performance of an airline is influenced by many external drivers. Special attention therefore must be paid to constantly managing an airline's cost position.

Airlines can control only parts of their operating costs

With regards to costs, many drivers lie out of an airline's control, so the remaining, mainly indirect, cost positions must be closely monitored and constantly reduced. Over the last 10 years, for example, European airlines have managed to reduce indirect operating costs by roughly 10%. This cost advantage has been completely absorbed by rising direct operating costs that an airline can only partly control (e.g. fuel or air traffic control (ATC) and landing fees). Figure 5 illustrates the cost structure of an exemplified A320.

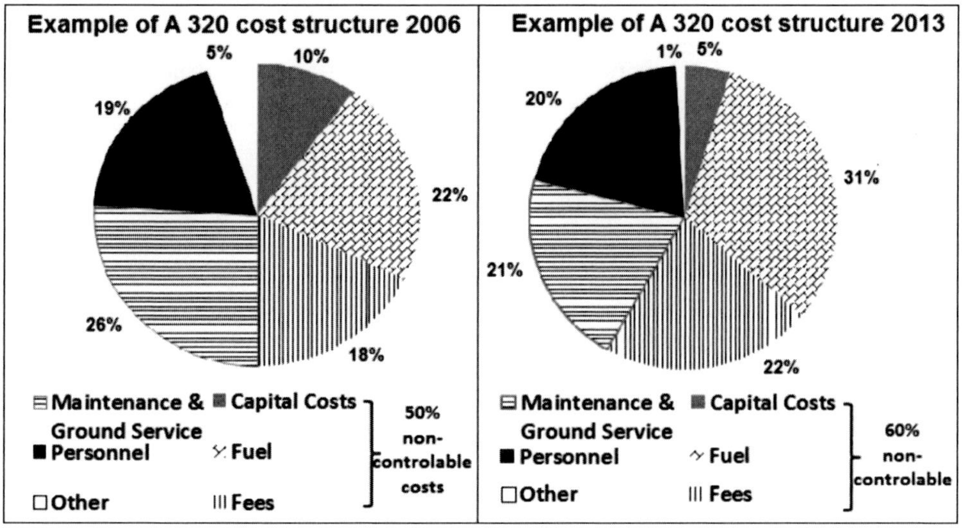

Figure 5: A 320 cost structures
(Own illustration based on Lufthansa data)

Production costs of an airline are highly dependent on the size of the deployed aircraft. Figure 6 shows that continental aircraft with 200 seats can produce roughly at 60% of the cost per seat compared to a 100-seat regional aircraft. The hub and spoke concept of network airlines helps to maximize load factors by combining different O&Ds in order to deploy as large an aircraft as possible.

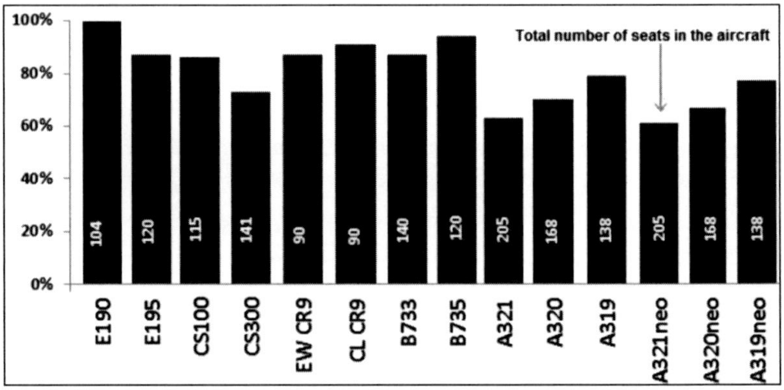

Figure 6: Production cost with regard to continental aircraft size (Own illustration)

C. NETWORK DEVELOPMENT

The framework for all long-term network development is an annually revolving planning system that defines market and competitive strategies.

C. 1 Market and competitor development

Sources for demand forecast

Different sources for demand forecast exist in the airline industry. Most common are the International Air Traffic Association (IATA) Forecast and the market outlooks of the two big aircraft manufacturers Boeing and Airbus:

- The IATA forecast focuses on the number and growth of O&D passengers between countries and bases its forecast on an evaluation of all its member airlines (Delphi Methodology). It usually forecasts no more than four consecutive years and tends to be relatively precise as the regional expertise of every relevant member airline is included
- The manufacturers combine historic aircraft demand with economic and passenger demand data and project their evaluations up to 20 years into the future. They focus primarily on the number and size of airplane-orders but also give indications on passenger growth and regional developments

Furthermore, larger airlines tend to establish more detailed forecasts. They tend to use own forecasting systems that combine historic O&D data and economic projections (GDP growth, imports/exports growth, population growth etc.).

Finally, universities and political institutions set up demand forecasts with a focus on providing data for traffic infrastructure planning.

Main information is market growth and competitor development

Airlines use these forecasts to determine the overall market growth (needed for capacity planning) and regional distribution of growth (needed for capacity planning and specific market strategies). For several years, forecasts for European network airlines for example have shown a general market growth of 4-7% and regional growth centers in traffic to/from Eastern Europe, the Middle East and Asia.

Development of the main competitors can also be derived from the regional information of market forecasts but is often enhanced by evaluating the published aircraft order books of the manufacturers.

Based on both, market and competitor development, a picture of the expected development in travel demand can be sketched. Within this framework an airline sets up several key strategies that determine future network and fleet development:

- Definition of key strategic markets
- Definition of its own growth rates and their regional distribution
- Definition of number, size and role of hubs

C. 2 Fleet dimensioning

Number and size of available aircraft is one of the most important factors influencing an airline's network development. The fleet development is basically driven by replacement and growth.

Reasons for aircraft replacement

Replacement needs for an airlines' leased aircraft fleet are clearly predetermined by the structure of existing lease contracts and the situation in the aircraft lease market. Whether or not an owned aircraft needs to be replaced is influenced by technological, economic, and strategic questions:

- Does an aircraft reach its technological life-cycle limit (e.g. operational stability is insufficient or large investments have to be made to continue operating etc.)?
- Does a replacement aircraft provide new technology that reduces operating costs significantly enough to justify the investment?
- Are new aircraft available from manufacturers/lessors?
- Does the airline's economic position allow for an investment?
- Will the older aircraft still be needed for future flexibility?

Market position and growth plans also determine the number and size of aircraft to be acquired

The number and size of aircraft to be acquired can be derived from the airlines' strategic positioning in the market described above. The O&D passenger growth rates an airline aims for can be translated into a growth in seats. Furthermore, regional distribution of capacity and the ratio of direct/connecting traffic are needed to calculate for an exact capacity target in the future.

Together with the envisaged productivity development, a total additional capacity can be calculated in relation to the existing seat capacity. Figure 7 shows an example for a calculation of a fleet development and the influencing factors.

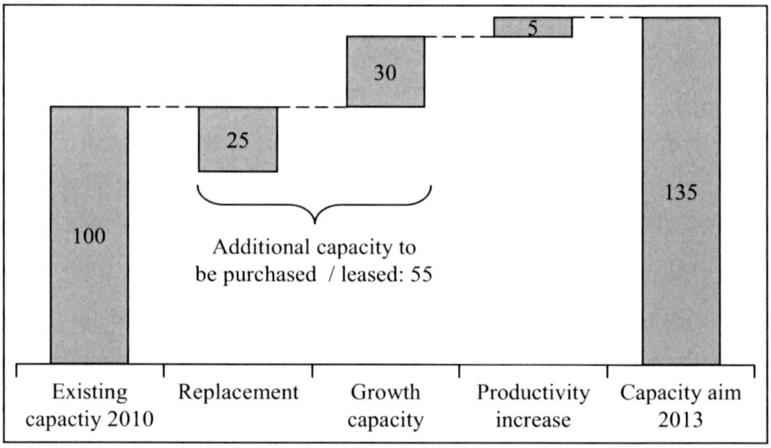

Figure 7: Example of fleet dimensioning

Size and type of replacement and growth aircraft are determined again by technological, economic and strategic questions, for example:

- Which aircraft meet the technological requirements?
- Which aircraft are available on the market?
- Which aircraft meet the economic requirements?
- Which aircraft size fits best into the fleet structure in order to keep up a sensible mix of small and large aircraft ('staggering')?

D. NETWORK SCHEDULING

D. 1 Economics of network scheduling

Network scheduling aims at a maximization of potential revenue at the lowest production cost possible with the currently existing fleet size and structure.

Network scheduling is about maximizing potential revenue and minimizing costs

By connecting different pairs of cities via one or several hubs, the number of servable routes for an airline is significantly increased compared to a network relying solely on local demand. Thus, potential revenue is maximized.

At the same time production costs are reduced when bundling passengers in hubs. This is because a significant part of a flight's cost is fixed and thus not affected by the number of passengers transported (i.e. travel cost and allowances for crew, maintenance cost, depreciation of aircraft etc.). Additional passengers can be transported at marginal costs (additional fuel, landing fees, catering etc.).

With limited local demand, the only possibility for network planning to make use of scale effect and to increase revenue potential is by establishing O&D connections (Figure 8).

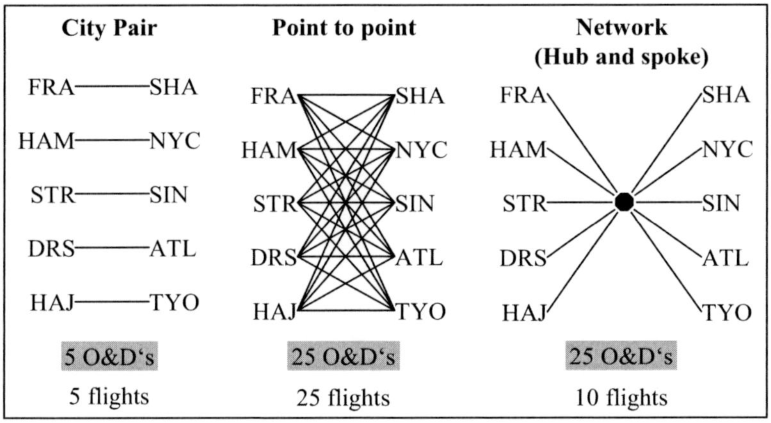

Figure 8: Maximization of potential revenue by establishing O&D connections (Own illustration)

Further possibilities for the reduction of production costs lie in the reduction of fixed costs. However, this is a general management task and is out of the control and planning horizon of network planning. Therefore, only the direct operating costs (DOC) are relevant for shaping an airline's network.

The following simplified example illustrated the economic mechanism behind hub systems (Figure 9).

Available A/C	Type 1	Type 2	Type 3
Seats	80	120	200
Revenue per Pax per day	40		
Fixed costs per flight	900	1000	1100
Variable costs per flown km	8	9	10
Total costs per flight	4.900	5.500	6.100

Assumptions

- Stage length: 500 km every flight
- Only four destinations exist: A, B, C, and D
- Potential Hub: B
- Required min. SLF: 60%,
- No preferences between direct and hub services

Revenue Potential

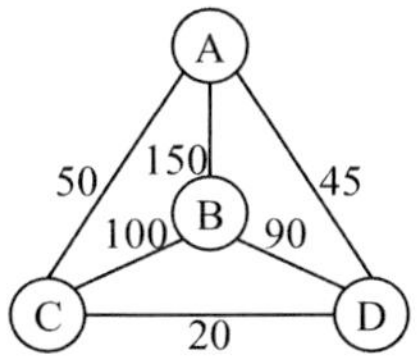

Results	Hub	Direct
Flights	3 (A-B, B-C, B-D)	4 (A-B, A-C, B-C, B-D)
Revenue	18.200 (150*40+100*40+90*40+ 50*40+45*40+20*40)	15.600 (150*40+100*40+ 90*40+50*40)
Cost	17.100 (6.100+2*5.500)	21.400 (6.100+5.500+2*4.900)
Profit	1.100	-5.800

Figure 9: Simplified example of hub economics (Own illustration)

The basis of this calculation is a hub and spoke system as opposed to a P2P-System with the following assumptions: there are only four destinations, every flight is 500 kilometers long, there are three different A/C types available, and direct flights are only offered if the passenger load factor (SLF) is at least 60%. Due to that the routes A to D and C to D are not served directly, but via a hub and spoke route structure allowing the airlines to bundle their passengers via a central hub. Advantages of this concept are better connectivity, a higher passenger load factor, and an increase in efficiency.

D. 2 Constraints in network scheduling

Ideally, network planning would be conducted as an optimization of the previously mentioned parameters of potential revenue and operating cost. This would mean connecting the highest possible number of O&Ds via one hub with an even utilization of production resources.

In reality, however, numerous constraints limiting an airline's possibilities to design the optimum network have to be considered, as illustrated in Figure 10:

Different factors influence network scheduling

- External factors (slots, spread of demand during day/week/season, traffic rights, airport infrastructure, competitors, customer preferences etc.)
- Internal factors (crew resources, aircraft performance, fleet structure, strategy etc.)

Some of them can be altered, but not in the time frame given for network planning periods. Thus, they are limiting factors that the network planning needs to take into account as a basis for planning.

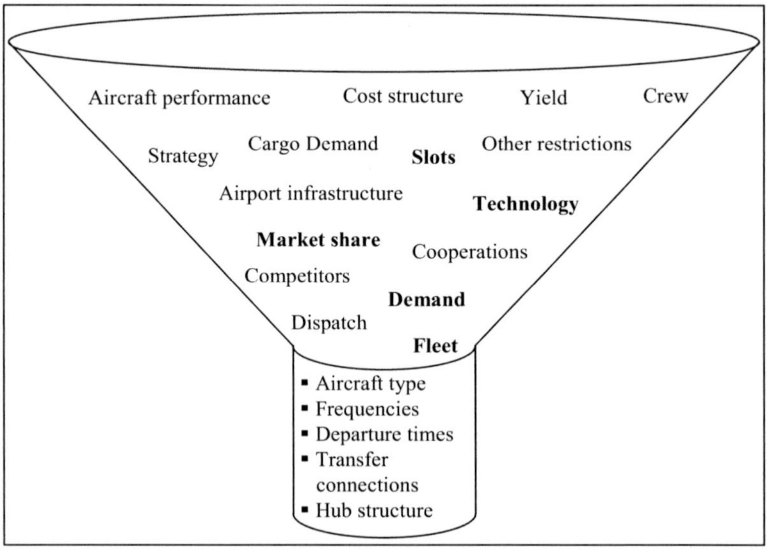

Figure 10: Constraints in network planning (Own illustration)

E. PROCESS OF NETWORK SCHEDULING

Four phases of network scheduling

Network planning is a continuous and revolving process. It can be divided into two parts consisting of the preparations for the two main flight plan periods in summer and winter. Both schedules undergo four basic phases of preparation:

- Basic schedule structuring
- Optimization
- Realization
- Implementation

E. 1 Basic schedule structuring

On the basis of an old flight plan, the new one is outlined

Roughly 12 to 18 months before the flight plan period starts, the first draft of a flight plan is worked out. Flights and destinations are planned with IT tools and a first rotation planning is made on the basis of demand estimations.

The typical bank structure of a hub is either extended into the future or altered in this phase. In a bank flight arrivals and departures are bundled and spread over the day in order to achieve attractive connection times for the passengers. Typical hubs spread their arrival and departure peaks over six or eight banks a day. Flights in need of a retiming are drawn from one bank to another in this phase. Figure 11 outlines the bank structure for the Munich (MUC) summer schedule 2014.

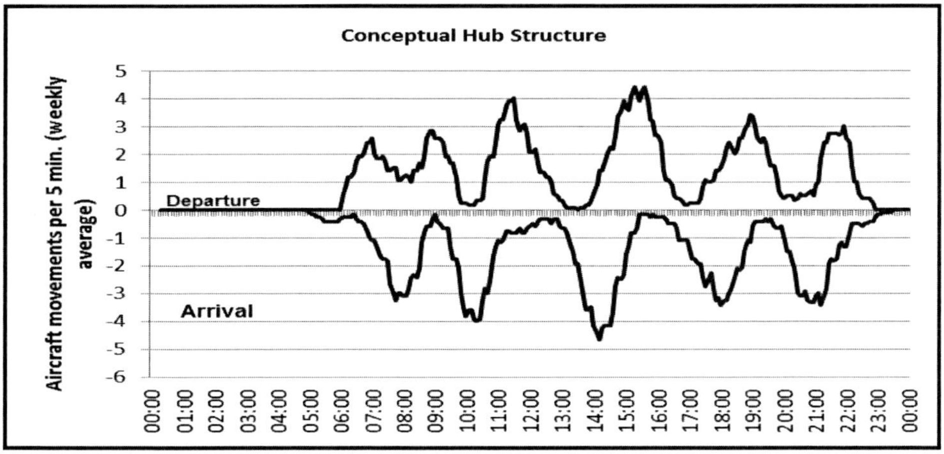

Figure 11: Conceptual bank structure of hubs (Own illustration)

Typical constraints

As soon as constraints are already known they will be incorporated into this early stage of flight plan. Typical constraints that are known in this phase are:

- Scheduled maintenance downtimes
- Historical slot restrictions
- Revolving peak and off-peak dates such as trade fairs or public holidays

- Planned new projects like destinations or additional frequencies
- Abandonment of destinations

E. 2 Optimization

Seven months before the flight plan period's start, an optimization process is begun on the basis of the previously mentioned pre-structured flight plan. The IT based optimization aims at maximizing the hub-connectivity in order to secure maximum potential revenue.

New information and further constraints are incorporated

Based upon historic and actual booking figures, it identifies O&D traffic with particularly high revenue potential. Connection times for these O&Ds are optimized – if necessary by also disconnecting other O&D traffic with less revenue potential. In addition, further restrictions in the possible aircraft rotations as well as known slot restrictions are incorporated.

At coordinated airports, airlines apply for desired slots

IATA slot conference

After this first optimization phase has ended, an iterative process begins in order to integrate the slot-framework into the schedule. At capacity coordinated airports, the airline applies for all the slots they need to produce the optimized flight schedule. Slots are allocated to the airline upon the basis of this first application. Because some of these slots are not the desired times the airline applied for, airlines have the opportunity to swap slots with other airlines and to negotiate slots with the relevant airport coordinators at the bi-annual IATA Slot Coordination Conference. After a period of roughly two months airlines have to return slots they do not intend to use in the upcoming schedule period by the 'slot hand-back deadline'.

E. 3 Realization

The realization phase begins approximately six months ahead of the schedule period.

Further optimization based on real slots

Firstly, another optimization process with current market data and results from the Slot Coordination Conference is run. Secondly, the preliminary slot assumptions are replaced by actual slots and, in the end, the optimized flight schedule is more precisely seasonally adjusted to accommodate to holiday times or bank holidays, for example. The realization phase ends one month before the schedule period begins.

E. 4 Implementation

The implementation phase starts one month ahead of the schedule period and lasts until its end. The structure of a flight schedule usually remains unchanged during implementation. However, ongoing changes are made with regard to aircraft-equipment, seasonality-adjustments or ad-hoc charters. These changes are more often made for continental traffic, because optimization flexibility is much higher with higher flight frequencies and aircraft types whereas intercontinental schedules typically remain rather unchanged for one season.

Every single month is planned in detail six weeks in advance

During implementation phase, the IT-based fleet assignment takes place every six weeks ahead of a scheduled month. It aims to achieve an optimum deployment of production resources throughout the whole network. Before this step, each flight in the schedule was dedicated to an aircraft that was ideal for its isolated revenue potential. After this step, it is possible that a single flight has to operate with an aircraft either too small or too large for the demand.

Fleet assignment parameters

However, in total, an optimum rotation in the whole network is established where the existing fleet is deployed to its best. Parameters for the fleet assignment are cost, demand, network effects, and planning guidelines (such as minimum ground times, crew restrictions on certain fleets etc.)

After the IT-based fleet assignment has taken place, a final schedule for the coming month is delivered to crew planning as a basis for the crew roster for each flight.

Finally, the operation center takes over responsibility and makes last adoptions

Responsibility for the schedule is handed over to the operations center one month before operation for the respective week on a weekly basis. The operations center will further adapt the schedule with regards to already known operational, regulatory or crew-planning issues until finally tail signs are assigned to each flight. Within 3 days before operation all short notice incidents, such as weather or maintenance requirements, are incorporated into the actual flight schedules.

The following figure shows an overview summarizing the process of network scheduling as described above.

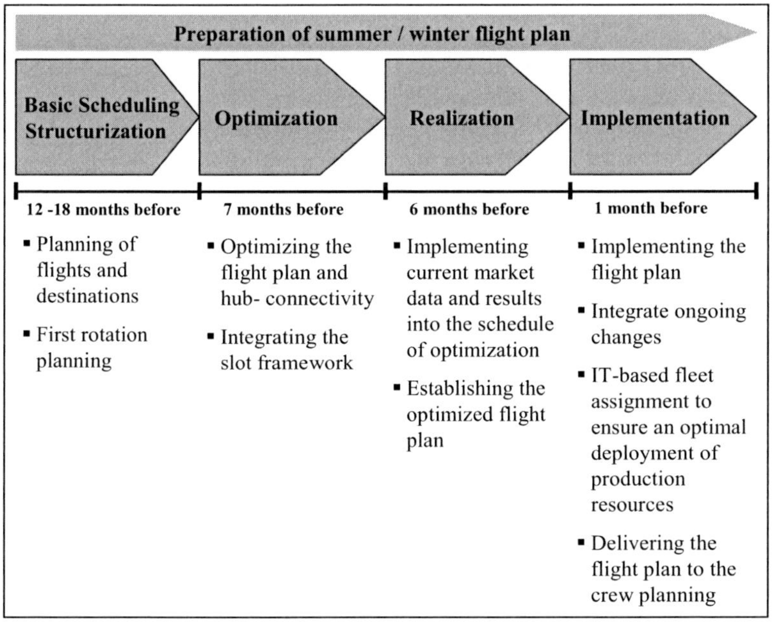

Figure 12: Process of network scheduling (Own illustration)

F. CURRENT TRENDS IN NETWORK PLANNING

F. 1 Network development

Shorter cycles make it more difficult to forecast capacity needs

Although the long-term development of demand still shows a constant growth trend, intermediate cycles have become shorter. This makes it increasingly difficult to make valid forecasts as a basis of precise capacity measures within a typical development time-frame of three to five years. Also, the risk of falsely predicted capacity measures has increased drastically: planned expansions that fall within a period of deep recession when the corresponding aircraft are finally delivered are as dangerous to an airline's cash position as lack of capacity is for an airline's market position when the market picks up despite a forecasted downturn.

Thus, flexibility is one goal of network development

Airlines therefore tend to plan in flexible terms rather than in precise capacities. For example, companies try to maintain both older and newer aircraft with a continuous phase-in of aircraft deliveries. This opens up possibilities for an earlier roll-over in times of decreasing demand as well as additional capacity in unforeseen boom times by extending older aircraft life-cycles. Also, delivery options at aircraft manufacturers allow airlines to decide as late as possible, with a clear picture of the market, whether they want to convert the option into firm deliveries without running the risk of missing production slots.

In isolated terms, this is often not the most economical way to secure future capacity. But, due to the high risk and uncertainty of long-term capacity planning, it is by far safer to invest in higher flexibility rather than in the least expensive capacity available.

In the light of alliances, network development becomes even more complicated

In addition, network development has become more complex because changes in alliances, joint ventures or in the ongoing consolidation process cannot be overseen in a typical development period of three to five years. Strategic decisions run the increasing risk of being proven wrong in the future because a new partner has been integrated or an established partner lost. Therefore, network development is increasingly required to evaluate strategic decisions in different partner and consolidation scenarios.

F. 2 Network planning

Due to increasing complexity, network planning is in danger of losing transparency

Due to the increasing size of Europe's main network airlines and the maximized use of IT tools, network planning has become increasingly complex. There is not only a threat to internal transparency over an airline's own network; IT-triggered network planning measures have also become increasingly difficult for customers to understand, when for example, daily varying aircraft types in different cabin layouts are deployed on the same flight number. This is especially true for passengers using only P2P-flights within a hub system, e.g. on large trunk routes. With increasing competition and rising number of direct connections network airlines can no longer afford to "force" local traffic into network hub structures.

A trend can therefore be seen in optimizing parts of the network on a stand-alone basis. For instance large trunk routes are operated on an "every hour on the hour" flight schedule in order to make the flight schedule most attractive to the high yield P2P-pax. The main criterion for optimization of those routes has hence become the local traffic rather than the connectivity of connecting traffic.

Local traffic has become the most important optimization criterion on highly competitive routes

Despite the economic advantages of hub-systems over direct flights, the P2P-Model of low-cost carriers has also forced network-carriers to reconsider their, often drastically reduced, decentralized route portfolio. Network carriers have rebuilt their position in large and important catchment areas outside their hubs in order to maintain good market positions for important corporate and private customers. This explains expansion strategies in decentralized catchment areas that would ideally be done via existing hub systems.

Low Cost oriented platforms within network-airlines become increasingly important

Often these approaches use a new production platform within or without the traditional network airline's structure. By this means, more competitive cost positions, e.g. through lower labour cost or higher density cabin layouts, can be achieved. With increasing competition also in the hubs it will be only a matter of time until parts of the incumbent hub-production will be done also by means of new production platforms. Network planning will then have to find new ways of coordinating classic hub-flights with low-cost oriented platform flights.

G. SLOT MANAGEMENT

G. 1 Types of slots

The term slot is used for two different subjects: the 'air traffic control' (ATC) slot (also 'airway slot') and the 'airport slot' (also 'runway slot'). Slot coordination processes do only apply to airport slots.

Air traffic slot

The ATC slot defines a time window for each departing flight on the actual day of operation and is mandatory for all flights operated under instrument flight rules. It is only valid for this specific flight and for a specific departure time window. The responsibility for ATC slots lies with the air traffic authorities, in Europe at Eurocontrol in Brussels.

Airport slot

The airport slot describes a specific time, on a specific weekday, for a specific interval for arrival and departure at airports where capacity is limited. It is usually allocated for a maximum of one schedule period and is used primarily for the planning purposes of airports and airlines in order to minimize airport congestion and thus potential delays. The following comments refer only to airport slots.

G. 2 Legal framework

International Air Traffic Association (IATA) has set up worldwide slot scheduling guidelines, which are the basis for the local procedures at airports in need of a slot management. For European airports the

Slot scheduling guidelines set the framework for an efficient and non-discriminating allocation process

regulations have been harmonized by the European Union (Council Regulation (EEC) No 95/1993, amended by regulations (EC) No 894/2002, 1554/2003, 793/2004 and 545/2009) which is based on the IATA guidelines. The aim of EU and IATA regulations/guidelines is to ensure that, where airport capacity is scarce, the available landing and take-off slots are used efficiently and distributed in an equitable, non-discriminatory and transparent way. The core of both is a classification scheme for airports and priority rules in the slot allocation process.

Airports are classified in three levels

The classification scheme distinguishes between three levels of airports:

Level one: non-coordinated airports

At level one airports, capacities are adequate and meet the demand of the airlines. An airline planning a flight to one of these airports needs to declare it at the airport corporation but needs no approval.

Level two: facilitated airports

Level two airports still offer sufficient capacity to the airlines but are approaching their capacity limits. A formal level of cooperation in the form of voluntary cooperation between the airlines is required to operate the airport efficiently. Airlines need to declare their planned arrival/departure times at the airport to the airport facilitator but need no approval.

Level three: coordinated airports

At level three airports demand for take-off/landing slots exceeds airport capacity. Therefore, formal procedures are implemented in order to allocate available capacity to the airlines and coordinate schedules. Airlines planning to operate to these airports need approval of their slots by the airport coordinator.

The EU and IATA documentation lays down objective criteria in which an airport can be classified as 'facilitated' or 'coordinated'. However, EU member states can designate any airport a 'coordinated airport'. For coordinated airports, each member state of the EU appoints an independent coordinator (natural or legal person, may be the same for several airports) who is responsible for:

- Neutral and transparent slot allocation according to predefined priorities
- Procedure of slot monitoring
- Imposition of sanctions in case of slot misuse

Today, approximately 150 of the world's airports are coordinated, the majority of them lie within the EU so that Europe's top 25 destinations are at coordinated airports, as shown in Figure 13.

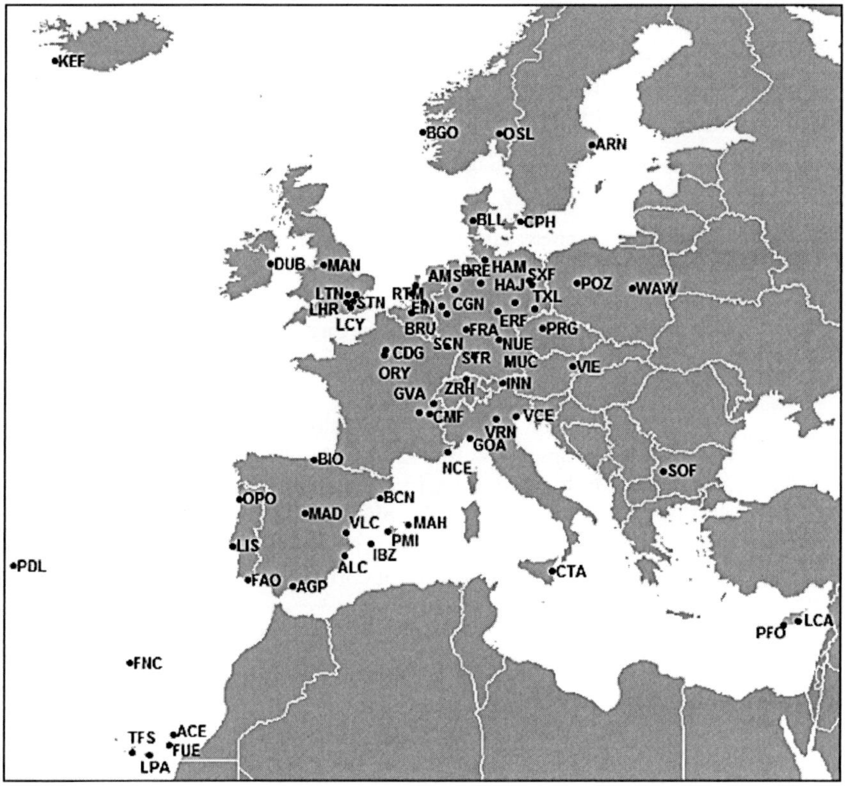

**Figure 13: Coordinated airports in Europe (excerpt)
(Own illustration)**

Slot allocation principles

Slot allocation is based on the 'use-it-or-lose-it' principle: airlines have first refusal on slots which they have already used in a past schedule period, the so called 'Grandfather Right'. This is supposed to give airlines planning reliability and ensure stable flight plans for the customers. Slots that are not used or additional slots are placed in a slot pool and allocated to the applicants according to predefined priorities by the airport coordinator. Slot allocation priorities at coordinated airports are (in order of descending priority):

Grandfather Rights

Previously used slot series (5 or more slots used in a sequence) have to be reallocated to incumbent airlines for the next equivalent schedule period,[1] if at least 80% of the slot-series have really been used in the past schedule period ('80/20' rule).[2] In case the 80%

---

1 Equivalent schedule periods are summer/summer and winter/winter periods.

2 The 80% quota can be reached by any combination of flights throughout the schedule period, i.e. cancelations can take place in a continuous time frame or distributed over the schedule period.

quota was not filled,[3] airlines can only claim historic slots if the reasons for failure to meet the quota lay beyond the control of the airline. Examples of these 'Force Majeure Criteria' are groundings of an aircraft type, industrial action or the closure of an airport.

Adjusted Grandfather Rights

These are previously used slots under the 80/20 rule that are retimed for the next equivalent schedule period upon the request of the airline. Slots that are not occupied due to grandfather or adjusted grandfather rights will go into a slot pool. These slots are further allocated after the following priorities.

New entrants

50% of slots in the pool are given to new entrants (unless requests by new entrants are less than 50%). An airline is considered a new entrant if it holds less than five slots per day or less than five per cent of the slot share, and if it plans to establish a flight on a route that is currently operated by maximum of two other carriers. The remaining slots are allocated according to the quality of the requested flight times.

All year ('Year Rounds')

Continuous services throughout a summer or winter schedule period are preferred over completely new services.

Daily services

Daily services are prioritized over flights on specific weekdays or shorter seasonal services.

The coordinator's slot monitoring comprises the compliance with the 80/20 rule, matching operations with the allocated slots and compliance with time slot cancelation procedures.

Possible sanctions are e.g. the deprivation of historical rights, lower priorities in the allocation process or monetary sanctions.

Slot exchange principles

Allocated slots may be exchanged for different routes within an airline. They may also be exchanged between different airlines on a 1:1 basis. A one-way transfer of slots from one airline to another is not allowed, except i.a. between parent and subsidiary companies, and between subsidiaries of the same parent company . Since 2008 1:1 slot exchanges may also be monetarily compensated.

G. 3 Slot management process

Slot management processes are linked to the two schedule periods in summer and winter, as illustrated in Figure 14. It begins with a compilation of possible grandfather rights for the coming season. Airlines then have to apply for their preferred slots which are then allocated by

---

[3] Irrespective of commercial or operational reasons for cancelations.

the airport coordinators. At the IATA Slot Coordination Conference, airlines negotiate with the coordinators and can exchange slots in order to optimize their slot portfolio.

Summer Schedule		**Winter Schedule**
until September	**Schedule Optimization Phase at airlines**	until April
September	**Airport coordinators post list of grandfather rights**	April
October	**First application deadline**	May
November	**First slot allocation by airport coordinators (14 days prior to conference)**	June
November	**IATA Slot coordination conference**	June
January 15th	**Slot-handback deadline (Handback of potentially non-utilized slots)**	August 15th
End of March	**Start of schedule period**	End of October
End of October	**End of schedule period**	End of March

Figure 14: Revolving slot management process (Own illustration)

G. 4 Current trends in slot management

Slot trading

The most important trend in slot management has been the clarification of the European Commission regarding its acceptance of slot exchanges with monetary compensations (slot trading) in April 2008. Monetary compensation without slot exchange is still not allowed in the EU.

Slot exchange with monetary compensation was practised at London-Heathrow Airport (LHR) even before the European Commission decided to tolerate the British practice, and is used fairly often due to the congested capacity at LHR. Since slot trading is still mostly focussed on LHR, the limited experience in practice makes it difficult to assess the success of the EU Commission's altered view.

Many questions remain unclear regarding fully legalized monetary slot trading: What is the value of a slot? Who is the legal owner of a slot? Are slot exchange prices subject to VAT? How are slots incorporated into the airline's balance sheets?

Therefore, it remains to be seen whether legitimized slot trading will really increase slot mobility in European slot management. It must be made clear that the solution of airport capacity constraints does not lie in slot management, with or without slot trading, but only in early demand-based expansion of relevant airports.

Review Questions

- What are the specific characteristics of the airline industry that are relevant for the process of network planning and why are they relevant?
- What are the factors that determine an airline's network?
- Explain how network development and network scheduling are connected?
- What happens in each phase of network scheduling?
- Explain why slot management is important for network scheduling?
- What are the underlying principles in slot management and who is responsible for executing them?

Airline Revenue Management

Thomas Dionisius

Table of contents

You should be able to

- name the pillars of successful revenue management
- describe the tools a pricing manager uses
- explain the relevant factors that influence a flight's demand forecast
- outline how prices and availabilities on code share flights are determined between airline partners
- explain how overbooking works

The author

Thomas Dionisius is director revenue management at Lufthansa German Airlines, Frankfurt / Main, Germany. He has worked in various functions within Revenue Management and currently heads the Pricing and Forecasting for short-haul flights, flights to the US and Canada and global price products.

Abstract

Within the network management of an airline, flight planning decides on the operated routes, the frequencies offered and the number of seats on each flight one year in advance. When all this has been agreed upon, the core task of the revenue management (RM) is to maximize the revenue within the network and to insure a satisfactory load factor.

RM consists of three main pillars:

- A pricing unit that defines the price structure by evaluating the demand structure of different customer groups for each O&D, market per market. The main goal is to ensure optimal customer segmentation by defining target-oriented price products
- A capacity management that decides which demand to accept and which demand to deny in order to sell the seats to customers with the highest willingness-to-pay
- An IT department that provides state-of-the art RM tools and allows effective analysis of demand and sales data

RM needs to stimulate demand in off-peak periods and to select the best paying customers in times of surplus demand. The ultimate goal is to maximize the unit revenue (Revenue per SKO or Revenue per seat). This can only be achieved with a mixture of efficient market segmentation, the choice to give the seats to the right (= best paying) customer and an efficient IT-infrastructure and data analysis.

A. INTRODUCTION

Core task of revenue management (RM)

The core task of revenue management (RM) is maximizing the unit revenue by using efficient market segmentation and optimal capacity steering. Each company has developed its own way of handling this task. Some have set up complicated revenue management systems and developed the underlying IT-infrastructure, while others have chosen to sell products at a unified price.

One traditional form of market segmentation is found in the classical bazaar: the vendor gauges the willingness of the potential buyer to pay during the sales pitch. Often, people that are not familiar with RM concepts complain about being charged a 'tourist price' in foreign (poorer) countries. However this type of price differentiation is the basis of all successful RM. The core skill for the vendor is to close the deal at a price that is just slightly below the maximum willingness of each customer to pay. The more skilful the vendor is at this task the higher the profit margin will be.

Airlines use RM to determine where and when a specific seat generates the most revenue

Airlines have the same goal and challenges as the aforementioned vendor: they want to sell tickets at a price that is just slightly below the willingness of each customer to pay; however, they also run the risk of losing the potential customer to a competitor. Additionally, since airlines normally sell tickets worldwide they have the potential to sell the same seat to various market segments simultaneously. These market segments are not linked to each other and can be spread over a significant number of points-of-sale. Therefore airlines need to define a price hurdle that is the minimum price they are willing to accept for a ticket at a given time. Defining this price hurdle implies that some demand is turned away. However, the revenue manager of an airline expects that the seat can be sold at a higher price to another customer.

Limited capacity is fundamental for RM to be beneficial

Successful RM is based on efficient capacity planning. If capacity is too high or 'unlimited', the vendor cannot choose the buyers with the highest willingness to pay and therefore needs to sell at any offered price level. In a situation where capacity is scarce, the vendor can achieve high revenue per unit but will let market opportunities go, resulting in potential customers choosing competitors' offers.

Demand prognoses are the basis of RM and flight planning

In the airline industry the demand prognosis is central to the success of optimal flight planning, the creation of efficient price products, and the optimal capacity steering. Long-term forecasts are necessary for allocating the right number of seats to each route. Consequently, efficient flight planning is the basis for all RM processes and a suboptimal capacity decision cannot be rectified by sophisticated RM.

RM decisions are based on mid- and short term forecasts

Mid-term and short-term forecasts are vital for pricing and capacity steering: the pricing has to create price products that reflect the willingness to pay in each market and, on the other hand, generate sufficient demand to fill the network of an airline. Based on the forecast, the capacity steering tries to select the customers at each given point in time that will contribute the most to the network and set rules for which demand to accept and for which demand to deny.

In Figure 1, you can see that revenue can be increased, if the airline is able to establish different prices and charge a price slightly below the maximum willingness to pay of each customer.

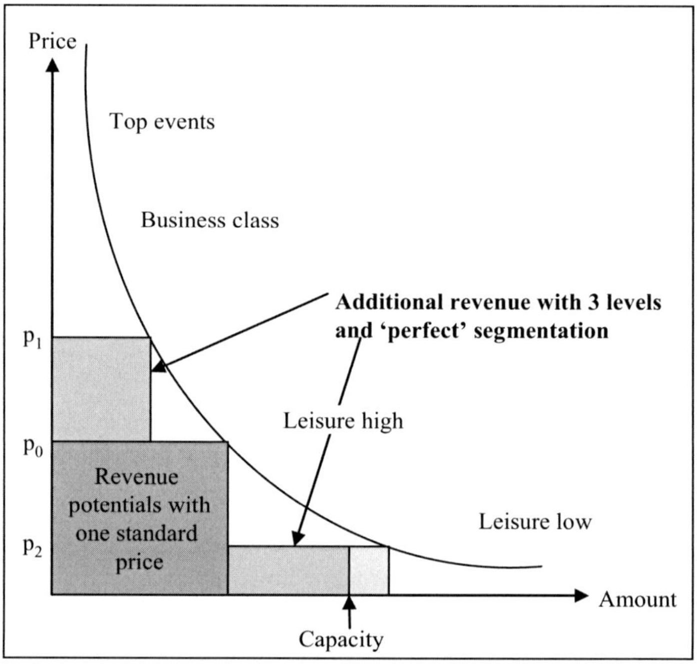

Figure 1: Demand curve in the airline industry (Own illustration)

B. BASIC OF REVENUE MANAGEMENT AND SPECIALTIES IN THE AIRLINE INDUSTRY

B. 1 The pillars for all revenue managers

Booking level rise varies between different routes

At most major airlines, the sales of airfare tickets start 360 days before the actual departure date. Therefore the booking level of each flights starts at zero and slowly rises towards the departure date. Depending on the demand pattern this booking curve varies: while intercontinental flights, with a high share of leisure travelers (e.g. Frankfurt – Miami), are sold relatively early, short-haul flights with a high share of business passengers (e.g. Düsseldorf – Geneva) are booked much closer to departure.

Two major mistakes

Revenue Managers can now make two major mistakes:

- They might sell the seats too early and too cheaply which results in a lack of seats for better paying customers who want to buy closer to departure. This would cause a flight to depart with a very high load-factor but the average ticket price ('yield per passenger') is below the optimum
- They might turn away cheap demand at the beginning of the sales period and later end up with empty seats at departure. The yield per passenger will be rather high but the capacity is not optimal: many seats are not sold; in RM terms they are called spoiled seats

B. 2 Basics of pricing

RM needs to separate market segments based on the willingness to pay

Beside the different booking processes, the creation of pricing products needs to find ways to separate market segments according to willingness to pay. In the airline industry a primary variable is the tariff conditions which are applied to each ticket and define restriction of usage.

Common tariff restrictions are:

- Minimum stay (e.g. customer needs to stay at least 3 days before the return journey)
- Penalties: the cost for rebooking or cancellation of a ticket (from 'free' to 'non-rebookable' / 'non-refundable')
- The possibility to combine tickets with other price products or fares from other airlines
- Advanced purchase (the latest date a ticket can be purchased before departure)

Tickets for specific user groups

Another powerful measure for segmentation is offering tickets to specific user groups either through bilateral contracts with large customers (corporate tickets, consolidator tickets) or through the definition of social-demographic criteria (e.g. student tickets, senior discounts).

B. 3 The market and demand forecast as key success factor

Price manager needs to know the market

The skill set of a good price manager is the precise judgment/knowledge of the market: he needs to know the (potential) target groups and their buying behavior as well as the available capacity and prices in the particular market. This includes the timeframe when tickets are booked as well as the willingness to pay of each segment. This knowledge leads to efficient pricing products. The more precise the judgment the more advantageous the slope of the demand-curve for the airlines becomes.

Price manager needs to react to competitors' price changes

Speed-to-market is crucial since the deregulation of the airline industry has led to millions of price changes per month on a global scale. Each player has to come up with solutions regarding which of these price changes they should react to and how exact the reaction should be. Normally, the focus is on a short reaction time for all major competitors and on major O&Ds. The pricing manager is then responsible to set a new price within 1 to 2 days and to answer the competitor's changes.

Difference to low-cost carriers

Since the 1980s the traditional network airlines have upgraded their RM systems and increased the sophistication of their pricing and capacity steering tools. In contrast, the emerging low-cost carriers established RM concepts that practically abandoned tariff restrictions and relied exclusively on the availability of a price product. This led to a significant decrease in complexity and a faster speed-to-market. The major disadvantage is the reduced possibility of segmenting the market and pushing certain offers to defined target groups.

B. 4 Basics of successful revenue management

Reliable data is the key

The basis of effective RM is professional and reliable data management. This includes booking and sales data as well as information about the customers and the usage of external data sources. Effective data handling and mining can be seen as the key to successfully defining the price product for the targeted customer group (Figure 2).

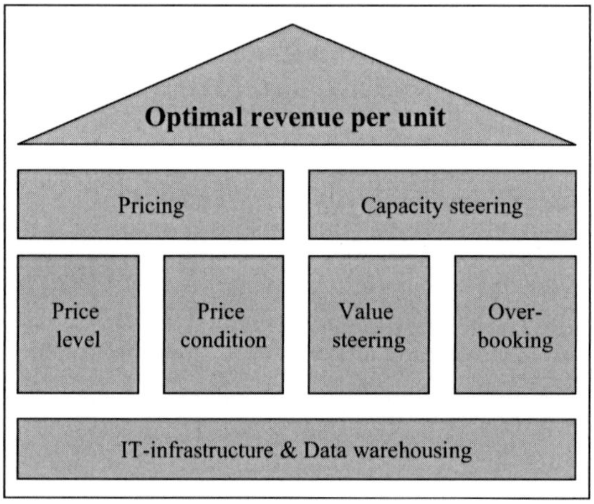

Figure 2: The house of RM (Own illustration)

B. 5 Cultural differences and the implications on RM

Cultural differences influence RM

Customer behavior is different at a global level. Cultural background must be integrated into the RM work, and this affects the philosophy behind pricing and steering. A common example is the time of ticket purchase. While in some cultures people plan their journeys far in advance and consequently buy airfare tickets early, in other markets the potential customers prefer to buy tickets close to departure. Imagine an airline operates a route from A (early booking market) to B (late booking market). The sales representative in B may be driven to sell expansive tickets since many tickets were purchased by market A early in the booking process and no contingency for inexpensive airfares is left late in the booking process. Consequently, RM has to find solutions to balance the cultural differences and allow each market its fair share within the available capacity.

A similar situation is faced when operating a route from a Muslim country to a Christian one. The weekend in the Christian country is Saturday/Sunday and therefore Friday is a major day for corporate travel. In the Muslim country Friday is the main holy day and corporate travel is rather limited. Capacity steering needs to balance the different traffic flows on the route in order to optimally fill the flight.

People's habits, customs and social values also shape the demand. These patterns are developed over time and reflect the social interaction of a society: likewise, it can be assumed that road traffic levels in a country also reflect the general demand pattern for domestic travel. As an example for the interaction between social values and the implications on demand let's look at Germany: the normal work pattern means roads are generally crowded on Friday afternoons and Monday mornings whereas there is little to no traffic on Sunday mornings. The demand for domestic airfares (and also train tickets) also show these travel preferences. In order to cope with these challenges, airlines establish a toolbox with tailor-made solutions for the various situations.

Peaks in automobile traffic are a good indicator for peaks in domestic air traffic

Figure 3 shows typical booking curves. Over time more tickets are sold and the booking level increases steadily. This curve is also influenced by cultural differences and shows different patterns for different O&Ds.

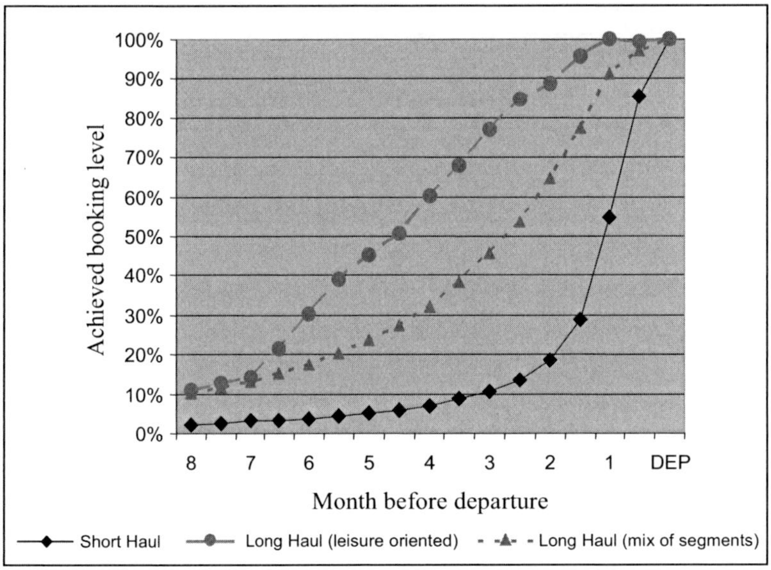

Figure 3: Booking curves for different flight types (Own illustration)

B. 6 The interaction with the global reservation systems

All defined RM parameters have to be transmitted to the globally operating computer reservation systems (CRS). The worldwide standardization is based on booking classes which are used to depict the airline's decision to sell a ticket in a certain value range. If a booking class is closed the agent cannot offer tickets located in that class. He can either book a waiting list and hope that the booking will be ac-

Computer reservation systems are the backbone for sales

cepted by the airline later or offer a more expensive ticket in a booking class that is open at the time of booking.

Booking classes

The use of some booking classes is globally harmonized, e.g. the F class is used worldwide for full fare tickets in the First compartment. Others are used by various airlines differently (so called private classes). In addition there are booking classes that are used identically within one airline alliance. For example, the W class at Star Alliance is generally used for promotional fares. For an overview of booking classes at Lufthansa see the following Figure 4.

F - First	F	Unrestricted First
	A	First Reduced
	O	First M+M (redemption), free and reduced travelling (ID/AD etc.)
C - Business	J	Unrestricted Business
	C	Business classic
	D	Business reduced
	Z	Business reduced
	P	Business reduced / Promo (since 2012)
	I	Business M+M (redemption)
	R	Business free and reduced travelling (ID/AD etc.)
E - Premium Eco	G	Unrestricted Premium Economy
	E	Unrestricted + restricted Premium Economy classic
	N	Premium Economy classic
M - Eco	Y	Unrestricted Economy
	B	Economy reduced
	M	Economy reduced
	U	Economy reduced
	H	Economy reduced
	X	Eco M+M (redemption) & Eco free and reduced (ID/AD etc.)
	Q	Economy reduced
	V	Economy reduced
	W	Economy reduced
	S	Eco reduced // IATA and OAL Carrier Fares (interline travel)
	T	Economy reduced
	L	Economy reduced // Special products + Catchment // Promotion
	K	Promotion

Figure 4: Booking classes at Lufthansa (effective 01.05.2014) (Own illustration)

Sales relies on auto pricing

The definition of price products is also globally standardized and therefore valid for all pricing managers that work with the traditional CRS systems. At the moment, the pricing manager can subsequently use 22 categories which define a price product, and these definitions are transmitted to the CRS and uniformly displayed all over the world. This standardization enables the reservation systems and internet engines to 'understand' the price product and automatically quote the correct price to the travel agent or customer (auto pricing).

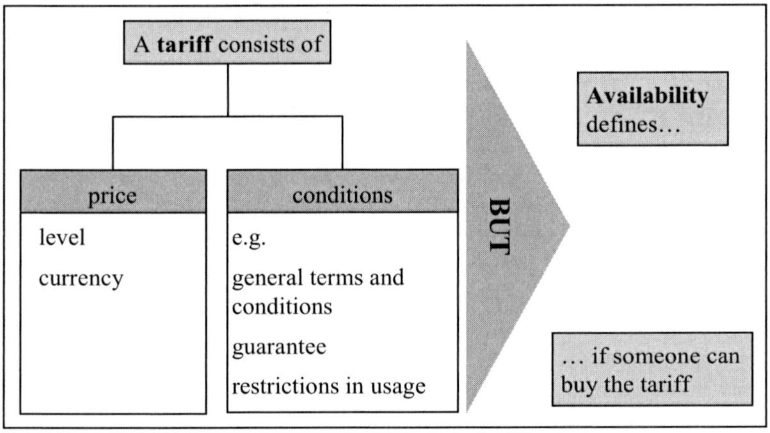

Figure 5: Pricing and steering together determine which price is available for the customer (Own illustration)

C. BASICS OF PRICING

C. 1 Traditional tariff conditions

Besides the price level, a price product is also made of price conditions

The primary task of each pricing manager is the creation of price products. Each price product consists of a price level (the price the customer needs to pay for a ticket) and the price conditions, which define the restrictions of the usage for one tariff. Airline pricing has defined standardized restrictions for a price product. New IT-development and market needs contribute to the development or modification of these categories over time.

The most important price conditions are:

Typical fare conditions

- **Advanced purchase**: defines how many days before departure the tariff has to be booked
- **Minimum stay**: dictates when the return travel may start
- **Maximum stay**: the latest date when the travel has to be completed
- **Penalty**: the cost for rebooking or cancelation
- **Combinability**: the right to combine a ticket with a another fare product
- **Application**: which operating airlines or flight numbers can be used
- **Channel**: restriction of sale to certain sales channels or travel agencies
- **Sales restriction**: sales period of a price product
- **Travel restriction**: defined travel period
- **Routing/mileage**: limits the routing (e.g. eastbound or westbound; via a certain hub, maximum length of routing etc.)

All prices are defined for an entire journey; airlines call it 'origin and destination' (O&D). This means that the pricing manager creates a

Process of price definition

tariff structure from an origin to a destination, regardless of the number of possible flights that fly on this particular O&D. The price product more or less neglects the available capacity of the airline but is oriented at the current market situation and customer structure. Let's be more precise: for a flight from Cairo (CAI) to Chicago (CHI) the pricing manager has to analyze the Egyptian market and know the pricing products, of the main competitors (benchmarks). Together with the estimated willingness to pay of the potential customers he then comes up with his own price products which are placed on the Egyptian market. Consequently, the prices for other O&Ds that could be part of a CAI-CHI routing such as the prices from Frankfurt to Chicago or from Cairo to Frankfurt are not considered The following fictitious example shows that the less expensive a tariff is the more restrictions apply (see Table 1).

Booking Class	Price level		Cost of refund	Cost of rebooking	Advanced purchase	Min. stay	Compartment
	One Way	Return					
C	900 €		free	free	-	-	Business
C		1,600 €	free	free	-	-	Business
C		1,200 €	free	free	3 days	2 days	Business
Y		1,400 €	free	free	-	-	Economy
B		1,100 €	free	free	3 days	2 days	Economy
M		800 €	100 €	100 €	3 days	3 days	Economy
H		600 €	100 €	100 €	7 days	3 days	Economy
Q		400 €	100 €	100 €	14 days	3 days	Economy
V		300 €	100 €	100 €	21 days	Sunday Return	Economy
W		220 €	200 €	200 €	28 days	Sunday Return	Economy

Table 1: Traditional pricing structure (so called 'upsell structure') (Own illustration)

Importance of benchmarks

Customers often do not understand why airlines offer cheaper prices on the heavily flown New York routes than on shorter connection to other destinations. The focus on benchmark prices rather than the production structure of the airline explains this phenomenon. This goes together with lean production structures in order to be competitive on frequently flown routes.

Coherence between price and tariff conditions

Traditionally the cheapest price comes with the most restrictive tariff conditions. The more a customer pays for an O&D the less restrictive the purchased tariff will be. At the top of the ladder we find the full flex tariff, which can be rebooked or refunded at no cost. Furthermore, his tariff can be sold up to departure, has no minimum stay and is placed in the highest booking class with the highest availability. At the bottom of the ladder we find restrictive tariffs that can neither be rebooked nor refunded. They are often called 'use it or lose it', since the tariff comes with no flexibility and is normally sold in the lowest booking class. Between the full flex and the special tariff in a typical pricing structure we find six to ten additional price products in the economy compartment.

Impact of seasonality

Setting the price level also depends highly on the seasonality of a market. While the core price structure remains more or less stable, the price level can vary significantly. A common pattern is three price levels for high, low and shoulder season which are tied to the demand pattern of the particular market. Since markets behave differently according to the season, this can lead to various seasonal patterns on the same route. While the high season for travelling commencing in the USA normally starts in the beginning of June, the high season for travel from Europe to the US starts later, depending on the vacation schedule of the particular year. As a result of different seasonal periods, prices in the US could already be at the high season level, while prices for north Atlantic journeys in France are still in the shoulder season.

Upsell concept

The previously described 'traditional' upsell concept (Table 1) can still be considered the base for pricing schemes from traditional network carriers. Nevertheless, a typical 'pure' upsell structure is very seldom seen and airlines have added new pricing ideas to the upsell concept or dropped some basic principles. The main target of the upsell concept remains to maximize the turnover by preventing a customer from buying a tariff that is significantly below his willingness to pay (also referred to as dilution or downsell).

C. 2 Other current pricing elements

Special prices are offered for vital target groups

Low demand or aggressive pricing behavior of main competitors drives the need for additional price products. The pricing manager then often adds special prices that undercut the lowest price level within the all-year structure. The sales period is often restricted to a certain period in order to fill the flights or secure market share.

Tariffs are grouped into fare families

Recently, it has become common to group some fares to fare families with identical fare conditions but different price levels. These fares can then be combined within one fare family on a half-return basis. Which of these fares is actually charged is determined by the lowest available booking class. This leads to higher prices on flights with a surplus demand and lower prices on low-demand flights. The airlines attempt to more evenly spread the actual demand across the entire network by offering lower fares on departures during off-peak hours. On short-haul services with direct competition this pricing scheme is also used to react quickly by adjusting price availabilities.

Special fares for internet sales

Another current trend is specifically reserved fare products for internet sales. Some carriers offer tariffs on the internet that are either less restrictive or cheaper than a corresponding fare sold through agencies. Other carriers charge a surcharge if the customer chooses not to book through the internet. Figure 6 shows an example of a fare concept for a certain O&D.

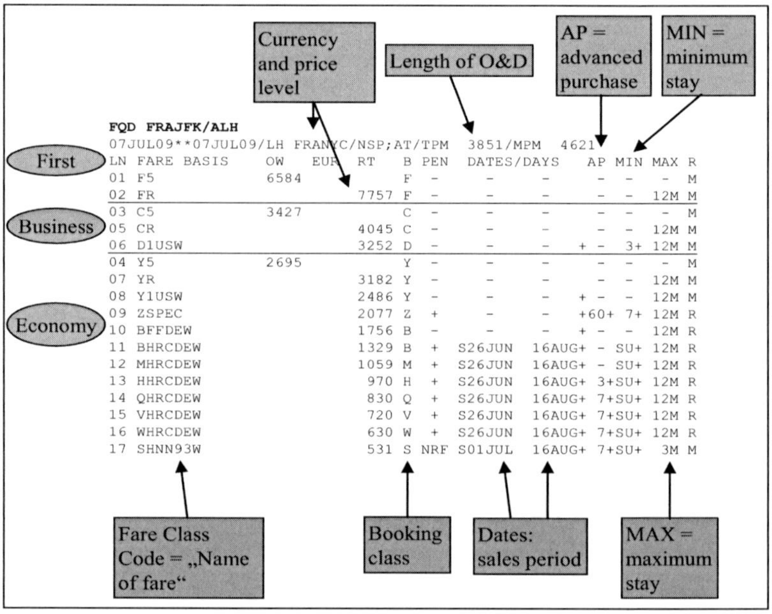

Figure 6: LH price concept Frankfurt – New York (CRS display, August 2009)

C. 3 Fare products for closed user groups

So far we have mainly discussed published fares, meaning fare products that are sold through open distribution channels and not restricted to a certain customer group. Besides these published fares airlines often tailor fare products that address the needs (and budget) of various customer groups (negotiated or private fares).

Corporate fares are one important group within the closed user group fares

The main focus of these unpublished tariffs is corporate fares. These fare products and fare levels are directly negotiated between the revenue management of an airline and define special prices for frequently used O&Ds of the customer. The corporate customer commits to use a certain amount of tickets in order to get the negotiated discount that is not shared publically. Corporate travel is quite vital to the airlines. Demand is fairly constant throughout the year with less seasonal ups and downs than other market segments and corporate customers account for the majority of demand in the premium cabin (first and business).

Consolidator or group tickets

Consolidator or group tickets are a further market segment that is very visible in the airline industry. This volume-oriented business requires completely different price products with an emphasis on inexpensive fares and an early booking window. Later in the booking process the consolidator then has to be granted a certain amount of flexibility to adjust the number of tickets. This business is important for the airlines for securing a base load in the beginning or the middle of the booking period. Airlines normally grant significant discounts when the business is secured and the tickets cannot be cancelled by the partner.

Other special fares for 'traditional' target groups include senior citizens, students or young professionals. The eligibility for these fares is tied to social-demographic parameters and takes into account these particular groups' lower willingness to pay. Other customers are excluded from purchasing these price products. Note that EU law prohibits price setting that offers discounts based on a customer's nationality, religion, sex or other discriminatory factors. Therefore some pricing programs (e.g. offers for agents that sell tickets exclusively to certain ethnic groups) had to been discontinued.

Segmentation by age

We have seen that the pricing manager has a powerful toolbox that allows him to find the appropriate market segment and use his analytical skills and creativity to compose the right price products. His goal is to offer attractive price products to the target groups and simultaneously prevent downsell of (potential) customers for tariffs that are too low. The examples of market segmentation in this chapter cover only a fragment of what really happens with pricing. The daily work comprises many more market segments and target groups.

Currently, Revenue Management is entering a new stage where recent developments in IT offer new opportunities for segmenting the market and creating innovative RM products. It is therefore difficult to predict which elements of traditional segmentation will remain and which new components will be added for use in demand management.

Future developments

D. BASICS OF CAPACITY STEERING

D. 1 Leg-based steering vs. network-based steering

Price products are placed in the market year-round and are revised at certain intervals. In contrast, the steering parameters determine which tariff is available on a certain sales date for a requested route or O&D and can change on a daily basis. The decision in a network airline is not only made for a route (flight from A to B) but also has to consider the entire flight pattern that the customer wants to travel (O&D). Therefore the customer's booking request has to be evaluated in relation to the value of the entire network.

Steering parameters determine available tariffs

This concept can be explained with the following example: the 8 am departure from Berlin (TXL) to Frankfurt (FRA) on a Monday morning combines two contrary market segments – high paying corporate travelers use it for a one-day trip to Frankfurt while (leisure) customers travelling to the US need to take the flight to connect to a huge number of US flights which depart from between 10 am and 1 pm from Frankfurt.

RM needs to combine contrary market segments

Capacity steering now needs to ensure seats are reserved for point-to-point (P2P) business travelers or network passengers connecting to an intercontinental flight. Subsequently, customers with inexpensive tickets on the P2P connection or to short haul flights should be steered to a later or earlier TXL-FRA flight. Steering therefore has to make

Optimization process

sure that seats are offered in the lower booking classes for the 12 o'clock departure in order to give customers paying less (but with more flexibility) the opportunity to purchase a ticket. This optimization process is illustrated in Figure 7.

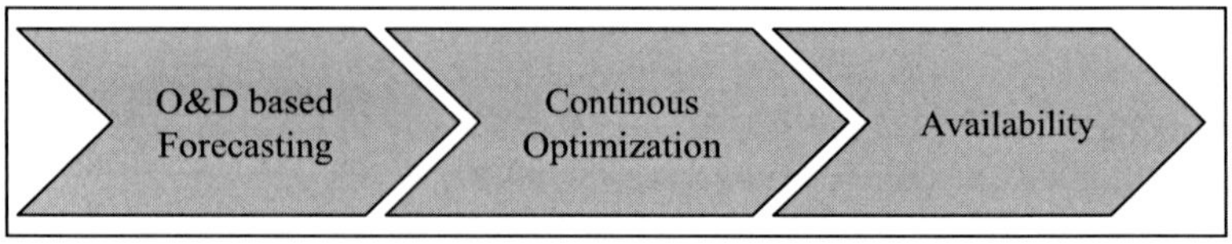

Figure 7: The optimization process (Own illustration)

Bid prices are the main criteria for the availability decision

Network airlines need to define an internal hurdle price which each customer has to pay in order to get a booking for a flight. This value is generally referred to as hurdle price, margin price or bid price in common publications. Mathematically, this hurdle price reflects the base of the current forecast and the margin value that an airline believes it can earn for the next seats.

Each request for a booking is now compared with the current hurdle prices for all requested flights. If the value of the requested booking exceeds the hurdle price, the request is confirmed and the customer gets the desired booking. If the hurdle price exceeds the value of the booking the airline denies the booking and the customer needs to pay a higher price in order to confirm the booking.

Let us look back to our example. Imagine the hurdle price for the TXL-FRA flight is 200 Euros. A customer from TXL to FRA must pay at least 201 Euros in order to get a seat. A customer with an itinerary from Berlin to Chicago (CHI) also needs to match or exceed the hurdle price for the FRA-CHI flight. Imagine the current hurdle price for FRA-CHI amounts to 170 Euros. Consequently, the customer needs to pay at least 371 Euros to get a booking from Berlin to Chicago via Frankfurt. This principle is illustrated in Figure 8.

As we now see, hurdle prices are always based on the forecasted demand and do not reflect the lengths of a route or even the cost for the flight.

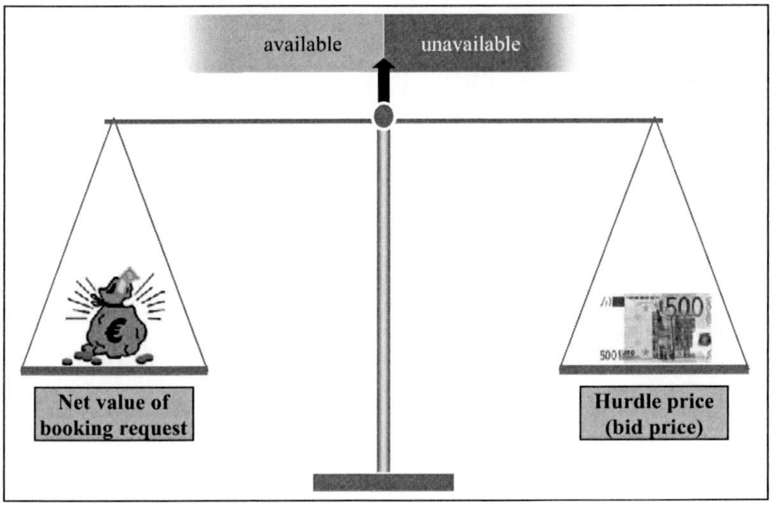

Figure 8: The principle of capacity steering (Own illustration)

Before network airlines switched to O&D based RM, the availability of a tariff was exclusively determined by the used booking classes. All pricing products were strictly attached to booking classes. The capacity manager would then define a lowest open booking class for each flight at a given point in the booking process. In order to get a ticket in a certain booking class, the requested booking class had to be open on each flight of the planned itinerary. The decisive disadvantage of this system was the inability to attach all pricing products with the mathematically correct value to the limited number of booking classes. If the price for a CAI-FRA flight in the Egyptian market was set at 500 Euros in H class and the corresponding price in the German market was set at 750 Euros, both booking requests would display the same availability on a given flight from CAI to FRA regardless of the value difference of 250 Euro. This led to non-optimal revenue steering for network traffic and preferred points-of-sale (POS) with lower price structure versus POS with higher prices.

Airlines that focus on point-to-point traffic still work with leg-based RM systems.

D. 2 Forecasts as the base of capacity steering

The base for all availability decisions is a precise forecast that includes the number of customers who will likely travel on a certain O&D and their estimated willingness to pay.

Process of continuous forecast adaption

The complexity of the 'correct' forecast derives from the long sales period. Therefore the revenue manager normally starts with a forecast that is almost exclusively based on historical data and assumes that the demand pattern will remain stable in the future. Throughout the booking period new information (internal and external) can then be incorporated into the forecast - decreasing or increasing it. Typical factors that are not depicted in a forecast based on historical data are changes in competitor's behavior (e.g. new entrant on a certain route), the business cycle, a shift of holiday periods or religious events (Easter, Ramadan) or the airline's own decision to increase or decrease capacity on a route.

Efficient capacity steering requires a forecast that estimates the potential number of customers that would theoretically be willing to fly on a certain O&D (unconstrained demand) and their theoretical willingness to pay regardless of capacity limitation.

Interface between forecast system and optimizing system

Let us return to our example for illustrating the importance of these forecasts: for the Monday morning departure from Frankfurt to Chicago in 30 weeks, the revenue management forecast system expects 5 customers from CAI. Two of them are willing to pay a mid-price economy tickets while 3 are waiting to buy a rock-bottom price special. The forecast also expects a demand of 7 customers from Berlin, which would connect to the CHI-flight. Two of them are business class customers who are willing to buy a full-flex ticket while 5 customers will not pay more that the cheapest offered economy fare. We can find a huge number of single O&D prognoses that affect the FRA-CHI flight. Altogether the unconstrained demand for the CHI-flight on this Monday morning is 533 while the actual capacity is restricted to 300. For each of these 533 potential customers their willingness to pay is estimated by the forecast system. This set of data is the basis for all availability decisions. The forecast data is now handed over to the optimizing systems. This system calculates which demand to accept and which to deny in order to achieving an optimal result for the entire network. Based on the forecast and the offered capacity the optimizing system calculates the minimum price for each ticket.

D. 3 Overbooking

Overbooking for optimization purposes

Besides the forecast the RM optimization process consists of a second tool: overbooking. Basically, overbooking gives the revenue manager the chance to optimize the loadfactor on a short-term basis.

Parameters of overbooking

Despite a confirmed booking or even a valid ticket a significant number of passengers do not show up for boarding on each flight. To compensate these so called no-shows, airlines accept more bookings than physical seats available. The actual overbooking level varies significantly between each flight, and major parameters that influence the overbooking level are the structure of demand, the day of travel and cultural diversity of the demand.

Compensation for no shows and late cancellation

The overbooking level must additionally compensate for late cancellations, since some passengers cancel their bookings shortly before departure. The total overbooking consequently consists of compensation for no-shows at check-in as well as a compensation for cancellation at the later stage of the booking process.

Other impacts

The higher the number of passengers holding flexible tickets, the higher the probability of no-shows. Therefore the overbooking level can be increased. But the capacity manager has to be careful with the overbooking level at the beginning of a vacation period in the days before Christmas or Ramadan or during major fairs and exhibitions. On these occasions the no-show rate drops (statistically) significant and overbooking has to be adjusted by the capacity manager.

Importance of historical data

In order to evaluate the described effects and derive the optimal overbooking rates, airlines need to collect and analyze historical data in order to find out which structural effects affect the overbooking level. The check-in employees at the airport also have to understand that despite a constant capacity (use of identical aircraft for each flight) the overbooking varies on the basis of these statistical parameters. A lack of understanding could lead to misinterpretation of the booking level and wrong decisions such as blocked seats during the check-in.

Figure 9 shows three different booking curves. It is obvious that successful RM steers overbooking and compensation for cancellation in a way that on the day of departure every seat in an aircraft is occupied and no customer has to be rejected from the flight he/she originally booked. If the airline does not make use of these two concepts demand will be turned away and potential revenue is lost.

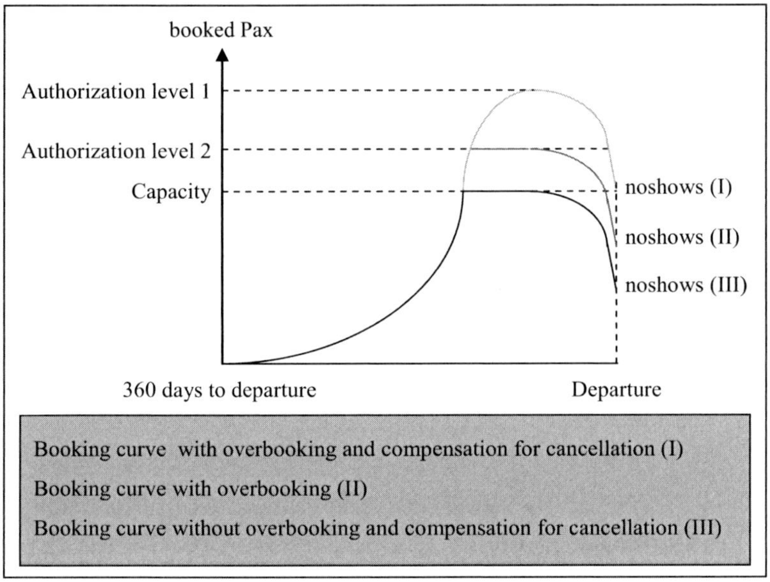

Figure 9: Overbooking curve (Own illustration)

Quality standards

Handling of denied boardings

Most airlines define quality standards for the overbooking level which is a trade-off between maximum revenue opportunities and good customer service. Generally, these standards define the number of denied boardings in relation to the number of transported passengers. In spite of all statistical processes and personal experience, denied boardings cannot be avoided on a small number of flights. Airlines then need efficient processes for handling this situation and offering customers an alternative connection. Passengers refused seats have to be transported with the most rapid connection to the final destination and the airline has to pay their food and accommodation at the airport as well as full compensation for the disservice. The actual amount paid varies from between 125 - 600 Euros and is defined for all flights within and from the EU by an EU-regulation. This regulation was issued in 2005 and is valid for all airlines that fly from or within the EU. Similar regulations are issued on other countries as well.

To summarize, Figure 10 shows parameters that determine the applicable overbooking level.

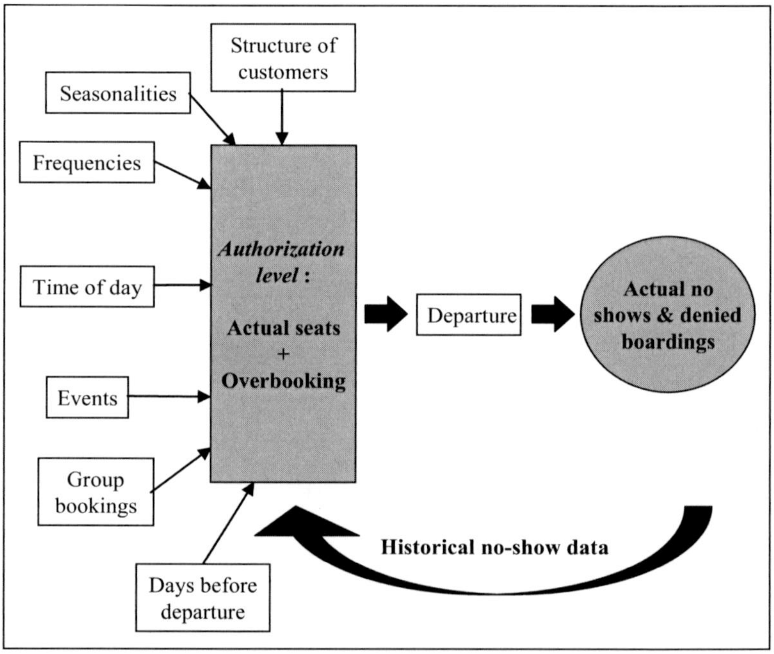

Figure 10: Parameters defining the overbooking level (Own illustration)

E. REVENUE MANAGEMENT AS PART OF AN AIRLINE

E. 1 Revenue management and airline alliances

Trend towards incorporating partners' networks

All described processes and principles focus on the own airline's network and have not taken into account the growing trend in the industry towards increased cooperation. This trend is driven in order to expand the network offered to the customer through the company's own sales organization.

Challenges through increased cooperation in RM

The exchange of (booking class) availabilities and interlineable pricing products is the base for commercially successful cooperation between airlines. This sensible development and the increasing number of codes have brought new challenges to the revenue management departments. On the pricing side cooperation is very limited due to compliance rules which prohibit the exchange of information and agreements about pricing conditions and fare levels. On the steering side the biggest obstacles are various IT-systems and steering philosophies that make the exchange of availabilities very cumbersome.

Anti-trust rules

Price fixing is one of the harshest violations of anti-trust rules and agreements are severely punished by anti-trust authorities. Consequently, even in a code share situation it to negotiate prices between different airlines is strictly forbidden.

Airlines only negotiate internal contracts that define how much an airline needs to pay in order to use its partners' flights (pro rate). After this has been agreed the pricing managers create pricing products that include the partners' networks. The set price level must take into account the amount the airline has to pay to the partner.

In the case of our example, our customer from Berlin wants to travel not only to Chicago but also to Des Moines (DSM). For the journey the customer uses Lufthansa (LH) flights on TXL-FRA and FRA-CHI and then changes to a United Airways (UA) flight to Des Moines. On this flight the customer can book an LH code share number (compare chapter 'Cooperation and Alliances') and subsequently buys one single ticket for the journey from Berlin to Des Moines. This pricing product was entirely defined by the LH pricing manager. On the other hand, the availabilities were set by LH for the first two flights and by the capacity steering of UA on the third leg (Figure 11).

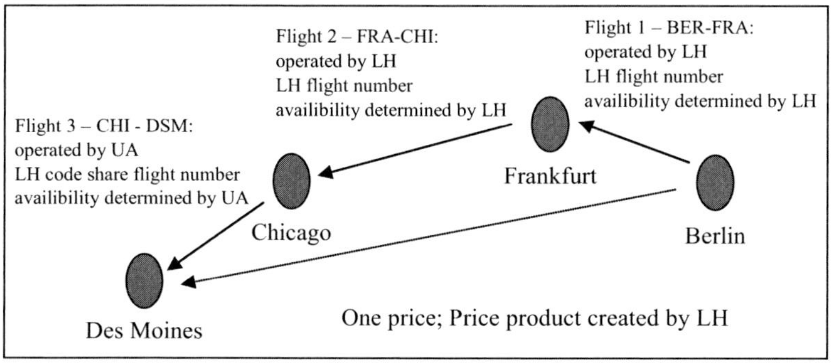

Figure 11: Three flights, two airlines, one price (Own illustration)

Compensation mechanism

After the journey is over, United Airlines wants to get its fair share of the ticket. Both airlines will have an agreement in place that defines how much Lufthansa has to transfer to United Airlines for the use of the Chicago – Des Moines flight.

In general, the most common constructions are:

- LH pays a fixed amount for the intra-American flight operated by United Airways; consequently the value of the LH ticket is of no relevance (fixed amounts)
- Both carriers split the ticket value using a standard procedure (algorithm) in the airline industry which divides the cash based on the lengths of all the flown sectors within the journey (straight rate prorate)

Class conversion between partner airlines

As previously mentioned the operating carrier defines which booking class is available and sends this information to the marketing carrier who now receives the right to market, namely to sell tickets in all available booking classes. Airlines agree which of the classes from their booking class set corresponds with the booking class set of the partner (a so called class conversion table). Using this class conversion table, the marketing carrier needs to ensure that the received availability message is displayed correctly on the marketing flight number and that the received information dealt with in the IT-infrastructure in real time.

Future challenges

One major challenge for revenue management systems in the next decade will be the establishment of more flexible availability exchange and commercial contracts. These processes must include the value of a (partner) feeder flight into the availability decision and the actual amounts that will be paid for the seat on the feeder flight.

E. 2 IT solutions as base for revenue management

Interaction of two IT solutions

The effective use of RM is closely tied to the usage of state-of-the-art IT-solutions. Generally speaking these solutions can be differentiated into two elements.

Data warehousing

All elements of data warehousing focus on available data from various sources and IT-solutions are needed to use this data easily and in a targeted way. This data includes information about the load factors of flights, the underlying booking curves and information about the used tickets as well as background information on the flying behavior of Frequent Flyer Program (FFP) members or the development of corporate travel and corporate contracts. The reports can normally be used on a broader level as management information and furthermore be extended down to detailed levels. This level of information is essential to revenue managers' decisions concerning pricing and steering. Another element of data warehousing is the observation of competitor behavior. This includes the monitoring of pricing products and the change in availability and route planning.

Forecasting and optimization

The second issue is the core of capacity steering and includes IT systems for forecasting and optimizing. The entire RM process is based on precise forecasts. Therefore an airline requires a state-of-the-art forecasting tool. The forecasting tool uses historical data and transforms it into forecasts for the upcoming flights. These forecasts are calculated on mathematical processes and have to be edited in order to include economic development or calendar changes (e.g. the period of Ramadan varies from year-to-year). These forecasts then need to be processed by an optimizing system which defines the optimal availabilities and determines which potential demand to accept and which to turn down. The optimizer also uses the expected no-show rate to determine the optimal overbooking level.

E. 3 Organizational implication within the company

Three core functions

The Revenue Management with the three key functions capacity management, pricing and IT- solutions are all central to the company's organization.

Capacity management and steering

The capacity management is responsible for all processes regarding an airline's inventory. With its decisions to grant or deny availability for certain pricing products at various points of sale, it may influence the turnover of a local sales organization. The capacity control has the delicate decision of determining which market is to be denied availability because the requested seat may be sold elsewhere at a higher price. The capacity management needs to be independent of particular interests of local sales organizations or single sales channels operating as a kind of referee. Consequently, the capacity management is normally considered to be a central and independent department within an airline.

Pricing

The role of pricing can be interpreted in different ways: some airlines link capacity steering closely to pricing and hold both departments responsible for the right pricing product and the optimal availability. Others place the responsibility of pricing with the sales department and consider it to be one of the airline's key marketing instruments, closely connected to the local sales organizations.

IT

IT can either be provided by a central IT department that bundles all IT hard- and software for the entire company together or dedicated IT, which can be developed as part of integrated revenue management.

F. OUTLOOK

The last decade has seen a significant improvement in forecasting and optimization solutions. This has been possible because more refined mathematical models could be implemented due to improved hardware solutions. Even for big network carriers it is now possible to shift from a leg-based forecasting and optimization towards network (or O&D-based) Revenue Management.

Pricing has faced new fare schemes with fewer fare conditions being brought into the market by emerging low-cost carriers. This has lead to a significant decline in fare restrictions and the creation of fare groups with identical fare conditions where sales possibilities are determined exclusively by booking class availability.

Currently two main trends are seen within Revenue Management:

1.) The price decision will be based on new or extended input parameters (such as the FFP status, customer value, historical buying behavior, time of the day, contractual agreements…). The border between defining a price product and determining availability for the customer will become increasingly indistinct. As the creation of price offers will become more dynamic it is often refered to as dynamic pricing or dynamic demand management.

2.) Airlines continue to unbundle their services and consequently the customer can chose various service packages as well as ancillary service for his travel. Generally, RM can than either define fixed service bundles or completely unbundle the travel from all additional features and sell them separately. In practice, neither of these two extremes are in use but airlines rely on a mix of two to five service bundles plus an offer of extra on top. At the moment, the prices differential is still based on the overall demand while ancillary services or upsells between service bundles are fixed. It is expected that price setting will become more dynamic in the future.

	Economy Bundle S	Economy Bundle M	Economy Bundle L	Business Bundle XL
Basic Service	✓ Travel	✓ Travel	✓ Travel	✓ Travel
Flexibility	✓ No rebooking: ✓ No refund ✓ No upgrade	✓ Rebooking: 50 € ✓ No refund ✓ Upgrade: 150 €	✓ Rebooking: free ✓ Refund: 100 € ✓ Upgrade: 100 €	✓ Rebooking: free ✓ Refund: free
Product Features / Services	✓25% miles	✓50% miles ✓1 drink ✓1 snack ✓1 checked bag	✓100% Meilen ✓2 drinks ✓1 snack ✓2 checked bags ✓Advanced seat reservation ✓Lounge-Access ✓Fast Lane	✓200% Meilen ✓Premium drinks ✓Premium meal ✓2 checked bags ✓Advanced seat reservation ✓Lounge-Access ✓Fast Lane
Price		Bundle S + 50 €	Bundle M + 80 €	Bundle L + 150 €

Figure 12: Fare Bundling – exemplary concept (Own illustration)

The opportunities and boundaries of this development are not clear yet, but they will be determined by upcoming IT-solutions, the capability within the RM organization of dealing with increasing complexity, new solutions for the airline co-operations and the ability to use big data solutions in RM.

Airlines started complex revenue management in the 1980s and have continued to be industry leaders in finding new and more sophisticated ways of segmenting their customers.

New technologies based on increasing computing power and underlying data sources will lead RM into the next century. It can be expected that RM decisions will become more dynamic based on pre-defined parameters and that the customer will be able to partly define the desired product or product bundle while historically the airlines defined a set of fixed services that where included in each and every ticket for the chosen compartment.

Review Questions

- Name five common tariff conditions that are used to define the restriction of a price product?
- What is the difference between a private and a published fare?
- In the case of airline cooperation, which airline defines the price level the customer has to pay for a ticket?
- Why do airlines overbook their flights and what happens if not all booked passengers can be granted a seat (denied boarding)?
- What is the main difference between an O&D-based and a leg-based optimization?
- What does a price product consist of?
- Explain the decision-making process that determines the acceptance or refusal of booking a request?

Bibliography and further reading

Abdelghany, A. / Khaled, A. (2007): Modelling air-carrier's portfolio of business travel, in: Journal of Revenue and Pricing Management, Vol. 6, No 1, p. 51-63.

Burger, B. / Fuchs, M. (2004): Dynamic Pricing – A future airline business model, in: Journal of Revenue and Pricing Management, Vol. 4, No 1, p. 39-53.

Cento, A. (2008): Airline Industry: Challenges in the 21st Century (Contributions to Economics), Heidelberg.

Clarke, K. (2004): Case study: Implementing a revenue management system at Malaysia Airlines, in: Journal of Revenue and Pricing Management, Vol. 3, No 1, p. 41-48.

Cutshall, C. / Weisbrodt, J. (2005): Implementing an O&D revenue management solution, in: Journal of Revenue and Pricing Management, Vol. 5, No 2, p. 128-134.

Diller, H. (2007): Preispolitik, Stuttgart.

Dunleavy, H. / Westermann, D. (2004): Future of airline revenue management, in: Journal of Revenue and Pricing Management, Vol. 3, No 4, p. 380-383.

Frank, M. / Friedemann, M./ Mederer, M. / Schroeder, A. (2005): Airline revenue management: A simulation of dynamic capacity management, in: Journal of Revenue and Pricing Management, Vol. 5, No 1, p. 62-71.

Grosser, S. (2006): Reward Management: The blind spot of bonus program theory, Saarbrücken.

Higle, J. L. (2006): Bid-price control with origin-destination demand: A stochastic programming approach, in: Journal of Revenue and Pricing Management, Vol. 5, No 4, p. 291-304.

Karadjov, Y. / Farahmand, M. (2007): Revenue Management circa 2020, in: Journal of Revenue and Pricing Management, Vol. 6, No 4, p. 291-292.

Klein, R. / Steinhardt, C. (2008): Revenue Management, Augsburg.

Klophaus, R. / Pölt, S. (2006): Airline overbooking with dynamic spoilage costs, in: Journal of Revenue and Pricing Management, Vol. 6, No 1, p. 9-18.

Lindenmeier, J. / Tscheulin, D. K. (2005): Kundenzufriedenheitsrelevante Effekte der Überbuchung im Rahmen des Revenue-Managements, in: Zeitschrift für Betriebswirtschaft, Vol. 75, No. 1, p. 101-123.

Maurer, P. (2003): Luftverkehrsmanagement: Basiswissen, Oldenburg.

Petrick, A. / Gönsch, J. / Steinhardt, C. (2008): Revenue Management mit flexiblen Produkten, in: WiSt Heft, Vol. 9, No. 1, p. 14-20.

Skugge, G. (2007): FUTURES: Future of Revenue Management: Capture your current potential!, in: Journal of Revenue and Pricing Management, Vol. 6, No 3, p. 241-243.

Spann, M. / Klein, J. / Makhlouf, K. / Bernhardt, M. (2004): Interaktive Preismaßnahmen bei Low-Cost-Fluglinien, in: Zeitschrift für Betriebswirtschaft, Vol. 74, No. 1, p. 53-78.

Vinod, B. (2005): Advances in inventory control, in: Journal of Revenue and Pricing Management, Vol. 4, No 4, p. 367-381.

Vinod, B. (2004): Alliance revenue management, in: Journal of Revenue and Pricing Management, Vol. 4, No 1, p. 66-82.

Wangenheim v., F. / Bayón, T. (2007): Behavioral Consequences of Overbooking Service Capacity, in: Journal of Marketing, Vol. 71, No. 1, p. 36-47.

Aviation Policy

Thomas Kropp

Table of contents

You should be able to

- recognize origins, actors and processes of national and international aviation policy
- describe the main aviation-related policy fields of regulation and legislation

The author

Thomas Kropp is Senior Vice President of Deutsche Lufthansa AG and head of Corporate International Relations and Government Affairs.

Abstract

Internationally operating airlines act in an environment which is strongly influenced by various types of stakeholders. The first two chapters offer an overview of the historical origins, actors and processes in aviation policy, its underlying legislation, and its significance to the aviation industry. The last three chapters deal with contemporary as well as future issues in aviation policy, among them environment and sustainability, safety and security and consumer protection.

A. INTRODUCTION TO AVIATION POLICY

A. 1 Subjects and goals

Complex airline environment and its stakeholders

The system of civil aviation, its industry and regulation is a complex conglomerate of various factors. Airlines act in an environment, which is strongly influenced by various types of stakeholders – different parts of society, with different and often conflicting backgrounds, with vested interests and varying levels of power. The main task in aviation policy consists then of identifying and analyzing existing interests, locating the best common solutions and developing political instruments for bringing about decisions and solutions. The following figure displays the complex system which influences civil aviation:

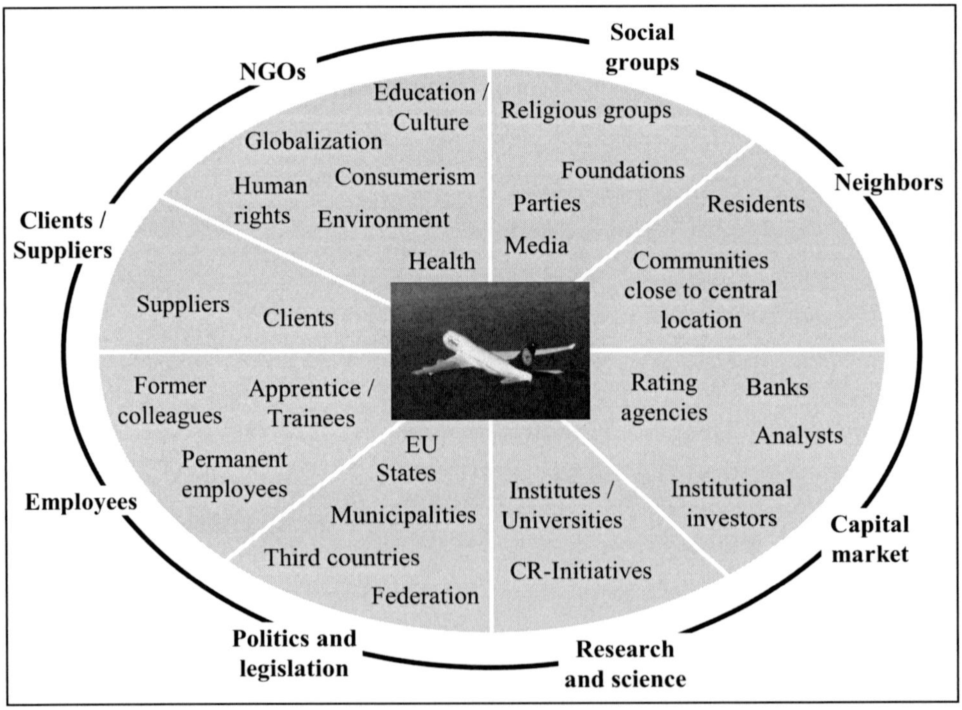

Figure 1: An airline's environment and its stakeholders (Own illustration)

Definition of aviation policy

In order to make this clearer it is helpful to look at the definition of the word policy. One of the most common definitions would be "a course or principle of action adopted or proposed by an organization or individual" (Oxford, 2009). Relating this to aviation, aviation policy incorporates the organization of objectives and instruments of civil aviation by national and supranational governmental institutions, international organizations, interest groups and companies in order to achieve political-economic (general) and company (specific) objectives. This means that a multitude of stakeholders and actors influence policy, all with different degrees of interest, investment and capability to influence decisions and translate them into action. Keep in mind that any kind of action – including non-action – can be part of a policy.

To summarize aviation policy combines the definition of objectives with the definition of strategies in a wide array of aviation-related policy fields – ranging from foreign and economic to environmental and consumer protection policy. It also influences and is influenced by other regulatory and financial policies, legal obligations (international public law) and long-term political goals. Besides the various actors that influence aviation policy, it is also influenced by the overall economic situation, the objectives of national and supranational aviation policy, multi- and international treaties (aviation policy of other states), vertical political and economic objectives, and activities within the aviation industry.

Yet any national aviation policy is always only one segment of a national transport policy, which, given the waning influence of national authorities, is decreasing in importance and independence due to globalization and increasingly strong supranational actors (e.g. the EU).

A. 2 Historical background

History as key to understand aviation policy

History is the key to understanding the current framework of aviation policy. Through the development of airplanes and their military potential in the early 20th century, sovereignty of airspace above a country's territory became an issue. Should the space above ground be considered to belong to a country or, like the open sea, should it be considered common international territory? The principles developed by the Grotian[1] tradition were of little use when dealing with the issue of freedom of airspace. Early tentative attempts and discussions among scholars were ended by world war 1and ultimately led to the Paris Convention of 1919.[2] This first multilateral approach by international

Paris Convention of 1919

---

[1] Hugo Grotius worked as a jurist in the Dutch Republic in the 17th century and formulated in his Mare Liberum (published 1609) on the principle that the sea was international territory and all nations were free to use it for seafaring and trade.

[2] The Paris Convention of 1919 (Convention relating to the regulation of areal navigation, signed in Paris on 13 October 1919) defined the status of

law relating to air navigation brought academic discussion to an end with the definition "that every power has complete and exclusive sovereignty over the air space above its territory".[3] Although this proposal is no longer in force, its concepts of aviation law were a pioneering contribution and its fundamental ideas survived. The principle of sovereignty of airspace "has become an axiom and a backbone of international air law ever since" (Milde, 2008).

Chicago Convention of 1944

In 1944, several allied states – who would later also found the United Nations – met at the Convention on International Civil Aviation in Chicago and agreed upon the so-called 'Chicago Convention', which set a milestone in aviation history from a political perspective. It was signed on 7 December 1944 by 52 states and went into effect on 4 April 1947, the same date the International Civil Aviation Organization (ICAO) was founded. ICAO is the UN agency dealing with civil aviation, bearing testament to the importance that aviation holds in international affairs.

Excursion:
Preamble to the Chicago Convention

"WHEREAS the future development of international civil aviation can greatly help to create and preserve friendship and understanding among the nations and peoples of the world, yet its abuse can become a threat to the general security;

WHEREAS it is desirable to avoid friction and to promote that cooperation between nations and peoples upon which the peace of the world depends;

THEREFORE, the undersigned governments having agreed on certain principles and arrangements in order that international civil aviation may be developed in a safe and orderly manner and that international air transport services may be established on the basis of equality of opportunity and operated soundly and economically;

Have accordingly concluded this convention to that end."

(Preamble, Convention on International Civil Aviation signed in Chicago on 7 December 1944)

Annexes

The original agreements of the Chicago Convention, have since then, been revised eight times, and have been supplemented by 18 annexes, covering all relevant major fields of modern air transport - from pilot licensing to aircraft operation rules; from the rules governing aerodrome design to safety and security issues. The content of those annexes is binding for all member states and has to be adopted into national law. Many of the elementary points of aviation policy, such as

international airspace and gave the authority to the commander of an aircraft to act in accordance with the law of the state of registration.

3 Paris Convention of 1919, Chapter I - General Principles, Article 1.

the decision to base cost-recovery in aviation (for infrastructure for example) on fees and not taxes (such as a fuel tax), stem from this time. This decision proves how far sighted the convention really was. Today, many countries have realized that letting users pay for infrastructure via tolls and fees is more efficient and less complex than introducing complex and less cost-oriented policy tools such as taxes.

Freedoms of the air

Not directly part of the Chicago Convention, but laid down in a side protocol are the 'Freedoms of the Air'. As of today, eight freedoms exist. The first two govern transit traffic and are written down in the International Air Services Transit Agreement. The other freedoms govern commercial rights and are largely subject to bi- or multilateral agreements.

Excursion:
The freedoms of the air

1st Freedom:	Airlines may fly over the territory of a signatory state without landing.
2nd Freedom:	Airlines may land in the territory of a signatory state for non-commercial purposes, such as refueling or emergency repairs.
3rd Freedom:	Passengers and cargo may be flown from the airline's own country to another signatory state.
4th Freedom:	Passengers and cargo may be picked up in another signatory state and transported to the airline's own country.
5th Freedom:	Airlines may transport passengers and cargo between one signatory state and a third state; however the flight must originate or terminate in the airlines own country.
6th Freedom:	Airlines may pick up passengers and cargo from abroad and fly them on to a third state after stopping in their own country.
7th Freedom:	Airlines may transport passengers and cargo between two signatory states without taking off or landing in their own country.
8th Freedom:	Also known as cabotage, this freedom allows airlines to conduct flights within a foreign country in which it is not domiciled.

State ownership and state intervention after WW II

Following the Chicago Convention, several events and developments in the political economy have had an impact on the airline industry, beginning with the end of World War II and the then new emerging world order. The Cold War and the internationalization within blocks fostered state influence and air transport became a strategic asset with tremendous political and economic importance. This led to state ownership and state intervention within the frameworks of ICAO and IATA – the then cartel-like International Air Transport Association. As a result, the overwhelmingly state-owned industry became a densely regulated and a non-competitive sphere. Domestic service was often monopolized by one carrier, and international traffic between two countries was divided between the two flag carriers of the respective countries. Prices were regulated and high, as destinations, frequencies, capacity and even types of service and product were subject to regulatory agreement or approval.

Deregulation in the USA

However as this system came to its factual limits – and demand for international mobility increased – political pressure led to step-by-step liberalization, starting in the US in the 1970s. A group of experts drafted a report expressing the opinion that too much regulation engenders inefficiency, lacks of innovation and other aspects. These discussions resulted in the Airline Deregulation Act of 1978, liberalizing entry to American airports, routes and the industries and introducing pricing flexibility. Subsequent market entries led to huge increases in capacity offered, triggered a dramatic collapse in prices and ultimately led to the collapse of many incumbents.

Liberalization in Europe

In Europe, deregulation and privatization of infrastructure networks was also becoming more prevalent, although it took the European Community almost 10 more years to start liberalization of the European market. Liberalization of market access and prices came about in three liberalization packages between 1987 (introduction of discount fares and first changes in the strict capacity rules) and 1992 (total deregulation of prices, routes and capacity). A common market in European aviation was finally completed through liberalization of ground services (1996) and full cabotage (1997, the 8th Freedom). This came in the midst of the political and economic reunification of the European continent, which also greatly increased demand for fast and reliable mobility within a much larger European Union.

Slowdown of liberalization trends in Europe

The crash of the New Economy on September 11th 2001 and the subsequent crisis for the airline industry marked the beginning of the 21st century. Scarcity of resources, increasing environmental regulations, and a further round of EU enlargement together with new EU regulatory powers have led to a slow-down or even partial reversal of liberalization trends. With new (perceived) need for increase in security, a focus on consumer protection, new business models and competitors and a continuing need for truly global mobility of people and goods, aviation policy has reached a complexity never seen before.

In spite of these events and developments, aviation policy is still essentially shaped by the original framework of 1944, based on the absolute sovereignty of each nation to govern its airspace. This implies and strengthens a natural regulatory interest of governments, whilst being shaped by the many individual goals, interests and trends briefly highlighted above.

B. AVIATION POLICY MAKING

Aviation policy is primarily shaped by national and supranational governments. Even though the industry itself is deregulated, various fields of it are still subject to regulation, and even partly subject to increasing regulation activities.

Main aviation-related objectives of state regulation

The main objectives of state regulation are:

- Utility (economic and social growth)
- Efficiency (cost-/resource-effectiveness) and environmental sustainability
- Functioning of markets
- Intermodal cooperation / traffic management
- International cooperation
- Security and safety (standardization)
- Consumer protection

Figure 2 shows the different fields of regulation and legislation concerning aviation.

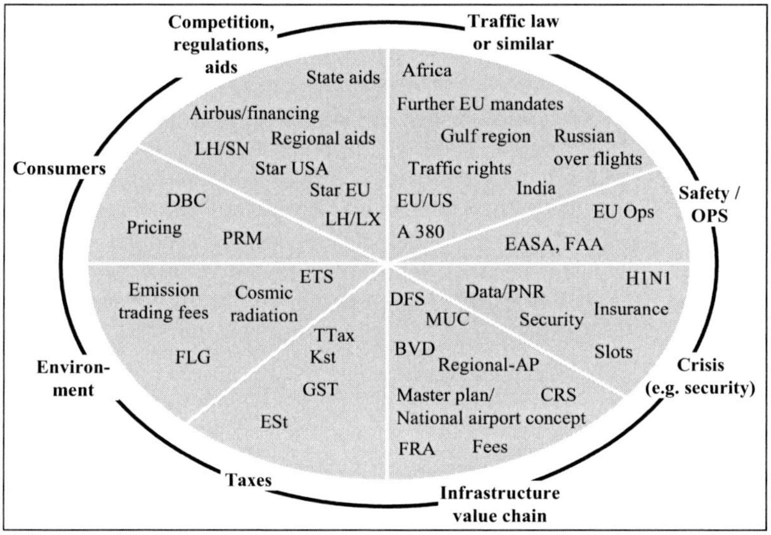

Figure 2: Different fields of regulation and legislation (Own illustration)

Instruments of aviation policy

While objectives such as utility and efficiency tend to find their philosophical foundation in the economic theory of imperfect markets, other objectives - including environmental sustainability and consumer protection - evolve in the context of a dialogue with different stakeholders. To reach those objectives, governments or their agents can use a variety of different instruments which all work in different ways. The four main groups of instruments for aviation policy – as displayed in Figure 3 – are fiscal, regulative, infrastructural and administrative.

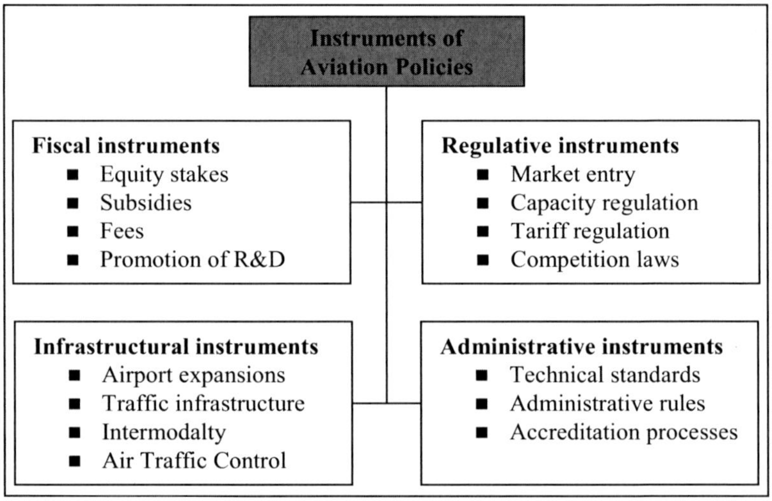

Figure 3: Instruments of aviation policy (Own illustration in relation to Pompl, 2002)

B. 1 Aviation policy making in Germany

Additional complexity at national, federal, and EU level

Aviation Policy making in Germany is not only complex because of the variety of stakeholders which are similar in at least all developed countries, but also due to division of power between the federal and state level (national) and the federal and European Union level (supranational). In a structure like this, a clear division of tasks is necessary, though often difficult and sometimes impossible. German constitutional law regulates the main legislative, executive and juridical aspects and responsibilities of aviation policy within the federal system of Germany (Figure 4).

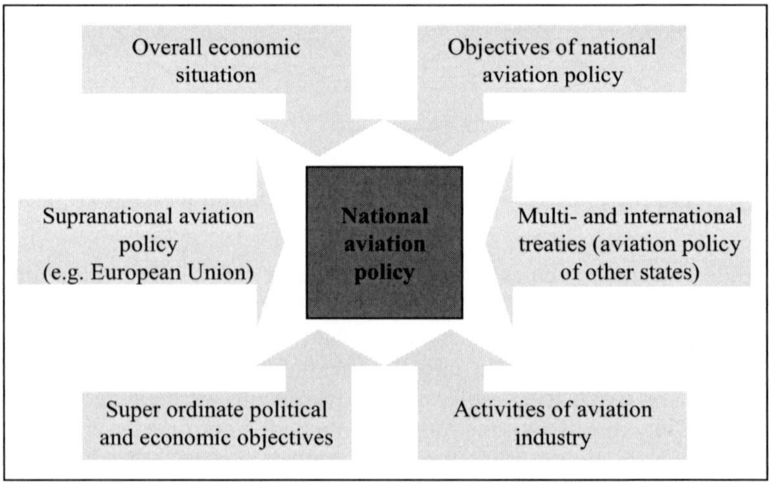

Figure 4: Aviation policy making in Germany (Own illustration in relation to Pompl, 2002)

Even though its administrative system and decision making process are complex, Germany has successfully developed as a hub for international air transport over the past few decades. Positive factors influencing this are its relatively big domestic market, central location within Europe, powerful and successful (export) economy, stable politics and sometimes even the complex political system itself, which brings greater balance and sometimes more reason to political decision making. Nowadays, the air transport industry is one of the key drivers and catalysts in German economic development.

B. 2 Aviation policy making in Europe

Responsibilities shifted from EU member states to the EU

With the creation of a single European market for aviation, many responsibilities shifted from the EU member states to the European Union (EU). European Aviation Policy is now mainly driven by the European Commission (EC).

Air transport had traditionally been a highly regulated industry, dominated by national flag carriers and state-owned airports. Due to the creation of a single market for aviation in the 1990s, nowadays all EU airlines may operate air services on any route within the EU. The internal market has removed all commercial restrictions for airlines flying within the EU, such as restrictions on the routes, the number of flights or the setting of fares.

Parallel to the opening-up of the market, the EC has developed a regulatory framework for the effective and safe operation of civil aviation. This regulatory framework is constantly evolving in the light of new developments in the aviation sector.

Aviation related fields of EU politics

Areas of (growing) EU competences and policies are for example:

- Market access
- Passenger rights
- Safety
- Security
- Environmental protection
- ATM
- Infrastructure
- Personnel and social issues
- Competition/state aids

However, airlines still have less commercial freedom when flying to countries outside the EU. International aviation has traditionally been governed by bilateral agreements between individual countries, restricting the number of airlines on the routes concerned, the number of flights and the possible destinations. To overcome these limitations, the EU is extending its aviation policy beyond its borders.

EU external aviation policy

The three pillars of the EU external aviation policy are:

- **Horizontal Agreements**: any bilateral agreements that are not in line with the freedom of operation deriving from the single mar-

ket need to be revised to ensure legal certainty and to put all EU airlines on an equal footing for flights to countries outside the EU (this can also be done bilaterally by the member states).
- **A Common Aviation Area with the EU's neighbors**: the EU is working to establish a common aviation area with neighboring countries in the Mediterranean and to the East by 2010.
- **Comprehensive agreements with global partners**: the EU is setting up open aviation areas with other key international partners.

These closer international relations not only open markets, but also allow the EU to ensure high standards of safety and security in international air transport and to work with others more effectively to address the impact of aviation on the environment.

B. 3 Influence of the airline industry

Important role of aviation industry associations

Political decisions often have a determining impact on the operations and thus ultimately the bottom-line of every airline affected. It is in the airline industry's own interest to participate actively in the policy making process. Naturally, the sphere of influence of each participant depends on the size, financial importance and number of employees, customers and communities served. However, it is often more convincing to speak with a common voice, which is why aviation industry associations are useful at all levels – global (e.g. IATA), European (e.g. AEA – Association of European Airlines) and national (e.g. BDF – Association of German Airlines).

Expertise of airline industry

The main task of these associations or of a company's political unit is to participate actively in the political process by acting as a link between the political and the company sphere. This includes picking up necessary information from both sides and delivering them in a useful way to the other party. It means giving the right information to the right people at the right time in the right place – which evidently requires the maintenance of many communication channels and relationships. However, by doing so, the airlines do not only follow their own interests. As government experts are often generalists, governments require external expertise in order to develop policy. Thus industry representatives – like academics and NGOs – are frequently invited by relevant government agencies to discuss their expertise, which on many issues can only be given in this case by airlines or airports operating in those areas on a daily basis.

The actual process can take different forms depending on the issues and people involved: informal contacts to formal hearings and procedures, questionnaires to media. However, decision making processes within government agencies are not the only points in the political process which are of interest to the industry. Other areas include the representation of industry interests abroad, which often involve crisis management by high level government officials (e.g. wars, epidemics, terrorist activities).

C. ENVIRONMENT AND SUSTAINABILITY

Aviation industry is not main contributor to climate change

Over the past few years public discussion about climate change and environmental protection has been intensifying. In this discussion, the aviation industry has often been identified by media and politicians as one of the main contributors to climate change. Despite the statistical evidence indicating that the impact of aviation-related emissions are not the main driver of climate change, the industry is still having to combat this false perception and deal with an increasing amount of regulatory provisions aimed at limiting aviation growth and improving its environmental performance. Regardless of the ongoing discussions, the airline industry itself is pushing forward with continuing efficiency measures due to intense competition and substitutability of different networks. Fuel costs are one of the main costs limiting this for most airlines and the inherent incentive to increase efficiency and thus reduce fuel costs is tremendous.

C. 1 Noise

Traffic noise as environmental issue

Besides climate change, other environmental issues surrounding aviation are contentious. According to studies by the Federal Environment Agency and the German Aerospace Center, more than 60% of the German population feels adversely affected by road traffic noise, about 30% by aircraft noise and more than 20% by rail noise (multiple complaints were possible) (Umweltbundesamt, 2007). Thus over the years, some of the world's strictest regulations on noise and gas emissions have been passed in Germany placing severe limits on airport development and usage in combination with costly bills for compensation for operators.

German aircraft noise protection act

The 'German aircraft noise protection act' of 2007, for instance, defines noise limits and noise contours around airports where owners receive compensation (noise insulation costs and additional compensation). Environmental regulations for new constructions or enlargements of airports are defined within the German air transport act, while local air quality standards in line with EU requirements are regulated by the federal Emission Protection Act.

European regulations on noise and gas emissions

Two regulations on noise and gas emissions are important at a European level. The directive on the establishment of rules and procedures with regard to the introduction of noise-related operating restrictions at community airports (2002/30/EC) defines procedures to identify noise-critical airports, and introduces the so called ICAO-Balanced Approach. To solve a noise problem at an individual airport, the following options should be equally analyzed: noise reduction at source, noise mitigation, land use planning and operating restrictions (e.g. phase out). The second regulation is the directive relating to the assessment and management of environmental noise (2002/49/EC). The aim of this regulation is to solve noise problems mainly in congested urban areas by means of strategic noise mapping and action plans based on noise maps. This directive was transformed into national law and is part of the 'German emission protection act' which is linked to the 'German aircraft noise protection act'.

It is interesting that, besides national and international regulations, technological innovations have led to drastic noise and emission reductions from engines and thus aircrafts. Over the last 60 years engine noise has been reduced by ~90% (-25 dB) through technological innovation.

Noise as the main limiting factor for aviation growth

Still, noise is the main limiting factor facing aviation growth. Many major European airports have restrictions, especially at night, which lead to capacity limitation at airports and thus limits on operational opportunities and efficiency. In the future more restrictive regulations may be expected (esp. at night) – even though some exceptions should be made for special segments of aviation – such as express cargo. Ultimately, high investments in new technologies will pay off, though, allowing a sustainable reduction of noise burden near airports.

C. 2 Emissions

Emissions reduction as environmental issue

Another political priority is the question of emissions reduction. At a political and economical level mainly fiscal or pseudo-market-approaches (such as ticket taxes, emissions related charges, kerosene taxes or the EU emissions trading scheme for airlines) have been discussed or already introduced. The basis for these instruments is agreements and regulations at regional, national and international levels which aim to reduce gas emissions. The goal of the Kyoto Protocol is to reduce greenhouses gases in developed countries by 5.2% between 2008 and 2012 by compared levels in 1990. With regard to the burden sharing principle within the Kyoto Protocol - which has so far been ratified by 188 states - the EU 15 have agreed on a reduction of 8% and the German government is even pursuing the goal of a reduction of greenhouse gases by 21%. Nevertheless, international aviation (together with shipping) was excluded from the industries covered by the Kyoto Protocol because of its comparatively small contribution and the mobility of its sources (Kyoto Protocol follows a territorial approach, with nations responsible for emissions from their territories, while aviation follows a nationality approach – see again Chicago Convention). This mobility makes attaching national responsibility to certain emissions impossible. This is also the reason why it is probably only sensible to introduce emissions trading – if at all – at a global level.

C. 2. 1 Emissions trading scheme

Aviation as a part of EU emissions trading scheme

In December 2008, the EU decided to include airline activities in its own EU emissions trading scheme (ETS), with a starting date of 2012. The idea of ETS is to create a market based instrument with economic incentives for emissions reduction. In this trading system, emissions limits (caps) are defined by a government agency and certificates are given to the industry by this agency (allowances). Next, the industry can trade those emission certificates, either to acquire further certificates (to offset a shortfall if emissions exceed allowances) or to sell for profit (in case of a surplus due to emissions reduction by the company). Demand and supply would create the trading price per ton CO_2 according to market rules (cap & trade system). An international and highly complex system of certificates is of course difficult to administer. It is not surprising that fears surrounding distortion of competition are high and the first reports of fraud are surfacing.

Underlying principles

From 2012 the EU-ETS will be applicable to all flights to or from EU airports. The cap was set at 97% in 2012 and 95% from 2013 respectively based on the CO_2 emissions for the years 2004-2006. These emissions are allocated to the airline industry as emission rights (allowances). 15% of the allocated rights (97% / 95% reduction on the years 2004-2006) will be auctioned by the member state to which an airline belongs.

Distortion of competition through the EU emissions trading scheme

Currently dependent on airlines themselves, airline operators are expecting to have to buy additional allowances for between 30% and 50% of their carbon exposure by 2012. This shows that the introduction of a European Emissions Trading Scheme would lead to a great financial burden for the European airline industry – money that would otherwise be available for investment in modern technology. The financial aspect, however, is amplified by the distortion of competition which a Europe-only approach to ETS brings: transfer flights from/to non-EU-countries via non-EU-hubs (e.g. New York-Dubai-Tokyo compared to New York-Frankfurt-Tokyo) will be entirely free of the additional cost. Similarly, transfers from Europe via non-EU-hubs will be partially free of the additional charges (e.g. Berlin-Istanbul-Mumbai versus Berlin-Munich-Mumbai). This distortion negatively affects EU carriers twice and benefits non-EU carriers and their longer – less environmentally friendly – routings. The unilateral introduction of ETS and the consequences would be an example of unwanted effects of regulation caused by the great complexity and internationality of aviation. The German government has so far promised to abstain from measures which distort competition and put German companies at an unfair disadvantage.

C. 2. 2 Industry approach – four-pillar strategy

Four pillar strategy

As mentioned, aviation has a keen self-interest in efficiency. It is also well ahead of most other industries in formulating and implementing a truly encompassing approach to limiting inefficiencies and emissions.

Over the past 40 years aviation's progress has led to a part elimination of soot particles, a reduction of noise emissions by 75% and improvement of Fuel / CO_2–efficiency by 70% (IATA, 2010a). In 2007, the international aviation industry passed an integrated approach for emission reduction, which has two main targets based on a four pillar strategy (Figure 5): Firstly, it is competition- and innovation-oriented, looking for win-win options, and secondly, it is sustainable, fulfilling social expectations. The corresponding four pillar strategy has been accepted widely at international (political) level.

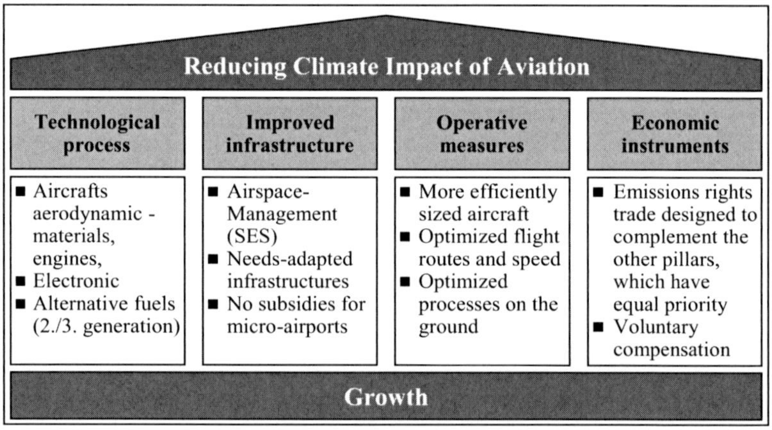

Figure 5: The Four pillar strategy for reducing climate impact of aviation (Own illustration)

Emissions reduction targets

Industry and research have already defined their targets. The IATA - Fuel Efficiency Goal states a reduction of specific fuel consumption (and therefore CO_2 emissions) of 25% by 2020 compared to 2006 (IATA, 2010b). Single European Sky (SES)[4] could add another 12% reduction of CO_2 emissions per year. The ACARE (Advisory Council for Aeronautics Research in Europe) aims to achieve a reduction of CO_2 emissions by 50%, a reduction of NO_x emissions by 80% and a reduction of average aircraft noise by 50% through new technologies by 2020 compared to the levels for reference year 2000 (Advisory Council for Aeronautics Research in Europe [ACARE], 2002).

The four pillar strategy is:

- Invest in new technology
- Build and use efficient infrastructure
- Fly more efficiently
- Use effective economic measures

The pillars focus on all industry players (airlines, airports, manufacturers, air navigation service providers) and the governments on addressing climate change together.

1st pillar: Invest in new technology

Innovative technology as first pillar promises to have the most potential for carbon reduction potential (Figure 6). Under technology aspects, IATA expects that the introduction of so called 2nd generation sustainable biofuels could provide 6% of aviation fuel use by 2020.

4 Single European Sky is an initiative by the European Commission.

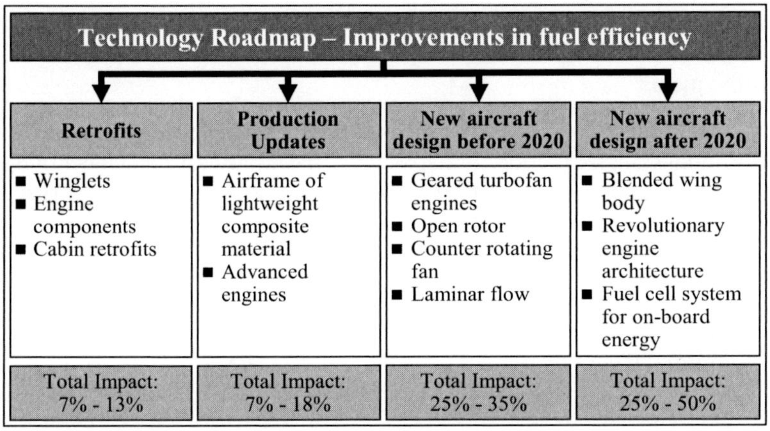

Figure 6: IATA TERESA-Project: Technology roadmap for environmentally sustainable aviation (Own illustration based on IATA, 2009)

2nd pillar: Build and use efficient infrastructure

A very important, and the most political, factor for an encompassing emissions reduction strategy is improved infrastructure. SES is the largest infrastructure and environmental protection project in Europe today. It aims to harmonize regulation on airspace within the European Union. This would benefit all airspace users by ensuring safer and more efficient utilization of airspace through better air traffic management and organization within and beyond the EU. Airspace management should be harmonized and decoupled from national territory. Instead new 'Functional Airspace Blocks' would run cross-border to maximize the efficiency of the airspace control throughout the European airspace. With an implemented approach to SES unnecessary detours of 468 million km (in 2007), equivalent to 5.4 million liters of kerosene per day (all airlines in EU traffic), could be avoided (Eurocontrol, 2007). Lufthansa, for example, uses more than 500,000 liters per day for such detours - with an average detour per flight of nearly 50 km. The more efficient navigation and flight management capabilities of new system technologies have a reduction potential of at least 6% - but it must be noted that these can only be realized if governments make the necessary investments to upgrade global air traffic management (ATM) systems.

Still, political decisions at a global level hinder the full effectiveness of the measures taken by the industry. The still fragmented nature of European air space and insufficient capacity at major EU hubs are among those obstacles. Others include the unnecessary overcapacity created elsewhere in the aftermath of political decisions such as subsidies for new aircrafts, regional airports or even airlines.

3rd pillar: Fly more efficiently

The third pillar includes operative measures like the use of more efficiently sized aircraft depending on routes, optimized flight routes and speed or optimized processes on the ground. Using aircraft efficiently makes a big difference. IATA Green Teams have completed 105 onsite assessments since 2005, helping airlines to identify savings in aircraft operations. IATA green teams and airlines like Lufthansa have saved 36.4 million tons of CO_2 since 2005 through operational improvements.

4th pillar: Use efficient economic measures

Support of positive economic measures is the fourth pillar of the aviation emissions reduction strategy. This means investment incentives, research funding or voluntary measures being undertaken by airlines including carbon offsets. Emissions Trading can also play a role as long as it is:

- Fair in comparison to other industries
- Global in scope
- Implemented by mutual consent between states

D. SAFETY AND SECURITY

Safety and security as important field of regulation and legislation

Safety and security are among the issues with the highest priority in daily operations – and highest on the agenda of regulators and legislators. The nature of air transport itself means every mistake can be fatal and nonreversible. The high media attention which follows every incident or accident draws public attention to the airlines involved, even though statistics prove that air transport is the safest of all modes of transport with the lowest number of fatalities per person/km. Furthermore, safety in air transport has considerably improved in terms of accidents per flight (Aviation Safety Network, 2006) over the last decades even though the traffic itself has multiplied.

Harmonizing role of EASA

To cope with the increasing air traffic and safety demands, especially in the European Union, the European safety administration was dramatically changed in 2003. Before, each country was responsible for aspects concerning safety and security. The only forum for mutual technical decisions was the Joint Aviation Authorities (JAA), where the Joint Aviation Requirements were released and the translation to national law was simply monitored. In 2003, however, the European Aviation Safety Agency (EASA) was founded, whose regulatory output, in contrast to JAA, does not require translation into its members' national law. With the foundation of EASA, European safety requirements are becoming substantially more harmonized. This results in a progressive transfer of responsibilities concerning e.g. safety issues from the certification of aircraft and the licensing of flight crews to the operation of aircraft to – the most recent extension of EASA competence – the safety aspects of aerodrome operation and air traffic management.

The main task of EASA is to find the necessary balance between harmonization in the European Union, administrative efficiency and global competition. In debates about new regulations on security and safety, the passenger's safety is always a strong argument, so that some regulations raise questions concerning the balance between security and safety on the one hand and operational needs and economic or competitive implications on the other.

Safety and security after Lockerbie and September 11

After Lockerbie and September 11 civil aviation experienced a flood of non-harmonized, often redundant or even contradictory national regulations on security. Airlines, as national symbols, and air transport as a life-sustaining system for economies and way of life have become targets for terrorists. Thus the security aspect has gained in public importance. Yet as security (also in Europe) is still a matter of national sovereignty – and aviation is seen as a crucial element of this - aviation security issues (i.e. protection against criminal acts) are still subject to national laws and authorities. Combined with limited confidence and insight into security matters of other states, a totally non-harmonized and poorly consulted network of often questionable measures around the world still exists.

The result is a costly security system which relies heavily on a non-transparent mix of public and passenger / airline funding, which impacts on service quality as well as operational efficiency. Examples - such as regulations on onboard liquids and the requirement to offload baggage if respective passengers do not board - abound. Both examples show that the consequences of these rules are often impractical and unreasonable. Especially in the case of baggage, modern screening technology can already successfully solve the problem. Thus, the need for a time-consuming offloading which interrupts operational processes is no longer necessary.

One-Stop-Security

To cope with these issues, the main task of aviation policy is to establish 'One-Stop-Security' areas (OSS). The main characteristic of OSS is to avoid redundant security measures, with only one state administering the necessary checks and other member states accepting these checks as sufficient for transfer and the continued journey. International coordination and recognition of foreign aviation security measures are of prime importance here. This automatically leads to higher creditability and acceptance among passengers and customers and improves operational efficiency. So far, first steps have been taken to accomplish OSS between Europe and North America, where a common OSS is being evaluated.

E. CONSUMER RIGHTS

Air passengers have comprehensive right

As in many service fields, the European Union is continuously widening consumer rights in commercial aviation. Thus, the regulation density has been growing at great speed and has now reached a truly unique level, with almost all fields of the consumer and airliner relationship covered by regulations in favor of the consumer.

Examples for air passenger-related regulations

Besides adding substantial cost and complexity, these regulations often level competitive differences and advantages, as most costumer rights are already service standards among quality carriers, while some network airlines and no-frills airlines have ignored such standards of service and often courtesy - often provoking regulatory action. Prominent examples include the 'Denied Boarding Regulation' (2004/261/EC), which determines the rights of air passengers in cases of flights being overbooked, canceled and delayed. The 'PRM-Regulation' (1107/2006/EC) refers to disabled persons and persons with reduced mobility and their right to assistance on board and at airports. The 'Fare Transparency Regulation' (2008/1008/EC) intends to stop price discrimination on the basis of place of residence and also counters non-transparent booking processes.

Besides leveling the competition, such regulations can also have the effect of distorting competition. Avoiding this uniform compliance and implementation of such regulations is necessary. However, not only compliance within the aviation industry is important – similar standards of service and liability have been introduced for passengers using other modes of transport. As a first step, an EC regulation on rail passenger rights and obligations entered into effect in December 2009.

Review Questions

- What is the legal basis of all air traffic activity, upon which international air transport relies?
- Which different specific instruments do you know regarding aviation policy?
- What is meant with the Freedoms of the Air?
- What opportunities, risks or other aspects do airlines see in context with the upcoming EU emissions trading scheme?
- What are the four pillars of IATA's integrated approach for emissions avoidance?
- What are the benefits of One-Stop-Security?
- Which air passenger-related EU regulations do you know?

Bibliography and further reading

Advisory Council for Aeronautics Research in Europe (ACARE) (2002): Strategic Research Agenda Volume 1, Brussels.

Aviation Safety Network (2006): Airliner Accident Statistics 2006.

Eurocontrol (2007): Performance Review Report 2007, Brussels.

Grotius, H. (1609): Mare Liberum (The Free Seas; from chapter 12 of De Indis), Leiden.

International Air Transport Association [IATA] (2010a): Aviation Environment, www.iata.org/whatwedo/environment, Montreal / Geneva, retrieved: 01/14/2010.

International Air Transport Association [IATA] (2010b): Aviation Environment – Fuel Efficiency, www.iata.org/whatwedo/environment/fuel_efficiency, Montreal / Geneva, retrieved: 01/14/2010.

International Air Transport Association [IATA] (2009): Technology Roadmap Report, Montreal / Geneva.

Milde, M. (2008): International Air Law and ICAO, Utrecht.

Oxford (2009): Policy in: Compact Oxford English Dictionary, Oxford.

Pompl, W. (2002): Luftverkehr - eine ökonomische und politische Einführung, 4th ed. Berlin / Heidelberg / New York.

Umweltbundesamt (2007): Environmental Data for Germany - environmental indicators, Dessau-Roßlau.

Air Cargo Management

Marc Oedekoven

Table of contents

You should be able to

- understand the importance of the air cargo industry
- be familiar with the major development trends of this industry
- display knowledge of the fast moving business environment
- describe the role of air cargo carriers within the logistics chain
- illustrate particularities of supply and demand for air cargo
- know relevant business models in the air cargo sector
- comprehend the core strategic marketing topics of this sector
- display knowledge of the relevant business challenges and draw appropriate conclusions for the successful management of the air cargo business

The author

Marc Oedekoven is the owner and MD of KIBIX Logistics GmbH in Cologne. He is also the Chairman of the IQS Group in Langenbach (Munich). Previously, he has held various management positions within the Lufthansa Group in Frankfurt, Dubai and Singapore. He holds a degree of Master of Economics and MBA and he is lecturer at the European Business School Oestrich-Winkel, at the International University of Bad Honnef as well as at the Europaeische Fachhochschule Bruehl/Cologne. Marc is married and father of two sons.

Abstract

Air cargo is the backbone of modern economies and companies in this sector face a correspondingly complex market environment. In this chapter I highlight the dynamics of the air cargo market and identify the general forces and constraints in air cargo development. Having determined the competitive intensity and attractiveness of the air cargo market, I subsequently derive implications for the management of companies in this sector.

A. THE SIGNIFICANCE OF AIR CARGO

The demands on companies are increasing steadily: customers are becoming more demanding and product life cycles are getting shorter due to strong competition, cost pressure and globalization. Overall, customers are demanding higher quality and improved services at lower prices.

Logistics are steadily gaining in importance

This same environment also creates an ever increasing demand on logistics as companies increasingly concentrate on their core competencies. A high degree of coordination is necessary in order to steer raw materials and parts flexibly, temporally and quantitatively across the globally linked logistic infrastructure. This is particularly relevant nowadays in a world where division of labor is increasingly international.

Especially high value goods are transported by air

Today, logistics takes more responsibility than ever in this complex environment, and in this respect, air cargo transport plays an increasingly important role within the transport chains of global trade. Although only one percent of globally transported goods are currently transported by air cargo, this accounts for more than 35% of the total value of global trade calculated by the value of goods shipped (aci.aero; Pompl, 2008, p. 106; Maurer, 2006, p.2; Schieck, 2008, p. 218).

Air freight is an inherent part of the logistics chain

Airplanes, ships as well as long distance trains on specific routes are employed for intercontinental transport, while trucks and the majority of trains compete with air cargo at a continental level. In the past, transport by plane was the exception, being utilized for either for high value or express freight only. Today, it is used for a wide range of goods and transport. Within the decentralized production and distribution of production facilities, air cargo plays a central role in the logistics chain.

Some industries do heavily rely on air cargo

Shippers and forwarders define the optimum balance between capital binding, production specific, and speed related factors on a daily basis. The fast and flexible bridging of huge distances is a unique feature which has supported the fast development of air cargo in its short history. Industrial and domestic life without air cargo is unconceivable today: cellphones, just-in-time production, the exact way the complexities of Formula 1 operate, mail order businesses or the availability of fresh mangos at any time of the year would not be possible without an air cargo system.

Some key industries, such as pharmaceuticals or fashion, would simply not exist in today`s shape without the present distribution channels provided by air cargo transportation. Figure 1 illustrates the high complexity of modern logistics chains.

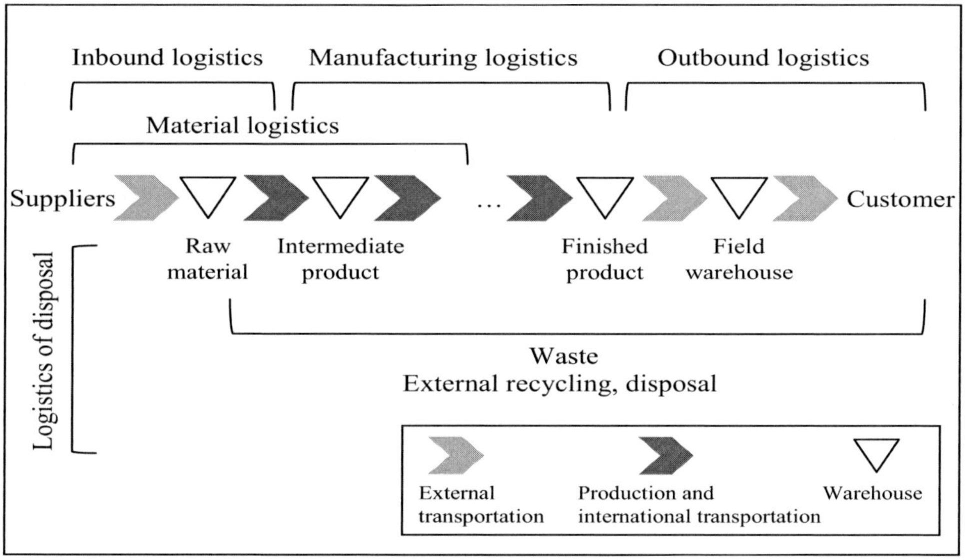

Figure 1: Air cargo as an integral part of logistics chains (Own Illustration based on Arnold, Isermann, Kuhn & Fuhrmans, 2008)

Air cargo has suffered severely from the recent economic downturn

In this globally interdependent context, the air cargo industry has suffered significantly during times of challenging market conditions:

- World air cargo traffic has averaged 5.2% growth per year since 1983 (Boeing, 2014)
- Growth slowed as fuel prices began to rise in 2005 and some shippers began to divert freight to less expensive modes of transport
- The global economic downturn, the worst economic contraction since the Great Depression, dragged down all modes of freight transport. World air cargo traffic dropped 13% over the two years ending in 2009
- From mid-2011 to early 2013, world air cargo traffic stagnated
- The routes which were affected most severely were those transporting air cargo between Europe and the US, between Germany and Asia, and between Asia and Germany[1]
- Average load factors of 49% (IATA, 2010a) have led to a reduction in the worldwide freighter fleet by more than 220 freighter aircraft (IATA, 2010b)

[1] Based on data from www.centreforaviation.com and www.iata.com.

- Air France-KLM took that as a starting point to group their freighter fleets together under the umbrella of their affiliated company Martinair (DVZ, 2009a / Airliners, 2009). Meanwhile Air France and KLM have abandoned their freighter operations, opening the way for a paradigm shift in business modeling within the air cargo industry.[2]

On the other hand, the global air cargo market was able to recover from periods of crisis:

- The growth rate exceeded 6% in several years throughout the 1980s, 1990s, and early 2000s
- Traffic jumped 19.4% in 2010 and gained a further 0.8% in 2011 (Boeing, 2014)
- The second quarter of 2013 brought a positive note and global air trade continued to gather momentum in 2014
- Even stronger growth is anticipated for the remainder of 2014

B. THE NATURE OF AIR CARGO

Mail and checked-in baggage are not counted as air cargo

All goods transported as freight shipments with an aircraft are defined as air freight. Traditionally, air mail plays a separate role as it is operated according to the regulations of the international mail organizations. Together, air freight and mail constitute air cargo. Luggage checked-in by passengers is not counted as air cargo (Klußmann & Malik, 2007, p. 156).

Air cargo traffic can be classified as follows (Grandjot, 2002):

Purpose	commercial	non commercial	military
Mode of transport	passengers	cargo	mail
Type of aircraft	freighters		belly aircraft
	wide body		narrow body
	jet aircraft		propeller aircraft
Length of haul	short	medium	long
Traffic area	regional	continental	intercontinental
Airspace	classified as per the freedoms of the air		
Regularity	line haul	charter	on demand
Business activities	AP-to-AP	D-to-D	other products

Figure 2: Morphological box of air cargo (Own illustration)

[2] For further elaboration on changing business models in the air cargo industry see also Airline Cargo Management March 2010, p. 16-28, as well as DVZ 27 June 2009, p. 1-5.

Air cargo is first choice for quick transportation

Compared to the economic efficiency of other modes of transport, air cargo is a poor choice for mass transportation. However, air cargo is particularly important for high value products requiring high speed transportation. These products require priority transportation, either because they are urgently needed (e.g. pharmaceutical products), or because they would otherwise perish over long distances (e.g. fruit or flowers) or because the value of the products is high and they bind capital (e.g. computer chips or diamonds).

Actors in air cargo transportation chain

Various actors are responsible for the management of the air transportation chain: amongst them are forwarders, customs agents, airports and the air cargo carriers themselves (Becker, 1999, p. 35-41). The air cargo carriers are accountable for the transport from airport-to-airport. The forwarders enlarge the transportation chain, enabling door-to-door delivery. In this context, the forwarder is the intermediary between shippers, air cargo carriers and consignees.

Different forms of carriers

Air transportation plays a central role in consolidation activities. It is also at the center of up- and downstream distribution processes. The air transportation chain is the entire process chain from the shipper to the consignee. Along this chain feeding, de-feeding and main leg processes can be differentiated. The main leg, which can be multi-segmented, is performed by aircraft. The operating companies are divided into so called belly-carriers (such as Swiss International Air Lines), carriers with a pure freighter fleet (such as Cargolux) and combined carriers (such as Lufthansa Cargo). In general, the distance covered by aircraft is the greatest related to the overall transportation chain whereas the time required is usually the smallest. In this context, the air cargo carriers are particularly important, as they add a high amount of value to the supply of logistics services.

Ground transportation

As mentioned above, air cargo is either co-loaded freight on passenger aircraft or transported by pure freighter aircraft. More than 50% of the worldwide air cargo volume is transported as co-loaded freight on passenger aircraft (Boeing, 2014 / Dahl, 2010, p. 82). The transportation of passenger and freight can therefore not be seen independently in terms of scheduling and network management. On traffic lanes with high air cargo volumes in conjunction with insufficient belly-hold capacities on passenger aircraft, pure freighter aircraft are employed.

Nature of goods transported

In addition, certain over-sized freight as well as freight of specific nature (e.g. radioactive, explosive, or dangerous goods) is flown on cargo aircraft alone. The amount of pure freighter flight worldwide as a percentage of all aircraft movements is about 5% (Boeing, 2008).

Feeding and de-feeding

Ground transportation between airports is often performed on behalf of the air cargo company by road feeder services. The feeding and de-feeding activities, which are the delivery to and collection from airports, complete the service for the shipper or consignee. These feeding and de-feeding activities are mostly organized and performed by the air cargo forwarders and agents.

Integrated transportation services are increasingly being provided in which the time for the entire transportation process from shipper to consignee is agreed upon.

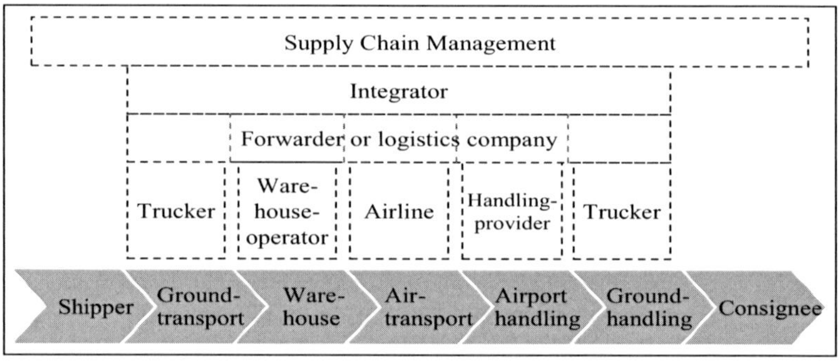

Figure 3: The role of air cargo carriers within the air cargo delivery system (Own illustration)

The changeover between means of transport takes place at airports which supply specific transportation, transit handling and warehousing services. Hence, apart from the transportation itself, the relevant elements of the air transportation chain are found at the airports. Airports are the most relevant air cargo specific logistics infrastructures. The following figure lists air cargo volumes amongst the top 15 airports worldwide in 2014.

RANK 2014	RANK 2013	AIRPORT CITY / COUNTRY / CODE	FREIGHT (Metric tonnes)	
			Loaded and unloaded	Percent change
1	1	HONG KONG, HK (HKG)	4 376 349	6.0
2	3	INCHEON, KR (ICN)	2 474 152	3.3
3	2	DUBAI, AE (DXB)	2 367 574	-3.1
4	4	SHANGHAI, CN (PVG)	2 334 368	8.1
5	6	TAIPEI, TW (TPE)	2 072 602	6.2
6	7	TOKYO, JP (NRT)	2 043 372	5.3
7	5	FRANKFURT, DE (FRA)	2 007 318	1.7
8	9	PARIS, FR (CDG)	1 858 482	1.3
9	8	SINGAPORE, SG (SIN)	1 843 800	0.3
10	10	ANCHORAGE AK, US (ANC)	1 787 287	6.6
11	11	MIAMI FL, US (MIA)	1 739 005	3.8
12	12	AMSTERDAM, NL (AMS)	1 633 195	6.7
13	13	LONDON, GB (LHR)	1 497 701	5.4
14	14	BANGKOK, TH (BKK)	1 193 300	0.3
15	15	LOS ANGELES CA, US (LAX)	1 044 835	5.6
16	16	NEW YORK NY, US (JFK)	1 002 569	3.7
17	17	DOHA, QA (DOH)	980 114	13.2
18	18	CHICAGO IL, US (ORD)	972 803	16.1
19	19	LEIPZIG, DE (LEJ)	840 987	3.0
20	20	ABU DHABI, AE (AUH)	797 069	12.8

Table 1: The world's busiest cargo airports, total international airfreight traffic 2014 (Airports Council International [ACI], 2015)

Carriers have focused global air cargo volume on an increasingly limited number of locations.

C. COMPLEX MARKET ENVIRONMENT

C. 1 Dynamic market development

Enormous growth

Over the last 20 years, the market volume for air cargo transportation has more than doubled, from 93 billions revenue tonne-kilometers (RTKs). in 1994 to 208 billions RTKs in 2014 (Boeing, 2014). In this context the fluctuation in a country's GDP strongly correlates with the development of air cargo (measured in revenue tonne-kilometers (RTKs)) as the following figure illustrates.

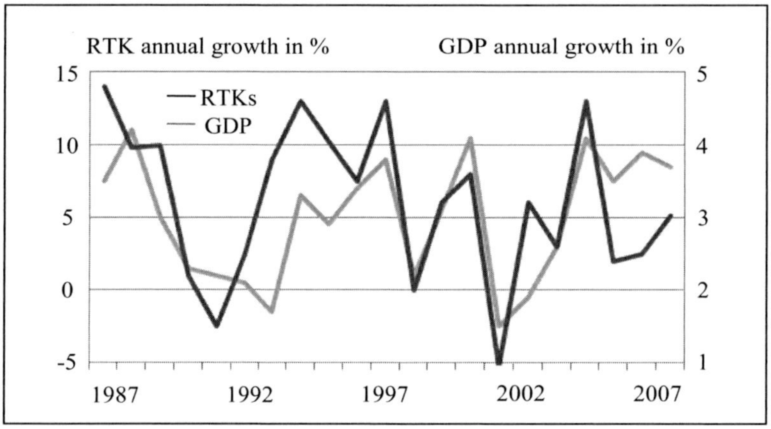

Figure 4: Correlation of GDP and air cargo development (Own illustration based on Boeing, 2008, p. 16)

Cyclicality of air cargo market

It can be observed that the development of air cargo is an early indicator for the subsequent development of the GDP. The course of the development of the air cargo market is extremly cyclical. Next to short term cycles with external causes, such as, SARS, bird flu, and the after effects of September 11 2001, mid- and long-term cycles can also be observed (Figure 5).

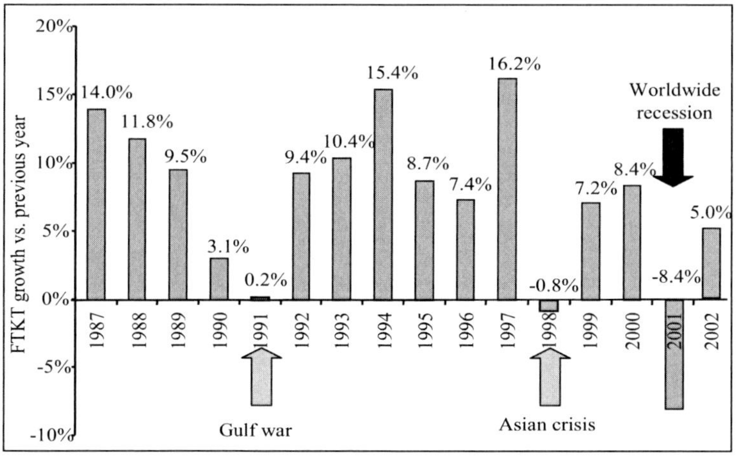

Figure 5: Air cargo is a strongly cyclical growth market (Own illustration based on IATA, 2003)

During a year, the market is subject to seasonal fluctuations in distribution and production.

Cyclicality of air cargo market

Express and standard cargo services are usually distinguished from each other. During the last years, the proportion of express products grew very quickly. The traffic lanes also known as trunk routes principally served on a global scale, are the routes between the regions of the triade (USA, EU, and Asia). Approximately 60% of all air cargo is flown on the lanes between the USA, the EU and Far East. The intra-Chinese market is the fastest growing one and the domestic US market is the largest single market for air cargo services (Boeing, 2014). The market development of air cargo is highly dependent on the geography and the infrastructure in a country or a group of countries. Factors for this are natural obstacles or the lack of well established rail and road networks which reduce the threat of substitutes for air cargo. Correspondingly, huge potential will emerge, particularly in intra-Asian air cargo market, compared to the already saturated intra-European air cargo market.

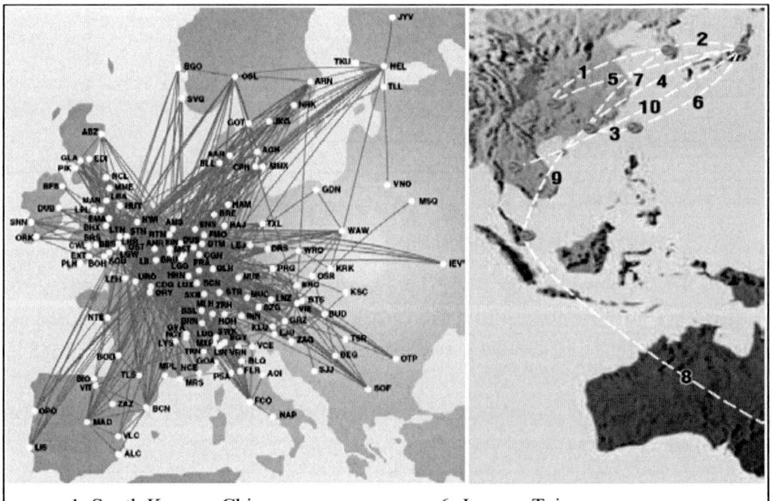

1. South Korea – China	6. Japan – Taiwan
2. Japan – South Korea	7. Hong Kong – South Korea
3. Hong Kong – Taiwan	8. Australia - Singapore
4. Hong Kong – Japan	9. Hong Kong – Singapore
5. Japan – China	10. Japan - Thailand

Figure 6: Intra-European and intra-Asian route development (Boeing, 2014)

Other factors influencing regional market development are GDP growth, customs regulations as well as regional trade agreements. The most relevant ones are highlighted in the next chapter.

C. 2 Forces and constraints for air cargo growth

Factors influencing air cargo business

In analyzing the macro-environment it is important to identify the factors that might in turn affect a number of vital variables likely to influence an air cargo organization's supply and demand levels and costs. The following checklist illustrates a selection of possible issues that might affect the air cargo industry (PEST analysis).[3] The analysis highlights the impact of each of these factors on the business. The results can then be used to take advantage of opportunities and to make contingency plans for threats when preparing business and strategic plans. The analysis is a useful strategic tool for understanding market growth or decline, business position, potential and direction for business operations.

PEST analysis

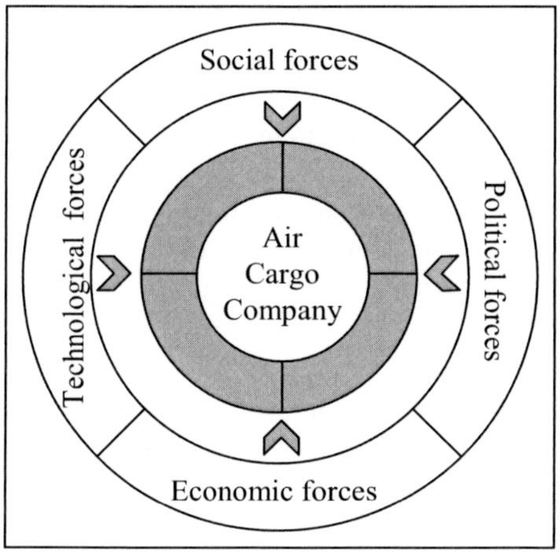

Figure 7: External factors influencing the operating environment within the air cargo industry (Own illustration)

Political factors:

Political factors

- **Legislation of traffic rights**. Despite the emergence of Open Sky treaties and market deregulation, the air cargo market still is regulated by national laws. This does not permit carriers to serve all routes (i.e. origin and destination) required.
- **Environmental protection laws**. The regulation of noise emissions (e.g. night curfews) as well as pollutant emissions has a direct impact on the production of air cargo carriers, e.g. the type of aircraft to be employed which affects the capacity available. The transportation of certain animals or radioactive materials is also controlled.
- **Foreign trade regulations** have a direct impact on the imports and exports of countries and their industries. The demand for air cargo capacity depends highly on these imports and exports.
- **IATA[4] regulations**. The use of IT systems, e.g. the paperless transmission of 'airway bills' or additional customs documents,

---

[3] An analysis of the external macro-environment in which the company operates can be expressed in terms of **P**olitical, **E**conomic, **S**ocial, and **T**echnological factors and is therefore called a PEST analysis.

[4] The mission of IATA (International Air Transport Association) is to represent and serve its members, some 230 airlines, the world's leading passenger and cargo airlines among them.

and the IATA agent declaration process, prerequisite to selling air cargo, are affected by IATA regulations.

Economical factors

Economic factors:

- **GDP trends**. With globally increasing GDP and trade, the air cargo market is likely to benefit from more demand in the future.
- **Energy availability** Fuel shortages will have direct impact on the cost of carriers and subsequently on air cargo rates.
- **Currency exchange rates** have a direct impact on international trade (Dieckheuer, 2001).
- **Globalization**. The harmonization of consumer needs, global production facility networks, and the standardization of marketing and sales activities lead to an increase in the movement and transport goods and therefore increase air cargo transportation (Meffert & Bolz, 2007)

Socio-cultural factors

Socio-cultural factors:

- **Demographics 1**. The industrialization of countries such as China is directly related to worldwide income distribution, which will have an effect on growth rates in these markets.
- **Demographics 2**: Countries with an aging population such as most European countries demand different consumer products and hence influence the air cargo demand with their buying behavior as well as with their travel habits.
- **Travel habits**. Air cargo capacities are also offered on passenger services as belly freight and therefore depend on the airlines' passenger networks.
- **Holidays:** Valentine's Day, Chinese New Year, Pilgrimages and other Holidays influence the offer and demand for air cargo capacities.

Technological factors

Technological factors:

- **The industry focuses on IT:** E-commerce, system links and interfaces (electronic data interchange), and e-communication (email etc.) require efficiently operating IT platforms.
- **Industry production changes considerably:** Product Life Cycles become shorter. As a result, last minute supply chain requirements, ECR[5] etc. become increasingly important.
- **Development of substitutes for air cargo services:** Faster and reliable long distance trains increasingly take market shares of the air cargo sector.
- **Efficiency of the air cargo production platform:** more fuel efficient engines and lighter aircraft bodies lower the cost of air transportation.

---

[5] Efficient Consumer Response (ECR) is a joint trade and industry body working towards making the grocery sector as a whole more responsive to consumer demand.

D. CHARACTER OF THE AIR CARGO INDUSTRY

D. 1 Attractiveness of the air cargo sector

Competitive forces by Porter

The attractiveness of the air cargo sector is determined by the following five essential competitive forces. Rivalry among existing competitors (central driving force), threat of new entrants (limitations to market entry), bargaining power of suppliers, and bargaining power of buyers and threat of substitute products or services. The more intense the threat of any of these five forces appears to be, the less attractive the sector is, and the more difficult it is to achieve sustainable competitive advantage (Porter, 1980, p. 150).

Competition between market players

The intensity of competition between the market players in the air cargo industry is high and it is primarily determined by the following:

- Many similar competitors (air cargo carriers) are active in this sector. They operate virtually identical means of production and their business models are comparable on a global scale.
- Capacity can only be added in larger increments. The fixed assets involved in air cargo logistics such as aircraft, warehouses and office buildings at airports etc. can only grow in larger and fixed steps.
- High strategic risks such as the development of energy generation.
- The barriers for exiting the air cargo market are high particularly due to specialized means of production, fixed costs of retirement and governmental barriers.

It is therefore highly likely to observe continuous overcapacities in the future and therefore an increase in competition for customers. Ceteris paribus, rates for air cargo services will decrease constantly and consequently profit margins will further fall and the attractiveness of the market decrease.

Market entry barriers

The existence of market entry barriers limits the number of companies in the air cargo market and consequently influences the rivalry amongst the existing competitors. If new companies appear on the market, competitive advantages are immediately influenced. The new service provider offers new additional capacities to the existing market. This additional capacity diminishes the profit margin of all market participants. The threat of new entrants is great if entry barriers are low. Three essential entry barriers can be observed in the air cargo market (which is valid for new pure cargo carriers, not, however, for the additional air cargo capacity offered by new passenger airlines):

- Existing carriers realize economies of scale by over proportionally decreasing the total cost while simultaneously increasing production capacity (i.e. freight ton kilometers offered) per period.
- Product diversity: the established companies may already have achieved high brand recognition, intense customer loyalty or similar marketing targets. In order to compete here, the new entrant must bear additional cost for sales support, advertising etc.

- Entry into the sector requires significant investment and capital. In terms of cost and capital expenditure, the risk of a business venture failing (sunk cost) presents a major hurdle for new entrants.

Suppliers

Suppliers can also pose a threat to the air cargo sector by increasing prices for their goods or services. Powerful suppliers could in this context reduce profitability for the companies operating within the sector, if they are unable to recoup this increase in cost through an increase of rates in their selling markets. The power of a supplier is generally determined by similar factors as those for the buyers. A supplier's sector such as aircraft manufacturing e.g. Boeing, Airbus or fuel producing companies is powerful because:

- The sector is dominated by only a few companies and it is more concentrated than the airlines.
- The goods and services delivered constitute an important contribution for the consuming air cargo sector.

Customers

Customers with a high market power compete with the air cargo sector as they put rates under pressure and demand better quality or the extension of the existing service range. This again reduces the profit margins of the air cargo sector.

As a customer group the forwarders are powerful because:

- High volume purchases combined with Pareto's 80:20 rule[6] lead to high consolidation effects within the market: the group of forwarders is highly concentrated, buying a large proportion of the total volume of the sector.
- The services and products purchased are standardized or undifferentiated for the vast majority of air cargo services.
- The forwarder's sector can credibly threaten the delivering air cargo carriers with upstream integration.
- The customer's sector benefits from full market transparency.
- The cost of changing a carrier is low and the services offered by the carriers are easily exchanged or substituted.

Substitutes

In a broader and more general perspective, all competitors in a sector compete with industries producing substitute services or products. Substitutes limit the profits within a sector as they determine the absolute level for rates that the sector can demand for their services and products. The influence of substitutes in the air cargo sector depends on more specific market segments. It is higher if air cargo services can relatively easily be switched from the original to the substitute (low product loyalty). The influence is also augmented if the incurred costs

---

[6] Pareto's principle states that in many situations only 20% are critical and 80% are less significant. In other words, the 80:20 rule means that the relationship between input and output is seldom, if ever, balanced. In this context it signifies that 20 percent of the forwarders control 80 percent of the business.

for this switch are relatively low and if the rates for air cargo transportation are relatively high compared to the performance of the substitute (e.g. slower speed of transportation by truck), which is acceptable to the consumer at a significantly lower rate.

D. 2 Determinants of air cargo

Characteristics of air cargo market

In general, air cargo is characterized by following features:

- The transportation offer cannot be stored
- Inflexibility of the offer on the production side, due to type of aircraft, airport locations, and fewer transport capacities in comparison with other means of transportation.
- High cost of transportation in the air and high proportion of fixed costs.
- Incomplete competition (private and public owned companies)
- Disparity between traffic (one way traffic flows)
- Heterogeneity of air cargo shipments
- Number of players on the demand side is limited
- Number of necessary players to produce offer is significantly high
- Volatility of demand (economic development, customer behavior)

Factors influencing demand

The demand for air cargo services is determined by the following factors:

- Speed of transportation
- Product life cycle of the products of shippers
- Emergencies on shipper or consignee side
- Just-in-time requirements (satisfaction of global sourcing and distribution)
- Capital turnover (dense value of transported goods)
- Light packaging
- Reduced cost of stock
- Reduced cost of insurance (e.g. through reduced risk of theft during transportation)
- Flexibility of disposition
- Simple documentation[7]

The challenge of derived demand

Demand within the air cargo industry occurs as a result of demand for another, so called derived demand. The derived demand occurs because the demand for logistics services depends on the production and distribution volumes of the shippers' markets. It depends on the demand for goods, as well as on the form of the market and the behavioral pattern within the markets for air cargo related goods. Figure 8 shows how demand is determined by the business-to-business relationship and the business-to-consumer relationship.

---

7 For further elaboration on the affinity of air cargo goods see Schieck (2008, p. 221).

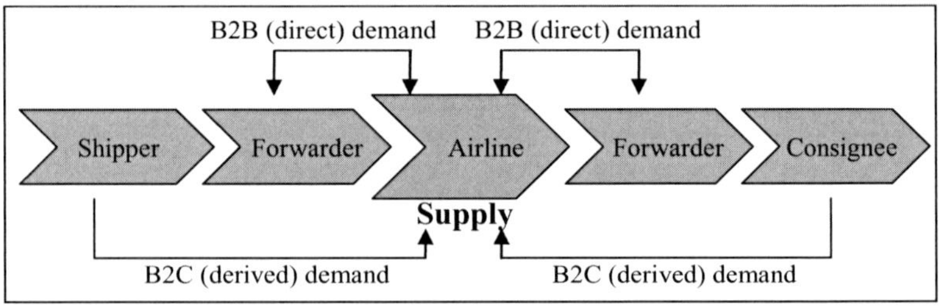

Figure 8: Derived demand in the air cargo industry (Own illustration)

A special character of the offer side is the organizational joint product. It is a result of the means of transportation delivering air cargo service, i.e. the aircraft, needing to return to its original location (return trip traffic). This traffic occurs in any case, regardless of whether there is existing demand for this traffic relation or not at this particular point in time.

Another form of joint product results from the cargo flown in the belly-hold capacities of passenger aircraft.

E. VALUE CHAIN MANAGEMENT OF AN AIR CARGO COMPANY

Value chain is influenced by special character of air cargo

The aforementioned properties of the air cargo market and the special character of air cargo have direct implications on the management of the value chain of an air cargo company. The basic structure of such a value chain of an air cargo company is illustrated in Figure 9.

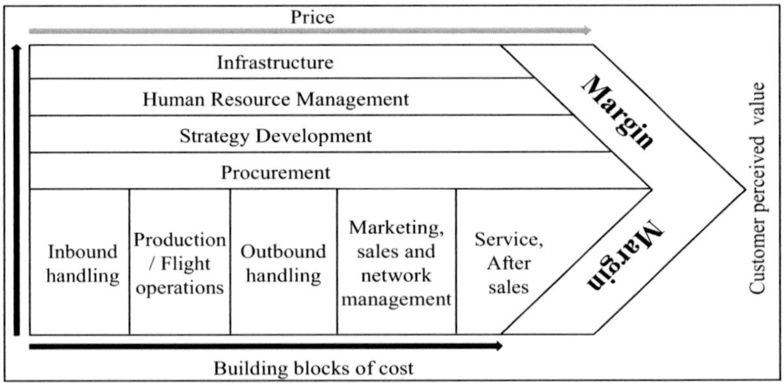

Figure 9: Value chain management in the air cargo industry (Own illustration)

Parts of the air cargo value chain

The value chain divides the mission of the company into strategically relevant activities and key management functions.[8] The functions for a typical air cargo company are listed below. For detailed information into the separate functions please see footnotes:

[8] For further information see (Ffis) Porter (1998, p. 41).

- Operations management: process management, operational handling and flight operations. The focus lies in managing:
  - The factors of production such as factory assets (e.g. warehouses),[9] aircraft (passenger aircraft and freighters),[10] infrastructure (routes and slots)[11] and airports[12]
  - Human assets (pilots, operation managers, ground personnel)
  - Production goods (Unit Load Devices etc.)[13]
- Sales management: the focus lies in managing:
  - Sales steering (optimizing freighter and belly-hold load factors, researching macro market and customer data)
  - Sales channel management and sales force administration
  - Revenue management[14]
- Strategic and operational marketing in a B2B environment[15]
- Shared services (e.g. Strategy development)
- Network Management (hub and spoke systems,[16] profitability measurement)

Support functions

Important support functions are the management of legal frameworks,[17] the management of the information technology (IT) and e-activities[18] as well as environmental topics.[19]

The overall target in managing the above is to:

- Identify cost drivers: successful companies in the air cargo industry relentlessly focus on reducing cost (this is one of only two ways to increase margins). Determining which cost drivers are applicable in the industry is key, e.g. kerosene, aircraft (ACMI)[20] and cost of personnel.
- Identify various factors as successful air cargo businesses will differentiate themselves from the competition; what are these factors and how do they apply to the company in question?

---

9 Ffis: Grandjot (2002, p. 89-96) / Arnold et al. (2008, p. 766-773).

10 Ffis: Maurer (2006, p. 148-271) / Arnold et al. (2008, p. 762-763).

11 The aviation industry has two different types of slots: the Air Traffic Control (ATC) slot is needed by each departing flight on the actual day of operation to avoid congested airways, and the Airport Slot is mandatory at coordinated airports for each movement (arrival and departure) and is valid for a specific time. This slot is used to plan the runway capacity to minimize airport congestion (Mensen, 2003, p. 58 / Klußmann, 2007, p. 231).

12 Ffis: Arnold et al. (2008, p. 766-775).

13 Ffis: Grandjot (2002, p. 61-88) / Arnold et al. (2008, p. 763-775).

14 Ffis: Becker (1999, p. 45-51).

15 B2B (business-to-business) marketing is the marketing of goods and services that businesses and other organizational customers require in order to resell or to support their operations.

16 Ffis: Becker (1999, p. 52-54).

17 Ffis: Grandjot (2002, p. 15-45 'Legal framework' / p. 46-60 'Institutions').

18 Ffis: Arnold et al. (2008, p. 776-778) / Grandjot (2002, p. 161-192).

19 Ffis: Grandjot (2002, p. 201-207).

20 ACMI: Aircraft, Crew, Maintenance and Insurance, so called wet lease.

- Leverage technology: How does an air cargo company apply technology to the components of the value chain?
- Review outsourcing: What parts of the Value Chain should be handed over to specialist firms who can perform the same function more cheaply, but at the same (or hopefully better) service levels?

Exemplary strategic (marketing) opportunities are:

- Cost Leadership (Kalitta Air Cargo)
- Focus - finding a niche (Swiss World Cargo)
- Differentiation (Lufthansa Cargo)

F. OUTLOOK

The air cargo industry environment will constantly change in the future. To quote from Charles Darwin (1809-1882) "It is not the strongest of the species that survives, nor the most intelligent that survives. It is the one that is the most adaptable to change." Adaption and flexibility of the air cargo players will be key to companies' success. The consideration of the following potential future developments can be necessary:

- The historical development of air cargo from being a by-product to becoming a joint-product maybe reversed, at least partially
- Management of the imbalance between offer and demand
- Cost pressure will demand high innovation from all industry participants
- Constant improvement of services quality will be demanded
- Pressure on automation of all relevant processes of air cargo operations. A 'business as usual' attitude will catapult many traditional players out of the market (Jahns & Schüffler, 2008)
- Efficiency increasing measures such as integrated transportation chains (von der Gracht, 2008)
- Innovative sales and marketing such as electronic sales (Lufthansa Cargo, 2009, p. 3-4)

G. CONCLUSION

In this chapter a brief introduction to the air cargo market environment was provided. The complex structures and its inherent challenges were outlined. Managing air cargo companies in the described interdependent structures needs a clear understanding of industry behavior. The low attractiveness of the air cargo sector has been summarized. Future developments will demand a steady adaption of strategies and value chain management.

Review Questions

- What are the general forces and constraints that influence air cargo growth?
- What is the special character of air cargo traffic?
- Which factors influence the attractiveness in the air cargo industry?
- What exactly is 'derived demand' within the air cargo industry?
- Which are the key determinants of air cargo demand?
- What are the main particularities of the supply side of air cargo services?
- What are the key differences in the development of the intra-European and the intra-Asian markets?
- How can the competitive situation in the air cargo sector be described?
- What could be a practical application of a generic strategy in the air cargo industry?

Bibliography and further reading

Airliners (2009): Martinair wird neuer Luftfrachtgigant, 09/16/2009, www.airliners.de/nachrichten/bereiche/management/strategie/martinair-wird-neuer-luftfrachtgigant/19109, retrieved: 05/17/2010.

Airports Council International [ACI], (2009): Outlook 2010 – Air freight Industry Impacted by Weak Global Economy.

Airports Council International [ACI], Webpage: www.aci.aero

Arnold, D. / Isermann, H. / Kuhn, A. / Furmans, K. (2008): Handbuch Logistik, 3rd ed., Berlin.

Becker, S. (1999): Reorganisation der Luftfrachtkonsolidierung – Eine Analyse strategischer Allianzen von Luftfrachtspeditionen, Göttingen.

Boeing (2008): World Air Cargo Forecast (WACF) 2008/2009, Seattle.

Boeing (2014): World Air Cargo Forecast (WACF) 2014/2015, Seattle.

Conway, P. (2009): Cargo crisis, 09/21/09, www.flightglobal.com/articles/2009/09/21 /332560/cargo-crisis.html, retrieved: 05/17/2010.

Dahl, R. V. (2010): Turbulence in the Cargo Arena, in: Aviation Week & Space Technology, Vol. 172, No. 3, p. 82-86.

Deutsche Logistik-Zeitung [DVZ] (2009a): AF-KLM trennt sich von 18 Frachtflugzeugen, http://www.dvz.de/content/news/transport/einzelseite/datum/2009/09 /15/af-klm-trennt-sich-von-18-frachtflugzeugen/print.html?type=98&cHash =88e6dbdb57, retrieved: 05/17/2010.

Deutsche Logistik-Zeitung [DVZ] (2009b): Air France-KLM stürzt tief in die Verlustzone, www.dvz.de/content/news/transport/einzelseite/datum/2009/11/18/air-france-klm-stuerzt-tief-in-verlustzone/print.html?type=98&cHash=1d46d7ca66, retrieved: 05/17/2010.

Dieckheuer, G. (2001): Internationale Wirtschaftsbeziehungen, 5th ed., Munich.

Erkes, J. (2008): Der deutsche Luftfrachtmarkt: eine Analyse der Entwicklungsmöglichkeiten, Hamburg.

von der Gracht, H. (2008): The Future of Logistics: Scenarios for 2025, Wiesbaden.

Grandjot, H.-H. (2002): Leitfaden Luftfracht. 2nd ed., Berlin.

Hamel, G. / Prahalad, C. K. (1996): Competing for the Future, Boston.

International Air Transport Association [IATA] (2010a): Worst Demand Decline in History – Encouraging Year-end Improvements, press releases No. 3 from January, 27th 2009, http://www.iata.org/pressroom, retrieved: 05/10/2010.

International Air Transport Association [IATA] (2010b): Cargo E-chartbook, Q1 2010, www.iata.org/whatwedo/Documents/economics, retrieved: 05/10/2010.

Jahns, C. / Schüffler, C. (2008): Logistik – von der Seidenstrasse bis heute, Wiesbaden.

Klußmann, N. / Malik A. (2007): Lexikon der Luftfahrt, 2nd ed., Berlin.

Koenen, J. (2009): Lufthansa verschärft Sparkurs, in: Zeit Online, 09/18/2009, http://www.zeit.de/wirtschaft/unternehmen/2009-09/lufthansa-sparkurs, retrieved: 05/17/2010.

Lufthansa Cargo (2009): eNews (electronic newsletter), 11/02/2009.

Maurer, P. (2006): Luftverkehrsmanagement: Basiswissen, 4th ed., Munich.

Meffert, H. / Bolz, J. (2007): Internationales Marketing Management, 4th ed., Stuttgart.

Mensen, H. (2003): Handbuch der Luftfahrt, Berlin.

Pompl, W. (2008): Luftverkehr: Eine ökonomische und politische Einführung, 5th ed., Berlin.

Porter, M. E. (1998): The competitive advantage of Nations, New York.

Porter, M. E. (1980): Competitive Strategy: Techniques for analyzing industries and competitors, New York.

Schieck, A. (2008): Internationale Logistik: Objekte, Prozesse und Infrastrukturen grenzüberschreitender Güterströme, München.

Sreenivasan, V. (2010): SIA confounds critics with strong Q3 profit, in: The Business Times at asiaone.com, 02/03/2010, http://www.asiaone.com/News/The%2BBusiness %2BTimes/Story/A1Story20100203-196464.html, retrieved: 05/17/2010.

Sterzenbach, R. / Conrady, R. / Fichet, F. (2008): Luftverkehr. Betriebswirtschaftliches Lehr- und Handbuch, München.

Wells, A. / Wensveen J. G. (2003): Air transportation: A management perspective, Belmont.

Section 4: General Management Functions in the Airline Business

Performance Measurement in the Airline Industry

Ronald Gleich, Alexander Tkotz, Peter Schentler

Table of contents

You should be able to

- explain what performance measurement is
- describe what KPIs are used for
- outline the different dimensions for airline performance measurement
- name the most important KPIs for each dimension
- explain the balanced scorecard and its benefits
- name further fields of aviation performance measurement besides airline performance measurement

The authors

Dr. Ronald Gleich is Professor and Head of the Strascheg Institute for Innovation & Entrepreneurship at EBS Universität für Wirtschaft und Recht, Wiesbaden, Germany and Managing Partner of the Horváth Academy, Stuttgart, Germany.

Alexander Tkotz works as a Managing Consultant in the Competence Center Controlling & Finance at Horváth & Partners Management Consultants. Besides that he is a doctoral candidate with the focus on innovation control at the SIIE at EBS Universität für Wirtschaft und Recht.

Dr. Peter Schentler is Senior Project Manager at Horváth & Partners Management Consultants in Vienna, Austria.

Abstract

In this chapter we provide an introduction to airline performance measurement (PM), an important part of aviation performance measurement. The theoretical basis includes a paragraph on key performance indicators (KPI) followed by a general overview of performance measurement and a discussion of the balanced scorecard as a well-established PM tool. The main contribution of this chapter represents the identification of numerous possible KPIs[1] in the airline context and their application in a balanced scorecard as a way of structuring airline PM.

A. INTRODUCTION

Prerequisites for airlines

The airline industry has some unique prerequisites compared to other industries. Firstly, the operation of aircraft is linked to high fixed costs on the one hand and relatively low marginal costs on the other. Secondly, flying is highly dependent on good weather and is regularly seriously disrupted by adverse conditions. Thirdly, the airline industry is extraordinary competitive. Some of the reasons are the large number of carriers worldwide and the fact that an airline's services can be copied easily by other airlines. In general the same applies for flight routes, although there may be restrictions due to slot shortage, at least in the short run. Thus, airlines are in a permanent struggle for customers and permanently endeavor to be better than their competitors, which ultimately leads to high cost pressure within the industry. The high degree of governmental involvement, (inter-)national regulations and high complexity of operations are also additional contributing factors (Francis, Humphreys, & Fry, 2005).

Need for airline performance measurement

To control and steer the above-mentioned aspects airlines require measures and measurement systems covering all aspects of their current and prospect performance. (Rouse, Putterill, & Ryan, 2002). Besides financial performance, other facets such as customer service, aircraft operations, human resources, and partner performance also have to be considered since they bear a high influence on the airlines performance.

Problems with existing systems

Existing measurement systems often do not meet the requirements of companies, because they focus on financial performance only. In order to establish a successful management system, a performance measurement system focusing on all aspects of actual and future performance can serve as a basis for such a controlling concept.

---

[1] Key Performance Indicator (KPI), indicator, metric, and measure are synonyms. In scientific literature metric is used more often; measure and (key performance) indicators are more common in practice. Since this chapter deals with the practical application of scientific viewpoints in airline performance measurement all three terms will be used interchangeably.

Airline performance measurement covers one aspect of aviation performance measurement and can be understood as a subsystem of the latter. Apart from airline PM there are some other interesting and important fields of aviation PM:

Other fields of aviation PM

- **Airport PM** is widely discussed by Humphreys, Francis & Fry (2002); Lin & Hong (2006); Oum, Yu & Fu (2003); Gillen & Lall (1997); and von Dietman (2008).
- **Air cargo PM** is addressed in Tangerman (1993) and Caplice & Sheffi (1995).
- An introduction to **alliance PM** can be found by Kleymann & Seristö (2004), Saramaa (1998), and Weber & Sparks (2004).
- **MRO**[2] **PM** is a well-covered topic. An introduction can be found by Linser (2005), and Rouse, Putterill & Ryan (2002).
- The field of **ground handling PM** is a rather new one, since liberalization of the ground handling market in Europe started only in the beginning of this millennium. Since then more and more operators have been trying to get a foothold in the market. Through the intensifying competition and thus lower profit margins, effective and efficient operations and therefore performance measurement are also gaining importance in this business area (Schmidberger et al., 2009).

B. PERFORMANCE MEASUREMENT

In this chapter we will lay the theoretical basis of performance measurement in brief. Every performance measurement system needs metrics and indicators, which will be discussed in the first section. Following, performance measurement is introduced in combination with a framework to determine the quality of a performance measurement system. The third part is dedicated to the balanced scorecard as a major performance measurement system.

B. 1 Key performance indicators

Measures show the company's performance

A key performance indicator is an index that helps to quantify a certain aspect of performance, process or state. KPIs and measurement systems are used to set goals and evaluate to what extent a company has achieved its goals.

In general, KPIs can be created in two different ways:

Ways of creating measures

- **Counting**: The simplest way to create a KPI is counting. Examples are passenger enplanements, lost baggage or destinations served. Unfortunately these KPIs often only have limited explanatory power and are difficult to compare.
- **Abstract measures:** Abstract measures or rather indicators are used if an event cannot be observed directly but only through the observation of other events. One way to discover such KPIs is to

[2] Maintenance, repair, and overhaul.

conduct a survey, e.g. passengers are questioned regarding satisfaction with the airline. Since this value cannot be counted it is quantified on a scale: 'very unsatisfied' to 'very satisfied'. If the 'very unsatisfied' is set to 0% and 'very satisfied' to 100% it is possible to calculate the overall satisfaction in per cent based on the quantity and distribution of the answers.

Counted and abstract measures convey much more information if they are placed in relation to another KPI (**relating KPIs**). Relating KPIs is not strictly a way to create KPIs in the first place, but a way of transforming already existing KPIs into another form and enriching them with more information. For example, is it possible to relate the total operating costs to available seat kilometers, which results in a measure of unit costs. This KPI is much more suitable for comparison than the total operating costs alone since these are influence by many different factors. A yearly comparison can be used to determine whether the unit costs change over the course of time, and, if so, in which direction. Time series comparison itself is a related KPI, since one year's/month's/week's KPI is related to the previous one(s).

It is important to choose the right measures

To find an appropriate set of KPIs, it is useful to find answers to some guiding questions:

- What information does a KPI need to deliver?
- According to what criteria can the amount of possible indicators be reduced to a convenient size?
- Are there standard KPIs for a certain task? What is the precise argument regarding whether certain KPIs are chosen or left out?

In order to answer these questions drafting a structured and complete requirement list is helpful (Küpper et. al., 2013; Müller-Stewens & Lechner, 2011.

Classification helps choosing balanced sets of measures

Airlines have an enormous pool from which to select KPIs. To classify a large amount of KPIs it is useful to have some classification criteria. Possible dimensions are: internal vs. external, strategic vs. operative, direct vs. indirect, lagging vs. leading or absolute vs. relative KPIs. It is important to have a well-balanced portfolio of KPIs when creating a performance measurement system. Classification helps in choosing KPIs that are balanced and reveals whether a set of KPIs focuses too much on one aspect alone. The example in Figure 1 demonstrates how classification can be conducted.

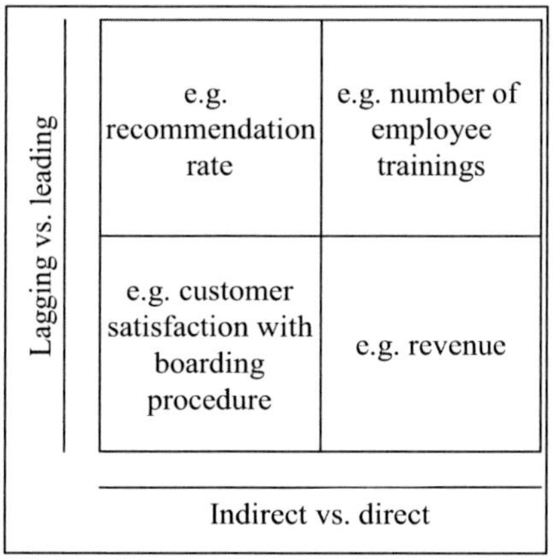

Figure 1: Possible classification of KPIs (Own illustration)

'Direct' means that an action or event can be gauged directly (e.g. number of passengers), 'indirect' means that an event can be observed only through an abstract or indicating measure, or indicator (e.g. if a customer recommends an airline to someone else, it cannot be observed from an airline's viewpoint but the customer can be asked if he / she intends to do so). The differentiation between leading and lagging KPI accounts for whether a KPI shows something that only affects the past performance, e.g. crew productivity in the previous year (lagging KPI), or something that will also affect the future performance, e.g. for customer service personnel training, which will influence the future service quality (leading KPI).

B. 2 An overview of performance measurement

Shortcomings of traditional measurement systems

Historically, financial KPIs had a dominating role in company steering, and still, many companies rely mainly on financial KPIs. The problem with financial KPIs is that they are usually lagging indicators. To predict a company's potential future financial performance leading indicators are required. Naturally these indicators are dominated by non-financial indicators. Therefore academia and practice have come to the conclusion that traditional, financially oriented measurement systems only have a limited benefit for the sustainable management and steering of a company (Raake, 2008). The criticism covers aspects such as a disregard of non-financial parameters, non-alignment to corporate strategy, a backwards-facing view, short-term perspective, insufficient customer orientation and misleading reference points for incentives (Gleich, 2011).

Performance measurement subsumes different new concepts

Several new concepts have been developed, which are subsumed under the term Performance Measurement (PM). PM should not only be used for evaluation and measurement of past actions, but should also focus on future-oriented management and steering activities (Gleich, 2011). This fosters target setting tailored to fit beneficiaries and performance levels, and the operationalization of strategy and its translation ino measurable goals (Gleich, 1997). It therefore involves the setup and use of several KPIs, e.g. costs, time, quality, ability to innovate, customer satisfaction and flexibility. These KPIs serve as a basis for the evaluation of the performance effectiveness and efficiency as well as for the performance potentials of different objects, or performance levels (e.g. organizational units, processes and employees). According to studies the Balanced Scorecard (see chapter B. 3) is the most prominent performance measurement system (Günther & Grüning, 2002).[3]

There still is no widely accepted PM definition

Although a lot of academic work was dedicated to research about performance measurement, different definitions are still being discussed (Raake, 2008; Weiss, Zirkler, & Guttenberger, 2008). Nevertheless it can be stated that performance measurement systems should comply with the following requirements (Brown & Leverick, 1994; Gleich, 1997, 2011; Müller-Stewens, 1998; Neely, Gregory, & Platts, 1995; Raake, 2008; Rummler & Brache, 1990):

- Provide past- and future-oriented management control information
- Reflect the demand of both internal and external stakeholders
- Provide management control information at all performance levels
- Allow considerations for improvement on a short- and long-term basis, as well as on corporate and divisional levels
- Contain financial KPIs, which can be amended by non-financial parameters, influencing the long-term financial performance capabilities of a company
- Contain not only quantitative (hard facts) but also qualitative information (soft facts)
- Provide strategic and operational KPIs
- Support continuous improvement

When applying this comprehensive understanding of PM, the question regarding whether PM is more than just another measurement concept, can be answered affirmatively. However, studies show that, in practice, performance measurement systems rarely meet the requirements stated in theory (Weiss, Zirkler, & Guttenberger, 2008).

Ten determinants to evaluate measurement systems

The ten determinants depicted in Figure 2 show the shortcomings that often exist in the practical implementation of performance measurement. In the past, most concepts were not structured along the lines of progressive performance measurement. Currently, performance measurement systems meet these new requirements to some extent. In the future, the development and implementation of progressive performance measurement will be needed in order to

[3] See chapter C. Other performance measurement systems are e.g. Data Envelopment Analysis, Tableau de Bord, Performance Pyramid, Quantum Performance Measurement, Productivity Measurement and Enhancement System see Gleich (2011).

tackle the increasing and multidimensional demands of markets and customers on the management structures of a company.

	Yesterday	Today	Tomorrow
Universal differentiation between performance levels	None	Weak	Strong
Strategic and operative targets and indicators	Predominantly financial	Financial and partly non-financial	Balance between non-financial and financial
Linking of strategic and operative planning	Not established	Partially established	Established
Reconciliation of targets and strategies	Low	On some performance levels	On all performance levels
Stakeholder influence	Dominated by shareholders	Average influence	strong influence
Choice of indicators and planned targets	Top Down	Partially autonomus on performance levels	Fully autonomus on performance levels
Flexibility/adaptability for change in indicators	Low	Medium	High
Indicators for performance targets	Unbalanced	Hardly balanced	Balanced
Allocation of roles of participants in Performance Measurement	Unbalanced	Hardly balanced	Balanced
Use of new managerial tools in Performance Measurement	No use	Some tools used	Many tools used

Figure 2: Development stages of performance measurement (Gleich, 2011)

Well tailored PM can improve profitability

Examples of progressive PM systems implemented in practice can be found only in isolated cases. But in these cases, progressive PM leads to higher profitability in comparison with other companies in the same sector with less developed PM systems (Gleich, 2011).

However, PM systems need to be tailor-made for each industry and company to be able to fit its strategy, organization, competition and constraints.

PM is a controlling subsystem with strong emphasize on strategy

Overall, the performance measurement and management control concepts in the English-speaking world and controlling concepts in German-speaking countries exhibit many interdependencies. The underlying goal behind these concepts is to steer or at least influence the behavior of members of an organization, especially managers, in such a way as to increase the likelihood of achieving goals (Flamholtz, 1996). Performance measurement – which forms an interface between planning, control, and information systems in the same way as controlling systems do – does not only enhance controlling in terms of time and target groups, but also by means of the format in which information is provided (qualitative as opposed to quantitative information) and by means of non-financial indicators (Müller-Stewens, 1998). Nevertheless, performance measurement should still be seen as an element (subsystem) of the controlling system with a special focus on supporting strategy implementation (Anthony & Govindarajan, 1998; Horváth et al., 1999).

B. 3 The balanced scorecard

In this section we present the balanced scorecard, which has been the most popular performance management tool of the last few decades.[4]

The BSC is special as it integrates different information and supports decision making

The underlying idea behind the balanced scorecard (BSC) is to integrate financial and non-financial KPIs into a single tool/report and relate them to a target value. Thus, the information (strategic) decision-makers require is presented from one source only and strongly supports decision-making. The goal is to enable managers taking decisions quickly in a target- and strategy-oriented way, and to translate strategic targets into operative action.

The strength of the BSC lies in the process of generating KPIs and focusing management's attention on them. The identification of suitable KPIs always starts with the business strategy. The first task is to identify KPIs which have a strong relation to the strategy goals. For the next step the relations between these KPIs are examined and only those are chosen that form a line of influence from the business processes to the target value. Furthermore, it is important to link targets to each KPI in order to be able to determine if the steps taken to reach the strategy have a positive or negative impact on the target value and achieving of strategic objectives in a later review. Another crucial aspect is to link business planning actions and employee's incentives to the targets in the BSC in order to put strategy into action (Kaplan & Norton, 1996).

A standard BSC in the original form contains four dimensions (see Figure 3) (Kaplan & Norton, 1998):

- The **financial perspective** embodies KPIs that are vital for a company and that reflect if the chosen strategy translates into financial success.
- **Customer perspective** provides KPIs that help to judge whether the customers' needs and wishes have been fulfilled. Categories are e.g. quality, price, time, and product performance.
- **Process perspective** focuses on the internal processes that are decisive to satisfy customers' needs. This category includes e.g. cost targets, skills and abilities of employees, and cycle times.
- **Capability perspective** - in order to generate growth in the future, innovation and operational improvement are necessary. Therefore, learning and development of employees is a crucial success factor.

4 For a detailed description of the Balanced Scorecard see Kaplan & Norton (1992) and Kaplan & Norton (2003).

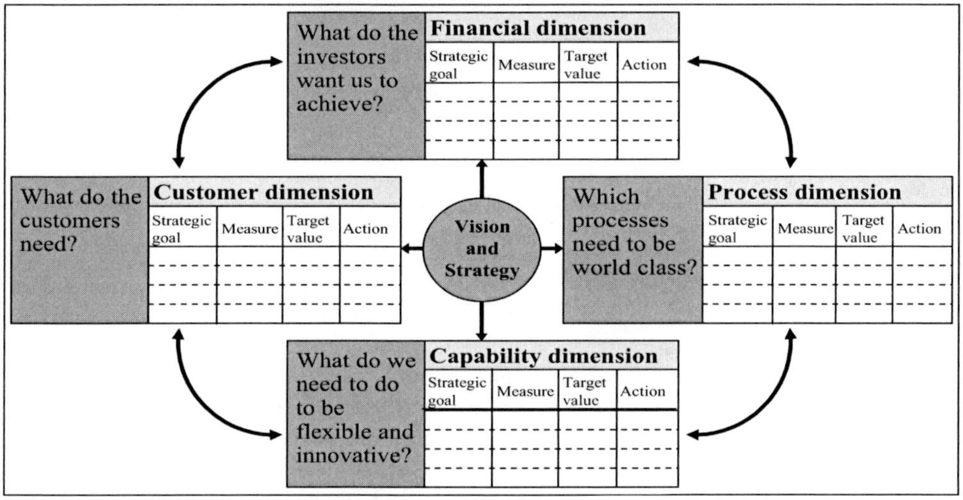

Figure 3: Perspectives of the original BSC (adapted from Kaplan & Norton, 1998)

Improvements of the BSC concepts

Since the time of development the BSC has been improved in several aspects. The first major improvement provided guidance on how to select KPIs. This was followed by the introduction of the 'strategy map', which will be used for the sample BSC in chapter D. The strategy map clearly displays causalities between KPIs and strategic goals.

C. AIRLINE PERFORMANCE MEASUREMENT

KPIs are individual for each company

In this section we are going to describe how to structure airline performance measurement along the BSC perspectives and present KPIs that are widely used and accepted. However, there is no ultimate set of KPIs that can be successfully applied to every airline. The decision about which KPIs an airline should choose is always an individual one and depends on the company's strengths and weaknesses as well as the corporate strategy. Nevertheless, the presented KPIs can be used as a blueprint and can be adapted to the individual needs of an airline.

C. 1 Overview

Before thinking about performance measurement systems, performance levels and single KPIs employed in the airline industry, it is helpful to think about which industries airlines can be assigned to. On the one hand, airlines provide a service (air travel), which classifies the airline industry as a service industry. This implies the use of KPIs such as customer satisfaction, customer loyalty, and service quality. On the other hand, airlines can also be assigned to the transport or logistics industry, since their service is to transport people (often together with mail and belly-freight) from one point (airport) to another.[5] This implies the use of KPIs like punctuality, operating performance, and transport performance.

Need for structurization

First of all it is necessary to structure possible KPIs. Holloway (2008), for example, structures his work on airline economics according to the following formula:

Operating performance
= Traffic x Yield – Output x Unit cost
= Profit (or Loss)

Operating and financial dimension

Operating performance is definitely one very important aspect of airline performance measurement, since it includes traffic, yield, output and costs among others. As discussed in the previous section, financial performance is at least equally important. Feng & Wang (2000) show that financial ratios are vital indicators of sustainable development and the airline's ability to succeed in this competitive market. Financial performance and operating performance therefore both take a share in airline performance measurement. However, these two dimensions are not sufficient to adequately measure an airline's performance.

Customer service dimension

Furthermore, airlines have a strong need to measure their performance in terms of customer orientation and service quality (Holloway, 2002), since both aspects have a strong influence on the future potential for financial success. Airlines are among the most customer-oriented industries worldwide, attaching high importance to customer service. It has been proven that high service quality and hence satisfied customers have a great influence on a company's financial situation and business success (Anderson & Mittal, 2000; Daniel, 2001; Matzler, Stahl, & Hinterhuber, 2008; Stauss, Dornach, & Coenen, 2006). Sim, Koh & Shetty (2006) even demonstrated that service quality and aircraft productivity positively correlate. Therefore it is crucial to use customer service quality as a separate dimension of airline performance measurement.

Capability dimension

A fourth dimension covers all future external potentials and internal capabilities. Capability can include KPIs concerning human resources, innovation, sustainability, marketing, competition, technology, ownership, and many more.

Consequently we have four dimensions of airline performance measurement: finance, operations, customer service and future capabilities. These dimensions are described in detail in the following paragraphs as a basis for the sample balanced scorecard presented afterwards.

---

[5] Cargo PM is not considered since this would exceed the focus of this article. Cargo airlines have their own set of specific KPIs which, to a large extent, differ significantly from those of passenger airlines.

C. 2 Financial dimension

Financial dimension is an integral part of performance measurement

Since Airlines are profit-oriented enterprises, which need to fulfill their shareholder's expectations, they have to measure their financial performance. Financial KPIs in the airline industry are pretty much the same as in other industries and companies. Many KPIs are predetermined by commercial and stock corporation law, especially if an airline is listed on the stock exchange. Nevertheless, the financial performance of airlines has some unique aspects. On the one hand airlines employ a lot of staff, invest heavily in infrastructure and aircraft, thus incurring high fixed costs; on the other hand the competition is very tough, because the numerous players and limited potential for building up and maintaining a unique selling position leads to declining yields and decreasing profits for the companies.

Financial reporting needs comprehensive KPIs

The simplest way to report financial KPIs is to report revenues and expenses detailed to single revenue sources and cost categories. Revenues include fees from passenger transport, cargo transport, or charter operations. Expenses are mainly driven by fuel, labor, maintenance, and service costs. Unfortunately reporting revenue and cost figures alone does not provide enough information on a companies' financial performance. It is necessary to create KPIs that are able to draw a realistic picture of a company's present and expected future financial situation (Kane, 2012). Morrell (2009) suggests working with four categories of financial KPIs:

- Performance and earning
- Risk and solvency
- Liquidity
- Market valuation

KPIs of performance and earning

Probably the most well-known KPI in the category performance and earning is 'operating ratio'. It indicates the management's performance in managing costs and maintaining or even increasing revenues. The operating ratio is calculated by dividing operating revenues by operating expenses. A value of at least one is desirable, but not necessarily an indicator of a good performance, since, in order to pay overhead costs, financial costs, and dividends to the shareholders, the revenues should exceed the costs by a certain amount. The operating profit can be distorted in several ways (e.g. by depreciation policy) and is thus not always a robust indicator.

The KPI 'net profit margin' relates operating revenues to profits after tax, yielding a percentage KPI. However, this KPI is not free from distortion, since it can be influenced through sales or depreciations of assets for example. A similar approach is followed by the KPI 'return on capital employed' (ROCE) which relates the net operating profits after taxes (NOPAT) to the employed average long-term capital. It shows the effectiveness of the management given the available capital. Again, distortions through changes in aircraft ownership or policy are possible. Finally, 'return on equity' (ROE) measures the management's performance in working with the capital entrusted by the company's shareholders. Profits after tax and interest are related to the average shareholders' equity, again yielding a percentage value.

Financial performance KPIs (performance & earning)

- **Operating ratio**: operating revenues / operating expenses.
- **Net profit margin**: operating revenue / profit after tax.
- **Return on capital employed**: net operating profit after taxes / invested capital.
- **Return on equity**: profit after tax and interest / average shareholders' equity.

KPIs of risk and solvency

The second category – risk and solvency – embodies two KPIs, showing the degree of risk of a company's financial situation. The first KPI, 'interest cover', shows whether a company is able to pay the interest on its debts. It is computed as profit before tax and net interest divided by net interest payable. The KPI should always be far above one. Otherwise there may not be enough cash position to pay dividends to shareholders or reinvest money in the company's future development. A value of less than one is perilous, because in such a situation a company does not have enough money to honor its debts and may be forced into bankruptcy. The second KPI is the 'debt to equity ratio' which shows the risk a company represents for a potential capital lender. The lower the debt to equity ratio the lower the risk is. In turn, the lower the debt to equity ratio the easier companies can raise money from a bank or investment agency.

Financial performance KPIs (risk and solvency)

- **Interest cover**: profit before tax and interest / interest payable.
- **Debt to equity ratio**: debt / equity.

KPIs of liquidity

The third category from the financial dimension is liquidity, where two KPIs are worth knowing: the 'current ratio' and the 'quick ratio'. The current ratio relates current assets to current liabilities. Normally a ratio of 1 is regarded as optimal. If the ratio falls substantially below 1 it may indicate that the business is not generating enough cash-flow and may be unable to pay its short-term obligations. If the ratio is well above 1 it may indicate that a company is preparing to acquire another company or is accumulating money to pay for future investments, in the case of the airline industry e.g. an aircraft delivery. It may also indicate that the management is unable to profitably invest all the cash earned and may be neglecting future growth potential. The 'quick ratio', also known as the 'acid test', measures a company's ability to quickly convert (near cash-) assets into cash in order to immediately pay back liabilities.

Financial performance KPIs (liquidity)

- **Current ratio**: current assets / current liabilities.
- **Quick ratio**: the sum of cash, cash equivalents, marketable securities, and accounts receivable / current liabilities.

KPIs of market valuation

The last category in the financial dimension is devoted to stock market KPIs (market valuation). One important KPI is 'dividend cover' which relates profits to dividends payable. There is no optimum for the value of this KPI, but it is advisable to keep the ratio well above 1 to prevent paying dividends from borrowed capital.

Another stock market oriented KPI is 'market capitalization'. This KPI is simply calculated by multiplying the current share price by the total number of shares. This KPI only has limited explanatory power, since share prices are subject to speculations and thus very volatile. Nevertheless the price fluctuation mirrors traders' current perception of the company's performance and expectations about future growth potential.

'Earnings per share' is a KPI very closely monitored by investment analysts. It shows how much profit a company generates per share. 'Price / earnings ratio' (PE-ratio) relates the current share price to the earnings per share and thus shows how much future profit the market believes a company will achieve. The bigger the expectations the higher the PE-ratio will be, since many traders order shares and increase the share price.

Financial performance KPIs (market valuation)

- **Dividend cover**: profits / dividends payable.
- **Market capitalization**: share price * number of shares.
- **Earnings per share**: profit after tax and interest / number of shares.
- **PE-ratio**: share price / earnings per share.

Airline specific financial performance KPIs

These financial performance KPIs are of general nature and may be applicable to most companies. Nevertheless airlines may also apply financial KPIs which are unique to the airline business. The most important of these airline-specific KPIs are introduced in the following box.

Airline specific financial performance KPIs

- **Revenue seat kilometers**: For every flight the number of seats that are occupied by paying customers is multiplied by the kilometers flown. When compared to available seat kilometers (see operational dimension) it measures the airline's ability to accurately predict demand and provide a suitable aircraft.
- **Cost per available seat kilometers (CASK)**: CASK is a measure of unit cost. The total operating costs are divided by the total available seat kilometers (see operational dimension).
- **Revenue per Workload-Unit (WLU)**: A WLU is equivalent to one passenger or 100 kg of freight. For every flight the revenue is divided by the total WLU. Airlines that transport passengers and freight convert passenger revenue and cargo revenue into revenue per WLU to be able to make comparisons on the same basis.

C. 3 Customer service dimension

Airlines should measure services even when they have been outsourced

Many of an airline's customer services are not carried out by the airline itself, but rather by outsourcing partners or airports. The question arises regarding why an airline should measure the performance of a service it does not perform. The answer is that customers do not differentiate between who exactly is responsible (and who is to blame in the case of a bad experience) for a certain service and ascribe the experienced service quality to the airline. Therefore airlines have to measure service levels for all offered services not only for the ones they operate on their own. Moreover, service KPIs help to control whether the outsourcing partner delivers the service quality agreed upon in the service level agreement (e.g. maximum waiting time during baggage reclaim) (Francis, Humphreys, & Fry, 2005). Another good argument for airlines to measure all offered services is that service delivery in general is highly prone to failure. This holds especially true in the airline business, since the service steps from buying a ticket, to arriving and checking in at the airport and finally leaving the destination airport are numerous and complex and the possibilities for failure are manifold (Holloway, 2002).

Service KPIs can be subjective and objective

Service quality can be measured in two different ways. KPIs can be objective, which means that they can be observed and are simply counted or computed without any subjective influence. Examples are number of delayed flights, customer complaints or flight cancelations. But objective KPIs disregard one important factor – the customer's perception – therefore, subjective KPIs are required. The pure information that a flight is canceled does not convey anything about the way customers experience and evaluate this cancelation (Zeithaml, Berry, & Parasuraman, 1996).

Objective customer service KPIs

- **On time performance**: percentage of flights that arrive and depart on time. Subgroups for different routes or countries can be useful.
- **Flight cancelation**: number or percentage of canceled flights, differentiated if a flight is canceled due to technical reasons or weather conditions. Subgroups for different routes or countries can be useful.
- **Overbooking level**: sold tickets in relation to available seats per flight.
- **Customer complaints**: number of customer complaints. To obtain a comparable measure, this number is divided by the total number of customers or expressed per 1,000 customers. Note that only a small percentage of dissatisfied customers actually complain about services provided by the airline.
- **Mishandled baggage**: amount of luggage that is mishandled, i.e. stays at the airport of origin, or is loaded to a wrong flight. A common formula is pieces per 1,000 passengers. A breakdown to single airports and service partners is useful.
- **Check-in waiting time**: average waiting time at check-in. Differentiating between airports and booking classes is recommended.
- **Baggage delivery time**: average time from start of unloading to delivery of luggage at the conveyor belt. Alternatively the time from start of unloading till the first / last piece of luggage arrives in the baggage claim can be used.

Ways to measure a customer's perception of the experienced service

An interesting question for airlines is whether the experienced service level will influence a customer's future booking behavior. Based on that information it is possible to estimate the economic effect of a certain service experience. This cannot be answered from objective KPIs alone but needs to be investigated in cooperation with customers. Typical instruments for this are surveys, interviews, and focus groups; often used KPIs are customer loyalty [schemes], customer satisfaction, and recommendation level (Bruhn, 2008). The KPI of customer satisfaction can be reduced to a more detailed level e.g. following the different phases of a flight (arrival at the airport, check-in, etc.).

Subjective customer service KPIs

- **Customer loyalty:** likelihood of booking the next flight with the same airline (often measured on a 5 or 7 point Likert-scale).
- **Recommendation level:** likelihood of recommending the airline to someone else (often measured on a 5 or 7 point Likert-scale).
- **Customer satisfaction:** measures how satisfied a customer was with the service. Again Likert-scales are used. A more precise measuring also accounts for the difference between expected and experienced service and thus offers the possibility to fine-tune a service offering. Components of customer satisfaction such as friendliness of staff, appearance and cleanliness of aircraft can be included, too.
- **Service quality:** relates the service expectation of a customer to the perceived service.

C. 4 Operational dimension

Operational performance has a strong influence on customer service and financial dimension

Having outlined the financial and customer service dimension the necessity of the operational dimension might be questioned, since the tracking of shareholders and customers interests is already considered in the first two dimensions. If these interests are satisfied the company is likely in a good position. However, the financial and customer service dimensions strongly depend on the performance results for the operational dimension. For example, good customer service is impossible to deliver if the operations do not run smoothly. This interrelationship is clearly visible in the sample BSC outlined in the next chapter.

Components of operational performance

Operations can include production and manufacturing, marketing and sales, delivery and purchase, and sometimes even administration, to name just a few. In the airline context this list could be augmented with ground handling, passenger processing, network planning, scheduling, and maintenance. Here the focus is on tasks linked to the operation of an aircraft.

Aircraft operation

The operation (of an aircraft) is perhaps one of the most complicated tasks that airlines have to perform. Aircraft operation in turn has a lot of possible KPIs to control for every little detail necessary to keep flight operations running, meet a certain performance level, and to be able to sense and steer even small performance deviations. The following description concentrates on ground handling and aircraft productivity. Other aspects include KPIs for MRO, safety and security, and coordination with airports.

Ground handling performance

One important area of aircraft operations is ground handling, which means servicing the aircraft during turnaround. The turnaround includes loading and unloading baggage and cargo, supplying the aircraft with fresh water, electricity and kerosene, waste disposal and cleaning (Meincke & Tkotz, 2015). Although most ground handling tasks are not performed by the airline itself but rather by service providers, airlines need to measure the ground handling performance. The argument here is pretty much the same as with the customer service tasks: the airline needs to ascertain whether the outsourcing partner delivers the service level that has been agreed upon. Moreover, it is only possible to determine what causes delays, for example, if all processes are tracked in the measurement system. The following box lists some ground handling performance KPIs.

Ground handling performance KPIs

- **Average turnaround time:** is the time needed to deplane passengers, prepare the aircraft and crew for the next flight, and enplane new passengers. This KPI should differentiate between short, medium, and long haul flights. Short haul flights often carry only a few business passengers with few luggage whereas long haul flights usually carry several hundred passengers, most of them traveling with at least one piece of luggage.
- **Working hours per aircraft turnaround:** sums up all working hours per single aircraft turnaround. This KPI may be detailed to length of flight, aircraft type, location, outsourcing partner, etc.
- **Labor cost per turnaround**: this KPI could also be used in the financial dimension, however, if used in a time series, as here, it indicates whether the airline is able to make productivity gains in ground handling. This should be reasonably differentiated by flight length and airport.
- **Staff injury:** shows how many injuries occur in a certain time period. This KPI must be related to some other KPI e.g. per 1,000 working hours or per take-off. For benchmarking reasons it is useful to differentiate between locations or even between teams of the same location.
- **Equipment damage:** is a similar KPI to staff injury but relates to the equipment used for aircraft servicing.
- **Loaded and unloaded amount of baggage:** again, detailing according to the above mentioned factors is useful. The same KPI may be employed for cargo handling where applicable.

Aircraft productivity

Another element of aircraft operations is the area of aircraft productivity. Here the different KPIs of availability, usability and seat kilometers are put into focus. The main question is how much performance the airline can expect from its resources. All KPIs presented in the following box may be detailed for different routes, aircraft, daytimes, weekdays, etc. (Radnoti, 2002; Sim, Koh, & Shetty, 2006).

Aircraft productivity KPIs

- **Available seat kilometers:** for every flight the number of seats in the aircraft available for passenger is multiplied by the flight distance. This yields a measure of supply.
- **Revenue seat kilometers:** measures all seats sold multiplied by stage length (distance between start and destination airport of a flight in kilometers).
- **Load factor:** revenue seat kilometers divided by available seat kilometers. States which portion of available seats was actually sold to passengers. Load factors must be considered together with yields. Otherwise it may be possible that load factors are only high because the yields are extremely low.
- **Breakeven load factor:** load factor that must be achieved to be able to earn money with a flight. Again the load factor varies in accordance with the yield level.
- **Direct operating cost (DOC) per block hour:** Although, this is a KPI of financial performance, it also indicates how much all operations cost the airline per produced block hour. Therefore, it is an indicator of operations efficiency.
- **Block hours:** number of hours an aircraft is not spending at turnaround or parking e.g. the hours between leaving the departure gate and arriving at the destination gate.
- **Flight hours:** this is the time an aircraft actually is in the air. This KPI should be related to a certain timespan e.g. per day.

C. 5 Capability dimension

The capability dimension includes KPIs for future internal and external potentials for generating revenue. Here we focus on partners (alliances), suppliers, human resources, and environmental issues.

C. 5. 1 Alliance performance

Alliances are important partners that strongly influence performance

Today, alliances are the dominating form of airline cooperation. They provide massive advantages to the participating airline as well as to the customers. For customers, an alliance offers a much bigger route network and a smoother journey due to synchronized schedules and seamless service offering. This means that a customer is more likely to choose an alliance for a planned journey, especially for exotic itineraries. Alliance airlines increase their market share and profit expectations (Oum, Yu, & Fu, 2003). Wang, Evans & Turner (2004) were able to prove that alliance airlines actually face less competition. Another aspect from an airline's point of view is the possibility of sharing resources with other airlines. Examples are lounges, IT systems, and check-in counters. Also, joint development tasks and shared administration are imaginable (Holtbrügge, Wilson, & Berg, 2006).

Alliance KPIs

- **Alliance integration**: number or percentage of code share flights.
- **Proportion of code share passengers**: number or percentage of own passengers that (also) use a partner's code share flight and vice versa.

C. 5. 2 Supplier performance

Suppliers as partners

Another group airlines have developed tight partnerships with is suppliers. They often play an important role in an airline's ability to offer a particular service or even directly deliver the service. Some examples for KPIs are displayed in the following box.

Supplier KPIs

- **Quality of delivered good and services:** is the degree to which quality expectations are met and agreed quality is delivered.
- **Supplier concentration**: the aim is to determine dependability on single supplier.
- **Speed of delivery:** how fast (days) is a certain order processed and delivered.
- **Punctuality of delivery:** percentage of deliveries that were delivered on time.

C. 5. 3 Human resource management performance:

Employees are the key to success

Service offerings of airlines are similar. An innovative service offering introduced by one airline is normally copied by another airline very soon. Airlines therefore require other ways to differentiate themselves from their competitors: their employees. The better educated and trained employees are the better the service quality will be perceived by the customers (Blyton et al., 2001; Hoffer Gittell et al., 2009). This is similar to nearly every service business, because the employees are crucial to delivering a good service for the customers.

Not only is the ground handling and management staff subject to measurement but also the work of the aircrew necessitates a variety of performance measures. Examples in this area are work productivity, the crew planning process and the measurement of its accurate realization. In HR management another factor is important; as with customers, employees are also company stakeholders. Therefore employee satisfaction and loyalty are interesting aspects for evaluating a company's HR performance.

Flight personnel performance is influenced by totally different determinants than other employee groups

Airlines have unique prerequisites in HR performance measurement, since the productivity of flight and cabin crews is influenced by many factors and restrictions that only exist in the airline industry. Crews on long haul flights in particular undergo very complicated crew planning processes, because crews require stop-over at the turnaround location. This stop-over is necessary to comply with crew duty time limitations and security issues. From a legal point of view crews are still on duty at the stop-over, but from an airline's point of view they are not generating revenue. Therefore a performance KPI of the crew planning process needs to be evaluated (Nubert, 2015).

Nearly all HR performance KPIs can be detailed for different business segments or employee groups.

Crew planning performance KPIs

- **Flight hours per day:** the higher this measure is the better is the fix cost digression, the lower are the DOC per block hour, and the better is the aircraft productivity.
- **Block hours/flight hour:** the closer this measure is to 100% the less time is wasted taxiing between gates and runway.
- **Block hours per duty day:** measures the productivity of the crew planning and assignment process. The better this measure the more productive the process work is.
- **Number of changes in crew assignments:** the more accurately the planning process is organized (have all restrictions been regarded) the less changes will occur.

Human resource performance KPIs

- **Headcount:** the total number of employees.
- **Number of managers / pilots / ...**: measures the number of a certain employee group. Can be related to another employee group or total headcount.
- **HR headcount ratio:** total headcount divided by number of HR staff. Measures how many employees one HR staff member in average is responsible for.
- **Training investment per employee:** How much money is invested to train employees? It can be related to total headcount to get a per person measure. Since training for aircrews is much more expensive than for other employee groups this measure should be differentiated according to staff group.
- **Training level:** Percentage of successful completed training needed for a certain position.
- **Employee satisfaction:** measures the satisfaction of employees with their working conditions on a Likert-scale similar to customer satisfaction.
- **Employee loyalty:** likelihood that an employee stays with the company.
- **Age structure:** distribution of employees within defined age groups.
- **Gender ratio:** ratio of female to male employees.
- **Fluctuation:** number of employees resigning divided by total headcount.
- **Application ratio:** number of applicants per open position. This KPI should be differentiated between applicants for inside and outside the company.
- **Internal filling ratio:** percentage of open positions that are filled with internal applicants.
- **HR service costs:** total cost of all HR activities.

C. 5. 4 Environmental performance

Environmental issues are gaining more importance

Airlines need to control their environmental impact, not only in terms of CO_2 emissions but also in terms of noise disturbance and waste disposal as well as simple slack of resource such as kerosene usage due to detours, congestions and delays. There are several incentives behind these issues.

Firstly, the airline industry and its emissions are highly visible to the public – be it the noise starting and landing aircraft produce or the ongoing public discussion about the airline industry's carbon footprint. Any negative publicity may harm an airline's commercial success. Secondly, airlines engage in environmental projects that have the side effect of cost saving and / or operational improvements (e.g. aircraft kerosene consumption or initiatives to minimize detours and delays) (Clarke, 2003).

Obviously environmental initiatives need to be evaluated in order to determine their success. Some exemplary KPIs are listed in the following box:

Environmental KPIs

- **Kerosene consumption per RPK/RTK:** The amount of used kerosene is divided by the total passenger kilometers. Of course this measure varies depending on the load factor. The measure may be related to ASK (available seat kilometers). Details for single routes or aircrafts are possible.
- **CO_2 emission in g/RTK:** kerosene consumed and converted into CO_2 to state how many grams of CO_2 are emitted per passenger- or freight-kilometer.
- **Population affected by aircraft noise:** counts all people that live in an area where the noise of starting or landing aircrafts exceeds a certain level. This measure differs with the type of aircraft and the climb-/descend-rate. Although this measure is more important for airport operators, airlines may use it to determine which aircraft to use for night operations. It is used by the airport operator to select more silent aircrafts or to calculate noise related landing fees at congested airports.
- **Percentage of waste recycled:** measures how much waste is recycled (e.g. plastic cups, newspapers, and glass bottles) and how much is directly thrown away. For some sorts of waste this is also an economic question since waste disposal may be more expensive than recycling.
- **Average fleet age**: This KPI indicates the age of the fleet and its consequent fuel consumption.

D. A SAMPLE BALANCED SCORECARD FOR THE AIRLINE INDUSTRY

To demonstrate how an airline performance measurement system may look like, we present the strategy map of a sample BSC for the airline industry. A strategy map is a good way of visualizing the cause-and-effect relationships between the learning or capability perspective and the financial perspective and provides a supplement to the original four perspective illustration (compare Figure 3). The BSC and the strategy map can help to set up and implement a strategy and to evaluate the performance of a company.

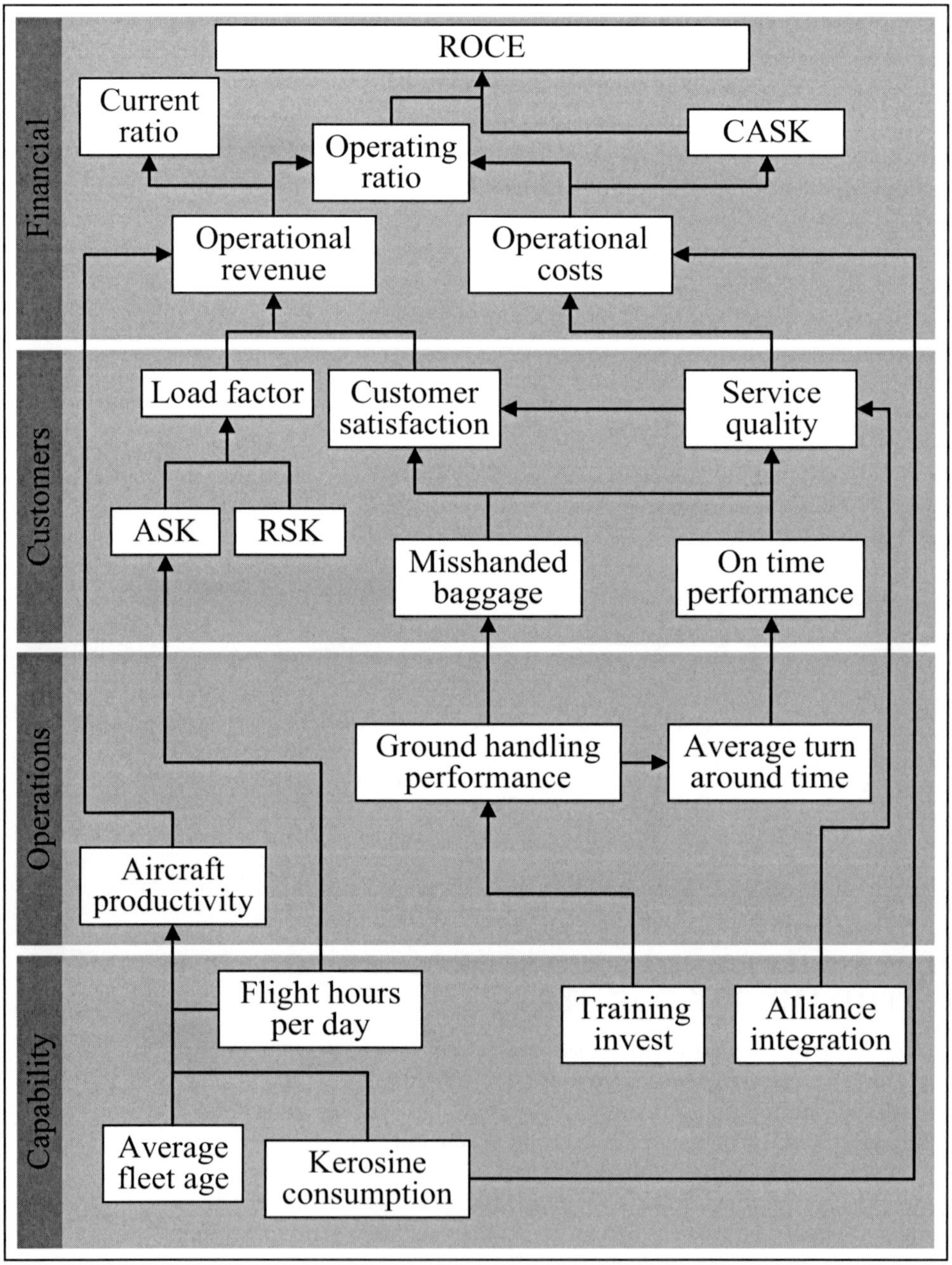

Figure 4: Sample BSC for the airline industry
Own illustration

E. OUTLOOK

Some words of warning

In this chapter we give an overview of different performance metrics for airlines and their integration in a strategy map. We provide a sample BSC to demonstrate the basic principles behind the BSC and the corresponding strategy map. Although the BSC proved to be a powerful and effective instrument in many industries, it has its limitations, as it always mirrors a company's individual strategy, target setting, available resources, and capabilities. It is the outcome of an intense discussion and the result of a challenging process to identify major target drivers and the interrelationships between them. A BSC is always tailored and customized to a specific situation and cannot be simply carried from one company to another. Our sample BSC serves as a generic model only. It needs to be adapted to the specific needs of a company.

Department or function specific PM

Besides the airline specific KPIs a further field of KPIs is linked to single departments or business units of airlines. For example a huge variety of KPIs exists in the field of marketing, supply chain management, or purchasing. These KPIs are generally not specific to the airline industry, but are used in many similar departments throughout different enterprises and industries. Starting points for these topics may be Zerres & Zerres (2006) for marketing PM, Choy et al. (2007) for supply chain PM.

KPIs are the key to good PM

Finally, we would like to emphasize that every KPI an airline wants to implement needs to be aligned to the company's specific situation and the objectives that are pursued with the use of a measurement system. An important part of performance measurement is the selection of the right KPIs.

Review Questions

- Describe the relation between airline PM and aviation PM and name further fields of aviation PM.
- Why do airlines (as most other companies) need to measure and evaluate their activities?
- What is the goal behind a measurement system?
- Name ways of creating KPIs and list advantages and shortcomings of KPIs created with each way.
- Why is classification an important tool when setting up a measurement system?
- What are the shortcomings of traditional measurement systems and how does performance measurement try to overcome them?
- Name the determinants of modern performance measurement systems.
- What is the strength of the balanced scorecard concept and how is it intended to support managers in decision-making?
- Which perspectives form the original balanced scorecard?
- List subcategories of the financial dimension and describe at least one KPI for each subcategory.
- What is a Work Load Unit (WLU) and why do airlines use this artificial unit?
- Why is the customer service dimension so important for airline performance measurement?
- Describe at least five KPIs of customer service dimension and explain why their nature is subjective or objective.
- Which operations of an airline can be part of the operational dimension?
- Why is the KPI 'load factor' central to aircraft profitability?
- List subcategories of the capability dimension and describe at least two KPIs of each subcategory.
- What is important to keep in mind when designing a performance measurement system?

Bibliography and further reading

Anderson, E. W. / Mittal, V. (2000): Strengthening the Satisfaction-Profit Chain, in: Journal of Service Research, Vol. 3, No. 2, p. 107-120.

Anthony, R. N. / Govindarajan, V. (1998): Management Control Systems, 9th ed., Boston.

Blyton, P. / Lucio, M. M. / McGurk, J. / Turnbull, P. (2001): Globalization and trade union strategy: industrial restructuring and human resource management in the international civil aviation industry, in: International Journal of Human Resource Management, Vol. 12, No. 3, p. 445–463.

Brown, D. M. / Leverick, S. (1994): Is Your Measurement System Well Balanced?, in: Journal for Quality & Participation, Vol. 17, No. 6, p. 6–11.

Bruhn, M. (2013): Qualitätsmanagement für Dienstleistungen: Grundlagen, Konzepte, Methoden, 9th ed., Berlin, Heidelberg.

Caplice, C. / Sheffi, Y. (1995): A Review and Evaluation of Logistics Performance Measurement Systems, in: The International Journal of Logistics Management, Vol. 6, No. 1, p. 61–74.

Choy, K. L. / Chow, H. K. H. / Lee, W. B. / Chan, F. T. S. (2007): Development of performance measurement system in managing supplier relationship for maintenance logistics providers, in: Benchmarking: An International Journal, Vol. 14, No. 3, p. 352–368.

Clarke, J. P. (2003): The role of advanced air traffic management in reducing the impact of aircraft noise and enabling aviation growth: Aviation and sustainability, in: Journal of Air Transport Management, Vol. 9, No. 3, p. 161–165.

Daniel, J. (2001): Ertragssteigerung durch Kundenzufriedenheit und Kundenbindung in: Wissenschaftsförderung der Sparkassenorganisationen e.V. (Ed.): Wissenschaft für die Praxis, Vol. 14, Stuttgart.

Von Dietman, N. (2008): Airport performance measurement: Kennzahlensystem zur Analyse und Bewertung von Flughafenprozessen in: Baumgarten, H. / Straube, F. / Klinker, R. (Eds.): Schriftenreihe Logistik der Technischen Universität Berlin, Vol. 5, Berlin.

Feng, C. M. / Wang, R. T. (2000): Performance evaluation for airlines including the consideration of financial ratios, in: Journal of Air Transport Management, Vol. 6, No. 3, p. 133–142.

Flamholtz, E. (1996): Effective organizational control: A framework, applications, and implications, in: European Management Journal, Vol. 14, No. 6, p. 596–611.

Francis, G. / Humphreys, I. / Fry, J. (2005): The nature and prevalence of the use of performance measurement techniques by airlines, in: Journal of Air Transport Management, Vol. 11, No. 4, p. 207–217.

Gillen, D. / Lall, A. (1997): Developing measures of airport productivity and performance: an application of data envelopment analysis, in: Transportation Research Part E: Logistics and Transportation Review, Vol. 33, No. 4, p. 261–273.

Gleich, R. (2011): Performance Measurement – Konzepte, Fallstudien und Grundschema für die Praxis, 2nd ed., München.

Gleich, R. (1997): Stichwort Performance Measurement, in: Die Betriebswirtschaft, Vol. 57, No. 2, p. 114–117.

Günther, T. / Grüning, M. (2002): Performance Measurement-Systeme im praktischen Einsatz, in: Controlling, Vol. 14, No. 1, p. 5–13.

Hoffer Gittell, J. / Nordenflycht, A. von / Kochan, T. A. / McKersie, R. / Bamber, G. J. (2009): Labor Relations and Human Resource Management in the Airline Industry, in: Belobaba, P. / Odoni, A. / Barnhart, C. (Eds.): The Global Airline Industry, Chichester, p. 275–312.

Holloway, S. (2002): Airlines: Managing to make money, Aldershot.

Holloway, S. (2008): Straight and level: Practical airline economics, 3rd ed., Aldershot.

Holtbrügge, D. / Wilson, S. / Berg, N. (2006): Human resource management at Star Alliance: Pressures for standardization and differentiation, in: Journal of Air Transport Management, Vol. 12, No. 6, p. 306–312.

Horváth, P. / Arnaout, A. / Gleich, R. / Seidenschwarz, W. / Stoi, R. (1999): Neue Instrumente in der deutschen Unternehmenspraxis: Bericht über die Stuttgarter Studie, in: Egger, A. / Grün, O. / Moser, R. (Eds.): Managementinstrumente und -konzepte: Entstehung, Verbreitung und Bedeutung für die Betriebswirtschaftslehre, Stuttgart, p. 289–328.

Humphreys, I. / Francis, G. / Fry, J. (2002): Performance Measurement in Airports: A Critical International Comparison, in: Public Works Management & Policy, Vol. 6, No. 4, p. 264–275.

Kane, R. M. (2012): Air transportation, 16th ed., Dubuque Iowa.

Kaplan, R. S. / Norton, D. P. (2003): The strategy-focused organization: How balanced scorecard companies thrive in the new business environment, Boston.

Kaplan, R.S. / Norton, D.P. (2000): Having Trouble with your Strategy? Then Map It, in: Harvard Business Review, Vol. 98, No. 9, p. 167-176.

Kaplan, R. S. / Norton, D. P. (1998): Balanced Scorecard: Strategien erfolgreich umsetzen, Stuttgart.

Kaplan, R. S. / Norton, D. P. (1996): Balanced Scorecard: Translating Strategy into Action, Harvard.

Kaplan, R. S. / Norton, D. P. (1992): The Balanced Scorecard: Measures That Drive Performance, in: Harvard Business Review, Vol. 70, No. 1, p. 71–79.

Kleymann, B. / Seristö, H. (2004): Managing strategic airline alliances, Aldershot.

Küpper, H. U. / Friedel, G. / Hofmann, C. / Hofmann, Y. / Pedell, B. (2013): Controlling - Konzeption, Aufgaben, Instrumente. 6th ed., Stuttgart.

Lin, L. C. / Hong, C. H. (2006): Operational performance evaluation of international major airports: An application of data envelopment analysis, in: Journal of Air Transport Management, Vol. 12, No. 6, p. 342–351.

Linser, A. (2005): Performance Measurement in der Flugzeuginstandhaltung, St. Gallen.

Matzler, K. / Stahl, H. K. / Hinterhuber, H. H. (2008): Die Customer-based View der Unternehmensführung, in: Hinterhuber, H. H. / Matzler, K. (Eds.): Kundenorientierte Unternehmensführung: Kundenorientierung - Kundenzufriedenheit - Kundenbindung, 6th ed., Wiesbaden, p. 3–33.

Meincke, P. A. / Tkotz, A. (2015): Airports - Types, Functions, Facilities, and Accessibility, in: Wald, A. / Fay, C. & Gleich, R. (Eds.): Introduction to Aviation Management, 3rd ed. in: Gleich, R. & Wald, A. (Eds.): Aviation Management, Vol. 3, Münster, p. 87–126.

Morrell, P. S. (2013): Airline finance, 4th ed., Aldershot.

Müller-Stewens, G. (1998): Performance Measurement im Lichte eines Stakeholderansatzes, in: Reinecke, S. / Tomczak, T. / Dittrich, S. (Eds.): Marketingcontrolling, St. Gallen, p. 34–43.

Müller-Stewens, G. / Lechner, C. (2011): Strategisches Management: Wie strategische Initiativen zum Wandel führen, 4th ed., Stuttgart.

Neely, A. / Gregory, M. / Platts, K. (1995): Performance measurement system design: A literature review and research agenda, in: International Journal of Operations & Production Management, Vol. 15, No. 4, p. 80–116.

Nubert, M. (2015): Aircraft - Types, Operations and Performance, in: Wald, A. / Fay, C. & Gleich, R. (Eds.): Introduction to Aviation Management, 3rd ed. in: Gleich, R. & Wald, A. (Eds.): Aviation Management, Vol. 3, Münster, p. 53–83.

Oum, T. H. / Yu, C. / Fu, X. (2003): A comparative analysis of productivity performance of the world's major airports: summary report of the ATRS global airport benchmarking research report 2002: Air Transport Research Society 2003 Special Issue, in: Journal of Air Transport Management, Vol. 9, No. 5, p. 285–297.

Raake, A. (2008): Strategisches Performance Measurement: Anwendungsstand und Gestaltungsmöglichkeiten am Beispiel des öffentlichen Personennahverkehrs in: Gleich, R. / Wald, A. (Eds.): Controlling und Management, Vol. 5, Berlin.

Radnoti, G. (2002): Profit Strategies for Air Transportation, New York, London.

Rouse, P. / Putterill, M. / Ryan, D. (2002): Integrated performance measurement design: insights from an application in aircraft maintenance, in: Management Accounting Research, Vol. 13, No. 2, p. 229–248.

Rummler, G. A. / Brache, A. P. (1990): Improving Performance. How to manage the white space in the organization chart, San Francisco.

Saramaa, T. (1998): Strategic Alliance Performance Measurement, Helsinki.

Schmidberger, S. / Bals, L. / Hartmann, E. / Jahns, C. (2009): Ground handling services at European hub airports: Development of a performance measurement system for benchmarking, in: International Journal of Production Economics, Vol. 117, No. 1, p. 104–116.

Sim, K. L. / Koh, H. C. / Shetty, S. (2006): Some potential issues of service quality reporting for airlines, in: Journal of Air Transport Management, Vol. 12, No. 6, p. 293–299.

Stauss, B. / Dornach, F. / Coenen, C. (2006): Zufriedenheitsmanagement in Deutschland: Von der Messung zur Unternehmenssteuerung, 1st ed., München.

Tangerman, N. A. (1993): The international logistics of freight forwarding: Performance measurement at the harper group, in: National Productivity Review, Vol. 13, No. 1, p. 107–114.

Wang, Z. H. / Evans, M. / Turner, L. (2004): Effects of strategic airline alliances on air transport market competition: an empirical analysis, in: Tourism Economics, Vol. 10, No. 1, p. 23–43.

Weber, K. / Sparks, B. (2004): Consumer attributions and behavioral responses to service failures in strategic airline alliance settings, in: Journal of Air Transport Management, Vol. 10, No. 5, p. 361–367.

Weiss, M. / Zirkler, B. / Guttenberger, B. (2008): Performance Measurement Systeme und ihre Anwendung in der Praxis. Ergebnisse empirischer Studien, in: Controlling, Vol. 20, p. 139–147.

Zeithaml, V. A. / Berry, L. L. / Parasuraman, A. (1996): The Behavioral Consequences of Service Quality, in: Journal of Marketing, Vol. 60, April, p. 31–46.

Zerres, C. / Zerres, M. P. (Eds.) (2006): Handbuch Marketing-Controlling, 3rd ed., Berlin, Heidelberg, New York.

Innovation in the Airline Business

Maximilian Rothkopf, Andreas Wald

Table of contents

You should be able to

- understand the importance for innovation in the airline industry
- explain different strategic approaches to innovations
- understand the specific challenges of service innovations
- explicate how innovations can create value for airlines
- sum up the main barriers for innovation
- show how the organizational processes and structures of airlines can reflect the importance of innovation

The authors

Dr. Maximilian Rothkopf is a partner at a leading top management consultancy. He focuses on strategic and commercial topics in transport and logistics industries.

Dr. Andreas Wald is professor of strategy at the School of Business and Law of the University of Agder in Kristiansand, Norway, and adjunct professor of aviation management at EBS Universität für Wirtschaft und Recht, Wiesbaden, Germany.

Abstract

Innovation is a key to success in many industries. In this chapter we elaborate on service innovation in general, introduce the specific traits of different services, and look at the implications for innovation in this sector. On this basis we consider innovation in the airline industry in more detail. We establish an airline specific definition for innovation and discuss the different categories of innovation in this industry. We show how airlines strategically approach innovation to generate value and explain how airlines can improve their organization and processes to facilitate innovation.

A. WHY CARE ABOUT INNOVATION?

Importance of innovation

Corporations and individuals compete against each other in various fields. Employees try to work better or harder than their colleagues in order to get promoted. Firms aim at delivering better or cheaper products and services than their competitors. The aim is to gain competitive advantage, i.e. to gain more customers who remain loyal or customers willing to spend more money with the company than with its rivals. A major means for achieving and securing competitive advantage innovation. Innovations can take the form of a completely new product or service offer. They can also be based on incremental modifications of existing solutions or on recombination. Innovations are not limited to product or services; they may also entail processes and entirely new ways of doing business, i.e. new business models (Tidd, Bessant & Pavitt 2001).

Triggers for innovations

The triggers for innovation are manifold but usually rooted in changes in the competitive environment of a firm. For instance, a changing customer base may force corporations to react by innovating. The ageing society in the Western world will bring about significant changes in the customers' needs. Another reason for innovation are technological changes (innovations) brought about by competitors. Finally, innovation can be spurred by regulative changes such as new laws or by technological developments. Regardless of the reason, innovations are a necessary precondition to survive and to stay ahead in every business. Although many famous and successful innovations were the result of fortune, creative acts of visionary entrepreneurs or quick reactions to critical situations, corporations cannot afford to abstain from the systematic management of innovation.

B. FUNDAMENTALS OF SERVICE INNOVATION

Diversity of services

Services are tremendously diverse both between and within sectors and the players are often smaller firms (Tether, Hipp & Miles, 2001). Services comprise fields as diverse as transport, government, education, healthcare, social and personal services, retail and wholesale, hotels and restaurants, banking and finance, telecommunication and management consulting (Oke, 2007). Over the last decades, the importance of the service sector has increased, and the sector accounts for the largest part of the Gross Domestic Product (GDP) in industrialized countries. In 2012, the share of the service sector of total GDP was 69% in Germany, 73% in Japan, and 79% in the U.S. Services are particularly labor-intensive, and therefore less prone to rationalization and job losses. On the other hand, many services strongly rely on low-skilled workers and offer only moderate incomes. The specific traits of services evoke a special approach in management. Fitzsimmons & Fitzsimmons (2006) describe the following fundamental traits of services:

Fundamental traits of services

- **Simultaneity**: services are usually produced and consumed at the same time. This results in an inability to produce services in bulk (e.g. universities cannot produce alumni in bulk).
- **Perishability**: as a result of the inability to inventory services, unused service offers perish and are gone forever. This gives rise to a special attention to a high degree of capacity utilization (e.g. an unsold airline seat).
- **Intangibility**: most services cannot be touched, seen or smelt. For the customer this makes it difficult to assess the quality of services, especially with complex and knowledge intensive services. As a consequence, the reputation of a firm and branding becomes very important, as decision criteria for the customers (e.g. the actual quality of surgery can hardly be assessed by the patient, however, the reputation of the surgeon gives some indication about his/her capabilities).
- **Heterogeneity**: The customer is usually directly involved in the service delivery process. There is a close interaction between the customer and the provider of services. This allows for an extensive adaptation of the service to the specific customers' needs (e.g. you will hardly find two women leaving the same hairdresser with a similar hairstyle).

Even though the service sector is by far the largest sector in advanced economies, research on innovation in this particular sector has only recently emerged (Miles, 2000; Chyi et al., 2010; Sakata et al., 2013). Innovation is a complex subject and its meaning is often unclear. A relatively fuzzy understanding of what constitutes innovation predominates. Therefore, several key definitions and key findings from existing research are outlined below.

B. 1 Innovation

Definition of innovation

There are a large number of definitions for innovation in the literature, which classify innovation in a business context depending on its degree of newness, how it is perceived, its combination of purpose and means, and its exploitation of new products or processes (Hausschildt & Salomo, 2007). The term 'innovation' has its etymological origin in the Latin expression 'novus' which means improvement, novelty or renewal, and refers to radical or incremental changes to products, services or processes (Seegy et al., 2008). Generally, innovation is the effort to create purposeful, focused change in an enterprise's economic or social potential (Drucker, 2002). It also involves a fundamental element of uncertainty (Dosi, 1988). Damanpour (1991, p. 556), who defines innovation as "adoption of an internally generated or purchased device, system, policy, program, process, product or service that is new to the adopting organization", stresses the fact, that an innovation does not have be new to the industry but only to the organization.

B. 2 Business model innovation

Elements of Business models

The most fundamental and comprehensive type of innovation is the business model innovation (BMI). This type of innovation is comparatively rare but it can be the source of a substantial competitive advantage. The most important BMI in the passenger airline business was the advent of the low-cost carrier (LCC). A business model (BM) is the conceptual model that describes the essence of how the business is conducted (Chesbrough, 2010; Teece, 2010). Although there is a multitude of different definitions of what exactly constitutes a BM, most definitions include the following elements (Osterwalder & Pigneur, 2010; Abdelkafi et al., 2013):

- Value proposition
- Value creation
- Value delivery
- Value capture

The value proposition describes the value the firm offers to the customer. For the example of the LCC business model, the value proposition lies in the offering of passenger flights that are significantly cheaper than those of established network carriers. Value creation refers to the process of the transformation of resources into goods and services. It also includes the organization and structure of the entire value chain/network. A typical element of the value creation in the LCC business model is point-to-point traffic between secondary airports by using only one (or very few) aircraft type(s). Value delivery describes how and to whom the value is delivered and how the value proposition is communicated to the customer and other stakeholders. In our example of LCCs, value delivery is simplified as booking alternatives are limited (online booking only) and communication and marketing activities are also streamlined and kept at low costs (see the chapter of Koch in this volume for more details). Finally, value capture explains how the revenues are generated, the cost structure and the transformation of revenues and costs into profits. The generation of profit in the LCC business model is based on strict cost optimization and the generation of additional revenues (luggage fees, food and drinks, priority check in).

Business model innovation

The four elements of a business model should not be developed in isolation but they must form a coherent pattern. A business model innovation therefore is not the simple modification of one or several elements, but an orchestrated improvement and modification of the entire pattern. BMI have a fundamental impact on the firm and often require significant organizational change. Therefore, they are less prevalent than product and service innovations. The latter are less complex and risky as they mostly pertain to only on element of the business model, - the value proposition.

B. 3 Service innovation

Types of service innovation

There is agreement in the literature that different types of innovations exist in service firms, but little agreement on what these different types are (Menor, Tatikonda & Sampson, 2002). Oke (2007) relates service innovations to variations in product delivery or add-on services establishing the service experience for the customer. A similar definition states that service innovation involves changes in the process of delivering existing services or the development of completely new kinds of services (Leiponen, 2005). Gadrey, Gallouj & Weinstein (1995) define service innovations as innovations in process and innovations in organization for existing service products. An alternative definition is offered by Seegy et al. (2008), who propose that, in a service industry context, innovation can affect three dimensions: the service potential, the service process and the service result. An example for an innovation in the first dimension would be the establishment of an additional contact point for customer complaints. The second dimension focuses on occurrence of innovations during the conduction of services, e.g. a new procedure in banking transactions. A new product from an insurance company is an example of the third dimension, which refers to the final outcome at the end of a service process. Also the goals firms pursue by service innovation differ. Tether (2003) lists several aims of service innovation, which are:

- Improve quality
- Open new markets
- Extend service range
- Improve flexibility
- Reduce labor cost
- Fulfill regulations
- Replace old services
- Reduce environmental damage
- Reduce energy use
- Reduce materials use

Service vs. manufacturing

Holloway (2002) suggests that service innovation motivates staff, generates incremental revenues, establishes points of differentiation, enhances brand image, closes quality or service gaps, revitalizes a brand or lowers costs. Still, as most of our understanding of innovation and innovation processes at the micro level has been derived from studies in manufacturing (Tether, Hipp & Miles, 2001), and as innovation in the service sector differs to some degree from innovation in manufacturing industries (van der Aa & Elfring 2002; Drejer 2004), the nature of service innovation can be described in more detail by pointing out key areas of difference to the manufacturing sector:

- A relatively low level of R&D is an important differentiator between service and manufacturing industry innovations (Howells, 2004)
- Human resources play a particularly important role in the generation of service innovations but also in the implementation phase
- Due to the high information content of many services, the widespread use of IT is the third characteristic of service innovations
- The high relevance of non-technological innovations, which is often seen as the most distinct feature of service innovations, even though this is only confirmed for some segments of the service sector (Hollenstein, 2003)
- In service industries there are usually more departments and project teams engaged in the innovation process than in the manufacturing sector (Hipp & Grupp 2005)
- The innovation behavior of actors is not always systematic and external actors play a minor role (Sundbo et. al. 2007)
- Services are difficult to protect and are easily imitated (von Stamm, 2008)

B. 4 Empirical findings on service innovation

Focus of innovation research on technology

The innovation literature has been traditionally technology-focused, mainly associated with new tangible product development in high-tech industries (Gallouj & Weinstein 1997; Alam & Perry 2002). Moreover, innovation management has played an increasing role in corporate competitive strategy (Roberts, 1998). One reason for the dominance of product innovation research might be that innovative developments in service industries seem to be difficult to explain in terms of traditional innovation theories and typologies (Damanpour, 1991). However, service innovation has recently become one of the key topics in innovation research (Sakata et al., 2013). Those studies are either focused on a specific sector (e.g. tourism) or on the whole service sector. Areas that attract the most attention are financial services, IT services and knowledge-intense business services (de Brentani, 2001). The main focus lies in innovation processes or in the differences to innovation in manufacturing industries (Gallouj, 2002; Tether, 2003; Vang & Zellner 2005; Orfila-Sintes & Mattsson 2009).

Innovation patterns in services

Services innovation follows patterns that are, to some degree, different from those in manufacturing (van der Aa & Elfring 2002; Drejer, 2004). According to Sundbo & Gallouj (1998) the following patterns can be identified as follows:

- The classic R&D pattern with a clear distinction between R&D and production is less frequent in service innovation
- The service professional pattern characterizes professional knowledge service firms where no formalized structures exist
- The organized strategic innovation pattern, i.e. a managerial model of organizing the innovation with no R&D department, but rather a strategy that determines the innovation policy. This is most typical within the service sector

- The entrepreneurial pattern is primarily focused on radical innovation in the creation of service firms
- The artisan pattern describes (small) service firms that focus on small changes and do not have any innovation strategy or R&D department
- The network patterns explain a situation where a number of service firms have created a common network firm with the purpose of innovating on behalf of the member firms

B. 5 New service development (NSD)

NSD process

From a conceptual side, the development of a new service is usually considered more complex than the development of new tangible products (Oke, 2004). The NSD for services is described as being generally an unsystematic search and learning process as compared to more formalized product development processes employed by manufacturing companies. It is understood that the NSD process, which often takes place in an ad-hoc manner, is a more chaotic process (Dolfsma, 2004; Sundbo. 1997). Furthermore, the innovation behavior is not always systematic, and external actors play a minor role (Sundbo et al. 2007). Also, internal organizational factors seem to be more important for NSD than for the development of new products. The interaction between NSD and service delivery is considered especially necessary (Nijssen et al. 2006).

The literature regards the existence of a formal innovation process and of a process management that systematically plans, controls and steers the innovation process as highly important. However, the nature of services also makes proven models for new product development in manufacturing like the Stage Gate Process difficult to use (Cooper, 1988; Cooper, 1994). Regardless of these differences between services and products, a few generic models for the business process generating service innovation have been suggested (Bowers, 1989; Edgett & Jones, 1991; Johnson et al. 2000; Stevens & Dimitriadis, 2005).

Phases of the NSD process

In Figure 1 we present a generic model by distinguishing four phases: concept, analysis, development and implementation. The innovation process usually starts in the concept phase with the definition of goals and strategies for services and development of new ideas. These ideas may come from customers, market-research, employees, suppliers of technology, industry associations, competitors and other sources. The ideas have to be assessed followed by a preliminary selection of the most promising ideas. First concepts will be developed and tested for these ideas. The prototypes are subjected to a more thorough examination in the analysis phase resulting in the authorization of the final new development projects. The following service design phase entails the design and testing of the service along with the adaptation of existing systems and infrastructure or the setup of new systems for the delivery of the services. In the implementation phase, the new service is introduced onto the market and the success of the launch needs to be monitored. In practice, these stages overlap and there are feedback-loops between prior and subsequent stages. Due to the extreme diversity of services and the competitive environment, context factors, like the market structure, the prevailing technology or the legal framework (Figure 1), will have a huge impact on the specific organization of the phases within the NSD-process. Irrespective of those characteristics, the involvement of expert frontline personnel and the implementation of a formal and planned launch program for the new service offer are essential. To summarize, a more formalized and non ad-hoc NSD will increase the chances of success (de Brentani, 2001).

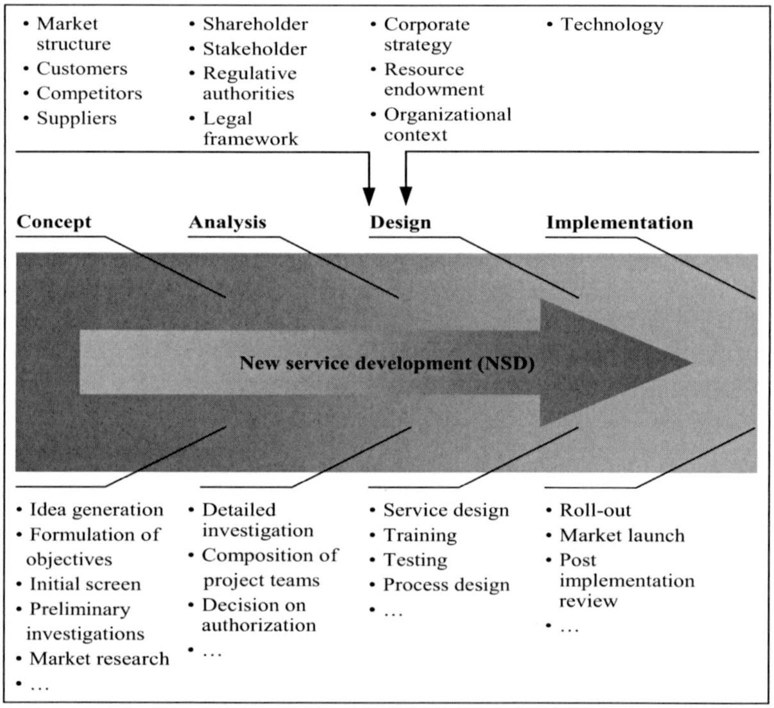

Figure 1: New service development process (Johnson et al. 2000)

Organization of Innovation

Services are often thought to be laggards in innovation, due to the fact that official statistics report that service companies do relatively little formal R&D (Salter & Tether, 2006). Indeed, the role of R&D for innovation in service industries differs. As described above, the classic manufacturing R&D pattern is the least frequent in services. This is in line with Barras (1986) who suggests that R&D investments are more strongly associated with successful manufacturing than services. Moreover, the existence of an in-house R&D in services is much less likely than in manufacturing firms. Several authors confirm that R&D strength is more important for a new product than service development (Howells, 2004; Nijssen et al. 2006). Overall, services place less emphasis on hard sources of technology and knowledge, such as R&D, and a greater emphasis on softer sources of knowledge and technology, such as the use of cooperation practices (Tether, 2005).

Organizational innovations

Innovations in services are often organizational in nature. Therefore the organization of innovation is an important topic. However, little research on this topic exists. In services, the capability to innovate is seen as a subject that involves the whole organization. As outlined above, the innovation may often take other forms than in manufacturing and may be organized differently. Hipp & Grupp (2005) point out that, in general, more departments and project teams are engaged in the innovation process in service industries than in the manufacturing sector. Also the organizational responsibilities and roles for innovation are typically less clear in services.

C. INNOVATION IN THE AIRLINE BUSINESS

Innovation in the transport sector

So far, little research on innovation in the airline industry exists. Therefore we approach innovation from a general transport angle, which lays the foundation for a better understanding of innovation in an airline context. Services are tremendously diverse, both between and within sectors. The transport sector contains firms like freight forwarders, bus companies, public transport providers, airlines, cruise liner, cargo ships and railways. It includes a large number of small-scale companies with a few employees, as well as some of the largest enterprises in the world. Even though the results of empirical studies vary, some common features for innovation in the transport industry can be identified:

- The main sources of innovation seem to be external, e.g. by suppliers, which is in line with the view that service innovations are supplier-dominated. Typically transport service firms are characterized as passive technology users and mere recipients of innovations in the manufacturing sector.
- Contrary to other service industries, transportation is engaged in much more stable activities (Tether, 2003) and put less emphasis on innovation than other service sectors. Most studies perceive transport firms as less innovative than other service firms.
- Transport and logistics industry show hardly any organizationally integrated innovation activities (Hipp & Verworn 2007). Some firms are innovating by simply copying their rivals or by adopting externally developed off-the-shelf technologies which requires little creativity and risk-taking.
- Generally, transport firms conduct limited structured R&D since innovations are rarely science based (Hipp & Grupp, 2005; Lopes & Dodinho, 2005).
- One of the most important areas of innovation in transport seems to be technological innovation. Also innovations in cost-efficiency play a major role in sustaining market growth, which is especially true for the logistics sector. Furthermore, information and communication technologies play an important role in transport sector innovation, as they help the operation and management of the physical transport and also give information and guidance to the users (Ongkittikul, 2006).

C. 1 An airline specific definition of innovation

Categories of innovations in the airline industry

In the following we present a framework for assessing airline innovations. Innovations in the airline industry are far from restricted to the development of improved maintenance and safety procedures, more potent power plants or new aircraft types (Hill, 2001). Innovations that are new to the airline industry are limited by nature. Therefore our definition of innovation comprises all implementations of novelties that are new to the airline under consideration and not necessarily new to the industry. Airline innovation leads to change and is intended to improve in some way what is currently already being done or offered; it requires some kind of investment, and has an unclear outcome. There are three main categories of innovations which are best applicable to the airline industry. This grouping of innovations applies to the frequently made distinction between product and process innovation – not meaning, however, that they are independent – and to both, incremental and radical innovations. The first group comprises innovation in the operations of an airline such as processes, IT or equipment. In a service context, it constitutes the necessary hardware and resources to provide the actual service, i.e. the transportation from A to B. The second group encompasses actual product and service innovations for the passenger, on the ground and in the air. The third group covers all innovations in the areas of organization and the business model. The three major innovation categories are briefly illustrated in Figure 2.

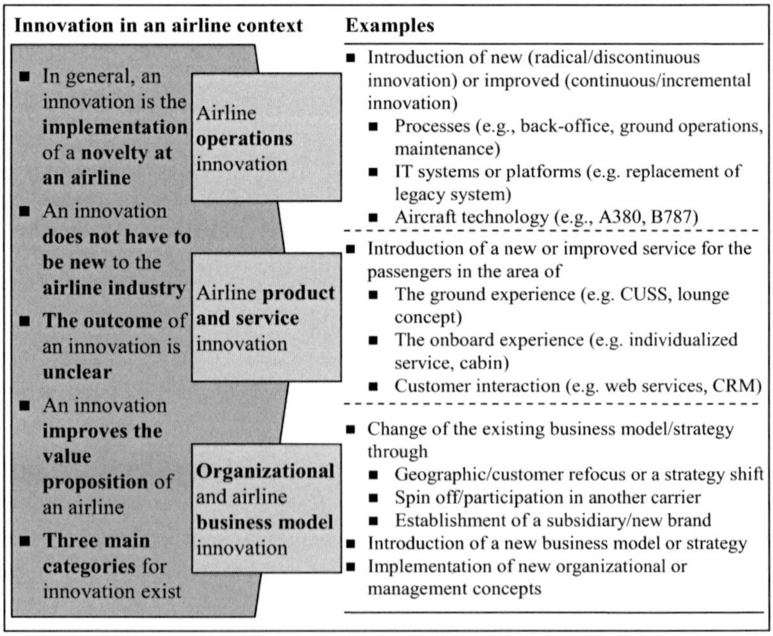

Figure 2: Innovation in the airline context (Rothkopf, 2009)

C. 2 Operational innovations

Important for the cost base

Operational innovations are important for the cost base of an airline, as cost advantages arise from performing particular activities more efficiently than competitors. Generally, operational (process) innovations have an internal focus and are efficiency driven. Process innovations are more systemic and complex than product innovations and also tend to be more internally sourced and more costly to implement (Gopalakrishnan, Bierly & Kessler, 1999). This area comprises technological innovations, IT innovations, innovations in ground and flight operations, and innovations in labor agreements. Generally, IT innovations are particularly important for all types of service firms in order to realize efficiency gains. Typically, innovations in these areas cannot be seen or experienced by the passengers as they occur in 'hidden' areas like the tools for revenue management described in the chapter by Thomas Dionisius in this volume. Technology and IT play a crucial role in the operations of the airline industry by supporting business objectives, as they enable innovation in a variety of areas. For example, IT can be used as a strategic tool in the customer relationship and internal management arenas. Besides fuel and ownership costs, labor is one of the biggest cost drivers for an airline. Unlike other service providers, airlines require a larger proportion of highly skilled workers, so innovations in the area of labor agreements or remuneration structures can have a large impact.

C. 3 Product and service innovation

Experiential service

Voss & Zomerdijk (2007) label an airline's service as an experiential service. This second category covers product and service innovations that passengers can experience onboard, on the ground and before or after a flight. Innovations in this second category of airline innovation have to also be perceived as an innovation for the passenger. The cabin environment offers the most significant opportunity for any airline to innovate and to be different (Tschechne, Eelmann & Becker 2008). Pilling (2003) highlights the ever shorter intervals of onboard service lifecycles. An analysis of the last 10 years shows that airlines on average implement some level of cabin innovation every four to seven years. However, there are a variety of other dimensions that have an impact on airline service quality. Elliot & Roach (1993) propose food and beverage quality, timeliness of luggage transport, seat comfort, check-in process and in-flight service as categories by which airline service quality can be measured. One could add to these the security process at the airport, the lounge experience for status passengers, the quality of the frequent flyer programs, punctual performance, the ease of transfer at hubs, boarding process, fare availability, and general attitude of the staff. All these areas offer ample opportunities for innovation. However, Pakdil & Aydin (2007) state that the services of an airline and the impact of innovations can be perceived in different ways by individuals with different backgrounds. Innovations in the area of product and service have the potential to increase loyalty and customer satisfaction, which are clear indicators for the success of an innovation (Burr, 2007).

Furthermore, airlines have discovered a large and important area for innovations, primarily on the ground, in e-services (Shon, Chen & Chang, 2003). The aim of e-services is to make travel an easier, faster and more transparent experience, whether in terms of booking, checking in, or boarding. Through computerization and automation, they offer a substitution for a range of previously labor intensive services, e.g. the check-in procedure.

C. 4 Business model and organizational innovations

The third airline innovation category subsumes business model and organizational innovations. Strategy innovation focuses on market innovation, i.e. the penetration of new markets or the innovation of target segments. Business model and strategy innovations can also include the transference of services to regional partners, franchises or alliances or the setting up of an LCC subsidiary (Dennis, 2007). The third category also includes innovations in distribution, e.g. innovations in pricing systems or fare structures and innovative distribution concepts. Moreover, organizational innovations are considered. These include, among others, innovations in the organizational structure of an airline (e.g. the redistribution of competencies across hierarchical levels), new management practices (e.g. the introduction of team-based work) or the reorganization of service delivery (e.g. outsourcing). This category also includes management innovations, i.e. new ways of mobilizing talent, allocating resources, and formulating strategies.

D. HOW AIRLINES STRATEGICALLY APROACH INNOVATION AND GENERATE VALUE

Recent research has shown that different strategic approaches and focus areas for airline innovation exist. They differ significantly regarding the extent and the way they create value for airlines (Rothkopf, 2009).

D. 1 Strategic approach to innovation

Innovation strategy

Airlines pursue a variety of strategic approaches towards innovation depending on their market position, economic situation, business model and their capabilities. According to the existing literature, an innovation strategy provides a clear direction and focuses the effort of the entire organization towards a common innovation goal (Oke, 2007). Moreover, an innovation strategy comprises all strategic declarations that provide an orientation for the total innovation activities in a firm, from which concrete innovation targets are derived (Seegy et al. 2008). On a more general level, Davila, Epstein & Shelton (2007) explicate an innovation strategy as the guide to how the organization will play the innovation game.

Our research has shown that despite the high importance of innovation and their innovation ambitions, surprisingly, few carriers have a clearly formulated or quantified innovation strategy or innovation goals as defined in the extant literature. Nevertheless, airlines implicitly have clear aspirations on what they want to achieve through innovation, which can change over time. Overall, four main different strategic aspirations for innovation are prevailing (Rothkopf, 2009), among airlines

- that they want to differentiate themselves from the competition through innovation in specific areas – e.g., Singapore Airlines,
- that they emphasize innovation as the key lever in turnaround situations to improve efficiency and/or the quality of the service offering, e.g. the successful turnaround of Air New Zealand;
- that they aim to secure their survival in cut-throat competitive markets by pursuing innovations in several areas;
- that they seek alignment with industry standards by copying 'must haves' in order to satisfy the basic needs of the market or the industry (e.g. airlines that introduced e-tickets at the earliest possible point in time).

Types of airline innovators

In line with the innovation framework put forward in the previous section, the most important innovation areas for airlines are the areas of business model and organizational innovations followed by product and service innovations. The different strategic innovation directions and the priority areas for innovation of airlines result in three types of airline innovators:

- **Focused innovator**: this type of airline focuses its innovation activities on one specific area for a certain period of time, typically two to three years. Innovation priorities alternate, but each of the three main innovation categories is prioritized at least once during a typical industry cycle. Prime examples in this category are large incumbent network carriers that regularly shift their innovation priorities between the three main categories defined in the previous section.
- **Unstructured innovator**: the second type displays unstable and unstructured innovation priorities over the cycle with no clear pattern. Carriers in this category typically produce few innovations over time and constantly change their innovation focus. Smaller and more focused airlines often fall in this category.
- **Undifferentiated innovators** are airlines that display very stable innovation priorities. These airlines hardly change their innovation priorities, independent of the carrier's economic performance and the state of the industry. A good example for this type is Virgin Atlantic, with its ongoing focus on product and service innovations.

D. 2 Value creation through innovation

Different impact on revenues and costs

Of course not all innovations actually create value for airlines. While some innovations only improve the image of an airline in the eyes of the passenger others have a direct impact on the bottom-line of the airline through increased revenues or lower costs. Airlines typically generate the biggest value through innovations in the area of business model and distribution. Particularly radical business model innovations implemented by large incumbent carriers and undifferentiated niche carriers have changed the traditional way of their doing business and had a massive financial impact (see the Chapter of Koch in this volume). Moreover, innovations to an airline's operational or IT systems have large value potential. Despite the fact that IT expenditures for an airline only account for a relatively small share in terms of total costs, they have often proved to have the potential to generate tremendous value by reducing complexity and increasing flexibility in the areas of revenue-, network-, process- or customer-management.

Low value of product and service innovations

Even though product and service innovations play a key role for many airlines, especially in the way the carrier is perceived and in the satisfaction of passengers' needs, studies have shown that this area generates comparably the lowest value contribution. In light of increasingly commoditizing airline markets, this is considered a very important area. However, airlines struggle to measure the impact of product and service innovations, which further complicates the value generation contribution. Furthermore, such innovations often mean more weight, which could add several extra tons to an aircraft, leading to higher fuel consumption and operating costs. Yet there are some examples where significant value could be created in this area. For example, through the First Class Terminal of Lufthansa and the extension of the service concept, the number of passengers in this service class could be increased by more than 50% within one year.

Potential for innovations in the airport environment

Most practitioners share a more or less unambiguous view on the potential of innovations in the future - they see more potential on the revenue than on the cost side in the future. The biggest potential for innovations – in terms of likelihood for implementation and value generation – is considered to be the airport environment and passenger ground processes, as passengers today often spend disproportionately large amounts of time at the airport. Airlines are likely to focus on creating a more stress-free travel experience and a more differentiated product offer, through process and ground product innovations. Cost cutting innovations no longer provide the largest value potential, as in recent years significant reductions were already achieved. Nonetheless there are two exceptions in this area. The first promising field of activity is aircraft technology innovations that reduce fuel consumption. The second exception is innovations in the area of labor, due to the fact that the airline industry is a labor-cost intensive industry facing a high union bargaining power. In light of further declining margins and an increasing commoditization, the potential of innovations in labor is high, even though the likelihood for large scale innovations is low. Furthermore, IT innovations will continue to be an important field for innovations, as the strong dependency on these legacy systems would be reduced through innovative systems that allow even simpler booking processes. The large airline alliances will also play a key role in driving such innovations, particularly in the development of more advanced pricing capabilities and a better exploitation of the large amount of passenger specific data to allow for more targeted and personalized customer relations.

E. HOW AIRLINES CAN ORGANIZE FOR INNOVATION

Organizational capability for innovation

For an airline the organizational capability to constantly innovate is a key to developing sustainable competitive advantages. However, developing successful innovations in the airline business is a complex task that requires an organization capable of developing innovations from idea generation to implementation. But there are specific barriers that are impeding innovations in the airline business.

E. 1 Organizational structures

Need for a structural and cultural fit

Until recently, few carriers had dedicated organizational structures and responsibilities around innovation. Often top management or certain individuals or departments were pushing for innovations, which led to uncoordinated innovation activities. Generally, corporate cultures that foster innovation have a positive impact on an airline's capability to innovate and the innovation success rate. Driven by an increasing need to develop innovations in increasingly competitive and commoditizing air travel markets, an increasing number of airlines are setting up dedicated organizations for innovation with systemic innovation processes. The typical innovation process in services along idea generation, concept development, market testing and implementation should therefore be reflected in an airline's organizational structure.

Systematic idea generation process

Many airlines try to systematically organize the idea generation process in order to ensure an ongoing flow of innovation projects. On the one side they use both external sources to generate ideas, in particular customers, which play an important role as idea source in all kind of service industries (Sørensen et al., 2013). Other carriers or service industries also play an important role as sources for ideas (e.g. the service processes in hospitality). However, most airlines consider internal idea sources as the key to successful innovations. Typically, service firms do not conduct structured R&D, which also holds true for most airlines. Therefore top management, employee suggestion schemes and market intelligence departments play a pivotal role as internal idea sources. The most important idea sources for airlines are summarized in Figure 3.

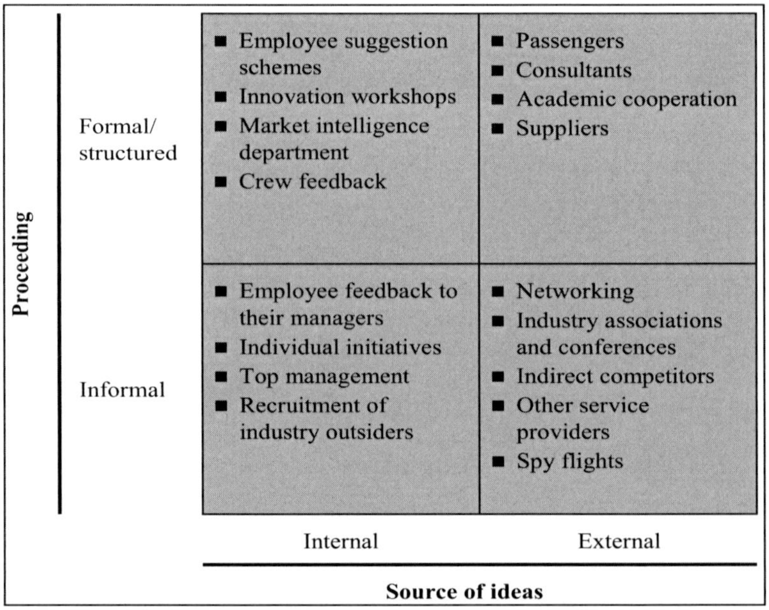

Figure 3: Overview of sources for innovation ideas (Rothkopf, 2009)

Project teams and innovation departments

Most airlines set up project teams to push an innovation through the concept development and market testing phase before it is handed over to the functional departments for implementation. Ideally, an airline sets up a centralized innovation department or responsibility close to a top executive to define structured innovation processes, develop and push new ideas forward and coordinate ongoing innovation projects.

E. 2 Internal and external barriers to innovation

It is challenging for every airline to achieve economically sound innovations as there are several key barriers that impede innovations. These barriers can be both internal (airline specific) and external. An overview of the key barriers facing airlines is shown in Figure 4.

Internal barriers

While external barriers can prevent or slow down innovation efforts, internal barriers constitute the biggest hindrance for innovation in an airline. In particular, disjointed legacy or home-grown IT systems, which are prevalent at most carriers, are considered a key internal barrier. They prevent many innovation ideas that require flexible, integrated, economical and standardized IT systems. Furthermore, a lack in innovation culture and the respective organizational processes and structures are a large barrier against innovation. The airline industry is characterized by the strong role of unions. For these reasons, inflexible labor agreements are also considered a key barrier.

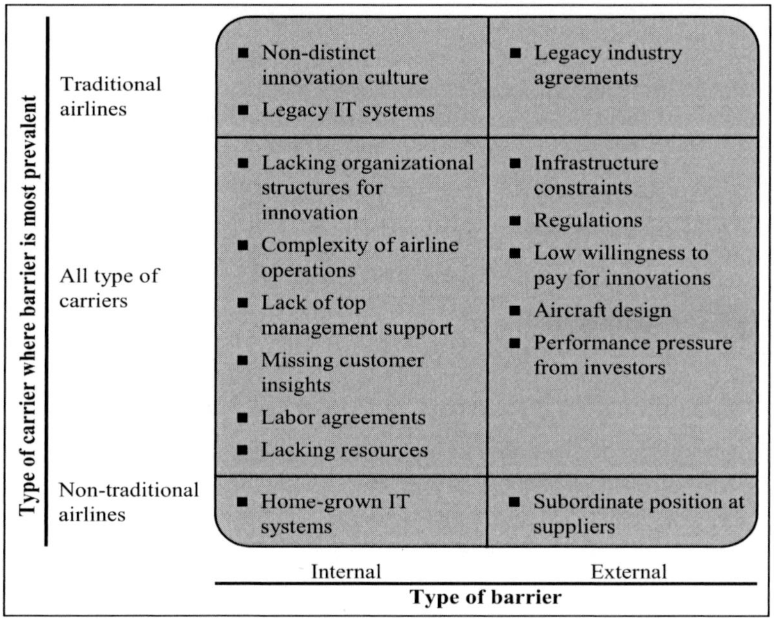

Figure 4: Barriers for innovation (Rothkopf, 2009)

External barriers

One of the key external barriers is the dependency on the infrastructure provided by often monopolistic entities (e.g. airports). In many cases this limits the possibilities for implementing innovative concepts. Despite the benefits offered by legacy industry agreements (e.g. interlining), their complex structures are often a barrier for pushing lean initiatives forward. Finally, the low willingness of passengers to pay for innovations introduced by the airlines is challenging all types of firm to prove the value of innovative ideas before being granted funds.

F. CONCLUSION

In this chapter we provided an introduction to innovation in the airline business. Although little research exists about innovation in this particular industry, there is clear evidence concerning the important role of innovation for value creation. However, the potential for, and the actual contribution to value creation vary across different categories of airline innovation (product/service, business model, organization). Airlines also differ with regard to their strategic approach to innovation. Regardless of these differences, airlines should establish dedicated organizational structures and processes to foster innovation and to overcome internal and external barriers.

Review Questions

- Name five key characteristics of service innovation.
- What do service firms want to achieve through innovation?
- What goals do companies want to achieve through innovations?
- Which stages are predominant in a typical process for new service development?
- What are key differences between innovation in manufacturing and service industries?
- What are common features for innovation in transport industries?
- Which elements should a properly formulated innovation strategy contain?
- Which are the most relevant external and internal barriers for airlines to pursue an innovation?
- What are typical strategic aspirations to achieve through innovation for an airline?
- Which main types of innovators exist in the airline business?
- What are the main barriers for innovation for airlines?

Bibliography and further reading

van der Aa, W. / Elfring, T. (2002): Realizing innovation in services, in: Scandinavian Journal of Management, Vol. 18, No. 2, p. 155-171.

Abdelkafi, N. / Makhotin, S. / Posselt, T. (2013): Business Model Innovations For Electric Mobility – What Can Be Learned From Existing Business Modell Patterns? International Journal of Innovation Management, Vol. 17, No. 1, pp. 1-41.

Alam, I. / Perry, C. (2002): A customer-oriented new service development process, in: Journal of Services Marketing, Vol. 16, No. 6, p. 515-534.

Barras, R. (1986): Towards a theory of innovation in services, in: Research Policy, Vol. 15, No. 4, p. 161-173.

Bowers, M. R. (1989): Developing new services: Improving the process makes it better, in: Journal of Services Marketing, Vol. 3, No. 1, p. 15-20.

Chyi, J. / Jyue-Yu, L., / Yi-Hsing, L., (2010): The determinants of new service development: Service characteristics, market orientation, and actualizing innovation effort, in: Technovation, Vol. 30, No. 4, p. 265–277.

de Brentani, U. (2001): Innovative versus Incremental New Business Services: Different Keys for Achieving Success, in: Journal of Product Innovation Management, Vol. 18, No. 3, p. 169-187.

Burr, W. (2007): Erscheinungsformen, Bedeutung und betriebswirtschaftliche Potenziale von Dienstleistungsinnovationen, in: Schmidt, K. / Gleich, R. / Richter, A (eds.): Innovationsmanagement in der Serviceindustrie - Grundlagen, Praxisbeispiele und Perspektiven, Freiburg, p. 73-93.

Chesbrough, H. (2010): Business Models Innovation. Opportunities and Barriers. Long Range Planning, Vol. 43, No.(2/3), pp. 354-363.

Cooper, R. G. (1994): Third-Generation New Product Processes, in: Journal of Product Innovation Management, Vol. 11, No. 1, p. 3-14.

Cooper, R. G. (1988): The New Product Process: A Decision Guide for Management, in: Journal of Marketing Management, Vol. 3, No. 3, p. 238-255.

Damanpour, F. (1991): Organizational innovation: A meta-analysis of effects of determinants and moderators, in: Academy of Management Journal, Vol. 34, No. 3, p. 555-590.

Davila, T. / Epstein, M. J. / Shelton, R. (2007): Making Innovation Work: How to manage it, Measure it and Profit from it, Upper Saddle River.

Dennis, N. (2007): End of the free lunch? The responses of traditional European airlines to the low-cost carrier threat, in: Journal of Air Transport Management, Vol. 13, No. 5, p. 311-321.

Dolfsma, W. (2004): The Process of new service development: Issues of formalization and appropriability, in: International Journal of Innovation Management, Vol. 8, No. 3, p. 319-337.

Dosi, G. (1988): Sources, Procedures, and Microeconomic Effects of Innovation, in: Journal of Economic Literature, Vol. 26, No. 3, p. 1120-1171.

Drejer, I. (2004): Identifying innovation in surveys of services: a Schumpeterian perspective, in: Research Policy, Vol. 33, No. 3, p. 551-562.

Drucker, P. F. (2002): The Discipline of Innovation, in: Harvard Business Review, Vol. 80, No. 8, p. 95-103.

Edgett, S. / Jones, S. (1991): New product development in the financial service industry: a case study, in: Journal of Marketing Management, Vol. 7, No. 3, p. 271-284.

Elliot, K. M. / Roach, D. W. (1993): Service Quality in the Airline Industry Are Carriers Getting an Unbiased Evaluation from Consumers?, in: Journal of Professional Services Marketing, Vol. 9, No. 2, p. 71-82.

Fitzsimmons, J. A. / Fitzsimmons, M. J. (2006): Service Management. Operations, Strategy, Information Technology, Boston.

Gadrey, J. / Gallouj, F. / Weinstein, O. (1995): New modes of innovation: how services benefit industry, in: International Journal of Service Industry Management, Vol. 6, No. 3, p. 4-16.

Gallouj, F. (2002): Innovation in services and the attendance old and new myths, in: Journal of Socio-Economics, Vol. 31. No. 2, p. 137-151.

Gallouj, F. / Weinstein, O. (1997): Innovation in services, in: Research Policy, Vol. 26, No. 4, p. 537-556.

Gopalakrishnan, S. / Bierly, P. / Kessler, E. H. (1999): A Reexamination of Product and Process Innovations Using a Knowledge-Based View, in: Journal of High Technology Management Research, Vol. 10, No. 1, p. 147-166.

Hausschildt, J. / Salomo, S. (2007): Innovationsmanagement. München.

Hill, L. (2001): Open seating: There's more to comfort in the cabin than meets the eye as the aircraft-interiors business becomes increasingly sophisticated, in: Air Transport World, Vol. 38, No. 5, p. 97-98.

Hipp, C. / Grupp, H. (2005): Innovation in the service sector: The demand for service-specific innovation measurement concepts and typologies, in: Research Policy, Vol. 34, No. 4, p. 517-535.

Hipp, C. / Verworn, B. (2007): Management des Innovationsprozesses in der Serviceindustrie - ein Überblick, in: Schmitz, B. / Gleich, R / Richter, A. (eds.): Innovationsmanagement in der Serviceindustrie - Grundlagen, Praxisbeispiele und Perspektiven, Freiburg, p. 93-110.

Hollenstein, H. (2003): Innovation modes in the Swiss service sector: a cluster analysis based on firm-level data, in: Research Policy, Vol. 32, No. 5, p. 845-863.

Holloway, S. (2002): Airlines: Managing to Make Money, Aldershot.

Howells, J. (2004): Innovation, Consumption and Services: Encapsulation and the Combinatorial Role of Services, in: Service Industries Journal, Vol. 24, No. 1, p. 19-36.

Johnson, S. P. / Menor, L. S. / Roth, A. V. / Chase, R. B. (2000): A Critical Evaluation of the New Service Development Process: Integrating Service Innovation and Service Design, in: Fitzsimmons, J. A. / Fitzsimmons, M. J. (eds.): New Service Development: Creating Memorable Experiences, Thousand Oaks, p. 1-32.

Leiponen, A. (2005): Organization of Knowledge and Innovation: The Case of Finnish Business Services, in: Industry & Innovation, Vol. 12, No. 2, p. 185-203.

Lopes, L. F. / Dodinho, M. M. (2005): Services Innovation and Economic Performance: An analysis at the firm level, DRUID Working Paper.

Menor, L. J. / Tatikonda, M. V. / Sampson, S. E. (2002): New service development: areas for exploitation and exploration, in: Journal of Operations Management, Vol. 20, No. 2, p. 135-157.

Miles, I. (2000): Services Innovation: Coming of Age in the Knowledge-Based Economy, in: International Journal of Innovation Management, Vol. 4, No. 4, p. 371-389.

Nijssen, E. J. / Hillebrand, B / Vermeulen, P. A. M. / Kemp, R. G. M. (2006): Exploring product and service innovation similarities and differences, in: International Journal of Research in Marketing, Vol. 23, No. 3, p. 241-251.

Oke, A. (2007): Innovation types and innovation management practices in service companies, in: International Journal of Operations & Production Management, Vol. 27, No. 6, p. 564-587.

Oke, A. (2004): Barriers to Innovation Management in Service Companies, in: Journal of Change Management, Vol. 4, No. 1, p. 31-44.

Ongkittikul, S. (2006): Innovation and Regulatory Reform in Public Transport, Erasmus University Rotterdam, Rotterdam.

Orfila-Sintes, F. / Mattsson, J. (2009): Innovation behavior in the hotel industry, in: Omega, Vol. 37, No. 2, p. 380-394.

Osterwalder, A . / Pigneur, Y. (2010): Business Model Generation, Hoboken.

Pakdil, F. / Aydin, O. (2007): Expectations and perceptions in airline services: An analysis using weighted SERVQUAL scores, in: Journal of Air Transport Management, Vol. 13, No. 4, p. 229-237.

Pilling, M. (2003): Price Promise in: Airline Business, Vol. 19, No. 4, p. 58-60.

Roberts, R. (1998): Managing innovation: The pursuit of competitive advantage and the design of innovation intense environments, in: Research Policy, Vol. 27, No. 2, p. 159-175.

Rothkopf, M. (2009): Innovation in commoditized service industries. An empirical case study analysis in the passenger airline industry, Münster.

Sakata, I. / Sasakia, H. / Akiyamaa, M. / Sawatanib, Y. / Shibatac, N. / Kajikawa, Y. (2013): Bibliometric analysis of service innovation research: Identifying knowledge domain and global network of knowledge, in: Technological Forecasting and Social Change, Vol. 80, No. 6, p. 1085-1093.

Salter, A. / Tether, B. S. (2006): Innovation in Services - Through the Looking Glass of Innovation Studies. Background paper for Advanced Institute of Management Research's Grand Challenge on Service Science.

Seegy, U. / Gleich, R. / Wald, A. / Mudde, P. / Motwani, J. (2008): The Management of Service Innovation: An Empirical Investigation, in: International Journal of Services and Operations Management, Vol. 4, No. 6, p. 672-686.

Shon, Z.-Y. / Chen, F.-Y. / Chang, Y.-H. (2003): Airline e-commerce: the revolution in ticketing channels, in: Journal of Air Transport, Vol. 9, No. 5, p. 325-331.

von Stamm, B. (2008): Managing Innovation, Design and Creativity, Chichester.

Sørensen, F. / Sundbo, J. / Mattson, J. (2013) Organisational conditions for service encounter-based innovation, in: Research Policy, Vol. 42, No. 8, p. 1446-1456.

Stevens, E. / Dimitriadis, S. (2005): Managing the new service development process: towards a systemic model, in: European Journal of Marketing, Vol. 39, No. 1-2, p. 175-198.

Sundbo, J. (1997): Management of Innovation in Services, in: The Service Industries Journal, Vol. 17, No. 3, p. 432-455.

Sundbo, J. / Gallouj, F. (1998): Innovation as a loosely coupled system in services, Lille.

Sundbo, J. / Orfila-Sintes, F. / Sørensen, F. (2007): The innovative behaviour of tourism firms - Comparative studies of Denmark and Spain, in: Research Policy, Vol. 36, No. 1, p. 88-106.

Teece, D.J. (2010): Business Models, Business Strategy and Innovation. Long Range Planning, Vol. 43, No. (2/3), pp. 172-194.

Tether, B. S. (2005): Do Services Innovate (Differently)? Insights from the European Innobarometer Survey, in: Industry & Innovation, Vol. 12, No. 2, p. 153-184.

Tether, B. S. (2003): The sources and aims of innovation in services: variety between and within sectors, in: Economics of Innovation & New Technology, Vol. 12, No. 6, p. 481-505.

Tether, B. S. / Hipp, C. / Miles, I. (2001): Standardisation and particularisation in services: evidence from Germany, in: Research Policy, Vol. 30, No. 7, p. 1115-1138.

Tidd, J. / Bessant, J. / Pavitt, K. (2001): Managing Innovation. Integrating Technological, market And Organizational Change, Chichester.

Tschechne, N. / Eelman, S. / Becker, A. (2008): A scenario-based approach towards deriving future cabin drivers along future airlines business models 2015. Paper presented at 12th ATRS World Conference, Athens.

Vang, J. / Zellner, C. (2005): Introduction: Innovation in Services, in: Industry & Innovation, Vol. 12, No. 2, p. 147-152.

Voss, C. / Zomerdijk, L. (2007): Innovation in Experiential Services – An Empirical View, in: DTI (ed.) Innovation in Services, London, p. 97-134.

World Bank (2014) World Development Indicators database 2014.

Aviation Project Management

Ulf Diefenbach, Benedikt Schnellbächer, Tim Brauer

Table of contents

You should be able to

- distinguish between different kinds of projects according to defined criteria
- name and describe the different project stakeholders as well as their expectations
- classify different projects regarding the project life cycle
- explain the evolution of project management
- describe the role, tasks and duties of the project manager
- explain success criteria and success factors
- apply the critical success factors system framework

The authors

Ulf Diefenbach is Research Assistant and Doctoral Candidate at the Aviation Management Center at EBS Universität für Wirtschaft und Recht, Wiesbaden, Germany.

Benedikt Schnellbächer is Research Assistant and Doctoral Candidate at the Strascheg Institute for Innovation and Entrepreneurship at EBS Universität für Wirtschaft und Recht, Wiesbaden, Germany.

Tim Brauer is Manager Corporate Sourcing at Deutsche Lufthansa AG, Frankfurt, Germany.

Abstract

Projects are a key instrument to enable organizations to continuously improve their processes as well as to adapt themselves to changes in the environment. Both features are indispensable to ensure sustainable success in organizations. This article describes the basics of projects and project management, including a brief overview of project standards, definition of project types, as well as evaluation techniques. The importance of project management within the aviation industry is addressed and types of aviation projects described.

A. INTRODUCTION

"The aviation industry is really a collective term for a number of different industries, each of which has its own distinct qualities and management needs." (Flouris & Lock, 2008, p. XVII)

Projects in the aviation industry

For those who design and make all kinds of aircraft or parts of them, the importance of projects and their management is unquestionable (Müller et al., 2012). But even in more service oriented branches, like aircraft operations, airport management or air navigation services, project management is viewed as an expedient instrument to improve efficiency and gain a competitive advantage.

Importance and use of projects grows continuously

The use of projects and project management continues to grow in our society and its organizations. Although, applying a general understanding of projects as temporary endeavor projects and their management exist for a long time, the popularity increased heavily in the 1960's and is doing so ever since. Businesses regularly use project management to accomplish unique outcomes with limited resources under critical time constraints.

This article focuses on projects in the aviation industry as an approach of dealing with increasingly complex challenges. Success in this regard is connected with an established and good project management. Parts of the project management are project planning, including the definition of work requirements or resources needed, and project monitoring including the tracking of processes, analyzing their impact and making adjustments. The evaluation of the project outcome should always be connected to the context that the project is conducted in.

B. AVIATION INDUSTRY OVERVIEW

B. 1 The Aviation Value Chain

Heckled airlines

According to Wittmer & Bieger (2011) the aviation value chain is composed of four major parts, which are the manufacturing industry and its suppliers, the airline industry, the airports, and the general service providers (see Figure 1). Main actors in this value chain are the airlines and the airports, since the airlines provide the direct service to the customer and the airports provide the infrastructure to enable airlines to offer this service. Characteristics of the different industries within the value chain vary significantly. The aircraft manufacturing industry, especially in the long haul market, is characterized by a duopoly of the two major players Airbus and Boeing. Airports in contrast can be considered as monopolists especially regarding large hub airports. The general service providers like air traffic control can be categorized as monopolists as well. Furthermore, in almost all European countries (except the United Kingdom) state-owned ground handling service providers were to various degrees partially privatized. Within the airline industry there are various actors that play a significant role. Prominent actors besides airlines are leasing companies like GECAS and ILFC, IT providers as the Computer Reservation Systems (CRS) Amadeus and Sabre, maintenance repair and overhaul providers (MRO) such as SR Technics and catering services such as Gate Gourmet. Market characteristics and profit margins of these actors differ significantly. Whereas the market for leasing companies, CRS and MRO companies is oligopolistic, the airline industry faces fierce competition in a polypolistic market. Therefore airlines often claim that their low profitability arises from a 'hostile' environment in which airlines are caught in a 'sandwich position' between monopolistic or oligopolistic providers that are able to generate much higher profit margins at the expense of the airlines (Wittmer & Bieger, 2011).

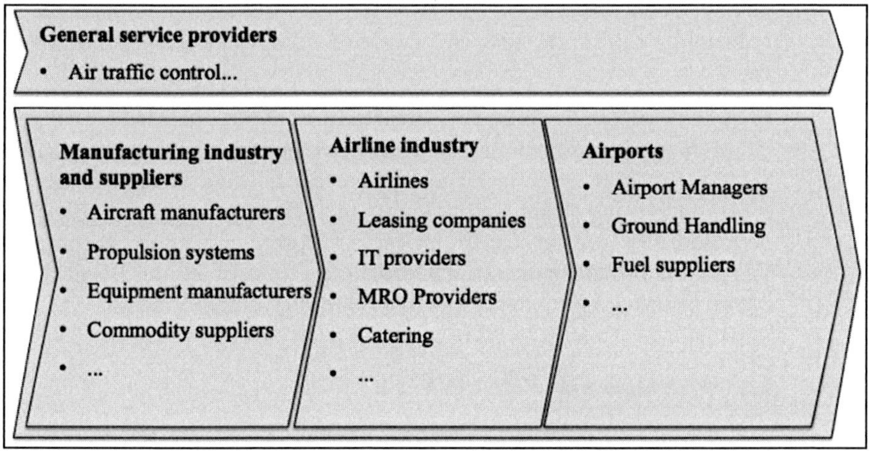

Figure 1: The aviation value chain (Wittmer & Bieger, 2011, p. 25)

B. 2 Projects in the Aviation Industry

Three types of projects common in the aviation industry

Projects are commonly used among all actors of the aviation value chain. According to Flouris and Lock (2008), the aviation industry is characterized mainly by three types of projects. Type 1 projects are **civil engineering and construction projects** and are most commonly executed by airports. Examples may be the construction of the Berlin airport or the construction of the third terminal in Frankfurt (Main),

Germany, by the Fraport AG. Construction projects are also executed or ordered by airlines. Lufthansa Cargo for example has built a new logistics center at Frankfurt International Airport. Type 2 projects are **manufacturing projects**. In contrast to engineering and construction projects, manufacturing projects are executed by all aircraft manufacturers and their suppliers. The manufacturing project of the A380 for example is most likely one of the most complex in the world. It bore high risk and great difficulties in control and coordination through its organizational complexity. Production of the A380 took place in four different European countries, and was two years behind the original schedule and greatly exceeded the planned budget. One major problem of this project had been the long-distance communication, the multiple languages, conflicting technical standards and foremost the incompatibility of the software between the different participating companies. When the different parts of the aircraft were finally put together, the engineers noticed that the wiring did not fit together, so everything had to be reworked at great cost (Flouris & Lock, 2008). The third type of projects, which is mainly common in the aviation industry are **IT projects and projects associated with management change**. They make up the majority of the projects among airlines but are undoubtedly important for all other actors as well. But due to the increased competition, airlines need to restructure their business, cut cost and increase revenue. IT systems are of high importance to achieve these objectives and therefore IT projects, building new or enhancing old IT systems, are common tasks for each airline nowadays.

Overall, any of the three described project types, or a mix of them, occur in the aviation industry. Many projects that are performed by airports, airlines and aircraft manufacturers fall into more than one of these categories adding complexity to their management. The construction of a new airport for example is foremost a construction project but also incorporates a manufacturing as well as an IT and management change project perspectives (Flouris & Lock, 2008).

C. BASICS OF PROJECTS

C. 1 Project Standards

Guidelines for Project Managers

Research on projects, and how they can be best managed, has been driven by scientists and practitioners within the last decades. The ultimate goal was to set up standards for project management to give clear guidance on how to organize projects and to increase the likelihood of project success. Over time different project management schools were established and published different project management standards. The most well-known standards today, are the Project Management Body of Knowledge (PMBOK) published by the Project Management Institute (PMI), the standards published by the International Project Management Association (IPMA), the standards for Projects in Controlled Environments (PRINCE), the open source standards published by the Global Alliance for Project Performance Standards (GAPPS) and the Guidance on project management (ISO/WD 21500) published by the International Organization on Standardization (ISO). At their core, all standards are quite similar and contain the same core issues. Nonetheless, there are differences in the details. The US standard PMBOK of the PMI is the most common used among firms nowadays. Therefore the following sections will concentrate on these standards.

C. 2 Definition of a Project

A temporary endeavor undertaken to create a unique product, service or result

The PMI has defined a project as "a temporary endeavor undertaken to create a unique product, service or result" (PMI, 2013). Projects differ from the regular activity of a business in the way that they aim at developing a unique solution that is outside the usual activity pattern of the firm. These unique solutions can be a new product or service but also an enhancement of an existing product or service, or just a result in the form of knowledge or a document. Due to the uniqueness of the project outcomes, more planning is necessary than in regular firm activities. Moreover, the project team needs to acquire and perform new tasks and activities within the project. Projects are temporary, because they always have a defined start and ending. Nonetheless, this does not denote that projects cannot last over long periods of time, but that they are terminated at some point in time. Termination of a project usually follows upon completion. However, some projects can also be terminated due to project failure or because the client or sponsor closed down the project, because the perceived utility of the project changed (PMI, 2013). The entire entity called a project is composed of several activities and processes, linked with each other, that need to be realized under the given circumstances in order to achieve the planned result. In many occasions projects are interlinked with other projects and consequently are organized in programs or portfolios (Mantel et al., 2011). Project programs are a collection of projects that are managed as one entity in order to achieve strategic business goals. Project portfolios are from an organizational point of view one level above programs and compile all projects within one business unit. These projects are not necessarily interconnected with each other. Portfolios are commonly managed by Project Management Offices (PMO), whose task it is to prioritize these projects according to their urgency and contribution to the overall business success, allocate resources, and track progress as well as time schedules (PMI, 2013).

C. 3 Classification of Projects

Projects can be classified by several characteristic criteria. Common criteria are for example the scope of a project, the position of the customer of the project, the degree of repetition, the number of involved organizational units and the degree of complexity. Table 1 gives an overview on different kinds of project classifications.

Criterion	Example
Project scope	• Mergers & Acquisitions • Incorporation projects • Marketing- & Strategy projects • Feasibility studies • Research projects • Product development • Organizational development projects • Investment projects (e.g. plant engineering) • Maintenance and repair projects
Position of project sponsor and customer	• Internal sponsor and internal customer • Internal sponsor and external customer • External sponsor and internal customer • External sponsor and external customer
Degree of repetition	• Unique projects • Similar / reoccurring projects
Number of involved organizational units	• Project within one department • Project across several internal departments • Project across departments and organizational boundaries
Degree of complexity	• High • Medium • Low

Table 1: Classification of projects (Patzak & Rattay, 1998)

C. 4 Project Stakeholders

Stakeholders interested in projects are either individuals, or groups, or organizations who may influence, or be influenced by a decision, activity or outcome of the project (PMI, 2013). These stakeholders need to be identified and managed by the project manager continuously throughout the entire project life cycle. Project stakeholders have different levels of authority and responsibilities; they can be internal or external, active or passive. They may have competing expectations of the project outcome, which in turn results in rising conflicts in the course of the project. Therefore the project manager's most critical task regarding the project stakeholders is to manage their expectations. The most common stakeholders in a project besides the project manager and his or her team are the project sponsor, customers and users, suppliers, organizational groups, and functional managers.

„A project is successful if all the stakeholders are happy." (Hartman, 2000)

The project team is composed of various employees as well as external personnel, depending on the organizational culture, scope and locality of the project. The team can be dedicated, meaning that they all work full-time on the project. In contrast the team or parts of the team can only work part-time on the project and keep their line function simultaneously (PMI, 2013). This is for example the case for pilots who reduce the time in the cockpit in exchange for project-based work in the office. **The project sponsor** who can be internal or external, is accountable for the entire project, and should provide sufficient resources and support for it. Moreover he or she is in charge of promoting the project to the upper management, other business units and the clients or users in order to receive support and acceptance. If a new runway at an Airport is planned, the project sponsor would be in most cases the upper management itself. **Customer and user** of the new runway would be the Airport, whereas the Airlines are just regarded as users in this respect. Hence customers and users can be external or internal to the company. The customer is the entity that approves and manages the project outcome, whereas the user is actually employing the product, service or result of the project. Sometimes these two entities are represented by the same person or organization. **Suppliers and contractors** are mostly external parties that deliver components or services for the project. For the new runway this would be the construction companies or the architect responsible for the building plan. Internal business units that are affected by the project directly are called **Organizational groups.** These mostly include the supporting activities like marketing and sales, human resources, legal services, finance and controlling, operations, manufacturing, and customer service. Another stakeholder playing a major role is the **general public**. Especially in aviation projects, public interest groups can have a huge impact on the project development and its success. The last important stakeholders are **functional managers**, since these are the heads of the business units, making the key decisions that impact the project work (PMI, 2013). Depending on the project there are other stakeholders that play an important role. All stakeholders can be classified by their impact on the project process and need to be treated accordingly to their influence and importance (Kloppenborg, 2009). Furthermore the different stakeholder groups are all interrelated as shown in Figure 2.

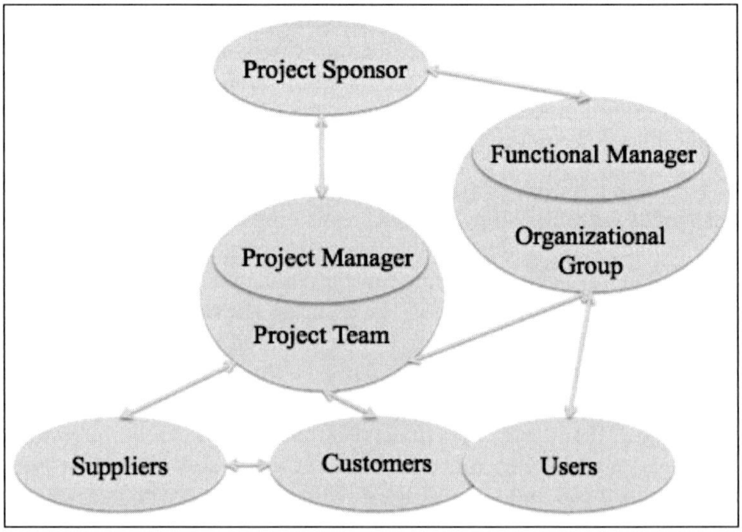

Figure 2: Project stakeholder interaction (Own illustration)

C. 5 Project Life Cycle

Four phases

The project life cycle is commonly referred to as the series of phases, which a project passes through from its initiation to its closure (PMI, 2013). It should not be confused with the product life cycle, which spans over the entire usage of the product, so from creation until obliteration. The project life cycle can be divided into any number of phases depending on the characteristics of the project and the executing organization. These phases are usually sequential but sometimes overlap in certain areas. The general model consists of four phases which are named Initiation, Planning, Execution and Closure (Abdomerovic, 2012). The **Initiation phase** is about the project idea and defining the broad project scope. In the **planning phase** the scope is then defined in more detail and budget and time schedule are formulated. The actual value is created in the **execution phase**, where the product, service or result is actually generated. The last phase is the **project closure**, where the evaluation takes place and the achievement of project goals is checked (Jugdev & Müller, 2005). These four phases are similar to the project management process groups, but are not the same. The difference is that these process groups include activities like monitoring and controlling that might be executed and reoccur within each phase of the project as well as for the project as a whole (PMI, 2013).

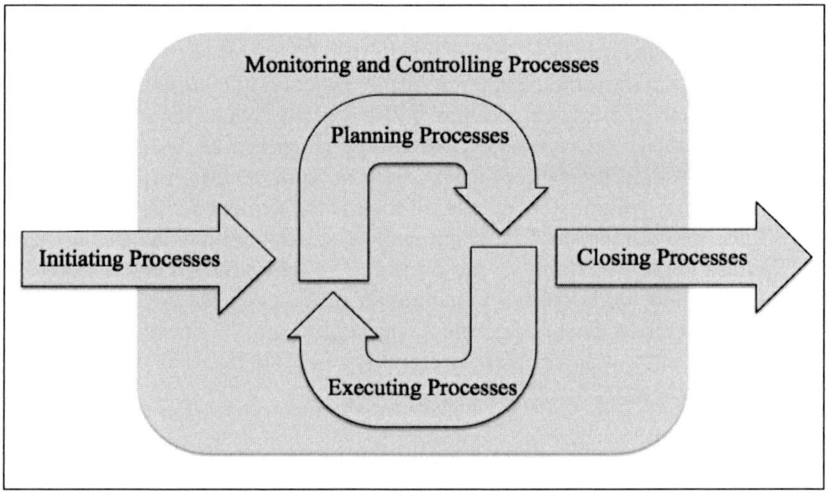

Figure 3: Project life cycle phases (PMI, 2013)

Reverse development of risk and cost of changes

The life cycle of a project has some general characteristics. In most of the projects the cost and the level of staffing are low in the initiation phase of the project, then gradually increase and have their peak in the execution phase. After this peak, they rapidly drop towards the closure phase of the project. On the other hand, risk and uncertainty are rather high in the initiation phase and decrease throughout the execution until the closure phase. The costs of changing the project scope are low in the beginning but increase significantly as the project progresses. Therefore mistakes that are corrected in the beginning of a project are less severe than towards the end of a project.

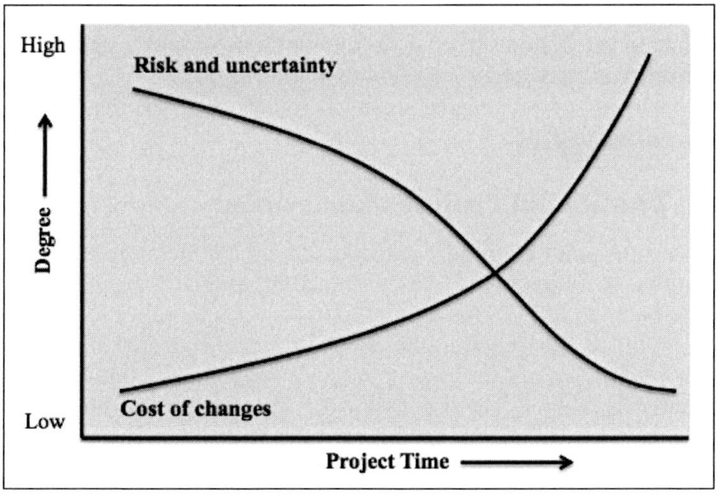

Figure 4: Development of risk and cost of changes in the project life cycle (PMI, 2013)

There are three different types of project life cycles. The previously described life cycle is called **predictive life cycle** in which the scope is set in detail at the beginning of the project and changes occur rarely. This type of life cycle is generally applied, when the deliverable is well understood. Another type is the **iterative & incremental** life cycle. In this, the project team repeats one or several project activities over time, whereby its understanding of the project scope is deepened. The iterative process is employed, when the project scope is rather broad in the beginning of the project. The **adaptive life cycle** goes one step further and adapts to changes in scope even faster. It is intended to react flexible to incremental changes and high stakeholder involvement and is therefore preferred, when operating in fast changing environments (PMI, 2013).

D. PROJECT MANAGEMENT

There are many books and journals on the topic of project management. Most of them tend to give advice to project managers on how they should organize and execute their projects. Others outline the most common mistakes done in project management and therewith try to give a reverse guide of which pitfalls to avoid (e.g. Pinto & Kharbanda, 1996). The vast literatures lead to different understandings and approaches of project management. Nonetheless, the different approaches share some common ground. Bødker, Kensing, and Simonsen (2004) understand project management "as establishing, maintaining, and overseeing the mutual commitments that make the project what it is". Such a broad comprehension reflects the uniqueness of projects itself. PMI defines **project management as "the application of knowledge, skills, tools, and techniques to project activities to meet the project requirements"** (PMI, 2013, p.47). The two definitions share the notion, that the starting point of project management is the project itself with its inherent "commitments" or "requirements". This view on project management is rather novel in the history of project management.

D. 1 Traditional Project Management

Begin of modern project management

The starting point of project management as a collection of standardized tools to support the successful completion of projects can be traced back to the 1930s (Garel, 2013). At the time, large, state-sponsored projects required the coordination of multiple stakeholders over long periods of time. Thus, project management's know-how was gradually developed. Nevertheless, such knowledge was concentrated in few, specialized and isolated firms with almost no dissemination of standardized practices (Garel, 2013). In the 1950s, this changed rapidly. At the time the cold war encouraged big investments in military and space research projects. These projects required the coordination of highly specialized experts in various technical fields as well as the management in uncertain conditions with limited time at their disposal (Ives, 2005). Hence, instruments with the capability to manage costs and time under these conditions were needed and subsequently created (Morris, 2013; Hornstein, 2015). Increased attention to the topic lead to the establishment of a research community and the foundation of the Project Management Institute (PMI) in 1969 for standardization and disseminating project management know-how (Garel, 2013; Morris, 2013).

Traditional project management

Over time project management practices were honed to handle projects in a consistent and comparable manner. These practices are known as traditional project management (Spundak, 2014). The basic assumption of traditional project management is that the successful completion of projects requires meticulous managing of inherent project risks, affected individuals and the change itself (Augustine et al., 2005). Consequently, traditional project management concentrates on planning as well as enhancing process transparency through documentation (Coram and Bohner, 2005). As a result of this focus the traditional process management is particularly well suited for linear, predictable projects, whose objectives are clearly defined (Saynisch, 2010). Typically, these characteristics can be found in large, long-lasting investment projects (Boehm and Turner, 2004).

Traditional project management consists of the active management of the project life cycle through five process groups: initiating, planning, executing, monitoring and controlling as well as closing. For this purpose, knowledge areas or tool boxes were defined to manage different project specifics, namely: integration, scope, time, cost, quality, human resource, communication, and risk as well as procurement (Sutherland and Ahmad, 2011). The task of the process group is to manage processes in these areas in coordination with each other, because the tasks are interdependent between the groups. Concretely, process outputs from one group are used as input by another (PMI, 2013).

At the onset of a project, the initiating process group is in charge of authorizing the project, thus "integrating" it in the organization by defining its objective, requirements, management as well as limitations. The second process group is tasked with designing a project plan and the management of the project. The group has to utilize all knowledge areas to execute activities like scope definition, schedule planning, quality and risk management as well as procurement planning. The third process group handles the project execution. A deep understanding of the knowledge areas integration, quality, human resource, communication and procurement is required for conducting the activities plan execution, quality assurance, team development, information distribution, and source selection. The main tasks of the fourth process group, monitoring and controlling, are controlling integration, schedules, costs and risk. The diverse nature of these activities means, that all knowledge areas are necessary for successful completion. Finally, the closing process group focuses on administrative closure as well as contract closeout. The associated knowledge areas are communication and procurement (PMI, 2013).

There is not one standard procedure for tackling projects in traditional project management. Nonetheless, probably the most famous approach is the waterfall model. The model stems from software development projects, but proved successful application in all types of projects (Rahmanian, 2014; Wysocki, 2014).

The waterfall model proposes the sequential processing of five phases: requirements, design, implementation, verification and maintenance (see Figure 5) (Dingsøyr et al., 2008; Cohen, 2010). In the beginning phase, requirements, meticulous planning is supposed to take place. Before the execution phases of the project, the exact requirements for as many tasks within the project as possible should be specified and documented (Hass, 2007). On the basis of this documentation a project plan is designed to reach the project goal. The plan contains the tasks and activities to be conducted. Consecutively, the plan is executed during the implementation phase and in the verification phase checked for shortcomings. Finally, the maintenance describes modifying and honing the implemented solution, because errors occurred or there might be the potential to increase the usability of the output (Rahmanian, 2014).

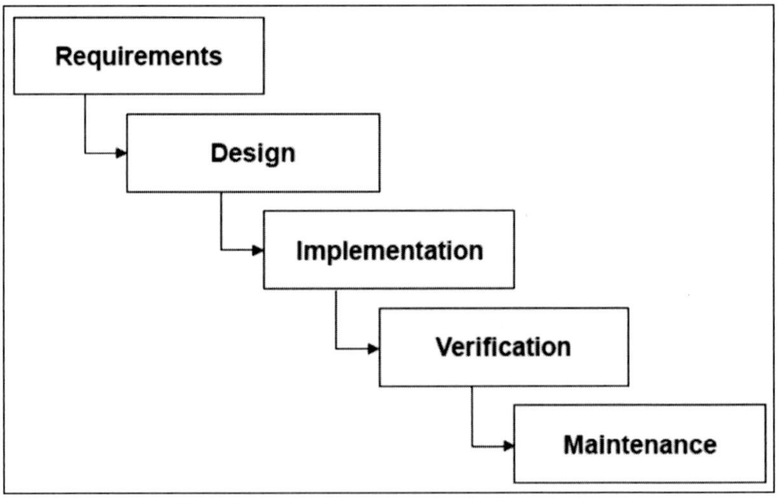

Figure 5: Waterfall model (Own illustration)

D. 2 Current Developments in Project Management

Drawbacks of traditional project management

While traditional project management proved itself over time, some drawbacks limit its application to specific contexts or settings. The approach relies on detailed planning, which is followed by consequent execution (Wysocki, 2014). Hence, the capability of the project manager to craft such plans and to forecast future developments is essential (Ives, 2005). A key challenge is the clear definition of the project objectives and requirements, because project stakeholders often are not able to sketch their needs or articulate them. Without such a clear understanding designing a robust project plan is hardly possible (Rajamanickam, 2005). This difficulty undermines the assumptions of traditional project management that its practices can be applied uniformly to all kind of projects (Spundak, 2014), because projects with higher complexity and uncertainty cannot be managed equally sufficient (Shenhar and Dvir, 2007; Wysocki, 2014). The shortcoming was intensified in the last decades through the trend to more complex projects in more and more volatile business environments. In such conditions the plans have often to be adjusted along the way and project management has to reflect this (Collyer et al., 2010). Traditional project management and its proposed practices have no convincing answer for this.

Agile project management

Against this background, new project management approaches were created and are still developed to this day. One new way of understanding the management of projects, which received vast and positive feedback, is agile project management. Agile project management is "a set of principles, whose goal is to render the process of project management simpler, more flexible and iterative in order to achieve better performance (cost, time and quality), with less management effort and higher levels of innovation and added value for the customer" (Conforto et al., 2014, p. 22). Several definitions of agile project management exist in the literature. Nonetheless, the common notion of these definitions is that this novel approach contains instruments to adapt to developments during project execution. Thus, projects can be managed, which solutions are unclear at the beginning of it (Wysocki, 2014).

Answering the calls for more flexible project management practices, agile project management focuses on repeating, iterative processes to handle tasks. This is reflected in its proposed project life cycle, the iterative project management life cycle (see Figure 6). The cycle consists of six phases: Scope, plan iteration, launch iteration, monitor & control iteration, close iteration and close project. The core idea of the cycle is to start off with the initial scope definition of the project followed by iterations in each of the different phases. Despite of the iterations, the goal of a phase is still to generate suitable project outcomes, but these solutions can be enhanced through additional iterations until the project clients are fully satisfied with the results. Not until in the close iteration phase the outcome is deemed fully satisfactory, the project is closed (Wysocki, 2014).

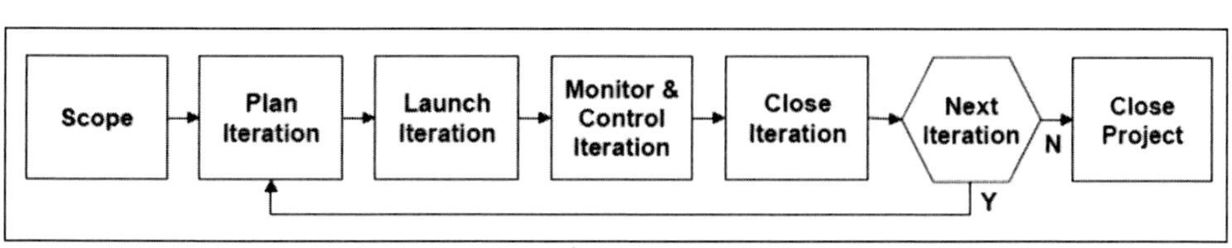

Figure 6: Iterative project management cycle (Adapted from Wysocki, 2014)

Many methods to manage agile projects are provided by the literature like adaptive software development (Highsmith, 2000), extreme programing (Beck, 2000) or feature driven development (Palmer and Felsing, 2002). However, the most famous method is undoubtedly scrum (Dingsøyr et al., 2012).

Scrum is a project management method, which relies heavily on iteration and team collaboration (Dybå and Dingsøyr, 2008). The project iterations are called "sprints". Depending on the project, a sprint lasts from one to four weeks (Salameh, 2014). Initially, a project description, stakeholders, a "scrum master", as well as a product vision are designated (Augustine, 2005; Salameh, 2014). The clients or customers of the project outcome design jointly with the project owner the product backlog. This document captures the needed requirements for the project outcome. The list is prioritized and frequently updated (Cohen, 2010; Salameh, 2014). The team uses the product backlog as input factor for creating a sprint backlog. Sprint backlogs are created before each sprint during the project. It states which features the next sprint is supposed to produce. It doesn't contain the entire product backlog. At the beginning of the project, the sprint backlog only consists of the main features of the product. Thus, earlier sprints result in project outcomes or products with only basic functions. Nevertheless, the customers receive the basic products and test them. This enables the customers to update the product backlog and the project team to refine the project result with each sprint (Stare, 2014). The close iteration phase of scrum consists of a sprint review and a retrospective meeting. While sprint reviews only consider the sprint at hand, retrospective meetings discuss potential improvements of the entire project and its processes (Salameh, 2014).

To estimate costs and time for the project the speed of the sprints and the requirements in the product as well as sprint backlogs are used as data bases (Cohn, 2010; Salameh, 2014). As the backlogs change over time, the estimates have to be adjusted accordingly (Salameh, 2014).

After completing a project outcome, which is satisfactory for customers and the team, the iteration is stopped and a lessons-learned meeting is conducted. Lessons-learned meetings aim to derive best practices for future endeavors (Salameh, 2014).

The advantages of agile project management can be summarized with time and cost reductions through minimized planning and documentation as well as increased satisfaction through transparency and as a result, superior output quality (Cohn, 2010; Salameh, 2014; Stettina and Hörz, 2015). Still, some drawbacks should be mentioned. The strength of the approach might also be considered as the core of its weaknesses. So is the possibility to start project execution without a clearly defined outcome an expedient way to deal with uncertainty, but many project clients may view the project as chaotic and don't provide support (Fernandez and Fernandez, 2008). Another weakness is the dependence on stakeholder involvement. Without strong commitment of stakeholders the approach cannot generate results and is not practical (Stare, 2014). Additionally, the neglect of documentation might lead to the failure to control for mistakes in the process, because controllers are not able to review results with no adequate documentation (Cohen et al., 2004; Fernandez and Fernandez, 2008). Last but not least, the assumption of collaboration and a joint team decision process requires effort, time and a single-focused project team. Some projects might rather flourish, if the project manager solely decides about the future course of the project (Nerur et al., 2005).

Considering project characteristics, agile project management is especially beneficial in explorative and unpredictable projects (Salameh, 2014; Wysocki, 2014). Additionally, small projects are rather suited for its application compared to large-scale ones (Coram and Bohner, 2005; Karlström and Runeson, 2006).

Furthermore, studies show innovative and less bureaucratic organizations are better aligned to the new management approach (Nerur et al., 2005; Salameh, 2014). Also smaller organizations are deemed more suitable for such projects due to the affinity of larger organizations towards formality and documentation (Mishra and Mishra, 2011).

Customers and team members are supposed to be located very close to each other, because an unhindered information exchange is necessary (Cohen, 2010; Salameh, 2014). The atmosphere has to foster trust and open communication (Augustine, 2005). Naturally, this depends greatly on the quality of the team members (Salameh, 2014), but an additional factor is the size of the team. Mutual trust is hard to create in larger teams. Literature suggests team numbers from seven to nine (Augustine, 2005).

E. EVALUATION OF PROJECTS

"Project success criteria" versus "Critical success factors"

Before evaluating a project outcome, it is very important to distinguish between two existing concepts about project success, i.e. project success criteria and critical success factors (CSFs). A criterion is a standard by which someone judges, decides about, or deals with something. A factor is a fact or situation that influences the result of something. Transferring these definitions to the field of project management one can define project success criteria as the standards to which the project outcome is judged. CSFs on the other hand, are the factors or variables that influence the project outcome. (Ika, 2009)

E. 1 Definition of Success and Failure

Usually success is seen as the degree of the accomplishment of a task towards an intended aim or purpose. Transferring this meaning to the context of project management, success can be defined as the accomplishment of the predetermined project goals (Lim & Mohamed, 1999). Although this definition seems to be clear and there are no doubts about its validity, in practice the concept of project success is by far more complex. Reviewing the literature there appears to be no common definition on what project success means (Ika, 2009). De Wit (1988) concluded that objectively measuring project success is impossible. Foremost, a clear distinction has to be made between the overall **project success**, also referred to as product success, and the **project management success** (Baccarini, 1999). Project management success enhances project success but it cannot prevent project failure. For example, if a new aircraft-type is designed and manufactured but delivered with a very heavy delay. The sales result of the new type can outweigh the time lag. The project itself would be seen as a success disregarding the poor project management.

De Wit (1988) agrees that project success can be measured by the accomplishment of the project objectives. The problem is that the project objectives of the various stakeholders in a project may differ. Moreover, project objectives often change throughout the different phases of the life cycle. Therefore it appears to be impossible to achieve thorough and overall project success. Overall, project success implies to meet the project mission and technical specification and satisfy all key stakeholders which are the project team, the organization and the clients.

The micro and the macro perspective on project success

Lim and Mohamed (1999) differentiate between the micro and the macro perspective on project success. **The macro perspective** of project success is in its core concerned about the users' satisfaction. It therefore needs to be examined, if the original concept is achieved. There are two phases within the project life cycle that are of importance for this evaluation: the planning phase and the closure phase. **The micro perspective** of project success is mainly concerned about the performance of the project within the execution phase. This measurement of success applies to the project manager and other contractual parties. Cleland and Ireland (2002) state that project success needs to be viewed from two different perspectives. They agree with previous studies that one significant evaluation aspect is the degree to which good project performance was achieved. Furthermore, they point out the significance of the strategic contribution of the project to the firm's mission. Jugdev and Müller (2005) go beyond the macro and micro perspective suggesting that project success needs to be measured outside the project life cycle, so that project management success is no longer independently measured of project success. Moreover, project success cannot be measured by a single criterion at one point in the project life cycle. The measure of success needs to be continuous. Additionally, project success is highly dependent on one's point of view. A project that is a failure for one stakeholder can be a success for another stakeholder. Project success therefore needs to be measured both continuously as well as inter-subjectively, across the project and product life cycle and from the perspective of the different stakeholders.

E. 2 Criteria to Evaluate the Project Outcome

Projects success

Based on the fact that there is no universal definition of project success, the criteria used to judge the outcome of a project are decisive. The criteria applied will determine if a project is viewed as success or failure, which subsequently has a great impact on the project manager, the client, all other stakeholders and at times the entire organization.

Among project managers and researchers there is great consensus that project success depends heavily on the balancing of the triangle of scope, cost, and time with quality in its center (e.g. Hab & Wagner, 2013).

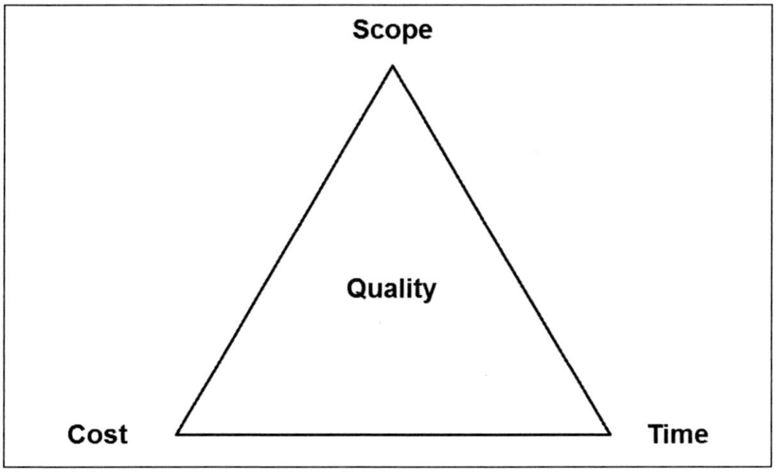

Figure 7: Project management triangle (Hab & Wagner, 2013)

Especially project managers measure the success of their project applying these four criteria. From this point of view projects are successful, if they were delivered within schedule, according to planned cost and when they meet all objectives set in the planning phase. Morris and Hough (1987) were the first to question this often called "iron triangle" as the universal set of evaluation criteria. They grouped project success in four different categories: project functionality ("does the project meet financial and technical requirements?"), project management ("did the project meet the budget, schedule, and specifications?"), contractors' commercial performance ("did the contractors benefit commercially?"), and project termination ("in the event that the project had to be cancelled, was this decision made reasonably and efficiently") (see also Jugdev & Müller, 2005). In 1990 Pinto and Mantel proposed measuring success based on three dimensions: success in the implementation process, the perceived value of the project and client satisfaction with the result.

Systematization of success criteria

The "Square Root" is a project evaluation framework that incorporates all the previously mentioned criteria (Atkinson, 1999). Foremost it distinguishes between two stages, the delivery stage and the post delivery stage. **The delivery** stage is about the process, so about doing it right. The classical criteria of the project management triangle or "iron triangle" are applicable there. **The post delivery** stage is about the system, so about getting it right. Most of the more recently developed success criteria such as client satisfaction apply here. The concept therefore appears to be not entirely new but provides a complete picture on all relevant criteria for the evaluation of project success summarizing them in four dimensions. **The first two dimensions**, called the "iron triangle" and the information system quality, measure if the project was "done right". The "iron triangle" again includes the classical criteria of cost, time and scope whereas the quality of the information system is measured by maintainability, reliability, validity and information quality use. **The third and fourth dimension**, benefits to the organization and benefits to the stakeholder community, are concerned about "getting it right". The benefits to the organization are measured by the criteria of improved efficiency and effectiveness, increased profits, organizational learning as well as preparing for the future, meaning the alignment with strategic goals. The benefits to the stakeholders highly depend on the stakeholders that are affected by the project. In general the criteria are satisfaction of the users, social and environmental impact, personal development, professional learning and others. The sub-criteria of the four dimensions can be extended according to the specific project, which is evaluated. The four dimensions themselves are exhaustive, since they incorporate all relevant areas of concern for the evaluation of a project. Recently conducted research agrees on the completeness of these criteria and rather focuses on the specific design of criteria for certain types of projects and groups of stakeholders (e. g. Shenhar et al., 2001).

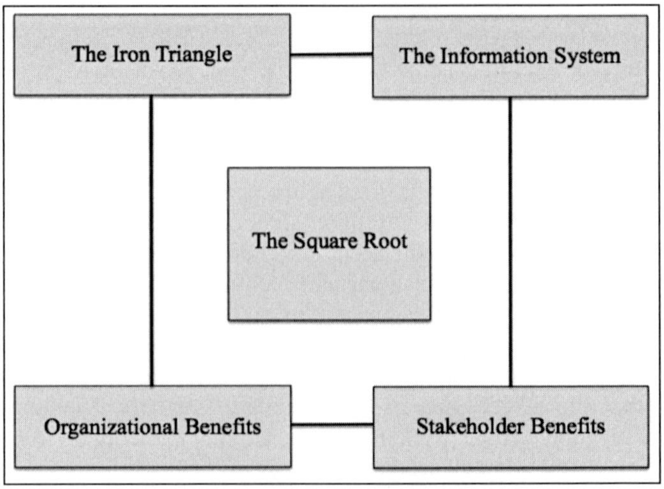

Figure 8: The square root (Atkinson, 1999)

E. 3 Evolution of Critical Success Factors in Project Management

On the search for a complete set of success factors

A lot of researchers have devoted themselves to write about CSFs in the past decades. Their ultimate goal was to develop a universal set of factors that can be applied to any project. The idea was to find and be able to manage these factors and therewith increase the likelihood of project success. Rubin and Seeling (1967) were the first ones to investigate the impact of a project manager's experience on the project outcome. According to their findings, the previous experience of the project manager has almost no impact on its outcome. Their study was followed by a theoretical study by Avots (1969), who examined the factors for project failure. Avots came up with three distinctive factors causing failure, which he named unsupportive top management, unplanned project termination and a bad project manager. Following research was then led by Archibald (1976), Martin (1976), and Cleland and King (1983), who came up with theoretical frameworks that relied on anecdotal factors, single-case studies or conceptual models. The problem was that most of these concepts were only applicable to specific projects and not a wide range of project types and situations. Further research was therefore devoted towards the empirical verification of these factors. Hughes (1986) focused on the manager's perspective and found out that the reasons for project failure were often not suitable managerial principles, meaning the reward of wrong actions and a shortcoming of communication of goals. Morris and Hough (1987) were the first to develop a CSF model addressing both objective and subjective dimensions, while studying eight large projects over many years. Concluding from their observation of these large projects that all failed, they came up with seven specific factors. Even though they have been retrieved from specific large projects, Morris and Hough argued that they were generally applicable to all projects, also ones of small scale. Moreover, they distinguished the importance of CSFs within the different phases of a project life cycle and the different stakeholder perspectives. Pinto and Slevin (1987) developed a concept that was based on an empirical study of over 400 projects, coming up with a set of ten CSFs that are generally applicable to project management. Might and Fischer (1985) studied structural factors of the firm, like the organizational structure, the size of the project and the level of authority that was delegated to the project manager and their impact on project success. Belassi and Tukel (1996) revised the concept of Pinto and Slevin and grouped the CSFs according to the different groups of stakeholders. Therewith, they generalized the original ten-factor model coming up with four dimensions: factors related to the project, factors related to the project manager and team members, factors related to the organization and factors related to the external environment. Up to that point the goal of researchers in the field of CSFs was still to find a general model that could be applied to all projects.

Comparing the literature on CSFs a clear evolution from a general more subjective analysis, over a general objective multi-factor empirical analysis towards a specific objective empirical analysis can be observed. In the early years of CSF research the ultimate goal has been to find one list of general CSFs that are applicable to all projects and therefore build the ultimate formula for project success. This has changed and researchers today argue that there is not one general list of CSFs that determine project success (Ika, 2009). The reason that CSFs differ significantly from one project to the next is due to the difference in variables of project scope, uniqueness and complexity (Wateridge, 1998). The majority of today's research focuses either on one specific factor and its relationship to project success or on specific project types or categories (e.g. Mir & Pinnington, 2014). Furthermore, efforts have been made to causally link project success criteria to project success factors (Westerveld, 2003).

E. 4 Critical Success Factor System Framework

Combining the studies of Martin (1976), Morris and Hough (1987), Pinto and Slevin (1987) and many others, Belassi and Tukel (1996) developed their CSF system framework. Their approach was to collect all possible CSFs and put them into categories according to the different stakeholders of the project. The authors argue that any CSF can be put into at least one of the four categories. The result was a model that showed the relationship between the different factors (see Figure 6). It greatly helps project managers to understand the cause-effect relationships and enables them to use the framework for their specific project in order to identify the major CSFs. Even though the framework has been developed almost two decades ago it is still valid for projects today and therefore is a very helpful tool.

Today it is known that CSFs go beyond having a common mission, top management support for resources, authority and power, but also include senior management commitment in order to provide the vision, strategy and sponsorship. Furthermore, success factors relate to the organization as well as the external environment (Jugdev & Müller, 2005).

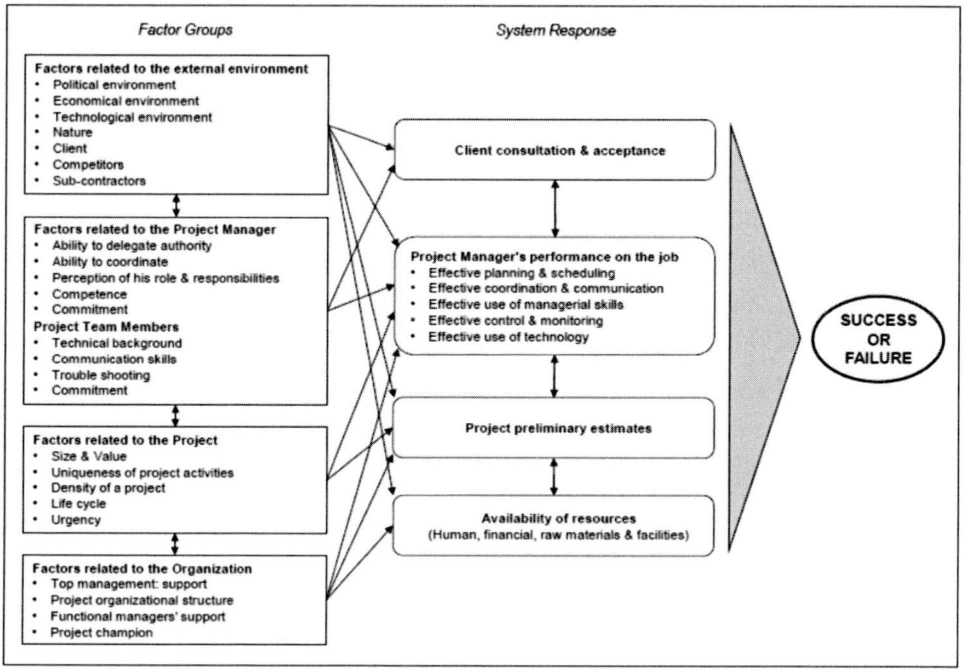

Figure 9: CSF system framework
(Belassi & Tukel, 1996)

F. CONCLUSION

The relevance of projects as part of the overall economic performance is increasing. As an approach to cope with shorter product and service life cycles as indicators for a rapidly changing business environment, it supports organizations to remain competitive and flexible.

This chapter provides an overview of the basics of projects as well as project management. Relevant standards for projects are discussed and the reasoning behind these standards explained. Building on the discussion regarding different types of projects and their stakeholders, a clear separation is drawn between project success criteria and critical success factors to be able to evaluate a project outcome.

By definition, no project is exactly like another. Therefore, it is of fundamental importance to adapt each and every step of the project management agenda to the particular circumstances. Projects in the aviation industry are diverse and manifold. No matter if it is the development of a new aircraft, the construction of an airport or just the implementation of a new baggage drop-off system, projects and their management are crucial for enabling sustainable success for all actors in this business.

Review Questions

- How is a project defined?
- Name and describe the project life cycle phases. How is the connection of these phases to risk and uncertainty and cost of changes of the scope of the project?
- Describe the limitations of project management.
- Describe the difference between traditional and agile project management.
- What is the difference between critical success factors and success criteria in general and with regard to projects?
- Discuss why trade-offs exist among the three primary objectives of project management.
- What are the distinctive features of projects in the aviation industry?

Bibliography and further reading

Abdomerovic, M. (2012): Project Management Life Span and Life Cycle Processes, in: PM World Today, 14(2), p. 1–15.

Archibald, R. D. (1976): Managing High-Technology Programs and Projects, New York.

Atkinson, R. (1999): Project management: cost, time and quality, two best guesses and a phenomenon, its time to accept other success criteria, in: International Journal of Project Management, 17(6), p. 337–342.

Avots, I. (1969): Why does project management fail, in: California Management Review, p. 77–82.

Augustine, S. (2005): Managing agile projects, Upper Saddle River.

Augustine, S. / Payne, B. / Sencindiver, F. / Woodcock, S. (2005): Agile project management: Steering from the edges, in: Communications of the ACM, 48(12), p. 85–89.

Baccarini, D. (1999): The Logical Framework Method for Defining Project Success, in: Project Management Journal, 30(4), p. 25.

Beck, K. (2000): Extreme programming explained: Embrace change, Boston.

Belassi, W. / Tukel, O. I. (1996): A new framework for determining critical success/failure factors in projects, in: International Journal of Project Management, 14(3), p. 141–151.

Bødker, K. / Kensing, F. / Simonsen, J. F. (2004): Participatory IT design: Designing for business and workplace realities (p. 27), Cambridge.

Boehm, B. / Turner, R. (2004): Balancing agility and discipline: A guide for the perplexed, New York.

Cleland, D. I., & Ireland, L. (2002): Project management: Strategic design and implementation (4th ed.), New York.

Cleland, D. I. / King, W. R. (1983): Systems Analysis and Project Management), New York.

Cohen, D. / Lindvall, M. / Costa, P. (2004): An introduction to agile methods, in: Advances in Computers, 62, p. 1–66.

Cohen, G. (2010): Agile excellence for product managers: A guide to creating winning products with agile development teams, Silicon Valley.

Cohn, M. (2010): Succeeding with agile, Boston.

Collyer, S. / Warren, C. / Hemsley, B. / Stevens, C. (2010): Aim, fire, aim – Project planning styles in dynamic environments, in: Project Management Journal, 41(4), p. 108–121.

Conforto, E. C. / Salum, F. / Amaral, D. C. / Silva, S. L. / Almeida, L. F. M. (2014): Can agile project management be adopted by industries other than software development?, in: Project Management Journal, 45(3), p. 21–34.

Coram, M. / Bohner, S. (2005): The impact of agile methods on software project management, in: Proceedings of the 12th IEEE International Conference and Workshops on the Engineering of Computer-Based Systems, p. 363–370.

De Wit, A. (1988): Measurement of project success, in: International Journal of Project Management, 6(3), p. 164–170.

Dingsøyr, T. / Dybå, T. / Abrahamsson, P. (2008): A preliminary roadmap for empirical research on agile software development, in: Proceedings of the Agile 2008 Conference, p. 83–94.

Dingsøyr, T. / Nerur, S. / Balijepally, V. / Moe, N. B. (2012): A decade of agile methodologies: Towards explaining agile software development, in: The Journal of Systems and Software, 85(6), p. 1213–1221.

Dybå, T. / Dingsøyr, T. (2008): Empirical studies of agile software development: A systematic review, in: Information and Software Technology, 50, p. 833–859.

Fernandez, D. J. / Fernandez, J. D. (2008): Agile project management: Agilism versus traditional approaches, in: Journal of Computer Information Systems, 49(2), p. 10–17.

Flouris, T.G. / Lock, D. (2008): Aviation Project Management, Burlington.

Garel, G. (2013): A history of project management models: From pre-models to the standard models, in: International Journal of Project Management, 31, p. 663–669.

Hab, G. / Wagner, R. (2013): Projektmanagement in der Automobilindustrie, Berlin.

Hartman, F.T. (2000): Don't park your Brain Outside, Newtown Square.

Hass, K. B. (2007): The blending of traditional and agile project management, in: PM World Today, 9(5), p. 1–8.

Highsmith, J. (2000): Adaptive software development: A collaborative approach to managing complex systems, New York.

Hornstein, H. A. (2015): The integration of project management and organizational change management is now a necessity, in: International Journal of Project Management, 33(2), p. 291–298.

Hughes, M. W. (1986): Why projects fail: The effects of ignoring the obvious, in: Industrial Engineering, 18, p. 14–18.

Ika, L. A. (2009): Project success as a topic in project management journals, in: Project Management Journal, 40(4), p. 6–19.

Ives, M. (2005): Identifying the contextual elements of project management within organizations and their impact on project success, in: Project Management Journal, 36(1), p. 37–50.

Jugdev, K. / Müller, R. (2005): A Retrospective Look at our Evolving Understanding of Project Success, in: Project Management Journal, 36(4), p. 19–31.

Karlström, D. / Runeson, P. (2006): Integrating agile software development into stage-gate managed product development, in: Empirical Software Engineering, 11(2), p. 203–225.

Kloppenborg, T. J. (2009): Contemporary Project Management, Mason.

Lim, C. / Mohamed, M. Z. (1999): Criteria of project success: an exploratory re-examination, in: International Journal of Project Management, 17(4), p. 243–248.

Mantel, S. / Meredith, J. / Shafer, S. / Sutton, M. (2011): Project Management in Practice (4th ed.), Hoboken.

Martin, C. C. (1976): Project Management. New York: Amacom Implementation Process, in: Journal of Management Studies, 27(3), p. 305–327.

Might, R.J. / Fischer, W.A. (1985): The role of structural factors in determining project management success, in: IEEE Transactions Engineering Management, 32 (2), p. 71–77.

Mir, F. A. / Pinnington, A. H. (2014): Exploring the value of project management: Linking Project Management Performance and Project Success, in: International Journal of Project Management, 32(2), p. 202–217.

Mishra, D. / Mishra, A. (2011): Complex software project development: Agile methods adoption, in: Journal of Software Maintenance and Evolution: Research and Practice, 23(8), p. 549–564.

Morris, P. / Hough, G. H. (1987): The Anatomy of Major Projects, New York.

Morris, P. (2013): Reconstructing project management – Reprised: A knowledge perspective, in: Project Management Journal, 44(5), p. 6–23.

Müller, A. / Wald, A. / Görner, A. (2012): Comparing Project Management Practices in New Product Development: A Study in the Automotive, Aerospace and Rail Transport Industry, in: International Journal of Project Organisation and Management, 4(3), p. 203–217.

Nerur, S. / Mahapatra, R. / Mangalaraj, G. (2005): Challenges of migrating to agile methodologies, in: Communications of the ACM, 48, p. 73–78.

Pinto, J. K. / Kharbanda, O. P. (1996): How to fail in project management (without really trying) , in: Business Horizons, 39(4), p. 45–53.

Pinto, J. K. / Mantel, S. J. (1990): The causes of project failure, in: IEEE Transactions on Engineering Management, 37, p. 269–276.

Pinto, J. K., / Slevin, D. P. (1987): Critical Factors in Successful Project Implementation, in: IEEE Transactions on Engineering Management, Vol. EM-34, p. 22–27.

Palmer, S. R. / Felsing, J. M. (2002): A practical guide to feature-driven development, New York.

Project Management Institute (2013): A Guide to the Project Management Body of Knowledge (PMBOK Guide) (5th ed.), Pennsylvania.

Rahmanian, M. (2014): A comparative study on hybrid IT project management: Using traditional project management and agile approach, in: International Journal of Computer and Information Technology, 3(5), p. 1096–1099.

Rajamanickam, D. (2005): Successful project management using agile methodology, in: Journal of the Quality Assurance Institute, 19, p. 15–18.

Rattay, G. / Patzak, G. (1998): Projekt Management, Vienna.

Rubin, I. M. / Seeling, W. (1967): Experience as a factor in the selection and performance of project managers, in: IEEE Trans Eng Management, 14 (3), p. 131–134.

Salameh, H. (2014): What, when, why, and how? A comparison between agile project management and traditional project management methods, in: International Journal of Business and Management Review, 2(5), p. 52–74.

Saynisch, M. (2010): Beyond frontiers of traditional project management: An approach to evolutionary, self–organizational principles and the complexity theory — Results of the research program, in: Project Management Journal, 41(2), p. 21–37.

Shenhar, A. J. / Dvir, D. / Levy, O. / Maltz, A. C. (2001): Project Success: A Multidimensional Strategic Concept, in: Long Range Planning, 34(6), p. 699–725.

Shenhar, A. J. / Dvir, D. (2007): Reinventing project management: The diamond approach to successful growth and innovation, Boston.

Spundak, M. (2014): Mixed agile/traditional project management methodology: Reality or illusion?, in: Procedia - Social and Behavioral Sciences, 119, p. 939–948.

Stare, A. (2014): Agile project management in product development projects, in: Procedia - Social and Behavioral Sciences, 119, p. 295–304.

Stettina, C. J. / Hörz, J. (2015): Agile portfolio management: An empirical perspective on the practice in use, in: International Journal of Project Management, 33(1), p. 140–152.

Sutherland, J. / Ahmad, N. (2011): How a traditional project manager transforms to Scrum: PMBOK vs. Scrum. Presented at Agile 2011, Salt Lake City.

Wateridge, J. (1998): How can IS/IT projects be measured for success?, in: International Journal of Project Management, 16, p. 59–63.

Westerveld, E. (2003): The Project Excellence Model®: linking success criteria and critical success factors. Selected Papers from the Fifth Biennial Conference of the International Research Network for Organizing by Projects. Held in Renesse, Seeland, The Netherlands, 28-31 May 2002, 21(6), p. 411–418.

Wittmer, A. / Bieger, T. (2011): Fundamentals and Structure of Aviation Systems, in: Wittmer, A. / Bieger, T. / Müller, R. (Eds.). Aviation Systems, Berlin, p. 5–38.

Wysocki, R. K. (2014): Effective project management: Traditional, agile, extreme (7th ed.), Indianapolis.

List of Abbreviations

A. GENERAL ABBREVIATIONS

AC	Average cost
AD	Agent discount (discount for travel agents)
AD	Airworthiness directive
ADI	Attitude director indicator
AIP	Airport improvement program
AMB	Alliance management board
AMC	Acceptable material of compliance
AOC	Air operators certificate
AP to AP	Airport to airport
APU	Auxiliary power unit
ASI	Air speed indicator
ASK	Available seat kilometers
ASU	Air start unit
ATA	Actual time of arrival
ATD	Actual time of departure
ATPL	Airline transport pilot license
BGB	Bürgerliches Gesetzbuch (German civil code)
BITE	Build in test equipment
BRS	Baggage security, baggage reconciliation system
BSA	Blocked seat agreement
BSC	Balanced scorecard
Bund	German Federation
Bundesländer	Federal States (of Germany)
CAME	Continuing aviation maintenance exposition
CAME	Continuing airworthiness management exposition
CASK	Cost per available seat kilometer
CDS	Credit default swap
CEO	Chief executive officer
CG	Center of gravity

CITP	Common IT Platform
CO_2	Carbon dioxide
CPL	Commercial pilot license
CR	Corporate research
CRM	Customer relationship management
CRS	Computer reservation system
CSF	Critical success factors
CUSS	Common user self service
D to D	Door to door
DBC	Denied boarding compensation
DEU	Display electronics unit
DOC	Direct operating costs
ECAM	Electronic centralized aircraft monitoring
ECR	Efficient consumer response
EFIS	Electronic flight instrument system
EICAS	Engine indication and crew alerting system
EoS	Economies of scale
EU-OPS	EU operations (Guidelines on aircraft operations)
ETA	Estimated time of arrival
ETD	Estimated time of departure
Etix	Electronic ticket
ETOPS	Extended-range twin engine operational performance standards
ESt	Einkommensteuer (Income tax)
ETS	Emissions trading scheme
EU	European Union
FCL	Flight crew licensing
FFP	Frequent flyer program
FH	Flight hours
FLG	Fluglärmgesetz
FMS	Flight management system
FODA	Flight operations data analysis
GG	Grundgesetz (German Constitution)
GDP	Gross domestic product

GDS	Global distribution system
GM	Guidance material
GST	General sales tax
GPU	Ground power units
H1N1	Swine flu
HHI	Hirschman-Herfindahl Index
ID	Industry discount (discount for airline employees)
IFR	Instrument flight rules
ISA	International standard atmosphere
IT	Information technology
JAR	Joint aviation requirements
JV	Joint venture
KPI	Key performance indicator
KSt	Körperschaftsteuer (Corporate tax)
LCC	Low-cost carrier
MC	Marginal costs
MCDU	Multi control and display unit
MCT	Minimum cost track
MDT	Minimum distance track
MEL	Minimum equipment list
MFD	Multi-function display
MFT	Minimum fuel track
MGT	More ground time
MRO	Maintenance, repair and overhaul
MTOW	Maximum take-off weight
MTT	Minimum time track
NAV/COM	Devices for the tuning of navigational and inter communicational radios
ND	Navigation display
NDC	New distribution capability
NOPAT	Net operating profit after taxes
NOTAM	Notification to airmen
NPIAS	National plan of integrated airport systems
NSD	New service development

O&D	Origin and destination
OFP	Operational flight plan
OSS	One-stop-security areas
P2P	Point-to-point
PAX	Passenger
P_{dyn}	Dynamic pressure
PE-ratio	Price / earnings ratio
PFD	Primary flight display
PM	Performance measurement
PMBOK	Project management book of knowledge
PMO	Project management office
PNR	Passenger name record
POS	Point of sale
PRM	Public relations management
P_{stat}	Static pressure
P_{total}	Total pressure
Q	Quantity
R&D	Research and development
RPK	Revenue passenger kilometers
RASK	Revenue per available seat kilometer
RM	Revenue management
ROCE	Return on capital employed
ROE	Return on equity
RTK	Revenue ton kilometers
SDR	Special drawing rights
SGT	Scheduled ground time
SKO	Seat kilometers offered
Slats	Wing mounted at the leading edge
SLF	Seat (passenger) load factor
STA	Scheduled time of arrival
STD	Scheduled time of departure
SVFR	Special visual flight rules
TAS	True airspeed

TBR	Time between removal
TC	Total costs
TCAS	Traffic collision avoidance system
TTax	Ticket tax
TTIP	Transatlantic trade and investment partnership
UGT	Unscheduled ground time
U.S.	United States
USP	Unique selling proposition
USA	United States of America
VAT	Value added tax
v_{flow}	Velocity of the flow
VFR	Visual flight rules
vs	versus
VSI	Vertical speed indicator
WLU	Workload unit
WWII	World War II
ZGB	Zivilgesetzbuch (Swiss civil code)

B. ORGANIZATIONS AND INSTITUTIONS

AA	Auswärtiges Amt
ACI	Airports Council International
ADV	German Airport Association
AEA	Association of European Airlines
ATAG	Air Transport Action Group
ATC	Air Traffic Control
ATM	Air Traffic Management
BARIG	Board of Airline Representatives in Germany
BDF	Association of German Airlines
BFU	Bundesstelle für Flugunfalluntersuchung
BGH	Bundesgerichtshof
BMI	Bundesministerium des Inneren
BMU	Bundesministerium für Umwelt, Naturschutz und Reaktorsicherheit
BMVBS	Bundesministerium für Verkehr, Bau und Stadtentwicklung

BMWi	Bundeswirtschaftsministerium für Wirtschaft und Technologie
BVD	Bodenverkehrsdienste (Ground handling traffic)
CAB	Civil Aeronautic Board
DFS	Deutsche Flugsicherung (German authority for air traffic control)
DLR	German Aerospace Center
DOT	US Department of Transportation
DWD	Deutscher Wetterdienst
EAP	Etihad Airways Partners
EASA	European Aviation Safety Agency
EBS	European Business School
EC	European Community
EEC	European Economic Community
ECAC	European Civil Aviation Conference
ECSC	European Coal and Steel Community
EU	European Union
EUGH	Europäischer Gerichtshof
Euratom	European Atomic Energy Community
Eurocontrol	European Organization for the Safety of Air Navigation
FAA	Federal Aviation Authority
FAI	Fédération Aéronautique Internationale
FAZ	Frankfurter Allgemeine Zeitung
FhKD	Flughafenkoordination Deutschland
GAAPS	Global Alliance for Project Performance Standards
GECAS	General Electric Commercial Aviation Services
GUC	German University in Cairo
IAEA	Association of European Airlines
IATA	International Air Transport Association
ICAO	International Civil Aviation Organization
ILFC	International Lease Finance Corporation
IOSA	IATA Operational Safety Audit
IPMA	International Project Management Association
ISO	International Organization on Standardization
JAA	Joint Aviation Authorities

LBA	Luftfahrtbundesamt
LuftVG	Luftverkehrsgesetz
NGO	Non-governmental organization
PMI	Project Management Institute
PRINCE	Projects in Controlled Environments
SIIE	Strascheg Institute for Innovation & Entrepreneurship
TRTO	Type Rating Training Organization
UN	United Nations
UNCLOS	United Nations Convention on the Law of the Sea
WTO	World Trade Organization

C. AIRLINE CODES

AB	Air Berlin
AF	Air France
AZ	Alitalia
BA	British Airways
KLM	Royal Dutch Airlines
LH	Lufthansa
LX	Swiss Air
OS	Austrian Airlines
SN	Brussels Airlines
TK	Turkish Airlines
UA	United Airways

D. AIRPORT CODES

ATL	Atlanta
CAI	Cairo
CDG	Paris Charles de Gaulle
CHI	Chicago
DFW	Dallas Fort Worth
DSM	Des Moines
DXB	Dubai International
FRA	Frankfurt

JFK	New York John F. Kennedy
LHR	London Heathrow
MUC	Munich
ORD	Chicago O'Hare International
TXL	Berlin Tegel

E. CURRENCIES

US$	U.S. dollar
€	Euro